Table of Contents

To be used in conjunction with the Summer 2007 and Winter 2008 BAR/BRI Bar Review Courses

CONSTITUTIONAL LAW

TABLE OF CONTENTS

CONSTITUTIONAL LAW

PART 1: POWERS OF THE FEDERAL GOVERNMENT

I. THE JUDICIAL POWER

A. ARTICLE III

Federal judicial power extends to cases involving:

1. ***Interpretation*** of the Constitution, federal laws, treaties, and admiralty and maritime laws; and

2. ***Disputes*** between states, states and foreign citizens, and citizens of diverse citizenship.

B. POWER OF JUDICIAL REVIEW

The Supreme Court may review the constitutionality of acts of other branches of the federal government. It may also review state acts pursuant to the Supremacy Clause.

C. FEDERAL COURTS

Only Article III courts (*i.e.,* courts established by Congress pursuant to Article III) are the subject of this outline. Congress has plenary power to delineate the original and appellate jurisdiction of these courts but is bound by the standards set forth in Article III as to subject matter and party jurisdiction and the requirement of a "case or controversy." Congress can also create courts under Article I (*e.g.,* tax courts). Judges in those courts do not have life tenure as do Article III judges, and Congress may not assign to Article I courts jurisdiction over cases that have traditionally been tried in Article III courts.

D. JURISDICTION OF THE SUPREME COURT

1. Original Jurisdiction

The Supreme Court has original jurisdiction in all cases affecting ambassadors, public ministers, consuls, and those in which a state is a party, but Congress has given concurrent jurisdiction to lower federal courts in all cases except those between states.

2. Appellate Jurisdiction

The Supreme Court has appellate jurisdiction in all cases to which federal power extends, subject to congressional exceptions and regulation. Cases can come to the Court by one of two ways:

a. Writ of Certiorari—Most Cases

The Supreme Court has complete ***discretion*** to hear cases that come to it by certiorari. The cases that come by certiorari are:

1) Cases from ***state courts*** where (i) the constitutionality of a federal statute, federal treaty, or state statute is in issue, or (ii) a state statute allegedly violates federal law.

2) All cases from ***federal courts*** of appeals.

b. Appeal—Rare Cases

The Supreme Court ***must*** hear cases that come to it by appeal. These cases are confined to decisions by three-judge federal district court panels that grant or deny injunctive relief.

E. CONSTITUTIONAL AND SELF-IMPOSED LIMITATIONS ON EXERCISE OF FEDERAL JURISDICTION—"STRICT NECESSITY"

Whether a case is "justiciable" (*i.e.,* a federal court may address it) depends on whether there is a "case or controversy." In addition to the "case or controversy" requirement, there are other limitations on federal court jurisdiction.

1. No Advisory Opinions

There must be specific ***present harm*** or threat of specific future harm. Federal courts can hear actions for declaratory relief if there is an actual dispute between parties having adverse legal interests. Complainants must show that they have engaged in (or wish to engage in) specific conduct and that the challenged action poses a ***real and immediate danger*** to their interests. However, the federal courts will not determine the constitutionality of a statute if it has never been enforced and there is no real fear that it ever will be.

2. Ripeness—Immediate Threat of Harm

A plaintiff is not entitled to review of a statute or regulation before its enforcement (*i.e.,* may not obtain a declaratory judgment) unless the plaintiff will suffer some harm or immediate threat of harm.

3. Mootness

A real controversy must exist at all stages of review. If the matter has already been resolved, the case will be dismissed as moot.

a. Exception

Controversies capable of repetition, but evading review are not moot. *Examples:* Issues concerning events of short duration (*e.g.,* abortion) or a defendant who voluntarily stops the offending practice but is free to resume.

b. Class Actions

A class representative may continue to pursue a class action after the representative's controversy has become moot if claims of other class members are still viable.

CMR **Exam Tip** Ripeness bars consideration of claims ***before*** they have been developed; mootness bars their consideration ***after*** they have been resolved.

4. Standing

A person must have a concrete stake in the outcome of a case.

a. Components

1) Injury

Plaintiff must show that she has been or will be ***directly*** and ***personally*** injured by the allegedly unlawful government action, which affects her rights under the Constitution or federal law. The injury ***need not be economic***.

2) Causation

There must be a causal connection between the injury and the conduct complained of.

3) Redressability

A decision in the litigant's favor must be capable of eliminating her grievance.

CMR **Exam Tip** Remember that standing just allows the plaintiff to get into court. Thus, a successful ruling on the standing issue does not mean that the plaintiff wins his suit; it merely means that he gets an opportunity to try it.

b. Common Standing Issues

1) Congressional Conferral of Standing
A federal statute may create new interests, injury to which may be sufficient for standing. However, Congress has no power to eliminate the case or controversy requirement and, thus, cannot grant standing to someone not having an injury.

2) Standing to Enforce Government Statutes
A plaintiff may have standing to enforce a federal statute if she is within the "***zone of interests***" Congress meant to protect.

3) Standing to Assert Rights of Others
Generally, one cannot assert the constitutional rights of others to obtain standing, but a ***claimant with standing*** in her own right may also assert the rights of a third party ***if***:

a) It is difficult for the third party to assert her own rights (*e.g.,* an association may attack a law requiring disclosure of membership lists, because members cannot attack the law without disclosing their identities); or

b) A special relationship exists between the claimant and the third party (*e.g.,* a doctor can assert a patient's rights in challenging an abortion restriction).

4) Standing of Organizations
An organization has standing if (i) there is an injury in fact to members that gives them a right to sue on their own behalf, (ii) the injury is related to the organization's purpose, ***and*** (iii) individual member participation in the lawsuit is not required.

5) No Citizenship Standing
People have no standing merely as "citizens" to claim that government action violates federal law or the Constitution. The injury is too generalized.

6) Taxpayer Standing Requisites
A taxpayer has standing to litigate her tax bill, but a taxpayer generally has no standing to ***challenge government expenditures***, because the taxpayer's interest is too remote. *Exception:* Suits attacking taxing and spending measures on First Amendment ***Establishment Clause*** grounds (*e.g.,* federal expenditures to aid parochial schools).

CMR **Exam Tip** For a taxpayer to have standing, the ***spending power*** must be involved. Thus, for example, there is no standing to challenge federal government grants of surplus property to religious groups.

5. Adequate and Independent State Grounds
The Supreme Court will not exercise jurisdiction if the state court judgment is based on adequate and independent state law grounds—even if federal issues are involved. State law grounds are adequate if they are fully dispositive of the case. They are independent if the decision is not based on federal case interpretations of identical federal provisions. When the state court has not clearly indicated that its decision rests on state law, the Supreme Court may hear the case.

6. Abstention

a. Unsettled Question of State Law
A federal court will temporarily abstain from resolving a constitutional claim when the disposition rests on an unsettled question of state law.

b. Pending State Proceedings
Federal courts will not enjoin pending state ***criminal*** proceedings (and in some cases pending state administrative or civil proceedings involving an important state interest), except in cases of proven harassment or prosecutions taken in bad faith.

7. Political Questions
Political questions will not be decided. These are issues (i) constitutionally committed to another branch of government or (ii) inherently incapable of judicial resolution.

a. Examples of Political Questions
Challenges based on the "Republican Form of Government" Clause of Article IV; challenges to congressional procedures for ratifying constitutional amendments; whether a person elected to Congress meets the age, residency, or vote requirements; and the President's conduct of foreign policy are political questions.

b. Compare—Nonpolitical Questions
Legislative apportionment, arbitrary exclusion of a congressional delegate, and production of presidential papers and communications are not political questions.

8. Eleventh Amendment Limits on Federal Courts
The Eleventh Amendment prohibits ***federal courts*** from hearing a private party's or foreign government's claims against a state government.

a. What Is Barred?
The prohibition extends to actions in which the state is named as a party or in which the state will have to pay retroactive damages. Similarly, the Supreme Court has held that the ***doctrine of sovereign immunity bars*** suits against a state government in state court, even on federal claims, unless the defendant state consents.

b. What Is Not Barred?
The prohibition does not extend to actions against local governments, actions by the United States or other states, or proceedings in federal bankruptcy courts.

c. Exceptions

1) **Certain Actions Against State Officers**
The following actions can be brought against state officers in federal court despite the Eleventh Amendment: (i) actions to enjoin an officer from future conduct that violates the Constitution or federal law, even if this will require prospective payment from the state; and (ii) actions for damage against an officer personally.

2) **State Consents**
A state may consent to a suit in federal court. Such consent must be express and unequivocal.

3) **Congress Removes the Immunity**
Congress can remove Eleventh Amendment immunity ***as to actions created under the Fourteenth Amendment***, but it must be unmistakably clear that Congress intended to remove the immunity.

II. LEGISLATIVE POWER

The federal government has limited powers. Every exercise of federal power must be traced to the Constitution.

A. ENUMERATED AND IMPLIED POWERS

Congress can exercise those powers ***enumerated*** in the Constitution plus all auxiliary powers ***necessary and proper*** to carry out all powers vested in the federal government.

1. Necessary and Proper "Power"

Congress has the power to make all laws necessary and proper (appropriate) for executing ***any*** power granted to ***any*** branch of the federal government.

CMR **Exam Tip** The Necessary and Proper Clause standing alone cannot support federal law. It must work in conjunction with another federal power. Thus, an answer choice that states that a law is supported by the Necessary and Proper Clause (or is valid under Congress's power to enact legislation necessary and proper) will be incorrect unless another federal power is linked to it in the question.

2. Taxing Power

Congress has the power to tax, and most taxes will be upheld if they bear some ***reasonable relationship to revenue production*** or if Congress has the ***power to regulate*** the activity taxed. However, neither Congress nor the states may tax exports to foreign countries.

3. Spending Power

Congress may spend to "provide for the common defense and general welfare." Spending may be for ***any public purpose***.

CMR **Exam Tip** The federal government can tax and ***spend*** for the general welfare; it cannot directly legislate for it. Thus, nonspending regulations cannot be supported by the General Welfare Clause.

Also recall that although the power to spend for the general welfare is broad (any public purpose), it is still limited by the Bill of Rights and other constitutional provisions.

4. Commerce Power

Congress has the ***exclusive*** power to regulate all foreign and interstate commerce. To be within Congress's power under the Commerce Clause, a federal law regulating interstate commerce must either:

(i) ***Regulate the channels*** of interstate commerce;

(ii) ***Regulate the instrumentalities*** of interstate commerce and persons and things in interstate commerce; or

(iii) ***Regulate activities that have a substantial effect*** on interstate commerce.

a. Intrastate Activity

When Congress attempts to regulate ***intrastate*** activity under the third prong, above, the Court will uphold the regulation if it is of ***economic or commercial activity*** (*e.g.,* growing wheat or medicinal marijuana even for personal consumption) and the court can conceive of a ***rational basis*** on which Congress could conclude that the activity ***in aggregate*** substantially affects interstate commerce. However, if the regulated intrastate activity is noncommercial and noneconomic (*e.g.,* possessing a gun in a school zone or gender-motivated violence), it cannot be regulated under the Commerce Clause unless Congress can factually show a substantial economic effect on interstate commerce.

5. War and Related Powers

The Constitution gives Congress power to declare war, raise and support armies, and provide for and maintain a navy.

a. Economic Regulation

Economic regulation during war and in the postwar period to remedy wartime disruptions has been upheld.

b. Military Courts and Tribunals

Congress is authorized to make rules for the government and regulation of armed forces.

1) Judicial Review

Regular federal (or state) courts have no general power to review court-martial proceedings.

2) Enemy Civilians and Soldiers

Enemy civilians and soldiers may be tried by military courts.

3) American Soldiers

Military courts have jurisdiction over ***all offenses*** committed by persons who are members of the armed services both at the time of the offense ***and*** when charged.

4) American Civilians

American civilians may be tried by military courts under martial law only if actual warfare forces the federal courts to shut down.

5) **Detention of Citizen Enemy Combatants**
Due process requires that a ***citizen held in the United States*** as an "enemy combatant" have a meaningful opportunity to contest the factual basis for his detention before a neutral decisionmaker.

6. **Investigatory Power**
The power of Congress to investigate is implied. Investigation must be expressly or impliedly authorized by the appropriate congressional house.

7. **Property Power**
Congress has the power to dispose of and make rules for territories and other properties of the United States. While there is no express limitation on Congress's power to ***dispose*** of property, federal ***takings*** (eminent domain) must be for the purpose of effectuating an enumerated power under some other provision of the Constitution.

8. **No Federal Police Power**
Congress has no general police power. However, Congress has police power type powers over the District of Columbia, federal lands, military bases, and Indian reservations (based on its power over the capital and its property power).

CMR **Exam Tip** If an answer choice attempts to support federal action on the basis of the police power (*e.g.,* "Congress can constitutionally act under the police power" or "the action is valid under the federal police power"), see whether the facts state that the action pertains to the District of Columbia or other federal possessions. If not, it is a wrong choice.

9. **Bankruptcy Power**
Congress's power to establish uniform rules for bankruptcy is nonexclusive; states may legislate in the field as long as their laws do not conflict with federal law.

10. **Postal Power**
The postal power is exclusive. Under the postal power, Congress may validly classify and place reasonable restrictions on use of the mails, but may not deprive any citizen or group of citizens of the general mail "privilege."

11. **Power Over Citizenship**
Congress may establish uniform rules of naturalization. This gives Congress plenary power over aliens.

a. **Exclusion of Aliens**
Aliens have no right to enter the United States and can be refused entry summarily because of their political beliefs. However, ***resident aliens*** are entitled to ***notice and a hearing*** before they can be deported.

b. **Naturalization and Denaturalization**
Congress has ***exclusive*** power over naturalization and denaturalization. However, Congress may not take away the citizenship of any citizen—native born or naturalized—without his consent.

12. Admiralty Power
Congress's admiralty power is plenary and exclusive unless Congress leaves maritime matters to state jurisdiction.

13. Power to Coin Money and Fix Weights and Measures
Congress has the power to coin money and fix standards for weights and measures.

14. Patent/Copyright Power
Congress has the power to control the issuance of patents and copyrights.

SOURCES OF CONGRESSIONAL POWER

Government Action	Source of Power
1. Congress enacts divorce laws for the District of Columbia.	General federal police power for D.C. (as well as military bases and federal lands).
2. Congress pays for highways.	Spending Power and Commerce Clause.
3. Federal income tax.	Taxing Power.
4. Congress conditions aid to states for medical programs on state funding of AIDS research.	Spending Power.
5. Congress adopts a tax to regulate banknotes rather than to raise revenue.	Power to coin money.
6. Congress prohibits hunting on federal lands.	Property Power.
7. Congress bars racial discrimination at places of public accommodation.	Commerce Clause.
8. Congress requires all employers, including state governments, to comply with federal minimum wage and overtime provisions.	Commerce Clause.

Note: The Amendments to the Constitution may also be a source of power (*e.g.,* the Thirteenth Amendment gives Congress power to outlaw badges of slavery; thus Congress may require a private seller to sell land to blacks as well as whites). (*See infra.*)

B. DELEGATION OF LEGISLATIVE POWER

Legislative power may generally be delegated to the executive or judicial branch as long as intelligible standards are set and the power is not uniquely confined to Congress (*e.g.,* powers to declare war, impeach).

Note: Congress may not appoint members of a body with administrative or enforcement powers (*see* III.A.1.a., *infra*).

CMR **Exam Tip** Although you should know that a valid delegation of legislative power requires "intelligible standards" for the delegate to follow (*see* above), in applying that rule almost anything will pass for an intelligible standard, and thus no legislative delegation has been invalidated since 1936.

C. SPEECH AND DEBATE CLAUSE—IMMUNITY FOR FEDERAL LEGISLATORS

Conduct that occurs in the regular course of the federal legislative process and the motivation behind that conduct are immune from prosecution.

Note: Immunity does not cover bribes, speeches outside Congress, or the republication in a press release or newsletter of a defamatory statement originally made in Congress.

D. CONGRESSIONAL "VETO" OF EXECUTIVE ACTIONS INVALID

A legislative veto is an attempt by Congress to overturn an executive agency action ***without*** bicameralism (*i.e.,* passage by both houses of Congress) or presentment (*i.e.,* giving the bill to the President for his signature or veto). Legislative vetoes of executive actions are invalid.

III. THE EXECUTIVE POWER

A. DOMESTIC POWERS

1. Appointment and Removal

a. Appointment Powers

The executive appoints "all ambassadors, other public ministers and consuls, justices of the Supreme Court, and all other officers of the United States whose appointments are not otherwise provided for," with advice and consent of the Senate. Congress, however, may vest the appointment of ***inferior officers*** in the President alone, the courts, or the heads of departments. Congress itself may ***not*** appoint members of a body with administrative or enforcement powers.

b. Removal of Appointees

1) By President

The President can remove high level, purely executive officers (*e.g.,* cabinet members) at will, without any interference by Congress. However, Congress may provide statutory limitations (*e.g.,* removal only for good cause) on the President's power to remove all other executive appointees.

2) By Congress

Congress may remove executive officers ***only*** through the impeachment process.

2. Pardons

The President may grant pardons for all federal offenses but not for impeachment or civil contempt. The pardon power cannot be limited by Congress.

3. Veto Power

If the President disapproves (vetoes) an act of Congress, the act may still become law if the veto is overridden by a ***two-thirds*** vote of ***each*** house.

a. Pocket Veto

The President has 10 days to exercise the veto power. If he fails to act within that time, the bill is automatically vetoed if Congress is not in session. If Congress is in session, the bill becomes law.

b. Line Item Veto Unconstitutional

The veto power allows the President only to approve or reject a bill ***in toto***; he cannot cancel part (through a line item veto) and approve other parts.

4. Power as Chief Executive

The President's powers over internal affairs are unsettled. Clearly the President has some power to direct subordinate executive officers, and there is a long history of Presidents issuing executive orders. Perhaps the best guide is as follows:

a. If the President acts with the express or implied authority of Congress, his authority is at its maximum and his actions likely are valid;

b. If the President acts where Congress is silent, his action will be upheld unless it usurps the power of another governmental branch or prevents another branch from carrying out its tasks; and

c. If the President acts against the express will of Congress, he has little authority, and his action likely is invalid (*e.g.*, the President has no power to refuse to spend appropriated funds when Congress has expressly mandated that they be spent).

B. POWER OVER EXTERNAL AFFAIRS

1. War

The President has ***no power*** to declare war but may act militarily in actual hostilities against the United States without a congressional declaration of war. However, Congress, under its power to enact a military appropriation every two years, may limit the President.

2. Foreign Relations

The President has paramount power to represent the United States in day-to-day foreign relations.

3. Treaty Power

The President has the power to enter into treaties with the consent of two-thirds of the Senate.

a. Supreme Law

Like other federal law, treaties are the "supreme law of the land." ***State*** laws that conflict are invalid.

b. Conflict with Federal Laws

A conflict between a congressional act and a valid treaty is resolved by order of adoption: ***the last in time prevails***.

c. **Conflict with Constitution**
Treaties are ***not*** co-equal with the Constitution; a treaty may not be inconsistent with the Constitution.

Exam Tip Treaties are subject to constitutional limits. Thus, no treaty (or executive agreement) can confer on Congress authority to act in a manner inconsistent with any specific provision of the Constitution.

4. **Executive Agreements**
Executive agreements are signed by the President and the head of a foreign country. They can be used for any purpose that treaties can be used for. They do ***not*** require the consent of the Senate.

a. **Conflict with State Laws**
If a state law conflicts with an executive agreement, the agreement prevails.

b. **Conflict with Federal Laws**
If an executive agreement conflicts with a federal law, the federal law prevails over the agreement.

HIERARCHY OF U.S. LAW

United States Constitution

prevails over

Treaties and Federal Statutes
(in a conflict between these two, the last in time prevails)

prevail over

Executive Agreements

prevail over

State Law

C. EXECUTIVE PRIVILEGE/IMMUNITY

1. Executive Privilege

The President has a privilege to keep certain communications secret. National security secrets are given great deference by the courts.

a. Exception

In criminal proceedings, presidential communiques will be available to the prosecution where a need for such information is demonstrated.

2. Executive Immunity

The President has ***absolute immunity*** from civil damages based on any action he took within his official responsibilities, but there is no immunity for acts that allegedly occurred before taking office. If presidential aides have exercised discretionary authority in a sensitive area, they may share in the immunity for suits brought concerning that area.

D. IMPEACHMENT

The President, Vice President, and all civil officers of the United States are subject to impeachment (the bringing of charges). Grounds include treason, bribery, high crimes, and misdemeanors. A ***majority*** vote in the House is necessary to invoke the charges of impeachment, and a ***two-thirds*** vote in the Senate is necessary to convict and remove from office.

PART 2: THE FEDERAL SYSTEM

IV. RELATIVE SPHERES OF FEDERAL AND STATE POWERS

A. EXCLUSIVE FEDERAL POWERS

1. Power of States Expressly Limited

Some powers are exclusively federal because the Constitution limits or prohibits the use of the power by states (*e.g.,* treaty power, coinage of money).

2. Inherent Federal Powers

Other powers are exclusively federal because the nature of the power itself is such that it can be exercised only by the federal government (*e.g.,* declaration of war, federal citizenship).

B. EXCLUSIVE STATE POWERS

All powers not delegated to federal government are reserved to the states. Note, however, that federal powers are given an expansive interpretation, and thus little state power is exclusive.

C. CONCURRENT FEDERAL AND STATE POWER—EFFECT OF SUPREMACY CLAUSE

Because of the Supremacy Clause, a federal law may supersede or preempt local laws.

1. Conflict Between State and Federal Laws

If a state law conflicts with federal law, the state law will be invalidated.

2. **State Prevents Achievement of Federal Objective**
If a state or local law prevents achievement of a federal objective, it will be invalidated. This is true even if the state law was enacted for some valid purpose and not to frustrate the federal law (*e.g.,* state law providing for suspension of driver's license of persons who fail to pay off an auto accident case judgment, regardless of the person's discharge in bankruptcy, is invalid).

3. **Preemption**
A valid federal statute or regulation may expressly or impliedly "occupy" the entire field, thus precluding any state or local regulation ***even if the state or local regulation is nonconflicting***. Factors considered here (if there is no express preemption) are (i) comprehensiveness of the federal scheme and (ii) creation of an agency to administer the law.

D. ABSENCE OF FEDERAL AND STATE POWERS
Some powers are denied to both Congress and the states. For example, the qualifications for serving in Congress are set by the Constitution and cannot be altered by Congress or the states.

E. INTERSTATE COMPACT CLAUSE
The Interstate Compact Clause concerns agreements between states. If the agreement increases the states' power at the expense of federal power, congressional approval is required.

F. FULL FAITH AND CREDIT CLAUSE
By virtue of the Full Faith and Credit Clause, if a judgment is entitled to full faith and credit, it must be recognized in sister states (*i.e.*, a party who loses a case in New York generally may not relitigate it in New Jersey; the New Jersey courts are bound by the New York ruling). This Clause applies only if: (i) the court that rendered the judgment had ***jurisdiction*** over the parties and the subject matter; (ii) the judgment was ***on the merits***; and (iii) the judgment is ***final***.

V. INTERSOVEREIGN LITIGATION

A. SUITS BY UNITED STATES AGAINST A STATE
The United States may sue a state without its consent.

B. SUITS BY A STATE AGAINST UNITED STATES
Public policy forbids a state from suing the United States without its consent. Congress can pass legislation that permits the United States to be sued by a state in given situations.

C. FEDERAL OFFICER AS DEFENDANT

1. **Limitation**
A suit against a federal officer is deemed to be brought against the United States itself if the judgment sought would be satisfied out of the public treasury or would interfere with public administration and therefore is not permitted.

2. **Specific Relief Against Officer**
Specific relief against an officer as an individual will be granted if the officer acted ultra vires (beyond his authority).

D. SUITS BY ONE STATE AGAINST ANOTHER

One state may sue another state without the latter's consent. The Supreme Court has exclusive original jurisdiction.

VI. INTERGOVERNMENTAL TAX AND REGULATION IMMUNITIES

A. FEDERAL TAXATION AND REGULATION OF STATE OR LOCAL GOVERNMENTS

1. Tax or Regulation Applying to Both State and Private Entities—Valid

Congress may subject state and local government activities to regulation or taxation if the law or tax applies to ***both*** the public sector and the private sector (*e.g.,* minimum wage laws).

2. Tax or Regulation Applying Only to States

A federal tax or regulation that is not applicable to private businesses and that merely taxes or regulates a purely state or local governmental activity may be limited by the Tenth Amendment (*e.g.,* requiring states to either regulate radioactive waste or take title to it is beyond Congress's power).

a. Exception—Civil Rights

Congress may restrict state activities that violate civil liberties.

b. Exception—Spending Power Conditions

Congress may "indirectly" regulate states through the spending power by imposing conditions on the grant of money (*e.g.,* federal highway funds will be given only to states with a 21-year minimum age for drinking of alcohol).

CMR **Exam Tip** As a practical matter, the Court almost never strikes down on Tenth Amendment grounds a federal regulation or tax that impacts on state or local government entities. Thus, a choice on an MBE question that suggests that the Tenth Amendment will invalidate a federal action is almost always wrong.

3. Commandeering State Officials

While not specifically resting on the Tenth Amendment, the Supreme Court has held that Congress may not require state executive officials (*e.g.*, the police) to enforce federal laws because such a requirement would upset the Constitution's "dual sovereignty" structure (*i.e.*, both the states and the federal government are sovereigns).

B. STATE TAXATION AND REGULATION OF FEDERAL GOVERNMENT

A state may not directly tax federal instrumentalities without the consent of Congress. However, ***nondiscriminatory***, ***indirect*** taxes are permissible if they do not unreasonably burden the federal government (*e.g.,* state income tax on federal employees). States may not regulate the federal government or its agents while performing their federal functions.

VII. PRIVILEGES AND IMMUNITIES CLAUSES

A. ARTICLE IV—PRIVILEGES OF STATE CITIZENSHIP

The Interstate Privileges and Immunities Clause prohibits discrimination by a state ***against nonresidents***.

Note: Corporations and aliens are ***not*** protected by this clause. (In contrast, corporations and aliens are protected by the Equal Protection and Due Process Clauses of the Fourteenth Amendment, as well as the Dormant Commerce Clause, discussed *infra.*)

1. Only "Fundamental Rights" Protected

Only "fundamental rights"—those involving important ***commercial activities*** (*e.g.,* the pursuit of livelihood) and ***civil liberties***—are protected.

2. Substantial Justification Exception

The state law may be valid if the state has a substantial justification for the different treatment. In effect, the state must show that nonresidents either cause or are part of the problem that the state is attempting to solve and that there are ***no less restrictive means*** to solve the problem.

3. Note—Relationship to Commerce Clause

Although the Article IV Privileges and Immunities Clause and the Dormant Commerce Clause may apply different standards and produce different results, they tend to mutually reinforce each other. Consequently, they both have to be considered in analyzing bar exam questions.

ARTICLE IV PRIVILEGES AND IMMUNITIES CLAUSE

Invalid Discrimination

1. Statute requiring $2,500 license fee from nonresident ***commercial fishermen***, while residents paid $25.
2. Statute giving resident creditors priority over nonresident creditors to assets of foreign corporations in receivership proceedings.
3. Statute imposing a residency requirement for abortion.
4. Rule limiting bar admission to state residents.
5. Statute requiring ***private sector*** employers to give hiring preference to residents.

Discrimination Upheld

Statute requiring nonresidents to pay $225 license fee, as opposed to $30 residents' fee, for ***recreational*** hunting.

B. FOURTEENTH AMENDMENT—PRIVILEGES OF NATIONAL CITIZENSHIP

States may not deny their citizens the privileges or immunities of ***national*** citizenship (*e.g.,* the right to petition Congress for redress of grievances, the right to vote for federal officers, and the right to interstate travel). Corporations are not protected by this Clause.

PART 3: STATE REGULATION OR TAXATION OF COMMERCE

VIII. REGULATION OF FOREIGN COMMERCE

With a few minor exceptions, the power to regulate foreign commerce lies exclusively with Congress.

IX. REGULATION OF INTERSTATE COMMERCE

A. REGULATION OF COMMERCE BY CONGRESS

1. Power of Congress to Supersede or Preempt State Regulation

When Congress regulates interstate commerce, conflicting state laws are ***superseded*** and even nonconflicting state or local laws in the same field may be ***preempted***. (*See* IV.C.3., *supra.*)

2. Power of Congress to Permit or Prohibit State Regulation

Congress may permit state regulations that would otherwise violate the Commerce Clause. Likewise, Congress may prohibit state regulations that could otherwise be upheld under the Commerce Clause. Congress may ***not***, however, permit states to violate civil liberties.

B. STATE REGULATION OF COMMERCE IN THE ABSENCE OF CONGRESSIONAL ACTION

If Congress has not enacted laws regarding the subject, a state or local government may regulate local aspects of interstate commerce. To do so, however, it must ***not discriminate against*** or ***unduly burden*** interstate commerce. If it does, the state or local regulation will violate the Commerce Clause.

CMR **Exam Tip** The examiners sometimes use the terms "Dormant Commerce Clause" and "Negative Commerce Clause." These are merely descriptive terms that reflect the above idea: even where Congress has not acted, the Commerce Clause restricts state regulation of interstate commerce; states may not favor local economic interests or unduly burden interstate commerce.

1. Discriminatory Regulations

State or local regulations that discriminate against interstate commerce to protect local economic interests ***are almost always invalid*** (*e.g.,* New York cannot ban California wines or tax them at a higher rate than local wines).

a. Exception—Important State Interest

A discriminatory state or local law may be valid if it furthers an important, noneconomic state interest and there are ***no reasonable nondiscriminatory alternatives***

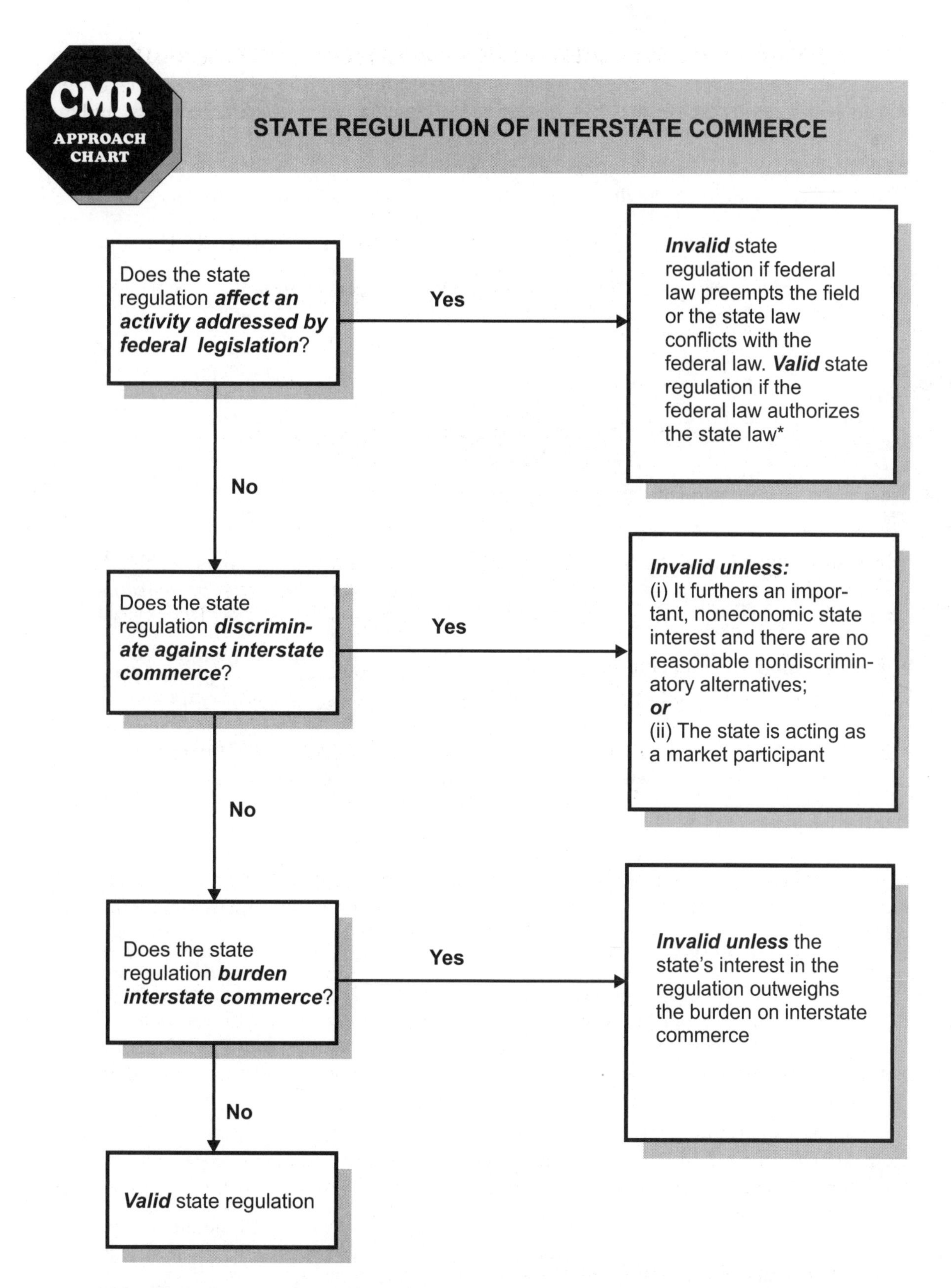

*Of course, Congress has no power to authorize legislation that would violate other constitutional provisions, such as the Privileges and Immunities Clause of Article IV.

available. *Example:* State could prohibit ***importation*** of live bait fish because parasites could have detrimental effect on its own fish population. However, state could not prohibit ***export*** of live bait fish when no major state interest was involved.

b. Exception—State as "Market Participant"
A state may prefer its own citizens when acting as a market participant (*e.g.,* when buying or selling, hiring labor, or giving subsidies).

Exam Tip Remember that discriminatory laws may also violate the Privileges and Immunities Clause of Article IV (*see* chart *infra*) or the Equal Protection Clause.

COMMERCE CLAUSE VS. ARTICLE IV PRIVILEGES AND IMMUNITIES

	Commerce Clause	Privileges and Immunities Clause of Article IV
State/local action *discriminates* against out-of-state entities	If the discrimination burdens interstate commerce and there is no applicable federal legislation, the action is ***invalid unless:*** (i) It furthers an ***important, noneconomic state interest*** and there are no reasonable nondiscriminatory alternatives; or (ii) The state is a ***market participant*** (*i.e.,* purchaser, seller, subsidizer).	If the action denies the out-of-state person important economic interests (*e.g.,* livelihood) or civil liberties, the law is ***invalid unless*** the state has a ***substantial*** justification and there are no less restrictive means.
State/local action does *not discriminate*	If the law burdens interstate commerce and the burden outweighs the state's interest in the action, the law is ***invalid***.	Privileges and Immunities Clause does not apply where there is no discrimination.
May an alien or a corporation be a plaintiff?	Yes	No
Is there a market participant exception?	Yes	No

Note: The Article IV Privileges and Immunities Clause is stronger than the Commerce Clause (no market participant exception), but it is much narrower in scope (applies only to discrimination against economic interest; does not protect corporations or aliens).

2. **Nondiscriminatory Laws—Balancing Test**
If a nondiscriminatory state law (*i.e.,* a law that treats local and out-of-state interests alike) burdens interstate commerce, it will be valid ***unless*** the burden outweighs the promotion of a legitimate local interest. The court will consider whether less restrictive alternatives are available. *Example:* An Iowa statute banning trucks over 60 feet was invalid because the state showed no significant evidence of increased safety and the burden on commerce was substantial.

a. **State Control of Corporations**
A different standard may apply to statutes ***adopted by the state of incorporation*** regulating the ***internal governance of a corporation.*** Because of the states' long history of regulating the internal governance of corporations that they create, and because of their strong interest in doing so, even a statute that heavily impacts interstate commerce may be upheld (*e.g.,* a state may deny voting rights to persons who acquire a controlling interest in a state corporation without approval from other shareholders, despite the impact that this may have on interstate commerce).

CMR Exam Tip When a bar exam question involves a state regulation that affects the free flow of interstate commerce, you should ask:

- Does the question refer to any ***federal legislation*** that might (i) ***supersede*** the state regulation or ***preempt*** the field or (ii) ***authorize*** state regulation otherwise impermissible?

- If neither of these possibilities is dispositive, does the state regulation either ***discriminate*** against interstate or out-of-state commerce or place an ***undue burden*** on the free flow of interstate commerce? If the regulation is discriminatory, it will be invalid unless (i) it furthers an important, noneconomic state interest ***and*** there are no reasonable nondiscriminatory alternatives, or (ii) the state is a market participant. If the regulation does not discriminate but burdens interstate commerce, it will be invalid if the burden on commerce outweighs the state's interest.

C. TWENTY-FIRST AMENDMENT—STATE CONTROL OVER INTOXICATING LIQUOR

1. **Intrastate Regulation**
State governments have wide latitude over the ***importation*** of liquor and the conditions under which it is ***sold or used*** within the state. However, regulations that constitute only an economic preference for local liquor manufacturers may violate the Commerce Clause.

2. **Interstate Regulation**
Liquor in interstate commerce is subject to the Commerce Clause.

3. **Federal Power**
Congress may regulate economic transactions involving liquor (*e.g.,* sales of alcoholic beverages) through the federal commerce power (*e.g.,* antitrust laws) or by conditioning grants of money (*e.g.,* highway funds given only to states with minimum drinking age of 21).

X. POWER OF STATES TO TAX INTERSTATE COMMERCE

The same general considerations that apply to state regulation of commerce (*see supra*) apply to state taxation of commerce.

A. GENERAL CONSIDERATIONS

Congress has complete power to authorize or forbid state taxation that affects interstate commerce.

1. Discriminatory Taxes

Unless authorized by Congress, state taxes that discriminate against interstate commerce (*e.g.,* tax on out-of-state businesses higher than tax on in-state businesses) violate the Commerce Clause. Note that these taxes may also violate other constitutional provisions (*e.g.,* the Privileges and Immunities Clause of Article IV or the Equal Protection Clause).

2. Nondiscriminatory Taxes

A nondiscriminatory tax will be valid ***if*** the following requirements are met:

a. Substantial Nexus

To be valid, the tax must apply to an activity having a substantial nexus to the taxing state; *i.e.,* there must be significant or substantial activity within the taxing state. (Lack of a substantial nexus might also violate the due process requirement of minimum contacts, but substantial nexus requires more in-state connections.)

b. Fair Apportionment

To be valid, the tax must be fairly apportioned according to a rational formula. However, the taxpayer has the burden of proving unfair apportionment. (An unfairly apportioned tax may also violate equal protection.)

c. Fair Relationship

To be valid, the tax must be fairly related to the services or benefits provided by the state.

B. USE TAXES

1. Permissible in Buyer's State

Use taxes are imposed on goods purchased outside the state but used within it. They are valid.

2. State May Force Seller to Collect Use Tax

An interstate seller may be required to collect a use tax ***if*** the seller has a ***sufficient nexus*** with the taxing state (*e.g.,* maintains offices in the taxing state). Merely soliciting orders by mail and shipping orders into the state is not sufficient.

C. SALES TAXES

Sales taxes are taxes imposed on the seller of goods for sales consummated within the state. They generally do not discriminate against interstate commerce; rather, the issue usually involves whether there is a substantial nexus between the taxpayer and the taxing state or whether the tax is properly apportioned.

D. AD VALOREM PROPERTY TAXES

Ad valorem property taxes are based on the assessed value of the property in question.

STATE TAXATION OF INTERSTATE COMMERCE

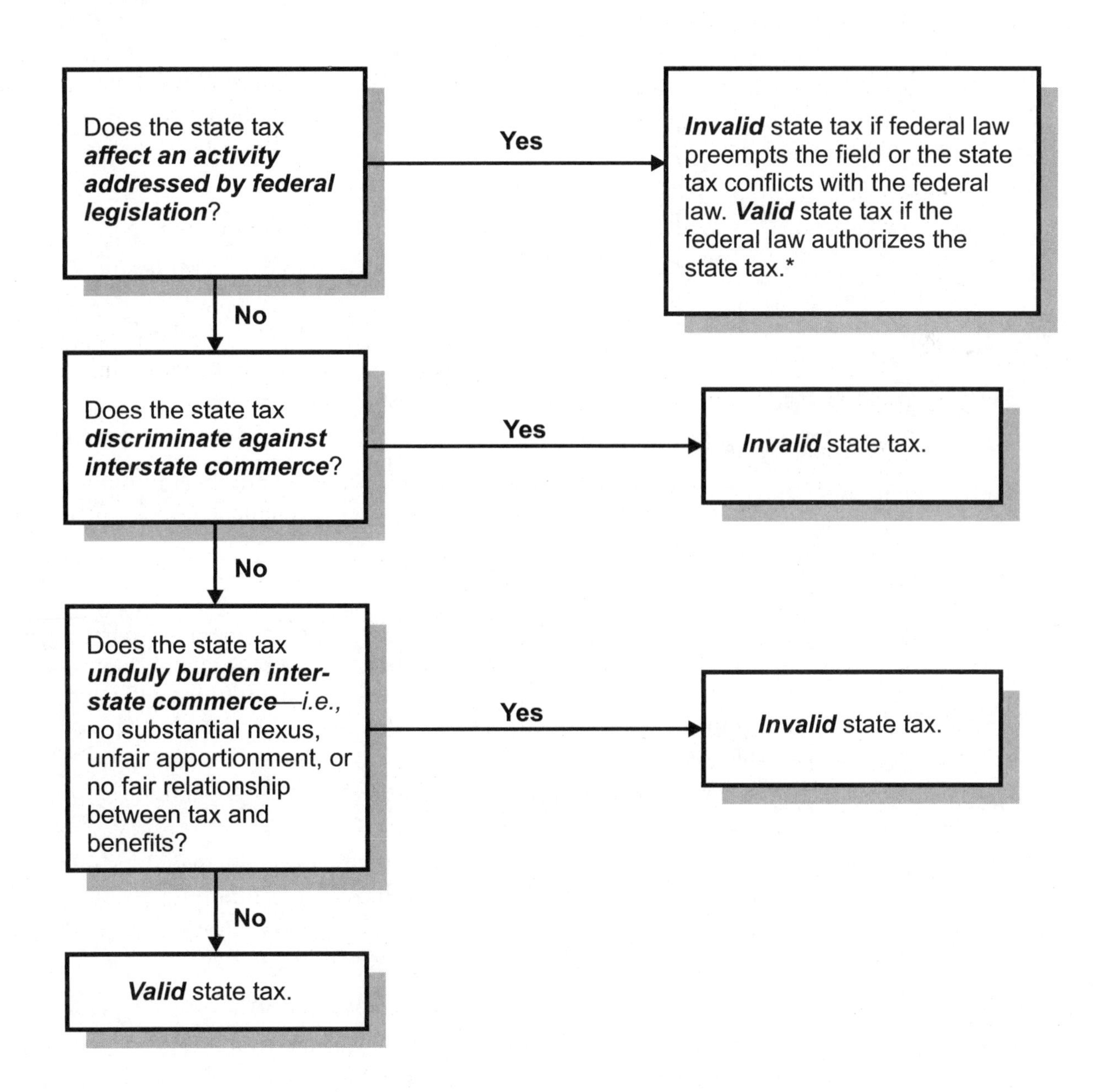

*Of course, Congress has no power to authorize taxes that would violate the Constitution (*i.e.,* go beyond Congress's taxing power).

1. **No Tax on Commodities in Course of Interstate Commerce**
Commodities in interstate transit are entirely ***exempt*** from state taxation.

a. **When Does Interstate Transportation Begin?**
Interstate transportation begins when the cargo (i) is delivered to an interstate carrier ***or*** (ii) actually starts its interstate journey.

b. **Effect of "Break" in Transit**
A break in the continuity of transit does not destroy the interstate character of the shipment unless the break was intended to end or suspend the shipment.

c. **When Does Interstate Shipment End?**
The interstate shipment usually ends when the cargo reaches its destination; thereafter the goods are subject to local tax.

2. **Tax on Instrumentalities Used to Transport Goods Interstate**
The validity of ad valorem property taxes on instrumentalities of commerce (*e.g.,* trucks or airplanes) depends on (i) whether the instrumentality has acquired a ***"taxable situs"*** in the taxing state (*i.e.,* whether there are sufficient "contacts" with the taxing state to justify the tax) and (ii) whether the value of the instrumentality has been ***properly apportioned*** according to the amount of the "contacts" with each taxing state.

a. **Taxable Situs**
An instrumentality has a taxable situs in a state if it receives benefits or protection from the state. (There may be more than one taxable situs). *Example:* An airplane was held to have a taxable situs in a state—even though the airline owned no other property in the state—because the airline made 18 regularly scheduled flights daily from a rented depot in the state.

b. **Apportionment Requirement**
A tax apportioned on the value of the instrumentality will be upheld if it fairly approximates the average physical presence of the instrumentality in the taxing state. The taxpayer's domiciliary state can tax the full value of instrumentalities used in interstate commerce unless the taxpayer can prove that a defined part thereof has acquired a "taxable situs" elsewhere.

E. PRIVILEGE, LICENSE, FRANCHISE, OR OCCUPATIONAL TAXES

These so-called doing business taxes are generally permitted. Such taxes may be measured by a flat amount or by a proportional rate based on contact with the taxing state. In either case, the basic requirements must be met: (i) the activity taxed must have a ***substantial nexus*** to the taxing state; (ii) the tax must be ***fairly apportioned***; (iii) the tax must ***not discriminate*** against interstate commerce; and (iv) the tax must ***fairly relate to services provided*** by the state.

CMR **Exam Tip** When a question involves state taxation that affects interestate commerce, you should ask:

1. Does the question refer to any federal legislation that might (i) ***forbid*** the state tax or ***preempt*** the field, or (ii) ***authorize*** state taxation?

2. If neither of these possibilities is dispositive, does the state tax ***discriminate*** against or ***unduly burden*** the free flow of interstate commerce? If the state tax discriminates or is unduly burdensome (no substantial nexus, unfair apportionment, or no fair relationship), it is invalid.

STATE TAXATION OF INTERSTATE COMMERCE—SPECIFIC TYPES OF TAXES

Type	Definition	Validity Under Commerce Clause
Use Tax	Tax on goods purchased outside of the state, but used within it	Valid unless higher than sales tax.
Sales Tax	Tax on the sale of goods consummated within the state	Generally valid if there is a substantial nexus to the taxing state and the tax is properly apportioned (if more than one state can tax the sale).
Ad Valorem Tax	Tax on the assessed value of some property	*Commodities:* Valid only if property is no longer in interstate commerce. *Instrumentalities:* Valid if instrumentality has "taxable situs" in state and tax is fairly apportioned. Full tax by domiciliary state valid unless taxpayer can prove a defined part has acquired taxable situs elsewhere.
Privilege, License, Franchise, and Occupational Tax	Tax placed on some activity ("doing business" tax)	Valid if (i) substantial nexus to taxing state, (ii) fairly apportioned, (iii) does not discriminate against interstate commerce, and (iv) fairly relates to services provided by the state.

XI. POWER OF STATES TO TAX FOREIGN COMMERCE

The Import-Export Clause and the Commerce Clause greatly limit the states' power to tax foreign commerce.

PART 4: INDIVIDUAL GUARANTEES AGAINST GOVERNMENTAL OR PRIVATE ACTION

XII. LIMITATIONS ON POWER AND STATE ACTION REQUIREMENT

A. CONSTITUTIONAL RESTRICTIONS ON POWER OVER INDIVIDUALS

1. Bill of Rights

By its terms, the Bill of Rights (the first 10 amendments to the United States Constitution) limits ***federal*** power. However, the Fourteenth Amendment Due Process Clause applies almost all provisions of the Bill of Rights to the states. *Exceptions:* The most notable exceptions to incorporation are: (i) the Fifth Amendment's prohibition of criminal trials without a grand jury indictment and (ii) the Seventh Amendment's right to a jury trial in civil cases.

2. Thirteenth Amendment

The Thirteenth Amendment prohibits slavery and involuntary servitude. Under the Thirteenth Amendment's Enabling Clause, Congress can prohibit racially discriminatory action by ***anyone*** (the government or a private citizen).

3. Fourteenth and Fifteenth Amendments

The Fourteenth Amendment prevents ***states*** from depriving any person of life, liberty, or property without due process and equal protection of law. The Fifteenth Amendment prevents both the ***federal and state governments*** from denying a citizen the right to vote on account of race or color. Generally, private conduct is not prohibited by these amendments—only where some ***state action*** is involved. (Purely private conduct may be prohibited, however, on a separate constitutional basis, such as the Commerce Clause.)

a. Scope of Congressional Power Under Fourteenth Amendment

Section 5 of the Fourteenth Amendment gives Congress the power to adopt ***appropriate legislation*** to enforce the rights and guarantees provided by the Fourteenth Amendment. Under Section 5, Congress may ***not*** expand existing constitutional rights or create new ones—it may only enact laws to prevent or remedy violations of rights already recognized by the courts. To adopt a valid law, Congress must point to a history or pattern of state violation of such rights and adopt legislation that is ***congruent and proportional*** (*i.e.,* narrowly tailored) to solving the identified violation.

4. Commerce Clause

Under the broadly construed commerce power, Congress may prohibit ***private*** racial discrimination in activities that might have a substantial effect on interstate commerce.

CMR **Exam Tip** Because almost any activity taken cumulatively might have a substantial effect on interstate commerce, the Commerce Clause is an important basis for civil rights laws.

5. **Rights of National Citizenship**
Congress has inherent power to protect rights of citizenship (*e.g.,* rights to interstate travel, assemble, and petition Congress for redress).

B. STATE ACTION REQUIREMENT

Because the Constitution generally applies only to governmental action, to show a constitutional violation "state action" must be involved. *Note:* This concept applies to government and government officers at all levels—local, state, or federal. Note, however, that state action can be found in actions of seemingly private individuals who (i) perform exclusive public functions or (ii) have significant state involvement.

1. **Exclusive Public Functions**
Activities that are so ***traditionally*** the ***exclusive*** prerogative of the state are state action no matter who performs them.

2. **Significant State Involvement—Facilitating Private Action**
State action also exists wherever a state ***affirmatively*** facilitates, encourages, or authorizes acts of discrimination by its citizens.

CMR EXAMPLE CHART

STATE ACTION VS. NO STATE ACTION

State Action	No State Action
Public Function	
Running a town	Running a shopping mall (does not have all the attributes of a town)
Conducting an election	Holding a warehouseman's lien sale
Significant State Involvement	
Enforcing restrictive covenants prohibiting sale or lease of property through use of state courts	Granting a license and providing essential services to a private club
Leasing premises to a discriminatory lessee where state derives extra benefit from the discrimination (*i.e.,* symbiotic relationship exists)	Granting a monopoly to a utility
Allowing state official to act in discriminatory manner under "color of state law"	Heavily regulating an industry
Administering a private discriminatory trust by public officials	Granting a corporation its charter and exclusive name

CMR **Exam Tip** On the bar exam, remember that the state must be "significantly involved" in the private entity; mere acquiescence by the state in private conduct is not enough. Also, states are not constitutionally required to outlaw discrimination. They are only forbidden to facilitate, encourage, or authorize it.

XIII. RETROACTIVE LEGISLATION

A. CONTRACT CLAUSE—IMPAIRMENT OF CONTRACT

The Contract Clause prohibits ***states*** from enacting any law that ***retroactively*** impairs contract rights. It does not affect contracts not yet entered into.

1. Not Applicable to Federal Government

There is no comparable clause applicable to the federal government, but flagrant contract impairment would violate the Fifth Amendment Due Process Clause.

2. Basic Impairment Rules

a. Private Contracts—Intermediate Scrutiny

State legislation that ***substantially impairs*** an existing ***private*** contract is invalid unless the legislation (i) serves an important and legitimate public interest and (ii) is a reasonable and narrowly tailored means of promoting that interest. *Example:* Imposing a moratorium on mortgage foreclosures during a severe depression did not violate the Contract Clause.

b. Public Contracts—Stricter Scrutiny

Legislation that impairs a contract to which the state is a party is tested by the same basic test, but the contract will likely receive stricter scrutiny, especially if the legislation reduces the contractual burdens on the state.

B. EX POST FACTO LAWS

The state or federal government may not pass an ex post facto law (*i.e.,* a law that ***retroactively*** alters ***criminal*** offenses or punishments in a substantially prejudicial manner for the purpose of punishing a person for some past activity). A statute retroactively alters a law in a substantially prejudicial manner if it: (i) makes criminal an act that was ***innocent when done***; (ii) prescribes ***greater punishment*** for an act than was prescribed for the act when it was done; or (iii) ***reduces the evidence*** required to convict a person of a crime from what was required when the act was committed. Note that the Due Process Clauses of the Fifth and Fourteenth Amendments similarly prohibit ***courts*** from retroactively interpreting criminal laws in an unexpected and indefensible way.

CMR **Exam Tip** The Ex Post Facto Clauses apply only to ***criminal*** cases. Thus, an answer choice that attempts to apply these prohibitions in a civil case (*e.g.,* regarding a denial of a professional license) is ***wrong.***

C. BILLS OF ATTAINDER

Bills of attainder are legislative acts that inflict punishment on individuals without a judicial trial. Both federal and state governments are prohibited from passing bills of attainder.

D. DUE PROCESS CONSIDERATIONS

If a retroactive law does not violate the Contracts, Ex Post Facto, or Bill of Attainder Clauses, it still must pass muster under the Due Process Clause. If the retroactive law does not relate to a fundamental right, it need only be rationally related to a legitimate government interest.

XIV. PROCEDURAL DUE PROCESS

A. BASIC PRINCIPLE

A ***fair process*** (*e.g.,* notice and a hearing) is required for a government agency to individually take a person's "life, liberty, or property." Only intentional—not negligent—deprivation of these rights violates the Due Process Clause.

B. IS LIFE, LIBERTY, OR PROPERTY BEING TAKEN?

1. Liberty

The term "liberty" is not specifically defined. It includes more than just freedom from bodily restraints (*e.g.,* it includes the right to contract and to engage in gainful employment). A deprivation of liberty occurs if a person:

a. Loses significant freedom of action; ***or***

b. Is denied a freedom provided by the Constitution or a statute.

2. Property

"Property" includes more than personal belongings and realty, but an abstract need or desire for (or a unilateral expectation of) a benefit is not enough. There must be a ***legitimate claim*** or "***entitlement***" to the benefit under state or federal law. Examples of property interests include continued attendance at public school, welfare benefits, and (in some cases) government employment.

Exam Tip At one time, due process protected a "right" but not a "privilege." This distinction has been rejected by the Court. Thus, an answer that uses that terminology (right versus privilege) should be discarded as a red herring. The proper terminology is "entitlement."

C. WHAT TYPE OF PROCESS IS REQUIRED?

The type and extent of required procedures are determined by a three-part balancing test that weighs:

(i) The ***importance of the interest*** to the individual; and

(ii) The value of specific ***procedural safeguards*** to that interest; against

(iii) The ***government interest*** in fiscal and administrative efficiency.

Presumably, fair procedures and an unbiased decisionmaker will always be required. Notice and chance to respond before termination of the liberty or property interest are usually required.

D. DUE PROCESS RIGHTS ARE SUBJECT TO WAIVER

As a general rule, due process rights are, presumably, subject to waiver if the waiver is ***voluntary and made knowingly***.

E. ACCESS TO COURTS—INDIGENT PLAINTIFFS

Government fees (*e.g.,* court filing fees) must be waived when imposition of a fee would deny a fundamental right to the indigent (*see infra,* for discussion of fundamental rights). Thus, for example, a marriage license or divorce court filing fee (privacy rights) or filing fee for candidates for electoral office (voting rights) must be waived. However, fees can be imposed when nonfundamental rights are involved (*e.g.,* fees for a bankruptcy discharge or review of welfare termination).

TYPE OF PROCESS REQUIRED

Interest Involved	Process Required
1. Commitment to Mental Institution	*Adults:* Prior notice and ***prior*** evidentiary hearing (except in emergency). *Children:* Prior screening by ***"neutral factfinder."*** (Parental consent alone insufficient.)
2. Welfare Benefits	Prior notice and ***prior*** evidentiary hearing.
3. Disability Benefits	Prior notice and opportunity to respond, and ***subsequent*** evidentiary hearing.
4. Public Employment (tenured or termination only "for cause")	Generally, prior notice and opportunity to respond, and ***subsequent*** evidentiary hearing.
5. Public Education (disciplinary suspension or academic dismissal)	Prior notice and opportunity to respond; ***no*** formal evidentiary hearing required.
6. Driver's License Suspension	Prior evidentiary hearing. *Exception:* Breathalyzer test suspension statutes.
7. Termination of Parent's Custody Rights	Prior notice and ***prior*** evidentiary hearing.
8. Civil Forfeitures	***Prior*** notice and evidentiary hearing for ***real property; subsequent*** notice and hearing for ***personal property.***

XV. THE "TAKING" CLAUSE

A. IN GENERAL

The Fifth Amendment provides that private property may not be taken for ***public use*** without

just compensation. This rule is applicable to the states via the Fourteenth Amendment. The Taking Clause is not a source of power for taking, but rather is a limitation. "Taking" includes not only physical appropriations but also ***some*** government action that damages property or impairs its use.

B. "PUBLIC USE" LIMITATION LIBERALLY CONSTRUED

If the government's action is ***rationally related*** to a ***legitimate*** public purpose (*e.g.,* for health, welfare, safety, economic, or aesthetic reasons), the public use requirement is satisfied. Authorized takings by private enterprises are included if they redound to the public advantage (*e.g.,* railroads and public utilities).

C. "TAKING" VS. "REGULATION"

The crucial issue is whether governmental action is a ***taking*** (requiring payment of just compensation) or merely a ***regulation*** (not requiring compensation). There is no clear-cut formula for making this determination, but the following general guidelines apply:

1. Actual Appropriation or Physical Invasion

An actual or physical appropriation of property will almost always amount to a taking. *Exception:* Emergency situations.

2. Use Restrictions

a. Denial of *All* Economic Value of Land—Taking

If a government regulation denies a landowner of ***all*** economic use of his land (*e.g.,* a regulation prohibiting any building on the land), the regulation amounts to a taking unless principles of nuisance or property law make the use prohibitable.

1) Temporary Denials of All Economic Use

Temporarily denying an owner of all economic use of property does not constitute a per se taking. Instead, the Court will carefully examine and weigh all the relevant circumstances—the planners' good faith, the reasonable expectations of the owners, the length of the delay, the delay's actual effect on the value of the property, etc.—in order to determine whether "fairness and justice" require just compensation.

b. Decreasing Economic Value—Balancing Test

Regulations that merely decrease the value of property (*e.g.,* prohibit the most beneficial use) do not amount to a taking if they leave an ***economically viable use for the property***. The Court will consider:

(i) The ***social goals*** sought to be promoted;

(ii) The ***diminution in value*** to the owner; and

(iii) The ***owner's reasonable expectations*** regarding the property.

The more drastic the reduction in value or the less it promotes public welfare, the more likely it is to be a taking.

CMR EXAMPLE CHART

"TAKING" VS. "REGULATION"

Government Action	Characterization
1. Condemnation of land to build highway	Taking
2. Creating public access easement on private property	Taking
3. Abolishing inheritance rights	Taking
4. Zoning ordinances that merely prohibit the most beneficial use of property	Regulation
5. Ordering destruction of diseased trees	Regulation
6. Landmark ordinances	Regulation

3. Remedy—"Just Compensation"
If the regulation amounts to a taking, the government must:

(i) ***Pay*** the property owner just compensation for the property (*i.e.,* fair market value); ***or***

(ii) ***Terminate the regulation and pay*** the owner for damages that occurred while the regulation was in effect (*i.e.,* temporary taking damages).

a. "Worthless" Property
Just compensation is measured by the ***loss to the owner***, not by the gain to the taker. Thus, while property that is worthless to the owner can be the subject of a taking, no compensation need be paid when it is taken.

XVI. INTRODUCTION TO SUBSTANTIVE DUE PROCESS AND EQUAL PROTECTION

A. RELATIONSHIP BETWEEN SUBSTANTIVE DUE PROCESS AND EQUAL PROTECTION

Both substantive due process and equal protection guarantees require the Court to review the substance of a law rather than the procedures employed.

1. Substantive Due Process
If a law limits liberty of ***all*** persons to engage in some activity, on the MBE it usually is a due process question.

2. Equal Protection
If a law treats a ***person or class of persons*** differently from others, on the MBE it usually is an equal protection problem.

B. WHAT STANDARD OF REVIEW WILL THE COURT APPLY?

Under either guarantee, the Court is reviewing the legitimacy of governmental acts. Three standards of review are used:

1. Strict Scrutiny (Maximum Scrutiny)

Regulations affecting ***fundamental rights*** (*i.e.,* interstate travel, privacy, voting, and First Amendment rights) or involving ***suspect classifications*** (*i.e.,* race, national origin, and alienage) are reviewed under the strict scrutiny standard: The law is upheld if it is ***necessary*** to achieve a ***compelling*** government purpose. This is a difficult test to meet, and so a law examined under a strict scrutiny standard will often be invalidated—especially if there is a ***less burdensome*** alternative to achieve the government's goal.

a. Burden of Proof

The government has the burden of proof.

2. Intermediate Scrutiny

Regulations involving ***quasi-suspect classifications*** (*i.e.,* gender and legitimacy) are reviewed under the intermediate scrutiny standard: The law is upheld if it is ***substantially related*** to an ***important*** government purpose.

a. Burden of Proof

It is unclear who has the burden of proof. It is probably the government.

3. Rational Basis (Minimal Scrutiny)

Regulations that do ***not*** affect fundamental rights or involve suspect or quasi-suspect classifications (most laws) are reviewed under the rational basis standard: The law is upheld if it is ***rationally related*** to a ***legitimate*** government purpose. This is a very easy standard to meet; therefore the law is usually valid—unless it is ***arbitrary*** or ***irrational***.

a. Burden of Proof

The person challenging the law has the burden of proof.

b. Classifications that Are Not Suspect or Quasi-Suspect

The rational basis standard is used to review regulations involving classifications that are ***not*** suspect or quasi-suspect, such as age, disability, and poverty.

CMR Exam Tip Many exam questions ask you about the standard that the Court will use to review governmental regulation. Therefore, you need to know which standard will apply in a particular case (*e.g.,* if a fundamental right is involved, strict scrutiny is applied). However, the choices may not ***name*** the standard ("strict scrutiny") but merely state it ("upheld if necessary to a compelling government interest"). Be prepared to recognize the standard by name ***or*** definition.

CMR Exam Tip Due process or equal protection questions also commonly test your knowledge of which party bears the burden of proof. Know the standards and their respective burdens.

XVII. SUBSTANTIVE DUE PROCESS

A. CONSTITUTIONAL SOURCE—TWO CLAUSES

The Due Process Clause of the Fifth Amendment applies to the federal government. The Due

Process Clause of the Fourteenth Amendment applies to state and local governments. The same tests are applied under each clause.

B. APPLICABLE STANDARDS

When a ***fundamental right*** is limited, the law or action is evaluated under the ***strict scrutiny*** standard. In ***all other cases***, the ***rational basis*** standard is applied.

C. A FEW IRREBUTTABLE PRESUMPTIONS MAY BE INVALID

If facts are presumed against a person so that she cannot demonstrate that she is qualified for some important benefit or right, the "irrebuttable presumption" may be unconstitutional.

CMR Exam Tip The Supreme Court no longer treats irrebuttable presumptions differently from other regulations or classifications. Thus, if an answer choice says "invalid because it is an irrebuttable presumption," it is probably wrong. You must consider whether it concerns a ***fundamental right*** or ***suspect or quasi-suspect class***, and judge it accordingly.

XVIII. EQUAL PROTECTION

A. CONSTITUTIONAL SOURCE

The Equal Protection Clause of the Fourteenth Amendment is limited to state action. However, grossly unreasonable discrimination by the federal government violates the Due Process Clause of the Fifth Amendment. The Court applies the same tests under either constitutional provision.

B. APPLICABLE STANDARDS

If a ***fundamental right*** or ***suspect classification*** is involved, the ***strict scrutiny*** standard is used to evaluate the regulation. If a ***quasi-suspect classification*** is involved, ***intermediate scrutiny*** is the applicable standard. If the classification does not affect a fundamental right or involve a suspect or quasi-suspect classification, the ***rational basis*** standard applies.

C. PROVING DISCRIMINATORY CLASSIFICATION

For strict or intermediate scrutiny to be applied, there must be ***intent*** on the part of the government to discriminate. Intent may be shown by:

(i) A law that is ***discriminatory on its face***;

(ii) A ***discriminatory application*** of a facially neutral law; or

(iii) A ***discriminatory motive*** behind the law.

Note: The third way to show intentional discrimination is the most difficult to prove. A discriminatory effect alone is ***not*** enough. The legislature's discriminatory motive must be shown (*e.g.,* by evidence of a history of discrimination).

D. SUSPECT CLASSIFICATIONS

Classifications are suspect if they are based on race, national origin, or alienage.

1. Race and National Origin

Classifications based on race or national origin are judged by a strict scrutiny standard.

a. School Integration

Only intentional segregation violates the Constitution. If school systems and attendance

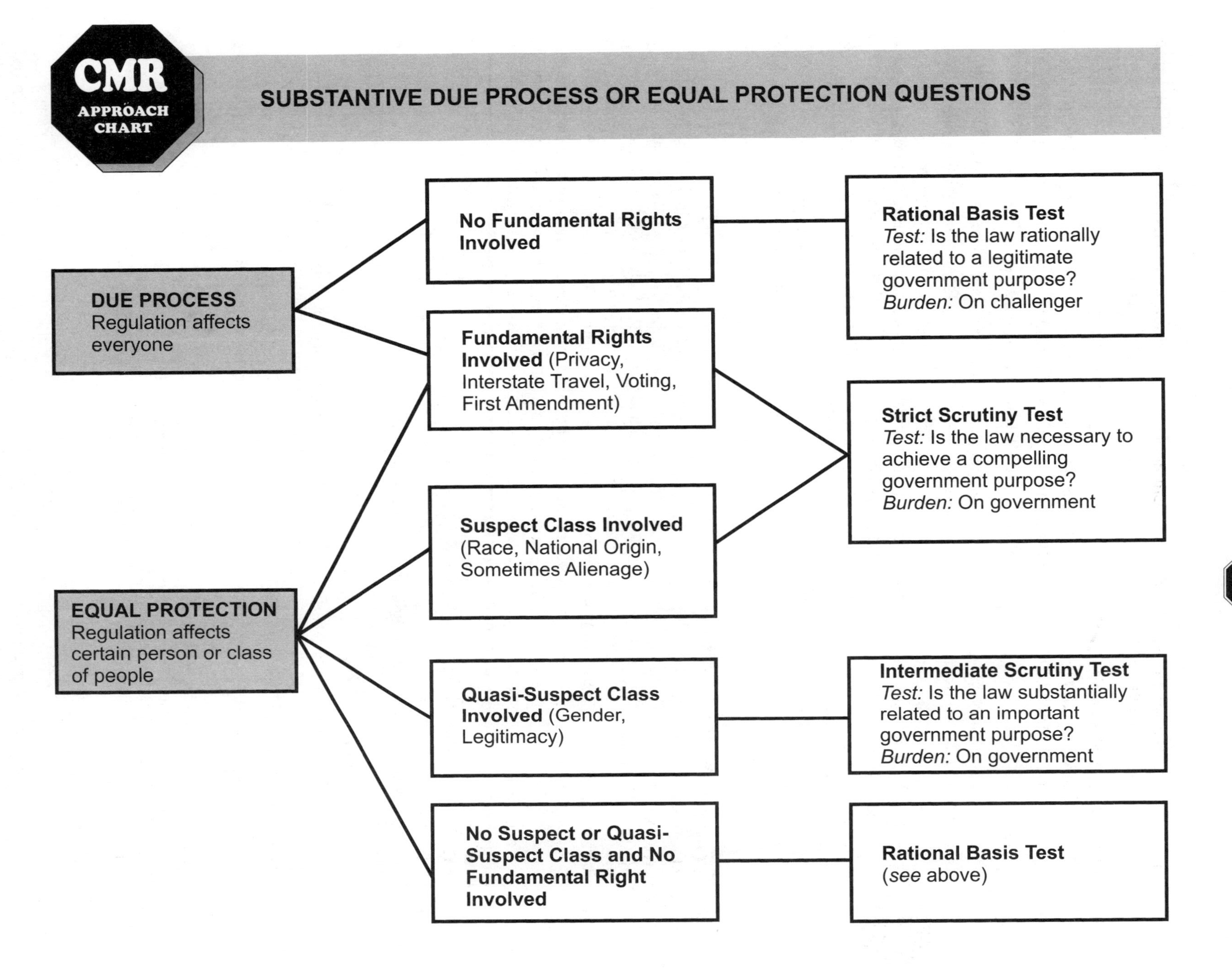
CMR
APPROACH
CHART
SUBSTANTIVE DUE PROCESS OR EQUAL PROTECTION QUESTIONS
DUE PROCESS
Regulation affects everyone
EQUAL PROTECTION
Regulation affects certain person or class of people
No Fundamental Rights Involved
Fundamental Rights Involved (Privacy, Interstate Travel, Voting, First Amendment)
Suspect Class Involved (Race, National Origin, Sometimes Alienage)
Quasi-Suspect Class Involved (Gender, Legitimacy)
No Suspect or Quasi-Suspect Class and No Fundamental Right Involved
Rational Basis Test
Test: Is the law rationally related to a legitimate government purpose?
Burden: On challenger
Strict Scrutiny Test
Test: Is the law necessary to achieve a compelling government purpose?
Burden: On government
Intermediate Scrutiny Test
Test: Is the law substantially related to an important government purpose?
Burden: On government
Rational Basis Test
(see above)

zones are established in a racially neutral manner, there is no violation. Thus, there is no violation if housing patterns result in racial imbalance in schools.

b. "Benign" Government Discrimination—Affirmative Action

Government action—whether by federal, state, or local governmental bodies—that ***favors*** racial or ethnic minorities is subject to the same strict scrutiny standard as is government action discriminating ***against*** racial or ethnic minorities.

1) Remedying Past Discrimination

The government has a compelling interest in remedying past discrimination against a racial or ethnic minority. The past discrimination must have been persistent and readily identifiable. A race-based plan ***cannot*** be used to remedy ***general*** past "societal discrimination."

2) Where There Was No Past Discrimination

Even where the government has not engaged in past discrimination, it may have a compelling interest in affirmative action. However, the governmental action must be ***narrowly tailored*** to that interest.

a) Diversity in Public Education

Public colleges and universities have claimed that they have a compelling interest in having a diverse student body—not to remedy past discrimination, but rather in its own right—because a diverse student body enhances learning. The Supreme Court has held that it will defer to a state college or university's good faith judgment that it has such a compelling interest. However, the Court has also held that each applicant to such schools must be considered as an individual. Although admissions officers may consider an applicant's race in making admissions decisions, race or ethnicity may only be deemed a ***plus among a range of factors***. If race or ethnicity is the defining criterion for admission, the admission policy will not be narrowly tailored to achieving the compelling interest of ensuring a diverse student body.

c. Discriminatory Legislative Apportionment

Race can be considered in drawing up new voting districts, but it ***cannot be the predominant factor***. If a plaintiff can show that a redistricting plan was drawn up predominately on the basis of racial considerations, the plan will violate the Equal Protection Clause unless the government can show that the plan is narrowly tailored to serve a compelling state interest.

2. Alienage Classifications

a. Federal Classifications

Because of Congress's plenary power over aliens, federal alienage classifications are ***not*** subject to strict scrutiny. Such classifications are valid if they are not arbitrary and unreasonable.

b. State and Local Classifications

Generally, state/local laws on alienage are suspect classifications subject to strict scrutiny. *Examples:* It is unconstitutional for United States citizenship to be required for welfare, civil service jobs, or to become a lawyer.

1) **Exception—Participation in Self-Government Process**
If a law discriminates against alien participation in state government (*e.g.,* voting, jury service, elective office), the ***rational basis*** standard is applied. Also, the rational basis standard is used for state and local laws limiting certain non-elective offices involving important public policy (*e.g.,* police officers, probation officers, and teachers).

c. **Undocumented Aliens**
Undocumented ("illegal") aliens are ***not*** a suspect classification. Thus, state laws regarding them are subject to a "rational basis" standard. (However, denial of free public education to undocumented alien children is invalid, and more than a simple rational basis standard was used by the Court.)

E. QUASI-SUSPECT CLASSIFICATIONS
Classifications based on legitimacy and gender are "quasi-suspect."

1. Gender Classifications
Gender classifications are reviewed under the intermediate scrutiny standard: They must be ***substantially related*** to an ***important*** government purpose. The government bears the burden of showing an "exceedingly persuasive justification" for the discrimination.

a. **Women**
Intentional discrimination ***against*** women generally is invalid. Classifications ***benefiting*** women that are designed to ***remedy past discrimination*** generally are valid.

b. **Intentional Discrimination Against Men**
Intentional discrimination against men is generally invalid. However, certain laws have been found to be substantially related to an important government interest (*e.g.,* statutory rape laws, all-male draft).

CMR EXAMPLE CHART

GENDER CLASSIFICATION

Classification	Status
Gender-based death benefits	Invalid
Gender-based peremptory strikes	Invalid
Alimony for women only	Invalid
State supported all-male or all-female schools	Invalid
Discriminatory minimum drinking age (women at 18, men at 21)	Invalid
Discriminatory statutory rape laws	Valid
All-male draft	Valid
Requiring American fathers (but not mothers) to prove their parentage of nonmarital children born abroad in order to obtain U.S. citizenship for them	Valid

Exam Tip The preceding chart spells out the most likely exam question topics. In any event, remember that most gender classifications are struck down. This is particularly true if they perpetuate stereotypes of economically dependent women.

2. Legitimacy Classifications

Legitimacy classifications are also reviewed under the intermediate scrutiny standard: They must be ***substantially related*** to an ***important*** government interest. Discriminatory regulations intended to punish illegitimate children (*e.g.,* law providing a benefit to legitimate children but not to illegitimate children) are invalid. *Example:* A law allowing only legitimate children to recover from their father's estate is invalid. *But note:* A law allowing illegitimate children to recover from their father's estate only if parenthood is established before the father's death is ***valid***.

F. OTHER CLASSIFICATIONS

All other classifications are evaluated under the ***rational basis*** standard. These include age, disability, and wealth classifications. For example, mandatory retirement ages may be established; and because education is not a fundamental right, there is no denial of equal protection when wealthier children can afford to pay for access to the best state-operated schools.

Exam Tip For the MBE, you must memorize the suspect classifications (race, national origin, and sometimes alienage), quasi-suspect classifications (gender and legitimacy), and the fundamental rights (right to interstate travel, privacy, voting, and First Amendment rights). Any other classification or any other right is ***not*** entitled to more than the rational basis test, and thus the government regulation will usually be valid. Do not let your personal feelings lead you to apply the wrong standard (and pick the wrong answer) because you think the right is important or the group is worthy.

XIX. FUNDAMENTAL RIGHTS

A. INTRODUCTION

Certain fundamental rights are protected under the Constitution. If they are denied to everyone, it is a substantive due process problem. If they are denied to some individuals but not others, it is an equal protection problem. The applicable standard in either case is strict scrutiny. Thus, government action must be ***necessary*** to protect a ***compelling*** governmental interest. (Remember that there must be no less restrictive means to achieve this goal.)

B. RIGHT OF PRIVACY

Various privacy rights including marriage, sexual relations, abortion, and childrearing are fundamental rights. Regulations affecting these rights are reviewed under the ***strict scrutiny*** standard.

1. Marriage

The right of a male and female to enter into (and, probably, to dissolve) the marriage relationship is a fundamental right. However, a statute restricting the rights of prison inmates to marry will be upheld if reasonably related to legitimate penological interests.

2. Use of Contraceptives

A state cannot prohibit distribution of nonmedical contraceptives to adults.

3. Abortion

The right of privacy includes the right of a woman to have an abortion without interference from the state under certain circumstances. However, normal strict scrutiny analysis cannot be applied because the state has two compelling interests here that often compete: protecting the woman's health and protecting the fetus that may become a child. In its latest abortion rights approach, the Supreme Court has adopted two basic rules: a pre-viability rule and a post-viability rule.

a. Pre-Viability Rule—No Undue Burdens

Before viability (a realistic possibility that the fetus could survive outside the womb), a state may adopt a regulation protecting the mother's health and the life of the fetus if the regulation does not place an "undue burden" on or substantial obstacle to the woman's right to obtain an abortion.

PRE-VIABILITY ABORTION REGULATION

No Undue Burden	Undue Burden
Requiring doctor to give woman relevant information to make ***informed consent***.	Requiring woman to ***notify spouse*** about abortion.
Requiring ***24-hour waiting period***.	Barring ***all*** partial-birth abortions.
Requiring ***parental consent*** or ***parental notice*** in order for minors to obtain an abortion, if there is a judicial bypass option.	
Requiring that abortions be performed only ***by licensed physicians***.	

b. Post-Viability Rule—May Prohibit Abortion Unless Woman's Health Threatened

Once the fetus is viable, the state's interest in the fetus's life can override the woman's right to obtain an abortion, but the state cannot prohibit the woman from obtaining an abortion if it is necessary to protect the woman's health or safety.

c. Remedy

When a court is faced with a statute restricting access to abortions that may be applied in an unconstitutional manner so as to harm the mother's health, it should ***not*** invalidate the statute in its entirety if the statute has valid applications. Instead, the court should attempt to fashion narrower declaratory and injunctive relief against the unconstitutional application.

d. Financing Abortions

The government has no obligation to pay for abortions.

4. **Obscene Reading Material**
The right to privacy includes freedom to read obscene material in one's home (except for child pornography), but not the right to sell, purchase, or transport such material.

5. **Keeping Extended Family Together**
Zoning regulations that prevent family members—even extended ones—from living together are invalid. However, this right does ***not*** extend to unrelated people.

6. **Rights of Parents**
Parents have a fundamental right to make decisions concerning the care, custody, and control of their children (*e.g.,* a parent has a fundamental right to send a child to private school or to forbid visitation with grandparents).

7. **Intimate Sexual Conduct**
The state has no legitimate interest in making it a crime for fully consenting adults to engage in private intimate sexual conduct (*e.g.,* sodomy) that is not commercial in nature.

8. **Collection and Distribution of Personal Data—No Privacy Right**
The state may reasonably gather and distribute information about its citizens. Thus, there is no privacy right to prohibit the accumulation of names and addresses of patients for whom dangerous drugs are prescribed.

C. RIGHT TO VOTE

The right to vote is a fundamental right. Thus, restrictions on that right, other than on the basis of residence, age, and citizenship, are ***invalid*** unless they can pass ***strict scrutiny***.

1. **Restrictions on Right to Vote**

   a. **Residency Requirements**
   Reasonable time periods for residency (*e.g.,* 30 days) are valid. Note that Congress may override state residency requirements in ***presidential*** elections and substitute its own.

   b. **Property Ownership**
   Conditioning the right to vote or hold office on ownership of property is usually invalid. *Exception:* Special purpose elections (*e.g.,* water storage districts); *see infra.*

   c. **Poll Taxes**
   Poll taxes are unconstitutional.

   d. **Primary Elections**
   States may require early registration to vote in primaries. However, states cannot prohibit political parties from opening their primary elections to anyone, whether or not registered with the party.

2. **Dilution of Right to Vote**

   a. **One Person, One Vote Principle**
   The "one person, one vote" principle applies whenever any level of government, state

or local, decides to select representatives to a governmental body by popular election from ***individual districts***.

1) **Congressional Elections**
States must use ***almost exact mathematical equality*** when creating congressional districts within the state. This is not true of Congress, however, when it apportions representatives among the states; Congress's good faith method for apportioning representatives commands more deference and is ***not*** subject to a precise mathematical formula, as are state plans.

2) **State and Local Elections**
For state and local elections, the variance in the number of persons included within districts must not be more than a few percentage points.

3) **Exception—Appointed Officials and Officials Elected "At Large"**
The apportionment requirement is inapplicable to officials who are appointed or elected at large.

4) **Exception—Special Purpose Election**
The one person, one vote principle does not apply to elections of officials who do not exercise "normal governmental authority" but rather deal with matters of special interest in the community (*e.g.,* water storage districts).

b. **Gerrymandering**
Race (and presumably other suspect classifications) cannot be the predominant factor in drawing the boundaries of voting districts unless the district plan can pass muster under strict scrutiny.

3. **Candidates and Campaigns**

a. **Candidate Qualifications**

1) **Fee Must Not Preclude Indigents**
States may not charge candidates a fee that results in making it impossible for indigents to run for office.

2) **Restrictions on Ability to Be a Candidate**
A ballot access regulation must be a reasonable, nondiscriminatory means of promoting important state interests. A state may require candidates to show reasonable support to have their names placed on the ballot.

b. **Campaign Funding**
The government may allocate more public funds to the two "major" parties than to "minor" parties for political campaigns.

D. **RIGHT TO TRAVEL**

1. **Interstate Travel**
An individual has a fundamental right to migrate from state to state and to be treated equally

after moving into a new state. However, not every restriction on the right to cross state lines is an impairment of the right to travel (*e.g.,* increased penalties for a father abandoning his children and leaving the state are valid). A problem arises when a state imposes a minimum durational residency requirement for receiving its benefits or otherwise dispenses state benefits based on the length of time a person has resided in the state. It is not clear whether the Court always reviews these regulations under the strict scrutiny standard. It may be best to just recall the following examples:

CMR EXAMPLE CHART

DURATIONAL RESIDENCY REQUIREMENT

Residency Requirement	Status
One-year residency to receive full welfare benefits	Invalid
One-year residency to receive state subsidized medical care	Invalid
One-year residency to vote in state	Invalid
Thirty-day residency to vote in state	Valid
One-year residency to get divorced	Valid

2. **Right to International Travel**
International travel is ***not a fundamental right***. It is, however, protected from arbitrary federal interference by the Fifth Amendment Due Process Clause; the rational basis standard applies.

PART 5: FIRST AMENDMENT FREEDOMS

The First Amendment prohibits Congress from establishing a religion or interfering with the free exercise of religion, abridging the freedoms of speech and press, or interfering with the right of assembly. These prohibitions are applicable to the states through the Fourteenth Amendment.

XX. FREEDOM OF SPEECH AND ASSEMBLY

A. GENERAL PRINCIPLES

Whenever the government seeks to regulate the freedoms of speech or assembly, the Court will weigh the great importance of speech and assembly rights against the interests or policies sought to be served by the regulation. Keep the following guidelines in mind:

1. **Content vs. Conduct**
Speech and assembly regulations can generally be categorized as either ***content*** regulations (regulations forbidding communication of specific ideas) or ***conduct*** regulations (regulations of the conduct associated with speaking, such as the time of the speech, sound level, etc.). Different standards are used to assess the validity of a regulation within each category.

   a. **Content**
   It is presumptively unconstitutional to place burdens on speech because of its content except for certain categories of speech (obscenity, defamation, etc.). Content-neutral speech regulations generally are subject to ***intermediate scrutiny***; *i.e.*, they must advance ***important*** interests unrelated to the suppression of speech and ***must not burden substantially more speech than necessary*** to further those interests.

   b. **Conduct**
   Conduct related to speech can be regulated by content-neutral time, place, and manner restrictions. (These rules will be discussed at B., *infra.*) Additionally, all regulations of speech are subject to the following restrictions.

2. **Reasonableness of Regulation**

   a. **Overbroad Regulation Invalid**
   If a regulation of speech or speech-related conduct punishes a ***substantial amount of protected speech*** in relation to its plainly legitimate sweep (*e.g.,* a regulation outlawing ***all*** First Amendment activity in an airport terminal; a regulation prohibiting all canvassers from going onto private residential property to promote ***any*** cause without first obtaining a permit), the regulation is ***facially invalid*** (*i.e.,* it may not be enforced against anyone—not even a person engaging in activity that is not constitutionally protected) unless a court has limited construction of the regulation so as to remove the threat to constitutionally protected expression. If the regulation is ***not substantially overbroad***, it can be enforced against persons engaging in activities that are not constitutionally protected.

   b. **Void for Vagueness Doctrine**
   If a criminal law or regulation fails to give persons reasonable notice of what is prohibited (*e.g.,* a prohibition of "lewd" speech), it may violate the Due Process Clause. This principle is applied somewhat strictly when First Amendment activity is involved.

   c. **Cannot Give Officials Unfettered Discretion**
   A regulation cannot give officials broad discretion over speech issues; there must be ***defined standards*** for applying the law. If a statute gives licensing officials ***unbridled discretion***, it is ***void on its face*** and speakers need not even apply for a permit. If the licensing statute includes standards, a speaker may not ignore the statute; he must seek a permit and if it is denied, he can challenge the denial on First Amendment grounds.

3. **Scope of Speech**
The freedom to speak includes the freedom ***not to speak***. Thus, the government generally cannot require people to salute the flag or display other messages with which they disagree (*e.g.,* a person need not display the motto "live free or die" on a license plate). The freedom can extend to ***symbolic acts*** undertaken to communicate an idea (*e.g.,* wearing a black armband

to protest the war), although the government may regulate such conduct if it has an ***important*** interest in the regulation ***independent*** of the speech aspects of the conduct and the incidental burden on speech is no greater than necessary (*e.g.,* to facilitate a smooth draft, the government can prohibit the burning of draft cards).

a. Mandatory Financial Support

Although the government may not compel a person to express a message, it may tax people and use the revenue to express a message with which they disagree (*e.g.,* a beef producer can be required to pay an assessment to support government sponsored generic advertising of beef even if the producer thinks generic advertising is a waste of money). However, it appears that people ***cannot*** be compelled to subsidize private messages with which they disagree (*e.g.,* while lawyers may be compelled to pay bar dues and government teachers can be compelled to pay union dues, they cannot be compelled to pay sums to such private associations that will be used to support political views that, or candidates whom, they do not endorse).

1) Exception—University Activity Fees

The government can require public university students to pay a student activity fee even if the fee is used to support political and ideological speech by student groups whose beliefs are offensive to the student, as long as the program is viewpoint neutral.

4. Funding vs. Regulation

Congress has more leeway when funding speech than it does when it is regulating speech. Congress may selectively fund programs that it believes to be in the public interest while denying funding to alternative programs. However, viewpoint restrictions generally are not allowed when the government funds private speech.

B. TIME, PLACE, AND MANNER RESTRICTIONS—REGULATION OF CONDUCT

The government has power to regulate the ***conduct*** associated with speech and assembly, although the breadth of this power depends on whether the forum involved is a public forum, a designated public forum (sometimes called a limited public forum), or a nonpublic forum.

1. Public Forums and Designated Public Forums

Public property that has historically been open to speech-related activities (*e.g.*, ***streets, sidewalks, and public parks***) is called a public forum. Public property that has not historically been open to speech-related activities, but which the government has thrown open for such activities on a permanent or limited basis, by practice or policy (*e.g.*, schoolrooms that are open for after-school use by social, civic, or recreation groups), is called a designated or limited public forum. The government may regulate speech in public forums and designated public forums with reasonable time, place, and manner regulations that:

(i) Are ***content neutral***;

(ii) Are ***narrowly tailored*** to serve a ***significant*** (important) government interest; and

(iii) Leave open ***alternative channels*** of communication.

Note: Almost every legitimate governmental interest satisfies the significant/important standard.

CMR **Exam Tip** Remember that even if a regulation meets the time, place, and manner requirements above, it could still be invalid if it is overbroad, vague, or gives unfettered discretion.

a. **Injunctions**
Injunctions against speech in public forums are treated differently from generally applicable laws. If the injunction is content based, it must be necessary to achieve a compelling interest. If the injunction is content neutral, it must burden no more speech than is necessary to achieve a significant government interest.

2. **Nonpublic Forums**
Speech and assembly can be more broadly regulated in nonpublic forums (*i.e.,* government-owned forums not historically linked with speech and assembly and not held open for speech activities, such as military bases, schools while classes are in session, government workplaces, etc.). In such locations, regulations are valid if they are:

a. ***Viewpoint neutral***; and

b. ***Reasonably related to a legitimate*** government purpose.

C. **UNPROTECTED SPEECH—REGULATION BASED ON CONTENT**
To be valid, restrictions on the content of speech must be ***narrowly tailored*** to achieve a ***compelling*** government interest. The government has a compelling interest in the following categories of speech, which are deemed "unprotected" speech under the First Amendment:

1. **Inciting Imminent Lawless Action**
Speech can be burdened if it creates a clear and present danger of imminent lawless action. It must be shown that imminent illegal conduct is ***likely*** and that the speaker intended to cause it.

2. **Fighting Words**
Speech can be burdened if it constitutes fighting words (personally abusive words that are likely to incite immediate physical retaliation in an average person). Words that are merely annoying are not sufficient. Note also that the Supreme Court will not tolerate fighting words statutes that are designed to punish only certain viewpoints (*e.g.,* proscribing only fighting words that insult on the basis of race, religion, or gender). However, the First Amendment does not protect "true threats," and, therefore, the Supreme Court has upheld a statute banning cross-burning when carried out with the ***intent to intimidate***.

Exam Tip While this classification of punishable speech exists in theory, as a practical matter, statutes that attempt to punish fighting words are usually vague or overbroad. Thus, on the examination, they generally should be regarded as ***invalid***.

3. **Obscenity**
Obscene speech is not protected.

a. **Elements**
Speech is obscene if it describes or depicts sexual conduct that, taken as a whole, by the average person:

1) ***Appeals to the prurient interest*** in sex, using a ***community standard***;

2) Is ***patently offensive*** and an affront to contemporary ***community standards***; and

3) ***Lacks serious value*** (literary, artistic, political, or scientific), using a ***national reasonable person standard***.

CMR **Exam Tip** Note the two different standards used in the obscenity test: appeal to the prurient interest and offensiveness are judged by contemporary ***community*** standards (local or statewide, not necessarily national standards), while value is judged on a ***national reasonable person*** basis.

b. Standard May Be Different for Minors

The state can adopt a specific definition of obscenity applying to materials sold to minors, even though the material might not be obscene in terms of an adult audience. However, government may not prohibit the sale or distribution of material to adults merely because it is inappropriate for children.

1) Pictures of Minors

To protect minors from exploitation, the government may prohibit the sale or distribution of ***visual*** depictions of sexual conduct involving minors, even if the material would not be found obscene if it did not involve children.

2) Compare—Simulated Pictures of Minors

The government may not bar visual material that only appears to depict minors engaged in sexually explicit conduct, but that in fact uses young-looking adults or computer generated images.

c. Land Use Regulations

A land use (or zoning) regulation may limit the location or size of adult entertainment establishments if the regulation is designed to reduce the secondary effects of such businesses (*e.g.*, rise in crime rates, drop in property values, etc.). However, regulations may not ban such establishments altogether.

d. Liquor Regulation

Under the Twenty-First Amendment, states have broad power to regulate intoxicating beverages. Laws relating to this power that affect free speech rights generally will not be set aside unless they are irrational.

e. Private Possession of Obscene Material

Private possession of obscene material ***in the home*** cannot be punished (except for possession of child pornography). However, the protection does not extend outside the home.

4. Defamatory Speech

Defamatory statements can be burdened. If the defamatory statement is about a ***public official*** or ***public figure*** or involves a ***public concern***, the First Amendment requires the plaintiff to prove all the elements of defamation ***plus falsity*** and some degree of ***fault***. (*See* Torts outline for detailed discussion.)

Exam Tip The First Amendment may also play a role in certain privacy actions. (*See* Torts outline.)

5. **Some Commercial Speech**
As a general rule, commercial speech is afforded First Amendment protection if it is truthful. However, commercial speech that proposes ***unlawful activity*** or that is ***misleading or fraudulent*** may be burdened. Any other regulation of commercial speech will be upheld only if it:

   a. Serves a ***substantial government interest***;

   b. ***Directly advances*** that interest; and

   c. Is ***narrowly tailored*** to serve that interest.

Exam Tip "Narrowly tailored" does ***not*** require the least restrictive means of accomplishing the legislative goal; there just must be a ***reasonable fit*** between the goal and the means chosen.

D. PRIOR RESTRAINTS
Prior restraints prevent speech before it occurs, rather than punish it afterwards. They are rarely allowed. The government has a heavy burden in justifying a prior restraint; it must show that some ***special societal harm*** will otherwise result.

1. **Procedural Safeguards**
To be valid, a system for prior restraint must provide the following safeguards:

   (i) The standards must be ***narrowly drawn***, ***reasonable***, ***and definite***;

   (ii) Injunction must ***promptly*** be sought; and

   (iii) There must be ***prompt and final determination*** of the validity of the restraint.

   A number of other cases, especially in the area of movie censorship, require that the ***government bear the burden*** of proving that the speech involved is unprotected.

VALID AND INVALID PRIOR RESTRAINTS

Valid	Invalid
Prohibiting publishing of troop movement ***in times of war***.	Prohibiting publication of *The Pentagon Papers* because it ***might*** have an effect on the Vietnam War.
Enforcing ***contractual prepublication review*** of CIA agent's writings.	Prohibiting grand jury witness from ***ever*** disclosing testimony.

2. Obscenity Cases

a. Seizures of Books and Films

Seizures of a single book or film may be made with a ***warrant*** based on probable cause, although if the item is available for sale to the public, a police officer may purchase a book or film to use as evidence without a warrant. Large-scale seizures must be ***preceded by a full scale adversary hearing*** and a judicial determination of obscenity.

b. Movie Censorship

The Court has found that time delays incident to censorship are less burdensome on movies than on other forms of expression. Thus, the Court allows the government to establish censorship boards to screen movies before they are released, as long as the procedural safeguards discussed above are followed.

c. Burden of Government

When the government adopts a content-based, prior restraint of speech, the government has the burden of proving that the restriction is ***narrowly tailored*** (*i.e.,* the ***least restrictive*** alternative) to accomplish its goal.

E. FREEDOM OF THE PRESS

Generally, the press has ***no greater First Amendment freedom*** than does a private citizen. Thus, the concepts discussed above apply.

1. Publication of Truthful Information

Generally the press has a right to publish truthful information regarding a matter of public concern, and this right can be restricted only by a sanction that is narrowly tailored to further an interest of the highest order.

2. Access to Trials

The First Amendment guarantees the public and press a right to attend criminal (and probably civil) trials. However, the right may be ***outweighed*** by an overriding interest stated in the trial judge's findings (*e.g.,* to protect children who are victims of sex offenses). The right includes the right to be present at voir dire and at other pretrial proceedings, unless the judge makes specific findings that closure was narrowly tailored to preserve a higher value.

3. Requiring Press to Testify Before Grand Jury

Members of the press may be required to testify before grand juries.

4. Interviewing Prisoners

The First Amendment does not give journalists a right to interview specified prisoners of their choice or to inspect prison grounds.

5. Business Regulation or Tax

The press and broadcasting companies can be subjected to ***general*** business regulations or taxes but cannot be targeted for special regulation or taxes. A tax or regulation impacting on the press or a subpart of the press cannot be based on the content of a publication (*e.g.,* a tax exemption cannot be given to "medical journals") absent a compelling justification.

6. Broadcasting Regulations

Radio and television broadcasting may be more closely regulated than the press. The paramount right is the right of ***viewers and listeners*** to receive information of public concern rather than the right of broadcasters to broadcast what they please. This paramount right allows government to forbid newspaper ownership of radio stations and to prohibit indecent speech over the airwaves.

a. Fairness Doctrine

The First Amendment does not require broadcasters to accept political advertisements. However, a radio station may constitutionally be required to offer free broadcasting time to certain individuals (*e.g.,* opponents of political candidates or views endorsed by the station, or persons who have been personally attacked in a broadcast).

7. Cable Television Regulation

While generally regulations of newspapers are subject to strict scrutiny, and regulations of the broadcast media are subject to less critical review, regulations of cable television transmissions generally are subject to review by a standard somewhere between these two (*e.g.,* a law requiring cable operators to carry local stations is subject to "intermediate scrutiny"—because it is content-neutral (*see* A.1.a., *supra*)—and is constitutional because it serves the important interest of preserving economic viability of local broadcasters). However, content-based restrictions (*e.g.,* a law forbidding sexually oriented cable programs before 10 p.m.) are subject to strict scrutiny.

8. Internet Regulation

The strict standard of First Amendment scrutiny, rather than the more relaxed standard applicable to broadcast regulation, applies to regulation of the Internet.

XXI. FREEDOM OF ASSOCIATION AND BELIEF

A. NATURE OF THE RIGHT

Although the freedom of association is not mentioned explicitly in the Constitution, it is clearly implied from the rights that are explicitly noted. Pursuant to this freedom, the government may neither prohibit politically unpopular groups nor unduly burden a person's right to belong to such groups. *But note:* This right is not absolute. Infringements of the right may be justified by a ***compelling*** state interest, unrelated to the suppression of ideas, if the infringements are the ***least restrictive means*** of protecting the government interest involved.

B. ELECTORAL PROCESS

Laws regulating elections might impact on the First Amendment freedoms of speech, assembly, and association. The Court uses a balancing test to determine whether a regulation of the electoral process is valid: If the restriction on First Amendment activity is severe, strict scrutiny is applied, but if the restriction is reasonable and nondiscriminatory, it generally will be upheld.

ELECTORAL REGULATIONS

Valid	Invalid
1. Requiring reasonable number of signatures to get on the ballot.	1. Prohibiting party from endorsing or opposing candidates in a primary.
2. Enforcing a party rule requiring a voter to be registered with a political party to vote in the party's primary.	2. Regulating party selection of delegates to national convention.
3. Requiring a voter to be registered in a political party or as an independent to vote in the party's primary (*i.e.,* prohibiting persons registered in one major political party from voting in the other party's primary).	3. Prohibiting ***any*** campaigning on election day (involves core political speech and is overbroad).
4. Prohibiting campaign activity within 100 feet of a polling place (involves core political speech but is narrowly tailored).	4. Requiring political parties to allow nonparty members to vote in the parties' primary elections.
5. Prohibiting individuals from appearing on the ballot as the candidate of more than one party.	5. Prohibiting judicial candidates from announcing their views on disputed legal and political issues.

1. Limits on Contributions

A statute limiting election campaign contributions is subject to ***intermediate scrutiny***—it must be closely drawn to match a "sufficiently important interest." To prevent corruption or the appearance thereof, laws may limit the amount of money that a person, group, or corporation can contribute to a ***political candidate***. However, the government may ***not*** limit the amount of money that may be spent to support or oppose a ***ballot referendum***, and there is an exception for groups or corporations formed specifically to participate in the political debate.

2. Limits on Expenditures

Laws may not limit the amount that a candidate or group spends on a political campaign.

3. Compare—Regulations of Core Political Speech

Regulation of "core political speech" (*e.g.,* electioneering, distributing campaign literature), rather than regulation of the process surrounding an election, will be upheld only if it passes muster under strict scrutiny.

C. BAR MEMBERSHIPS AND PUBLIC EMPLOYMENT

1. Restraints on Conduct

If a government employer seeks to fire an employee (or to terminate a relationship with an independent contractor) for speech-related conduct, one of two tests will apply, depending on whether the speech involved a matter of public concern. If a matter of public concern is involved, courts must carefully balance the employee's rights as a citizen to comment on a matter of public concern against the government's interest as an employer in efficient performance of public service. If the speech did not involve a matter of public concern, the courts should give a wide degree of deference to the government employer's judgment concerning whether the speech was disruptive.

a. **Official Duty Exception**
A government employer may punish a public employee's speech whenever the speech is made pursuant to the employee's official duties, even if the speech touches on a matter of public concern.

b. **Participation in Political Campaigns**
The federal government ***may*** prohibit federal executive branch employees from taking an active part in political campaigns.

c. **Bans on Receiving Honoraria**
A provision banning government employees from accepting an honorarium for making speeches, writing articles, or making appearances was held to violate the First Amendment when applied to "rank and file" employees. Such a rule deters speech within a broad category of expression by a massive number of potential speakers and, thus, can be justified only if the government can show that the employees' and their potential audiences' rights are outweighed by the necessary impact the speech would have on actual operation of the government.

d. **Patronage**
A public employee may not be hired, fired, promoted, transferred, etc., based on party affiliation except as to policymaking positions, where party affiliation is relevant.

e. **Must Not Be Vague**
A standard for conduct must not be vague (*e.g.,* a prohibition against "treasonable or seditious" utterings is vague).

2. **Loyalty Oaths**
The government may require employees to take loyalty oaths, as long as the oaths are not overbroad or vague.

a. **Overbreadth**
An oath cannot prohibit membership in the Communist Party or require abstention from advocating overthrow of the government ***as an abstract doctrine***.

b. **Vagueness**
An oath requiring employees to support the Constitution and to oppose the ***unlawful*** overthrow of the government is valid; but an oath requiring public employees to support the flag is invalid (because refusal to salute the flag on religious grounds might conflict with the oath).

3. **Disclosure of Associations**
The government may not force disclosure of every organizational membership in exchange for a government employment or other benefit; it may only inquire into those activities that

are relevant to the employment or benefit sought. Even here, however, a person can exercise his Fifth Amendment right to remain silent if the disclosure would be incriminating.

XXII. FREEDOM OF RELIGION

A. CONSTITUTIONAL PROVISION

The First Amendment prohibition on establishment of religion and its protection of the free exercise of religion is applicable to the states through the Fourteenth Amendment.

B. FREE EXERCISE CLAUSE

1. No Punishment of Beliefs

The Free Exercise Clause prohibits government from punishing someone on the basis of her religious beliefs. For example, the Clause forbids:

(i) State governments from requiring office holders or employees to take a ***religious oath*** (the federal government is similarly restricted by Article VI);

(ii) States from ***excluding clerics*** from holding public office; and

(iii) Courts from ***declaring a religious belief to be false***.

The Supreme Court has not defined what constitutes religious belief, but it is clear that religious belief need not come from an organized religion or involve a supreme being. The Court has never held an asserted religious belief to be not religious for First Amendment purposes.

CMR **Exam Tip** Technically, the government may deny benefits to or impose a burden on someone based on her religious beliefs ***if there is a compelling interest***. However, the Supreme Court has ***never*** found an interest so compelling that it justifies such action.

2. General Conduct Regulation—No Religious Exemptions Required

The Free Exercise Clause cannot be used to challenge government regulation unless the regulation was ***specifically designed*** to interfere with religion (*e.g.,* a law that prohibits the precise type of animal slaughter used in a ritual by a particular religious sect is unconstitutional). Moreover, the Free Exercise Clause does ***not require religious exemptions*** from generally applicable governmental regulations that happen to burden religious conduct; *i.e.,* a law that regulates the conduct of ***all*** people can be applied to prohibit the conduct of a person despite the fact that his religious beliefs prevent him from complying with the law.

a. Exception—Unemployment Compensation Cases

A state cannot refuse to grant unemployment benefits to persons who quit their jobs for religious reasons (*i.e.,* the work or conditions of work conflict with tenets of the worker's religion). The worker need not even belong to a formal religious organization in such a situation, as long as the belief is sincere.

b. Exception—Right of Amish Not to Educate Children

The Supreme Court has granted the Amish an exemption from a law requiring compulsory school attendance until age 16, based on the Free Exercise Clause ***and*** the fundamental right to educate one's children.

CMR **Exam Tip** To summarize, the Free Exercise Clause prohibits government interference with religious ***beliefs***, but it generally does ***not*** prohibit regulation of ***conduct***. If the governmental action regulates ***general conduct***—including religious conduct—it is ***valid*** (*e.g.,* banning any use of peyote is valid even though a group's religious beliefs require its use during its ceremonies). The only exceptions to this rule are those pertaining to unemployment compensation and the education of Amish children.

C. ESTABLISHMENT CLAUSE

The Establishment Clause prohibits laws respecting the establishment of religion.

1. Sect Preference

If a government regulation or action includes a preference for one religious sect over another, it is invalid unless it is ***narrowly tailored*** to promote a ***compelling*** interest.

CMR **Exam Tip** Although you should know the standard (narrowly tailored to promote a compelling interest) for government preference of a religious sect (or sects), it is unlikely that the government could ever have a compelling interest in preferring one religious group.

2. No Sect Preference

If a government regulation or action contains no sect preference, it is ***valid*** under the Establishment Clause ***if*** it:

(i) Has a ***secular purpose***;

(ii) Has a ***primary effect that neither advances nor inhibits religion***; and

(iii) Does not produce ***excessive government entanglement*** with religion.

a. Cases Unconnected to Financial Aid or Education

A good rule of thumb here is that a law favoring or burdening religion or a specific religious group will be invalid (*e.g.,* exempting certain religious groups—traditional religions—from state registration requirements), but a law favoring or burdening a large segment of society that happens to include religious groups will be upheld (*e.g.,* a Sunday closing law).

b. Cases Involving Financial Benefits to Religious Institutions

The Supreme Court applies the three-part test above with greater strictness when government financial aid is going to a religiously affiliated ***grade or high school*** than it does when the aid is going to another type of religious institution.

1) Recipient-Based Aid

The government may give aid in the form of financial assistance to a defined class of persons as long as the class is defined without reference to religion or religious criteria. Such a program is valid even if most of the people receiving the aid use it to attend a religiously affiliated school.

ESTABLISHMENT CLAUSE CASES

Valid	Invalid
Nonfinancial Aid and Education Cases	
Legislature's employment of a chaplain.	Delegation of zoning power to religious organization.
Granting religious organizations exemptions from employment discrimination laws where contrary to the organization's beliefs.	Requirement that all employers grant all workers their Sabbath day off.
Christmastime display that includes religious symbols and nonreligious symbols (*e.g.,* nativity scene along with a Christmas tree or Santa).	Christmastime display of ***only*** religious symbols (*e.g.,* nativity scene or menorah only).
Displaying Ten Commandments when purpose is not predominantly religious.	Displaying Ten Commandments when purpose is predominantly religious.
Recipient-Based Aid	
Tax credits for parents of ***all*** students for educational expenses.	Tax credits only to parents of ***private school*** students for educational expenses.
Tuition vouchers for poor students that can be used at participating ***public and private schools***.	
Aid to Religious Grade and High Schools	
Reimbursement to private schools for ***compiling*** state-required data or ***administering*** standardized achievement tests.	Reimbursement to private schools for ***writing*** achievement tests.
Providing government employees to ***test*** private school students for health or learning problems and to ***provide*** on-site auxiliary services, such as remedial education, guidance, or job counseling.	Providing private schools with ***teachers***, or money to pay teachers, of secular classes.
Exemption from property tax for religious, charitable, ***and*** educational property.	Tax exemption ***only*** for religious associations or activities.
Transportation ***to and from school*** for all students.	
Providing all students with state-approved ***textbooks*** or lending religiously neutral instructional material (*e.g.,* computers) to private as well as public schools.	
Religious Activities in Public Schools	
Ending classes early to allow students to attend ***off-school*** religious classes.	Ending classes early to give voluntary ***in-school*** religious classes.
Allowing religious student groups to meet in unused classrooms ***as any other*** student group.	***Prayer, Bible reading, or posting Ten Commandments*** in classrooms or at school football games.
	Requiring that "***creation science***" be taught.

2) Aid to Colleges and Hospitals
Aid to colleges or hospitals will be upheld as long as the government program requires the aid to be used ***for nonreligious purposes*** and the recipient so agrees.

3) Aid to Grade Schools and High Schools
Aid to religious grade schools and high schools is usually found to have a secular purpose, but may fail the other parts of the test. For example, if the program has detailed administrative regulations to prevent the effect of advancement of religion, the law will be stricken for excessive government entanglement.

c. Religious Activities in Public Schools
School ***sponsored*** religious activity is ***invalid***, but school ***accommodation*** of religion is ***valid***. Moreover, if a public school allows members of the public and private organizations to use school property when classes are not in session, it cannot deny a religious organization permission to use the property for meetings merely because religious topics will be discussed.

CONTRACTS

TABLE OF CONTENTS

CONTRACTS

I. WHAT IS A CONTRACT?

A. GENERAL DEFINITION

A contract is a promise or set of promises, for breach of which the law gives a remedy, or the performance of which the law in some way recognizes as a duty.

B. LAW GOVERNING CONTRACTS

Generally, contracts are governed by the common law. Contracts for the sale of ***goods*** (movable, tangible property) are governed by Article 2 of the Uniform Commercial Code ("U.C.C.") as well as the common law. In such contracts, when Article 2 conflicts with the common law, Article 2 prevails. (*See* Sales outline for more detail on Article 2.)

C. TYPES OF CONTRACTS

Contracts are classified by how they are formed and how they can be accepted.

1. Classified by Formation

Contracts may be ***express*** (formed by language, oral or written) or ***implied*** (formed by manifestations of assent other than oral or written language, *i.e.,* by conduct).

a. Quasi-Contract

A quasi-contract is ***not a contract***, but rather is a way to avoid unjust enrichment. Thus, even if an agreement does not qualify as a contract, under a quasi-contract, a party can recover the benefit she has conferred on the other party.

CMR EXAMPLE CHART

THEORIES OF CONTRACT LIABILITY

Theory	Description	Example
Express Contract	Promises are communicated by ***language***.	X promises to paint Y's car in return for Y's promise to pay X $100.
Implied Contract	Parties' ***conduct*** indicates that they assented to be bound.	(i) X fills her car with gas at Y's gas station. There is a contract for purchase and sale of the gas. (ii) X watches Y paint X's house, knowing that Y mistakenly thought they had an agreement for Y to be paid for it.
Quasi-Contract (Not a contract at all)	One party is ***unjustly enriched*** at the expense of the other party, so that the enriched party must pay restitution to the other party equal to the unjust enrichment.	X contracts with Y to build a house for Y. X becomes ill and is unable to continue after completing a third of the work. X cannot sue on the contract, but may recover the benefit conferred on Y.

2. Classified by Acceptance
Contracts are either ***bilateral*** or ***unilateral***. Bilateral contracts require an exchange of promises. Unilateral contracts require the exchange of an act for a promise. Under the modern view, most contracts are bilateral. Unilateral contracts are limited to two circumstances: (i) where the offeror clearly indicates that performance is the ***only manner of acceptance***; or (ii) where there is an ***offer to the public*** clearly contemplating acceptance by performance (*e.g.,* a reward offer).

3. Void, Voidable, and Unenforceable Contracts
Certain contracts may not be enforceable:

a. ***A void contract*** is one ***without any legal effect*** from the beginning (*e.g.,* an agreement to commit a crime).

b. ***A voidable contract*** is one that a party may ***elect to avoid or ratify*** (*e.g.,* a contract by a minor).

c. ***An unenforceable contract*** is one otherwise valid but for which some ***defense*** exists extraneous to formation (*e.g.,* the Statute of Frauds).

CMR Exam Tip The distinction between void and voidable contracts is sometimes important to an exam question. The key thing to remember is that ***void*** contracts cannot be enforced, but a party may ***elect*** to enforce a ***voidable*** contract.

D. CREATION OF A CONTRACT
Three elements are required to create a contract:

1. ***Mutual assent***, *i.e.,* offer and acceptance;

2. ***Consideration*** or a substitute; and

3. ***No defenses*** to formation.

CMR Exam Tip Contract formation is a major topic on the exam. For any contract question, be sure that there really is an enforceable contract; *i.e.,* ***all three*** of the above elements must be present. Fact patterns sometimes greatly emphasize some elements (*e.g.,* offer and acceptance) to try to fool you into thinking that a contract has been formed, but on closer examination, you find that another element (*e.g.,* consideration) is missing. Remember to check carefully for all three elements. (Of course, if the ***facts state*** that one or more of the elements is present—or that a valid contract has been formed—don't waste your time analyzing elements already given to you.)

II. MUTUAL ASSENT—OFFER AND ACCEPTANCE

A. IN GENERAL
For an agreement to be enforced as a contract, there must be mutual assent. In other words, one party must accept the other's offer. Whether mutual assent is present will be determined by an objective standard; *i.e.,* did words or conduct manifest a present intention to enter into a contract?

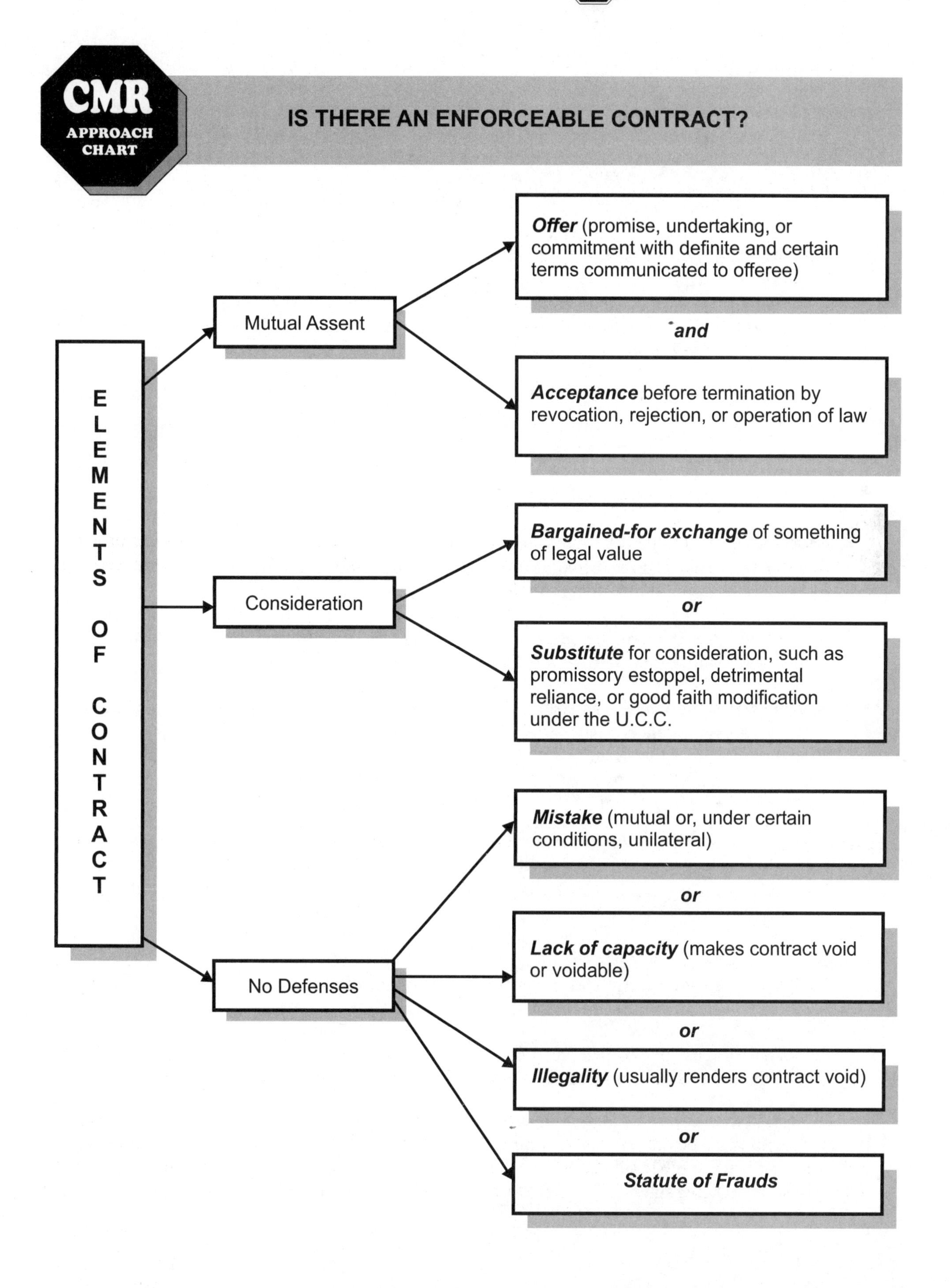
CMR
APPROACH CHART
IS THERE AN ENFORCEABLE CONTRACT?
ELEMENTS OF CONTRACT
Mutual Assent
Offer (promise, undertaking, or commitment with definite and certain terms communicated to offeree)
and
Acceptance before termination by revocation, rejection, or operation of law
Consideration
Bargained-for exchange of something of legal value
or
Substitute for consideration, such as promissory estoppel, detrimental reliance, or good faith modification under the U.C.C.
No Defenses
Mistake (mutual or, under certain conditions, unilateral)
or
Lack of capacity (makes contract void or voidable)
or
Illegality (usually renders contract void)
or
Statute of Frauds

B. THE OFFER

An offer creates a power of acceptance in the offeree. To be valid, an offer must be: (i) an expression of ***promise*, *undertaking*, *or commitment*** to enter into a contract; (ii) ***definite and certain*** in its terms; and (iii) ***communicated*** to the offeree.

1. Promise, Undertaking, or Commitment

It is important to distinguish between preliminary negotiations (not offers) and promises (offers). Consider:

a. The ***language*** used;

b. The ***surrounding circumstances***;

c. The ***prior relationship*** of the parties;

d. The ***method of communication***—the broader the communicating media (*e.g.,* an advertisement), the less likely it is an offer;

e. The ***custom*** in the industry; and

f. The ***degree of definiteness and certainty*** of terms.

CMR Exam Tip Most offers are fairly easy to spot, but watch out for language that sounds like an offer but really is an invitation to deal. For example, advertisements often sound like offers but usually are just invitations for people to come in and deal. The more definite the language (*e.g.,* "I'll sell for . . ." or "I'll pay you $10 for . . ."), the more likely the statement is an offer. However, you need to examine the other factors (surrounding circumstances, prior relationship of parties, etc.). Don't be too hasty in your determination.

CMR Exam Tip If there has been a series of communications between the parties, pay attention to the legal significance, if any, of each statement. For example, if you determine that A's first statement to B is not an offer but an invitation to deal, then B's response cannot be an acceptance (because there was nothing to accept). You must then consider whether B's response is an offer or another invitation to deal. Keep checking until you find an offer and an acceptance.

2. Terms Must Be Definite and Certain

Enough of the essential terms of a contract must be provided to make it capable of being enforced.

a. Identification of Offeree

The offer must sufficiently identify the offeree or class of offerees to justify the inference that the offeror intended to create a power of acceptance.

b. Definiteness of Subject Matter

Whether the subject matter is sufficiently definite depends on the kind of contract.

(i) ***Real estate transactions*** require identification of ***land*** and ***price*** terms.

(ii) In contracts for the ***sale of goods***, the ***quantity*** must be certain or capable of being made certain. ("Requirements" and "output" offers are generally sufficient, as a good faith intendment is usually read into the contract. The subject matter is also sufficiently identified if the offer specifies a reasonable range of choices.)

(iii) In an ***employment*** contract, the ***duration*** of the employment must be specified.

1) Reasonable Terms Supplied by Court
Certain ***missing*** terms may be supplied by the court if they are consistent with the parties' intent. Under the U.C.C., a reasonable price term and a reasonable time for performance may be supplied by the court.

2) Vagueness and Terms to Be Agreed On
A ***vague*** term may defeat formation of a contract unless acceptance or part performance makes the vague term clear. Formation fails if an offer provides that a material term will be agreed on at a future date.

3. Communication Requirement
The offer must be communicated to the offeree.

C. TERMINATION OF OFFER

An offer may be accepted only as long as it has not been terminated. It may be terminated by (i) an act of either party or (ii) operation of law.

1. Termination by Acts of Parties

a. Termination by Offeror—Revocation
The offeror terminates an offer if he: (i) directly communicates the revocation (*i.e.,* retraction of the offer) to the offeree; or (ii) acts inconsistently with continued willingness to maintain the offer, and the offeree receives correct information of this from a reliable source. Offers made by publication may be terminated only by use of comparable means of publication.

1) Effective When Received
Revocation is effective when received by the offeree (but publication of revocation is effective when published).

2) Offeror's Power to Revoke
Offers not supported by consideration or detrimental reliance ***can be revoked at will*** by the offeror, even if he has promised not to revoke for a certain period of time.

a) Limitations
The offeror's power to revoke is limited if:

(1) There is an ***option contract*** supported by consideration (*i.e.,* the party with the power of acceptance has paid for the offer's irrevocability);

(2) There is a ***firm offer under the U.C.C.*** (a signed writing by a merchant—*i.e.,* one who deals in goods of the kind sold or who has specialized knowledge of the business practices involved—promising to hold the offer open for some period of time);

(3) The offeree has ***detrimentally relied*** on the offer and the offeror could ***reasonably have expected*** such reliance; or

(4) In the case of a ***unilateral contract***, the offeree has embarked on performance (this is usually construed as an option contract giving the offeree reasonable time to complete performance).

b. Termination by Offeree—Rejection or Lapse of Time

1) Rejection

An offeree may reject an offer (i) expressly or (ii) by making a counteroffer (as distinguished from a mere inquiry).

CMR **Exam Tip** Remember that a counteroffer is ***both*** a rejection and a new offer. It terminates the original offer and reverses the roles of the parties: the offeree giving a counteroffer becomes the offeror of a new offer, which the other party may accept or reject. Thus, if A offers to sell his property, Blackacre, to B for $100,000, and B says, "I'll buy it for $90,000," what has happened? A's offer has been rejected and B has made an offer for $90,000, which A may accept or reject. B cannot later say to A, "All right, I'll take Blackacre for $100,000," and accept A's offer. It no longer exists because it was rejected. (Of course, A could accept B's new offer to buy it for $100,000.)

a) Effective when Received

A rejection is effective when received. Once an offer has been rejected, the original offer is not valid (*i.e.,* cannot be accepted); however, if the offeror restates the offer after it has been rejected, the offeree has the power to accept the new offer.

b) Rejection of Option

Rejection of an option does ***not*** terminate the offer; the offeree is still free to accept the offer within the option period ***unless*** the offeror has ***detrimentally relied*** on the offeree's rejection.

2) Lapse of Time

An offer may be terminated by the offeree's failure to accept within the time specified by the offer or within a reasonable period if no deadline was specified.

2. Termination by Operation of Law

The following events will terminate an offer:

a. ***Death or insanity of either party*** (unless the offer is of a kind the offeror could not terminate, *e.g.*, an option supported by consideration). Death or insanity need ***not*** be communicated to the other party;

b. ***Destruction*** of the proposed contract's ***subject matter***; or

c. ***Supervening illegality***.

CMR SUMMARY CHART

TERMINATION OF OFFER

	Revocation by Offeror	Rejection by Offeree	Termination by Operation of Law
When Effective	Effective when received	Effective when received	Effective when the death or insanity of either party, the destruction of the subject matter, or the supervening illegality occurs
Methods	Express revocation or implied (*e.g.,* offeree discovers offeror sold subject matter to someone else)	Express rejection, counteroffer, or lapse of reasonable time	Death or insanity of either party, destruction of subject matter, or supervening illegality
Limitations on Power to Terminate	Option contract, merchant's firm offer, detrimental reliance, beginning performance on unilateral contract	Generally cannot reject if already accepted	

D. THE ACCEPTANCE

Valid acceptance of a bilateral contract requires: (i) an ***offeree*** with the power of acceptance; (ii) ***unequivocal terms of acceptance***; and (iii) ***communication*** of acceptance.

1. Who May Accept

The person to whom the offer was addressed has the power of acceptance, as does a member of the class to whom the offer was addressed. Although the right to accept most contracts cannot be assigned, option contracts supported by consideration can be assigned to a "new" offeree.

2. Acceptance Must Be Unequivocal

a. Common Law

Acceptance must mirror the offeror's terms, neither omitting nor adding terms. Otherwise, it may be a counteroffer (*i.e.,* a rejection).

b. U.C.C. Rules

In contracts involving the sale of goods, an acceptance need ***not*** mirror the offer's terms (*i.e.,* an acceptance that deviates from the offer is ***not*** necessarily a rejection and counteroffer). Any acceptance that indicates an intention to enter into a contract is valid unless it is made conditional on the acceptance of new or different terms. Whether the offer terms or the acceptance terms govern depends on the status of the parties.

1) **Nonmerchants—Terms of Offer Govern**
If one of the parties is not a merchant, the terms of the offer control. The new or different terms are considered mere proposals.

2) **Merchants—Acceptance Terms Usually Included**
In transactions between merchants (*i.e.*, ***both*** parties are merchants), ***additional*** terms proposed in the acceptance ***become part of the contract*** unless they ***materially alter*** the agreement, the offer ***expressly limits acceptance*** to the terms of the offer, or the offeror ***objects within a reasonable time*** to the additional terms. Additional terms that materially alter the agreement do not prevent contract formation, but become part of the contract ***only if*** the offeror expressly assents to inclusion. There is a split of authority over whether ***different*** terms in the acceptance become part of the contract. Some courts treat different terms like additional terms, and they use the above test to determine whether the different terms should be part of the contract. Other courts follow the "knockout rule," which states that conflicting terms in the offer and acceptance are knocked out of the contract and the terms instead are provided by the U.C.C.

3) **Writings that Do Not Create a Contract—Effect of Performance**
If the original offeror's form contains an objection to the addition of any new or inconsistent terms, and the offeree's response proposes new terms and states that the response is not an acceptance unless the offeror expressly consents to the new terms, no contract arises ***unless performance begins***. Where the writings of the parties do not create a contract, but the parties behave as if they have one (*i.e.*, begin to perform), there is a contract consisting of all terms on which their ***writings agree***, plus supplementary terms supplied by the U.C.C.

3. **Generally Acceptance Must Be Communicated**
Acceptance is judged on an objective standard (*i.e.,* would a reasonable person think there was an acceptance?); the offeree's subjective state of mind is irrelevant. The modern rule and the U.C.C. permit acceptance by ***any reasonable means*** unless the offeror unambiguously limits acceptance to particular means.

a. **"Mailbox Rule"**
Under the mailbox rule, if acceptance is by mail or similar means and properly addressed and stamped, it is ***effective at the moment of dispatch***. (If it is improperly sent, it is effective upon receipt.)

CMR **Exam Tip** The mailbox rule ("effective upon dispatch") applies only to ***acceptance***. It does not apply to other events in the contract setting, such as rejection or revocation.

1) **Limitations on Mailbox Rule**
The following limitations apply to the mailbox rule:

a) The rule does not apply if the ***offer stipulates*** that acceptance is not effective until received.

EFFECT OF REJECTION OR REVOCATION ON OFFER

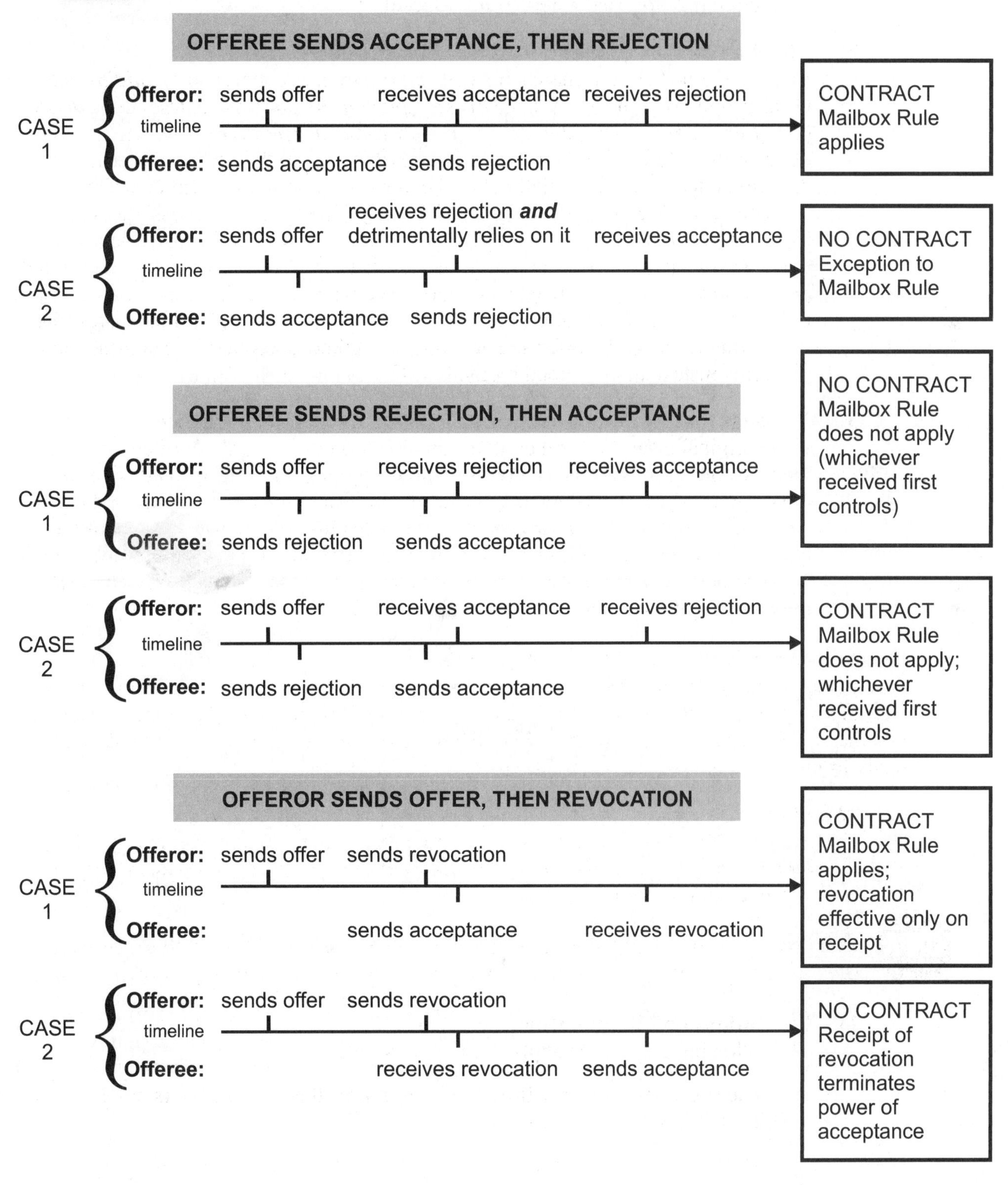

b) The rule does not apply if an ***option contract*** is involved (acceptance is effective upon receipt).

c) If the offeree sends a ***rejection and then sends an acceptance***, whichever arrives first is effective.

d) If the offeree sends an acceptance and then a rejection, the acceptance is effective (*i.e.,* the mailbox rule applies) ***unless the rejection arrives first and*** the offeror ***detrimentally relies*** on it.

b. Acceptance by Unauthorized Means

An acceptance transmitted by unauthorized means is effective if it is actually received by the offeror while the offer is still in existence.

c. "Crossing" Offers

Because an offer is effective on receipt, offers stating the same terms that cross in the mail do not give rise to a contract.

d. Exception—Acceptance Without Communication

An executory bilateral contract may be formed without communication of acceptance where (i) there is an express waiver of communication in the offer; (ii) the offer requires an act as acceptance; or (iii) the offeree silently takes the offered benefits.

E. UNILATERAL OR BILATERAL CONTRACT

1. Interpreting Contract as Unilateral or Bilateral

In a unilateral contract, the offeree accepts by performing a stipulated act. In a bilateral contract, the offeree accepts by promising to do a stipulated act. Modern courts generally interpret an offer as unilateral only if its terms clearly warn that an act is required for acceptance. If the offer is ambiguous, the Second Restatement and the U.C.C. allow acceptance by either an act or a promise.

2. Formation Problems

a. Unilateral Contracts

Generally, the offeree of a unilateral contract must act ***with knowledge of the offer and be motivated*** by it. There is a duty to give notice of performance to the offeror if he requests notice or if the act would not normally come to his attention; otherwise, there is no duty to notify.

CMR **Exam Tip** Keep in mind that the offeree of a unilateral contract ***must know of the offer*** to accept it. If the "offeree" acts without knowledge and learns of the offer later, her acts were not an acceptance. Thus, if A finds O's watch and returns it to O without knowledge of O's reward offer, A has no contractual right to the reward.

b. Bilateral Contracts

An offeree's ignorance of certain contractual terms may be a defense to formation of a bilateral contract. Also, oppressive terms or provisions contrary to public policy may prevent contract formation. Blanket form recitals that state that the offeree has read and understood all terms will not prevent a court from holding that there is no contract if a reasonable person would not understand the provisions.

III. CONSIDERATION

A. INTRODUCTION

Courts will enforce a bilateral or unilateral contract only if it is supported by consideration or a substitute for consideration.

B. ELEMENTS OF CONSIDERATION

Consideration involves two elements: (i) "***bargain***"; and (ii) ***legal value***.

1. Bargained-for Exchange

The parties must exchange something. In the case of a bilateral contract, they exchange promises. In the case of a unilateral contract, they exchange a promise for an act.

a. Gift

There is no bargain involved (*i.e.,* no consideration) when one party gives a gift to another.

1) Act or Forbearance by Promisee

An act or forbearance by the promisee will be sufficient to form a bargain ***if it benefits*** the promisor.

2) Economic Benefit Not Required

If one party gives the other peace of mind or gratification in exchange for something, it may be sufficient to establish a bargain.

b. Past or Moral Consideration

A promise given in exchange for something already done does not satisfy the bargain requirement.

1) Exceptions

Where a past obligation is unenforceable because of a technical defense (*e.g.,* statute of limitations), that obligation will be enforceable ***if a new promise*** is made ***in writing*** or is ***partially performed***. Also, under the modern trend, if a past act was performed by the promisee at the promisor's ***request***, a ***new promise*** to pay for that act will be enforceable.

CMR **Exam Tip** Beware of questions that use the word "consideration" to refer to something already done, as in "In consideration of your having done X, I promise you $1,000." Under the general rule, this promise is not enforceable because the promise is given in exchange for past acts.

2. Legal Value Element

a. Adequacy of Consideration

In general, courts do ***not*** inquire into the adequacy or fairness of consideration. However, if something is entirely devoid of value (token consideration), it is insufficient. Sham consideration (recited in the contract, but not actually paid) may also be insufficient. Where there is a possibility of value in the thing bargained for, consideration will be found even if the value never comes into existence.

b. **Legal Benefit and Legal Detriment Theories**
The majority of courts require that a party incur ***detriment*** (by doing something he is not legally obligated to do or by refraining from something he has a legal right to do) to satisfy the legal value element. Under the minority rule, conferring a benefit on the other party is also sufficient.

c. **Specific Situations**

1) **Preexisting Legal Duty**
Traditionally, performing or promising to perform an existing legal duty is ***insufficient*** consideration.

a) **Exceptions**
The preexisting legal duty rule is riddled with exceptions; there is consideration if:

(i) ***New or different*** consideration is promised;

(ii) The promise is to ***ratify a voidable obligation*** (*e.g.,* a promise to ratify a minor's contract after reaching majority, a promise to go through with a contract despite the other party's fraud);

(iii) The preexisting duty is ***owed to a third person*** rather than to the promisor;

(iv) There is an ***honest dispute*** as to the duty; or

(v) There are ***unforeseen circumstances*** sufficient to discharge a party.

A ***good faith*** agreement modifying a contract subject to the ***U.C.C.*** needs ***no consideration*** to be binding.

CMR **Exam Tip** Although payment of a smaller sum than due on an existing debt is generally ***not*** sufficient consideration for a promise by the creditor to discharge the debt, courts will attempt to avoid this result by applying the above exceptions. Thus, see if there is new or different consideration given in the facts (*e.g.,* payment ***earlier*** than required or payment in ***stock*** instead of cash); this change in performance could make the payment of a smaller amount sufficient consideration.

2) **Forbearance to Sue**
A promise to refrain from suing on a claim may constitute consideration if the claim is valid or the claimant ***in good faith*** believed the claim was valid.

C. MUTUAL AND ILLUSORY PROMISES—REQUIREMENT OF MUTUALITY

Consideration must exist on both sides of a contract (although the benefit of the consideration generally need not flow to all parties). If only one party is bound to perform, the promise is illusory and will not be enforced. Courts often supply implied promises (*e.g.,* a party must use her best efforts) to infer mutuality.

1. **Examples**
The following are common examples of contracts that satisfy the mutuality requirement:

   a. Requirements and output contracts;

   b. Conditional promises, unless the condition is entirely within the promisor's control;

   c. Contracts where a party has the right to cancel, if that right is somehow restricted (*e.g.*, a party must give 60 days' notice);

   d. Voidable promises (*e.g.*, one made by an infant);

   e. Unilateral and option contracts; and

   f. Gratuitous suretyship promises made before consideration flows to the principal debtor.

Exam Tip Closely analyze the wording of contract terms; language can make a big difference here. For example, a valid requirements or output contract term will say, "all the widgets I require" or "all that you produce," but a term such as "all the widgets I want" or "all you want to sell me" is illusory.

2. **Right to Choose Alternative Courses**
A promise to choose one of several alternative means of performance is illusory ***unless every alternative*** involves legal detriment to the promisor. The promise will not be found illusory if: (i) at least one alternative involves legal detriment and the power to choose rests with the promisee or a third party, or (ii) a valuable alternative (*i.e.*, one involving legal detriment) is actually selected.

D. NO REQUIREMENT THAT ALL CONSIDERATION BE VALID

There is no requirement that each of the promises given as consideration be sufficient as consideration (*i.e.*, one promise may be defective and another sufficient).

E. SUBSTITUTES FOR CONSIDERATION

In some special situations, consideration as defined above is not necessary to create contractual liability. In these cases, a "substitute" for consideration will suffice.

1. **Promissory Estoppel or Detrimental Reliance**
Promissory estoppel is a sufficient substitute. The following elements must be present: (i) the promisor should ***reasonably expect*** her promise ***to induce action or forbearance***, (ii) of a ***definite and substantial*** character, and (iii) such action or forbearance is ***in fact induced***.

Exam Tip A valid contract is better than an agreement that can be enforced only by promissory estoppel because some states limit recovery under promissory estoppel to that which "justice requires." Thus, in a question asking whether a party can prevail based on an agreement, always check first to see if there is a valid contract. Only if there is not should you consider promissory estoppel as a proper choice.

2. **Modification Under the U.C.C.**
Under the U.C.C., consideration is ***not*** necessary to a good faith written modification of a contract.

3. Promises to Pay Legal Obligations Barred by Law
If a legal obligation is not enforceable under law (*e.g.*, a debt barred by the statute of limitations), a new promise to fulfill the legal obligation is enforceable if in ***writing***. However, it will be enforceable only according to ***the new terms***, not the terms of the original legal obligation.

4. Seal
In many states and under the U.C.C., a seal is ***no longer a substitute*** for consideration.

IV. REQUIREMENT THAT NO DEFENSES EXIST

A. DEFENSES TO FORMATION

1. Absence of Mutual Assent

a. Mutual Mistake
A mistake by ***both parties*** is a defense if:

(i) The mistake concerns a ***basic assumption*** on which the contract was made;

(ii) The mistake has a ***material adverse effect*** on the agreed-upon exchange; and

(iii) The adversely affected party ***did not assume the risk*** of the mistake.

1) Assumption of Risk
Note that when the parties know that their assumption is doubtful (so-called conscious ignorance), mutual mistake is not a defense—the parties will be deemed to have assumed the risk that their assumption was wrong.

2) Mistake in Value Generally No Defense
A mistake in value generally goes unremedied, as courts presume parties assume the risk of determining value. *But note:* There are exceptions (such as when the parties rely on a third party to establish value).

b. Unilateral Mistake
Whether it be of identity, subject matter, or computation, a mistake by one party is generally ***insufficient*** to make a contract voidable. However, if the nonmistaken party knew or should have known of the mistake, the contract is voidable by the mistaken party.

c. Mistake by Intermediary (Transmission)
Where there is a mistake by an intermediary (*e.g.,* a telegraph company makes a mistake), the message usually will be operative ***as transmitted*** unless the party receiving the message should have been aware of the mistake.

d. Latent Ambiguity Mistakes
If the contract includes an ambiguous term, the result depends on the parties' awareness of the ambiguity:

(i) Neither party aware—no contract unless both parties intended the same meaning;

(ii) Both parties aware—no contract unless both parties intended the same meaning;

(iii) One party aware—binding contract based on what the ignorant party reasonably believed to be the meaning of ambiguous words.

Ambiguity is one area where subjective intent is taken into account.

e. **Misrepresentation**
If a party induces another to enter into a contract by using ***fraudulent misrepresentation*** (*e.g.,* by asserting information she knows is untrue) or by using ***nonfraudulent material misrepresentation*** (*e.g.,* by asserting information that she does not know is untrue but that would induce a reasonable person to enter into a contract), the contract is ***voidable*** by the innocent party if she ***justifiably relied*** on the misrepresentation. *Distinguish:* If there is ***fraud in the factum*** (*i.e.,* if a party is tricked into assenting without understanding the significance of her action) rather than fraudulent misrepresentation (which is a type of ***fraud in the inducement***), the contract is ***void,*** rather than voidable.

2. **Absence of Consideration**
If promises exchanged at the formation stage lack elements of bargain or legal detriment, no contract exists.

3. **Public Policy Defenses—Illegality of Contract**
If the ***consideration or subject matter*** of a contract is illegal (*e.g.,* a contract to commit a murder), the contract is void. *Exceptions:* (i) the plaintiff is unaware of the illegality while the defendant knows of the illegality; (ii) the parties are not in pari delicto (*i.e.,* one party is not as culpable as the other); or (iii) the illegality is the failure to obtain a license when the license is for revenue-raising purposes rather than for protection of the public. If only the ***purpose*** behind the contract is illegal, the contract is ***voidable*** by a party who was (i) unaware of the purpose; or (ii) aware but did not facilitate the purpose ***and*** the purpose does not involve serious moral turpitude (*e.g.,* murder).

B. DEFENSES BASED ON LACK OF CAPACITY

In most jurisdictions, ***persons under age 18*** lack capacity to contract. (Some exceptions exist, *e.g.,* contracts providing for the incapacitated party's necessities.) Upon reaching majority, the infant may affirm her contractual obligation (if there is no express disaffirmance, this will be construed as affirmance). A contract between an infant and an adult is voidable by the infant but binding on the adult. ***Insane persons*** lack capacity, although such persons may contract during a lucid interval. ***Intoxicated persons*** may also lack capacity if the other party has reason to know of the intoxication. Contracts induced by ***duress and coercion*** are voidable.

CMR **Exam Tip** Duress usually requires ***more*** than one party's taking economic advantage of another (*e.g.,* by charging a high price for something the other party desperately needs).

C. DEFENSES TO ENFORCEMENT

1. **Statute of Frauds**

a. **When Agreement Is Unenforceable**
Certain agreements ***must be in writing*** (evidenced by a memorandum) to be enforced. These agreements are:

1) Promises by ***executors or administrators*** to pay estates' debts ***out of their own funds***;

2) Promises to ***answer for the debt or default of another*** (*i.e.,* to act as a surety);

3) Promises made in consideration of ***marriage***;

4) Promises creating an ***interest in land*** (but leasehold interests for one year or less generally are not subject to the Statute);

5) Promises that by their terms ***cannot be performed within one year*** (the year runs from the date of agreement, not the date of performance; lifetime contracts are not within the Statute because they could be performed within a year); and

6) Agreements for the ***sale of goods for $500 or more, except*** (i) specially manufactured goods, (ii) a written confirmation of an oral agreement between merchants, (iii) admission in pleadings or court that a contract for goods existed, or (iv) partial payment or delivery made and accepted.

CMR **Exam Tip** Statute of Frauds issues are often raised in MBE questions. Remember that the Statute does not apply to all contracts. You must check the facts to see whether the contract falls within any of the covered areas (above). An easy way to remember agreements covered by the Statute of Frauds is by using the acronym ***MY LEGS***: Marriage, (within one) Year, Land, Executor (or Administrator), Goods (for $500 or more), Surety.

b. Memorandum Requirements

The Statute is satisfied if the writing contains the following:

1) The ***identity of parties*** sought to be charged;

2) Identification of the ***contract's subject matter***;

3) ***Terms and conditions*** of the agreement;

4) Recital of the ***consideration***; and

5) The ***signature of the party to be charged*** or his agent.

CMR **Exam Tip** To be sufficient under the Statute of Frauds, something ***in writing*** must show the above items. The writing need not be a full-fledged contract, nor need it even be one piece of paper. Thus, several pieces of correspondence between the parties could be a sufficient memorandum of the agreement; a fax or a memo written on a napkin also could suffice. The key is that there is something in writing.

CMR **Exam Tip** Also note that the memorandum does ***not*** need to be signed by both parties to the contract. Only the party to be charged (*i.e.,* the person to be sued) must sign. Thus, if a fact situation has an otherwise sufficient writing that is signed by the seller but not the buyer, if the buyer is suing the seller, the writing is enough for the Statute of Frauds. However, if the seller sued the buyer, there would not be a sufficient memorandum. (*Compare:* One signature may be enough for ***merchants'*** contracts under the ***U.C.C.;*** *see* Sales outline.)

c. **When Statute Is Not Applicable**
Noncompliance with the Statute renders a contract unenforceable. The Statute is not applicable to the extent of admissions in court that a contract was formed or to the extent there was part performance. For a ***sale of goods***, part payment or acceptance and receipt of part of the goods takes the contract out of the Statute to the extent of the part payment or partial acceptance and receipt of goods. For a ***sale of land***, most jurisdictions do not apply the Statute if there is performance that unequivocally indicates that the parties contracted for the sale of land. Most jurisdictions require two of the following: payment (in whole or in part), possession, and/or valuable improvements. *Note:* In cases where it would be inequitable to allow the Statute of Frauds to defeat a meritorious claim, courts will occasionally use the doctrine of ***promissory estoppel*** to remove the contract from the Statute.

2. **Unconscionability**
A contract may be voidable where the clauses are so one-sided as to be unconscionable. This includes contracts with inconspicuous risk-shifting provisions (*e.g.,* disclaimers of warranty buried in fine print) and contracts of adhesion ("take it or leave it"). Unconscionability is tested ***at the time the contract was made***, not later (*i.e.,* the contract must have been unfair when it was entered into). The defense is often applied where one party has substantially superior bargaining power.

CMR **Exam Tip** Unconscionability is seldom a good defense on the MBE. That a contract turned out badly for one party is insufficient in itself to give rise to unconscionability. Look for great differences in bargaining power (*e.g.,* big company vs. average consumer).

V. RIGHTS AND DUTIES OF NONPARTIES TO CONTRACT

A. INTRODUCTION
Nonparties to a contract may have rights or duties in connection with the contract.

B. THIRD-PARTY BENEFICIARIES
In the typical third-party beneficiary situation, A (the promisee) contracts with B (the promisor) that B will render some performance to C (the third-party beneficiary).

1. **Who Is Third-Party Beneficiary?**

a. **Intended vs. Incidental Beneficiary**
Only intended beneficiaries have contractual rights, not incidental beneficiaries. In determining if a beneficiary is intended, consider whether the beneficiary (i) is ***identified*** in the contract, (ii) ***receives performance directly*** from the promisor, or (iii) has some ***relationship with the promisee*** to indicate intent to benefit.

b. **Creditor vs. Donee Beneficiary**
There are two types of intended beneficiaries: (i) a creditor beneficiary—a person to whom a debt is owed by the promisee, and (ii) a donee beneficiary—a person the promisee intends to benefit gratuitously.

2. When Does Beneficiary Acquire Contractual Rights?

A third party can enforce a contract only when his rights have vested. This occurs when he (i) ***manifests assent*** to a promise in the manner requested by the parties; (ii) brings a ***suit to enforce*** the promise; or (iii) ***materially changes position*** in justifiable reliance on the promise. Prior to vesting, the promisee and promisor are free to modify or rescind the beneficiary's rights under the contract.

3. Who Can Sue Whom?

a. Third-Party Beneficiary vs. Promisor

A beneficiary may sue the promisor on the contract. The promisor may raise against the third-party beneficiary any defense that the promisor has against the promisee. Whether the promisor may use the defenses the promisee would have against the third-party beneficiary depends on whether the promisor made an absolute promise to pay or only a promise to pay what the promisee owes the beneficiary. If the promise is absolute, the promisor cannot assert the promisee's defenses; if the promise is not absolute, the promisor can assert the promisee's defenses.

b. Third-Party Beneficiary vs. Promisee

A ***creditor*** beneficiary can sue the promisee on the existing obligation between them. She may also sue the promisor, but may obtain only one satisfaction. A donee beneficiary has no right to sue the promisee unless grounds for a detrimental reliance remedy exist (*see* III.E.1., *supra*).

c. Promisee vs. Promisor

A promisee may sue the promisor both at law and in equity for specific performance if the promisor is not performing for the third person.

C. ASSIGNMENT OF RIGHTS AND DELEGATION OF DUTIES

1. Assignment

In the typical assignment situation, X (the obligor) contracts with Y (the assignor). Y assigns his right to X's performance to Z (the assignee).

a. What Rights May Be Assigned?

Generally, all contractual rights may be assigned. *Exceptions:* (i) an assignment that would ***substantially change*** the obligor's duty or risk (*e.g.*, personal service contracts where the service is unique, requirements and output contracts where the assignee will substantially vary the quantity); (ii) an assignment of future rights to ***arise from future contracts*** (not future rights in already existing contracts); and (iii) an assignment ***prohibited by law*** (*e.g.*, wage assignments).

1) Nonassignment Provisions

A clause prohibiting assignment of ***"the contract"*** will be construed as barring only delegation of the assignor's duties. A clause prohibiting assignment of ***contractual rights*** generally does not bar assignment, but merely gives the obligor the right to sue for damages. However, if the contract provides that attempts to assign ***will be void***, the parties can bar assignment. Also, if the assignee has notice of the nonassignment clause, an assignment will be ineffective.

b. **What Is Necessary for an Effective Assignment?**
For an assignment to be effective, the assignor must manifest an intent to immediately and completely transfer her rights. A writing is usually not required to have an effective assignment. The right being assigned must be adequately described. It is not necessary to use the word "assign"; any accepted words of transfer will suffice. A gratuitous assignment is effective; consideration is not required.

c. **Is Assignment Revocable or Irrevocable?**
An assignment for ***consideration*** is irrevocable. An assignment not for consideration is generally revocable. However, a gratuitous assignment is irrevocable if: (i) the obligor has already performed; (ii) a token chose (*i.e.,* a tangible claim, such as a stock certificate) is delivered; (iii) an assignment of a simple chose (*i.e.,* an intangible claim, such as a contract right) is put in writing; or (iv) the assignee can show detrimental reliance on the gratuitous assignment (*i.e.,* estoppel). A revocable gratuitous assignment may be terminated by: (i) the death or bankruptcy of the assignor; (ii) notice of revocation by the assignor to the assignee or the obligor; (iii) the assignor taking performance directly from the obligor; or (iv) subsequent assignment of the same right by the assignor to another.

1) **Effect of Assignment**
The effect of an assignment is to establish privity of contract between the obligor and the assignee while extinguishing privity between the obligor and the assignor.

d. **Who Can Sue Whom?**

1) **Assignee vs. Obligor**
The assignee can sue the obligor, as the assignee is the real party in interest; *i.e.,* the assignee—not the assignor—is entitled to performance under the contract. (The obligor has as a defense against the assignee any defense inherent in the contract, *e.g.,* failure of consideration and other defenses that came into existence before the obligor had knowledge of the assignment.) The obligor cannot raise by way of defense any defenses the assignor might have against the assignee.

2) **Assignee vs. Assignor**
The assignee can sue the assignor for wrongfully exercising the power to revoke in an irrevocable assignment situation. An action by the assignee against the assignor may also lie where the obligor successfully asserts a defense against the assignor in an action brought by the assignee against the obligor to enforce the obligation. The assignor will not be liable to the assignee if the obligor is incapable of performing.

e. **What Problems Exist If There Have Been Successive Assignments of Same Rights?**
If the first assignment is revocable, a subsequent assignment revokes it. If it is irrevocable, ***the first assignment will usually prevail*** over a subsequent assignment. Several exceptions exist (***if*** the second assignee has ***paid value and taken without notice*** of the first assignment): (i) the subsequent assignee gets the first judgment against the obligor; (ii) the subsequent assignee gets the first payment of a claim from the obligor; (iii) the subsequent assignee gets delivery of a token chose; (iv) the subsequent assignee is the party to a novation releasing the assignor; or (v) the subsequent assignee can proceed against the first assignee on an estoppel theory (estoppel could, of course, operate against the subsequent assignee as well).

2. Delegation of Duties

In the typical delegation situation, Y (the obligor/delegator) promises to perform for X (the obligee). Y delegates her duty to Z (the delegate).

a. What Duties May Be Delegated?

Generally, all duties may be delegated. *Exceptions:* (i) the duties involve ***personal judgment and skill***; (ii) delegation would ***change the obligee's expectancy*** (*e.g.*, requirements and output contracts); (iii) a ***special trust*** was reposed in the delegator by the other party to the contract; and (iv) there is a ***contractual restriction*** on delegation.

b. Requirements for Effective Delegation

The delegator must manifest a present intention to make a delegation. There are no special formalities to be complied with to have a valid delegation. It may be written or oral.

CMR **Exam Tip** Although "assignment" and "delegation" have precise meanings (rights are assigned and duties are delegated), on the MBE the terms are often used loosely. Thus, a question might state initially that "Y assigned his rights in the contract to X," but the facts later show that duties were also delegated.

c. Rights and Liabilities of Parties

The obligee must accept performance from the delegate of all duties that may be delegated. The delegator remains liable on the contract; thus, the obligee may sue the delegator for nonperformance by the delegate. The obligee may sue the delegate for nonperformance, but can require the delegate to perform ***only if*** there has been an ***assumption*** (*i.e.,* the delegate promises he will perform the duty delegated and this promise is supported by consideration or its equivalent). This promise creates a contract between the delegator and the delegate in which the obligee is a third-party beneficiary.

d. Terminology

Today, words assigning "the contract" or "all my rights under the contract" are usually construed as including an assumption of the duties by the assignee, unless a contrary intention appears.

D. NOVATION DISTINGUISHED

Novation substitutes a new party for an original party to the contract. It requires assent of all parties and completely releases the original party. (*See* VII.C.7., *infra.*)

VI. RULES OF CONTRACT CONSTRUCTION AND THE PAROL EVIDENCE RULE

A. RULES OF CONTRACT CONSTRUCTION

A contract is construed as a "whole," and according to the ordinary meaning of words. If there is an inconsistency between provisions, written or typed provisions prevail over printed provisions.

Ambiguities are construed against the party preparing the contract, absent evidence of the intention of the parties. Courts look to the custom and usage in a particular business and in a particular locale to determine the parties' intent when it is unclear. Courts generally will try to reach a determination that a contract is valid and enforceable.

B. PAROL EVIDENCE RULE

Evidence of ***prior or contemporaneous*** negotiations and agreements that contradict, modify, or vary contractual terms is inadmissible if the written contract is intended as a ***complete and final expression*** of the parties. A "merger clause" (recital that the contract is complete on its face) strengthens the presumption that the written document is final.

1. Exceptions

Evidence of the following is admissible: (i) ***formation defects*** (*e.g.,* fraud, duress, mistake, illegality); (ii) the existence of a ***condition precedent*** to a contract; (iii) the parties' intent regarding ***ambiguous terms***; (iv) ***consideration problems*** (*e.g.,* consideration stated in the contract was never paid); (v) a prior valid agreement which (as by mistake) is ***incorrectly reflected in the writing***; (vi) a ***collateral agreement*** if it does not contradict or vary the main contract and if it is not so closely connected as to be part of the main contract; and (vii) ***subsequent modifications***.

VII. INTERPRETATION AND ENFORCEMENT OF THE CONTRACT

A. INTRODUCTION

Two basic questions must be asked: (i) whether a present duty to perform has arisen (*i.e.,* is there an absolute promise ***or*** have all conditions been met or excused); and (ii) whether the duty to perform has been discharged. If a present duty to perform has arisen and has not been discharged, nonperformance will be a contractual breach.

B. WHEN HAS A CONTRACTING PARTY'S DUTY TO PERFORM BECOME ABSOLUTE?

1. Distinction Between Promise and Condition

a. Definitions

A ***promise*** is a commitment to do or refrain from doing something. It may be conditional or unconditional. A ***condition*** is an event the occurrence or nonoccurrence of which will create, limit, or extinguish the absolute duty to perform; it is a promise modifier.

b. Interpretation of Provision as Promise or Condition

It is not always clear whether a contract provision is a promise or a condition. The basic test is the "***intent of the parties***," as judged by the words of the agreement, the prior practices of the parties, and custom in the business. In doubtful situations, the courts prefer a promise, because a promise will support the contract.

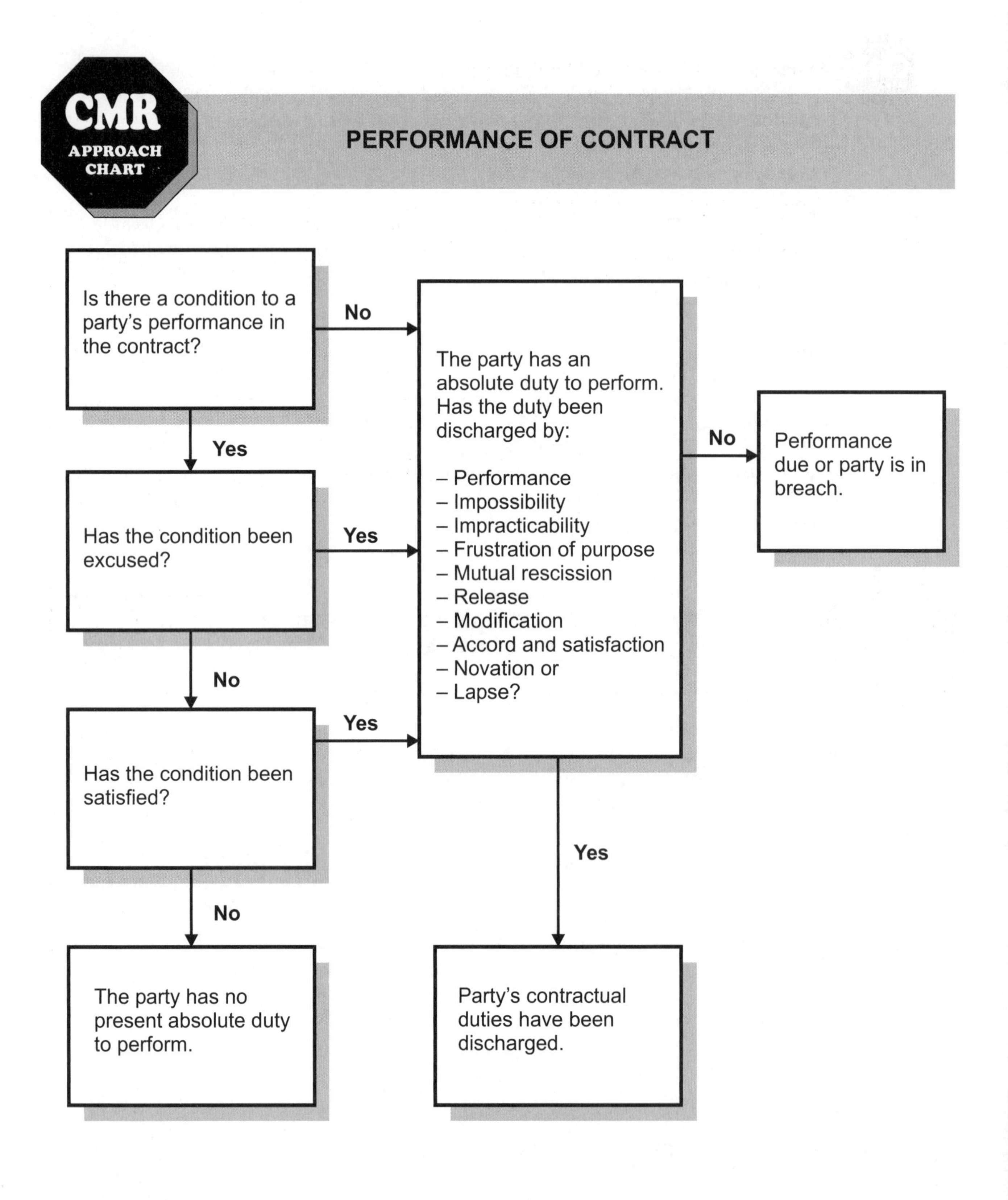
CMR
APPROACH CHART
PERFORMANCE OF CONTRACT
Is there a condition to a party's performance in the contract?
No
Yes
The party has an absolute duty to perform. Has the duty been discharged by:
– Performance
– Impossibility
– Impracticability
– Frustration of purpose
– Mutual rescission
– Release
– Modification
– Accord and satisfaction
– Novation or
– Lapse?
No
Performance due or party is in breach.
Has the condition been excused?
Yes
No
Has the condition been satisfied?
Yes
No
Yes
The party has no present absolute duty to perform.
Party's contractual duties have been discharged.

CMR **Exam Tip** The distinction between a promise and a condition is important, because the failure of a ***promise*** gives rise to a ***breach***, whereas the failure of a ***condition relieves*** a party of the obligation to perform.

c. **Condition or Promise**
A provision may be a promise for one party ***and*** a condition for the other, as in an exchange where the second party's duty to pay is conditioned on the first party's performance of her promise. A provision may also be both a promise and a condition for the same party, as where a party is under a duty to reasonably ensure that a condition comes about (*e.g.,* to secure financing).

2. **Classification of Conditions**

a. **According to Time of Occurrence**
A condition ***precedent*** is one that must occur before an absolute duty of performance arises in the other party. Conditions ***concurrent*** are those that are capable of occurring together, as where property is tendered in exchange for cash. A condition ***subsequent*** is one that cuts off an already existing duty of performance.

CMR SUMMARY CHART

CONDITIONS—TIME OF OCCURRENCE

Type	Definition	Effect of Occurrence of Condition	Example
Condition Precedent	Condition must occur before performance is due.	Performance due.	Agreement to pay $10,000 "if my house is sold by April 1." No payment unless house is sold by April 1.
Conditions Concurrent	Conditions to occur at the same time.	If one condition has occurred, performance of the other is due.	Agreement to pay $100,000 for Blackacre. Money and deed exchanged in same transaction.
Condition Subsequent	Condition cuts off already existing duty.	Duty to perform is excused.	Agreement to buy Blackacre for $100,000 unless zoning is changed. If zoning is changed, no duty to pay $100,000 or transfer deed.

CMR **Exam Tip** Theoretically, it is the plaintiff's burden to plead and prove that all conditions precedent to the defendant's duty have been performed, and it is the defendant's burden to plead and prove that a condition subsequent has cut off his duty. In practice, however, pleading rules, presumptions, and the court's discretion in the interest of justice may shift these burdens.

b. Express, Implied, and Constructive Conditions

Express conditions are those expressed in the contract. ***Implied*** conditions (called "implied in fact" conditions) are those to be inferred from evidence of the parties' intention. ***Constructive*** conditions (called "implied in law" conditions) are those read into a contract by the court ***without regard to the parties' intention*** in order to ensure that the parties receive what they bargained for. Constructive conditions may relate to the time of performance, *i.e.,* which party performs first.

3. Have the Conditions Been Excused?

A duty of performance becomes absolute when conditions are either ***performed or excused***. Conditions may be excused in several ways:

a. Excuse of Condition by Failure to Cooperate

A party who wrongfully prevents a condition from occurring will no longer be given the benefit of it.

b. Excuse of Condition by Actual Breach

An actual, material breach by one party excuses the other's duty of counterperformance. (A minor breach might suspend the duty, but will not excuse it.)

c. Excuse of Condition by Anticipatory Repudiation

Anticipatory repudiation must be unequivocal, not just an expression of doubt. It applies ***only if*** there are ***executory*** (unperformed) ***duties on both sides*** of a bilateral contract. (If the nonrepudiating party has nothing further to do at the time of repudiation—he has performed his part of the contract—he must wait until the time originally set for performance; the repudiator may change his mind up to that time.) Anticipatory repudiation gives the nonrepudiating party four alternatives:

(i) Treat the contract as totally repudiated and ***sue immediately***;

(ii) ***Suspend his own performance*** and wait until the performance is due to sue;

(iii) Treat the repudiation as an ***offer to rescind and treat the contract as discharged***; or

(iv) ***Ignore*** the repudiation and urge performance (but note that by urging the repudiating party to perform, the nonrepudiating party is ***not*** waiving the repudiation—she can still sue for breach and is excused from performing unless the repudiation is retracted).

Repudiation may be retracted until the nonrepudiating party has accepted the repudiation or detrimentally relied on it.

d. Excuse of Condition by Prospective Inability or Unwillingness to Perform

A party might have reasonable grounds to believe the other party will be unable or unwilling to perform when performance is due.

1) **Distinguish from Anticipatory Repudiation**
Prospective inability to perform merely ***raises doubts*** about performance; thus, it does not meet the unequivocality requirement of anticipatory repudiation.

2) **What Conduct Will Suffice?**
Conduct is judged according to a reasonable person standard.

3) **Effect of Prospective Failure**
The innocent party may ***suspend*** her own performance until she receives adequate assurances of performance. If these are not forthcoming, she may treat the failure as a repudiation.

4) **Retraction**
Retraction is possible, but may be ineffective if the other party has changed her position in reliance on the prospective failure.

e. **Excuse of Condition by Substantial Performance**
Where a party has almost completely performed his duties, but has breached in some minor way, the rule of substantial performance avoids forfeiture of a return performance.

1) **Application**
The rule is generally applied only where ***constructive*** conditions are involved; applying it to express conditions might defeat the express intent of the parties that performance be perfect. Substantiality of performance is judged by the same standards as materiality of breach. (*See* VIII.B.1., *infra.*) The rule is usually ***not*** applied if the breach was ***willful***.

2) **Damages Offset**
The substantially performing party may be required to pay damages to compensate the other party for the incomplete performance.

3) **Applicability of Substantial Performance to Sale of Goods**
Although the U.C.C. sets forth a "perfect tender rule," it is subject to exceptions, such as the provision for a seller's right to cure defective tender.

f. **Excuse of Condition by Divisibility of Contract**
Where a party performs one of the units of a divisible contract, she is entitled to the agreed equivalent for that unit even though she fails to perform the other units.

1) **What Is a Divisible Contract?**
Three tests must be met to find that a contract is divisible:

a) The performance of each party is divided into two or more parts under the contract;

b) The number of parts due from each party is the same; and

c) The performance of each part by one party is the agreed equivalent of the corresponding part by the other party.

2) **Installment Contracts**
Under the U.C.C., a contract that authorizes or requires delivery in separate lots is an installment contract. The buyer may declare a total breach only if defects in an installment are such as to substantially impair the value of the ***entire contract***.

g. **Excuse of Condition by Waiver or Estoppel**

1) **Estoppel Waiver**
A party may "waive" a condition by indicating that he will not insist on it. However, such a waiver may be retracted at any time unless the other party relies on the waiver and changes her position to her detriment. Upon such detrimental reliance, the waiving party is estopped from asserting the condition.

2) **Election Waiver**
If a condition is broken, the party who was to have its benefit may either terminate his liability or continue under the contract. If he chooses the latter, he is deemed to have waived the condition.

3) **Conditions that May Be Waived**
If no consideration is given for the waiver, the condition must be one that is ancillary or collateral to the main purpose of the contract. Otherwise, the waiver amounts to a gift and is thus not enforceable.

4) **Right to Damages for Failure of Condition**
Waiving a condition does ***not*** waive one's right to damages for the other's defective performance.

h. **Excuse of Condition by Impossibility, Impracticability, or Frustration**
Conditions may be excused by impossibility, impracticability, or frustration of purpose according to the tests described under discharge. (*See* C.4., *infra.*)

C. HAS THE DUTY TO PERFORM BEEN DISCHARGED?
Once it is established that there is an immediate duty to perform (either because the duty is unconditional or the condition has been satisfied or excused), that duty must be discharged.

1. **Discharge by Performance or Tender of Performance**
The duty may be discharged by complete performance or tender of performance, assuming the tendering party possesses the present ability to perform.

2. **Discharge by Condition Subsequent**
The duty may be discharged by occurrence of a condition subsequent.

3. **Discharge by Illegality**
The duty may be discharged by supervening illegality of the subject matter.

4. **Discharge by Impossibility, Impracticability, or Frustration**

a. **Discharge by Impossibility**
The duty may be discharged by impossibility (measured by an ***objective standard***—

nobody could perform according to the terms of the contract). This impossibility must arise after the contract was entered into. A party who has rendered part performance prior to the impossibility may recover in quasi-contract. Impossibility examples include: (i) ***death or physical incapacity*** of a person necessary to effectuate the contract, (ii) a subsequently enacted law rendering the contract subject matter ***illegal***, and (iii) ***subsequent destruction of the contract's subject matter*** or means of performance, as long as the promisor was not at fault and it is truly impossible to fulfill the terms of the contract at any price.

CMR **Exam Tip** A contract is ***not*** discharged by the death or incapacity of the person who was to perform the services if the services are of a kind that can be delegated. Thus, if the contract was for personal services of a ***unique*** kind (*e.g.,* the painting of a portrait by a famous artist), the death or incapacity of that person could make performance impossible, but if the services are not unique (*e.g.,* the painting of a farmer's barn), the death or incapacity of that person would ***not*** make performance impossible.

CMR **Exam Tip** Be sure to distinguish destruction of the subject matter of a contract to build from destruction of the subject matter of a contract to repair. When a ***contract to build's*** subject matter is accidentally destroyed (*e.g.,* a house that is almost finished being built is destroyed by accidental fire), the builder's performance is ***not*** discharged by impossibility because the builder is still capable of starting over and rebuilding. However, when a ***contract to repair's*** subject matter is accidentally destroyed (*e.g.,* a house getting a new roof is destroyed by accidental fire), the repairer's performance is discharged by impossibility because there is nothing left to repair.

b. Discharge by Impracticability

Modern courts will also discharge a duty because of impracticability (subjective test). Impracticability requires that a party encounter ***extreme and unreasonable*** difficulty or expense that was ***not anticipated***. A mere change in the difficulty or expense due to normal risks that could have been anticipated (*e.g.*, increase in price of raw materials) will ***not*** warrant discharge by impracticability.

c. Discharge by Frustration of Purpose

A duty may also be discharged by frustration of purpose. This requires (i) a ***supervening event***; (ii) that was ***not reasonably foreseeable*** at the time of entering into the contract; (iii) which completely or almost completely ***destroys the purpose*** of the contract; and (iv) the purpose was understood ***by both parties***.

5. Discharge by Rescission

a. Mutual Rescission

Duties may be discharged by mutual rescission, *i.e.,* where both parties expressly agree to it. The contract to be rescinded must be ***executory on both sides***. A mutual agreement to rescind will usually be enforced where a bilateral contract has been partially performed. Where the contract is unilateral, a contract to mutually rescind where only one party still has a duty to perform will be ineffective (unless there is an offer of new consideration by the nonperforming party, there are elements of promissory estoppel, or the original offeree manifests an intent to make a gift of the obligation owed her).

Mutual rescission may be made ***orally*** unless the subject matter is within the Statute of Frauds or it involves a contract for the sale of goods requiring a rescission to be in writing.

CMR **Exam Tip** Although mutual rescission generally discharges the parties to a contract, watch out for a third-party beneficiary case. Where the rights of a third-party beneficiary have ***already vested***, a contract will ***not*** be discharged by mutual rescission by the promisor and promisee.

b. **Unilateral Rescission**
Rescission may be unilateral where only one of the parties to the contract desires to rescind it. In this case, that party must have adequate legal grounds (*e.g.*, mistake, misrepresentation, or duress).

6. **Partial Discharge by Modification of Contract**
A duty may be discharged partially by modification of the contract. There must be mutual assent to the modifying agreement. Generally, consideration is necessary, although courts will usually find it where ***each party*** has limited his right to enforce the original contract. Consideration is not necessary where the modification is only a correction, or for a modification of a contract for the sale of goods.

CMR **Exam Tip** Remember this important difference between the common law and the U.C.C.—under the U.C.C. a contract modification is enforceable if made in good faith, ***even without consideration***. Of course, keep in mind that the U.C.C. applies only to contracts for the sale of goods. Modification of other contracts must be supported by consideration.

7. **Discharge by Novation**
A duty may be discharged by a novation, *i.e.*, a new contract substituting a new party for one of the parties to the original contract. Necessary elements are: (i) a previous valid contract; (ii) an agreement among all parties, including the new party; (iii) immediate extinguishment of contractual duties as between the original contracting parties; and (iv) a valid new contract.

8. **Discharge by Cancellation**
Duties may be discharged by cancellation of the original agreement.

9. **Discharge by Release**
Duties may be discharged by a release and/or covenant not to sue. The release must be in ***writing*** and supported by ***new consideration*** or ***promissory estoppel*** elements.

10. **Discharge by Substituted Contract**
There is a discharge by substituted contract where the parties to a contract enter into a second contract that expressly or impliedly ***immediately*** revokes the first contract.

11. **Discharge by Accord and Satisfaction**

a. **Accord**
An accord is an agreement in which one party to a contract agrees to accept performance different from that originally promised. Generally, an accord requires consideration. Consideration less than that of the original contract will be sufficient if it is of a

different type or is to be paid to a third party (*e.g.*, an accord agreement to exchange a $500 TV set for a $700 cash debt is valid).

1) **Effect**
An accord does not discharge a contractual duty. It merely suspends the other party's right to enforce it.

2) **Partial Payment of Original Debt**
Payment of a smaller amount than is due on a claim is valid consideration if it is made in good faith and there is a ***bona fide dispute*** as to the claim. This is often accomplished by tendering a check conspicuously marked "payment in full."

b. **Satisfaction**
Satisfaction is the performance of the accord. It discharges both the accord and the original debt.

12. **Discharge by Account Stated**
Duties may be discharged by an account stated; *i.e.*, parties agree to an amount as a final balance due from one to the other as settlement of all previous transactions between them. It is necessary that there have been ***more than one prior transaction***. A writing is required only if one or more of the original transactions was subject to the Statute of Frauds.

13. **Discharge by Lapse**
Duties may be discharged by the lapse of time if each party's duty is a condition to the other's duty and neither party performs her duty.

14. **Discharge by Operation of Law**
Duties may be discharged by operation of law (*e.g.*, the contractual duty of performance is merged in a court judgment for breach of the duty; discharge in bankruptcy bars any right of action on the contract).

15. **Effect of Running of Statute of Limitations**
Where the statute of limitations on an action has run, it is generally held that an action for breach of contract may be barred.

CMR **Exam Tip** Note the difference between a discharge by lapse and the effect of a statute of limitations. Although both have to do with time and the end result may be similar, technically, lapse ***discharges*** a contract while the statute of limitations merely ***makes it unenforceable*** in court.

VIII. BREACH OF CONTRACT AND AVAILABLE REMEDIES

A. WHEN DOES BREACH OCCUR?

If (i) the promisor is under an absolute duty of performance and (ii) this duty has not been discharged, then this failure to perform in accordance with the contractual terms may be held to be a breach of contract.

B. MATERIAL OR MINOR BREACH?

A breach is material if, as a result of the breach, the nonbreaching party does not receive the substantial benefit of her bargain. If the breach is material, the nonbreaching party (i) may treat the contract as at an end (any duty of counterperformance is discharged), and (ii) has an ***immediate right*** to all remedies for breach of the entire contract, including total damages. (Note that a minor breach, if coupled with anticipatory repudiation, is treated as a material breach.)

CMR **Exam Tip** The distinction between a material and a minor breach is important. A minor breach may allow the aggrieved party to recover damages, ***but*** she still must perform under the contract. If the breach is a material one, the aggrieved party need not perform.

1. Tests for Materiality

In determining whether a breach is material or minor, courts look at:

(i) ***The amount of benefit received*** by the nonbreaching party;

(ii) ***The adequacy of compensation*** for damages to the injured party;

(iii) ***The extent of part performance*** by the breaching party;

(iv) ***Hardship*** to the breaching party;

(v) ***Negligent or willful behavior*** of the breaching party; and

(vi) ***The likelihood that the breaching party will perform*** the remainder of the contract.

The nonbreaching party must show that he was both willing and able to perform.

2. Timeliness of Performance

Failure to perform by the time stated in the contract is generally not a material breach if performance is rendered within a reasonable time. However, if the nature of the contract makes timely performance essential, or if the contract expressly provides that time is of the essence, then failure to perform on time is a material breach.

C. REMEDIES FOR BREACH

There are several remedies for breach of contract, *e.g.,* damages, specific performance, and rescission and restitution.

1. Damages

There are three kinds of damages: compensatory, nominal, and punitive. Most important for bar examination purposes are compensatory damages. The goal of compensatory damages is to put the nonbreaching party into ***as good a position*** as the party would have been in had the other party fully performed. There are two kinds of compensatory damages and the nonbreaching party may recover both: the "standard measure" (cost of a substitute) and consequential damages.

a. Standard Measure of Damages

In most cases, the standard measure of damages will be expectation damages that would permit the plaintiff to buy a substitute. In cases where expectation damages are speculative, the plaintiff may recover reliance damages (*i.e.,* the cost she has incurred by performing).

CMR **Exam Tip** Note that damages must be reasonably certain; a court will not award damages that are speculative in nature. A typical example concerns a new business that fails to open on time due to the defendant's breach. Lost profits of such businesses generally are too speculative to recover, although modern courts may allow recovery if the plaintiff can present evidence of comparable business profits.

1) Contracts for Sale of Goods

Damages are measured by the difference between the contract price and the market price when the seller tenders the goods or when the buyer learns of the breach. If the ***buyer breaches***, under the U.C.C. the seller may withhold delivery or stop delivery by the carrier, resell the goods and recover the difference, or recover ordinary contract damages for nonacceptance. If the buyer has already accepted the goods, or if the seller is unable to resell identified goods, the seller may recover the contract price. If the ***seller breaches***, under the U.C.C. the buyer may reject nonconforming goods, cancel, cover, recover goods identified to the contract, obtain specific performance (in some cases), or recover damages for nondelivery. If the buyer accepts the nonconforming goods, the buyer may recover the difference between the value that the goods would have had if they had been as warranted and the actual value of the goods.

2) Contracts for Sale of Land

Damages are measured by the difference between the contract price and fair market value.

3) Employment Contracts

If an employment contract is breached by the ***employer***, the measure of damages is the full contract price (less wages actually earned elsewhere after the breach); if breached by the ***employee***, the measure is whatever it costs to replace the employee. The modern view allows the employee to offset any monies due from work done to date.

4) Construction Contracts

If a construction contract is breached by the ***owner***, the builder will be entitled to profits that would have resulted from the contract plus any costs expended. (If the contract is breached after construction is completed, the measure is the full contract price plus interest.) If the contract is breached by the ***builder***, the owner is entitled to the cost of completion plus reasonable compensation for the delay. Most courts allow the builder to offset or recover for work performed to date to avoid unjust enrichment of the owner. (If the breach is only late performance, the owner is entitled to damages incurred because of late performance.)

5) Contracts Calling for Installment Payments

If a contract calls for payments in installments and a payment is not made, there is only a partial breach. The aggrieved party is limited to recovering only the missed payment, not the entire contract price. However, the contract may include an acceleration clause making the entire amount due on any late payment, in which case the aggrieved party may recover the entire amount.

b. Consequential Damages

Consequential damages are awarded in addition to the standard measure and will be given if a ***reasonable person*** would have foreseen at the time of entering the contract that such damages would result from the breach. Note that the plaintiff bears the burden of proving the foreseeability of damages where "special circumstances" are involved (*i.e.,* whether those special circumstances were made clear to the other party at the time of contract formation).

c. Punitive and Nominal Damages

Punitive damages are generally ***not*** awarded in commercial contract cases. Nominal damages (*e.g.,* $1) may be awarded where a breach is shown but ***no actual loss*** is proven.

d. Liquidated Damages

A liquidated damages provision will be valid if (i) damages were ***difficult to ascertain at the time the contract was formed***, and (ii) the amount agreed upon was a ***reasonable forecast*** of compensatory damages. If these requirements are met, the plaintiff will receive the liquidated damages amount even though no actual money damages have been suffered. If the liquidated damages amount is unreasonable, the courts will construe this as a penalty and will not enforce the provision.

1) U.C.C. Rule

Under the U.C.C., a court can consider the ***actual damages*** incurred in determining whether a liquidated damages clause is valid.

e. Duty to Mitigate Damages

The nonbreaching party has a duty to mitigate damages. If she does not do so, her damages will be reduced by the amount that might have been avoided by mitigation. In employment contracts, the employee is under a duty to use reasonable diligence to find a like position. In sale of goods contracts, cover must be reasonable, in good faith, and without unreasonable delay. In construction and manufacturing contracts, mitigation requires the builder or manufacturer to cease work unless completion would decrease damages, *e.g.,* finishing partly manufactured goods.

CMR **Exam Tip** Keep in mind that the duty to mitigate only reduces a recovery; it does not prohibit recovery. Thus, if a fact pattern shows a clear breach and the plaintiff does not attempt to mitigate damages, she can recover for the breach, but the recovery will be reduced by the damages that would have been avoided by mitigation.

2. Suit in Equity for Specific Performance

Where the legal remedy (*i.e.,* damages) is inadequate, the nonbreaching party can seek specific performance—essentially an order from the court to perform or face contempt of court charges. The legal remedy is considered inadequate when the subject matter of the contract is rare or unique.

a. Available for Land and Unique Goods but Not for Services

Specific performance is always available for contracts involving the sale of land (because all land is considered unique) and for contracts for the sale of unique or rare goods (*e.g.,* a unique painting or gasoline in short supply because of an embargo).

However, even where services are unique, specific performance will not be granted in a service contract because of difficulty in supervision and because the courts feel it is tantamount to involuntary servitude. *Note:* Even though a court may not be able to grant specific performance of a service contract, it may ***enjoin*** a breaching employee from working for a competitor throughout the duration of the employment contract if the services contracted for are rare or unique.

b. Equitable Defenses Available

In addition to standard contract defenses, an action for specific performance is subject to the equitable defenses of:

1) ***Laches***—a claim that the plaintiff has delayed bringing the action and that ***the delay has prejudiced the defendant***;

2) ***Unclean hands***—a claim that the party seeking specific performance is guilty of ***wrongdoing in the transaction being sued upon***; and

3) ***Sale to a bona fide purchaser***—a claim that the subject matter has been ***sold to a person who purchased for value and in good faith***.

3. Rescission and Restitution

The nonbreacher may rescind (*i.e.,* cancel) and sue for damages at law or in equity. If the nonbreacher transferred a benefit to the breacher while attempting to perform, the non-breacher is entitled to restitution for the benefit transferred.

4. Quasi-Contractual Relief

If there is no contractual relief available under the rules discussed in this outline, quasi-contractual relief might be proper.

a. Unenforceable Contract

Where quasi-contractual relief is used to remedy a failed contract, all that is necessary is that the failed contract ***results in unjust enrichment of one of the parties***. Even the breaching party may be able to recover in quasi-contract, as long as the breach did not involve seriously wrongful or unconscionable conduct.

b. Material Breach of Contract

Where there is an enforceable contract that is materially breached, restitutionary damages may be awarded in lieu of expectation damages.

c. No Contract Involved

Where there is no contractual relationship between the parties, quasi-contractual relief requires that:

(i) The plaintiff has ***conferred a benefit*** on the defendant by rendering services or expending properties;

(ii) The plaintiff conferred the benefit with the ***reasonable expectation of being compensated*** for its value;

(iii) The ***defendant knew or had reason to know*** of the plaintiff's expectation; and

(iv) The defendant would be ***unjustly enriched*** if he were allowed to retain the benefits without compensating the plaintiff.

d. Measure of Quasi-Contractual Recovery

The measure of damages in quasi-contract where there has been an unenforceable contract or where no contract is involved is the value of the goods or services provided. The measure of restitutionary damages where there is a material breach of contract is the reasonable value of the benefit conferred on the defendant prior to the breach, normally determined by the market value of the plaintiff's performance rather than by the value of the actual enrichment to the defendant.

CMR **Exam Tip** Always keep the quasi-contract remedy in the back of your mind. Look first for a valid contract allowing the plaintiff relief. But if there is no valid contract, a quasi-contract will provide a remedy if the plaintiff has suffered a loss or rendered services.

SALES

TABLE OF CONTENTS

CRIMINAL LAW

TABLE OF CONTENTS

CRIMINAL LAW

I. JURISDICTION AND GENERAL MATTERS

A. JURISDICTION

Generally, a state has jurisdiction over a crime if: any act constituting an element of the offense was committed in the state, an act outside the state caused a result in the state, the crime involved the neglect of a duty imposed by the law of the state, there was an attempt or conspiracy outside the state plus an act inside the state, or there was an attempt or conspiracy inside the state to commit an offense outside the state.

B. SOURCES OF CRIMINAL LAW

There is no federal common law of crimes; all federal crimes are statutory. A majority of the states retain common law crimes. The modern trend is to abolish common law crimes either expressly by statute or impliedly by the enactment of comprehensive criminal codes.

C. THEORIES OF PUNISHMENT

Theories justifying criminal punishment include incapacitation of the criminal, special deterrence of the criminal, general deterrence of others, retribution, rehabilitation, and education of the public.

D. CLASSIFICATION OF CRIMES

There are two classes of crimes: felonies and misdemeanors. Felonies are generally punishable by ***death or imprisonment for more than one year***; other crimes are misdemeanors.

E. VAGUENESS AND OTHER CONSTITUTIONAL LIMITATIONS

Due process requires that a criminal statute not be vague. There must be (i) ***fair warning*** (*i.e.,* a person of ordinary intelligence must be able to discern what is prohibited), and (ii) ***no arbitrary and discriminatory enforcement***. The Constitution places two substantive limitations on both federal and state legislatures—no ex post facto laws and no bills of attainder.

F. INTERPRETATIONS OF CRIMINAL STATUTES

Criminal statutes are construed strictly in favor of defendants. If two statutes address the same subject matter but dictate different conclusions, the more specific statute will be applied rather than the more general. The more recently enacted statute will control an older statute. Under new comprehensive codes, crimes committed prior to the effective date of the new code are subject to prosecution and punishment under the law as it existed at the time the offense was committed.

G. MERGER

1. Common Law

At common law, if a person engaged in conduct constituting both a felony and a misdemeanor, she could be ***convicted*** only of the felony. The misdemeanor merged into the felony.

2. Modern Law—No Merger

There is no longer any merger ***except*** that one who solicits another to commit a crime may not be convicted of ***both the solicitation and the completed crime*** (if the person solicited does complete it). Similarly, a person who completes a crime after attempting it may not be convicted of ***both the attempt and the completed crime***. Conspiracy, however, does not merge with the completed offense (*e.g.,* one can be convicted of both robbery and conspiracy to commit robbery).

3. **Rules Against Multiple Convictions for Same Transaction**
Double jeopardy prohibits trial or conviction of a person for a lesser included offense if he has been put in jeopardy for the greater offense. However, a court can impose multiple punishments at a single trial where the punishments are for two or more statutorily defined offenses specifically intended by the legislature to carry ***separate punishments***, even though the offenses arise from the same transaction and constitute the same crime.

II. ESSENTIAL ELEMENTS OF A CRIME

A. ELEMENTS OF A CRIME
A crime almost always requires proof of a physical act (actus reus) and a mental state (mens rea), and concurrence of the act and mental state. It may also require proof of a result and causation (*i.e.,* that the act caused the harmful result).

B. PHYSICAL ACT
Defendant must have either performed a ***voluntary*** physical act or failed to act under circumstances imposing a legal duty to act. An act is a ***bodily movement***.

CMR **Exam Tip** Remember that the act must be ***voluntary***. In the past, the bar examiners have set up very unlikely scenarios to test this point—*e.g.,* they have an unconscious person shoot a victim. Don't be fooled by these odd facts; if the facts tell you that the defendant was unconscious, the act was not voluntary, and thus defendant cannot be convicted of a crime based on this act. (The only exception to this rule would be if the defendant knew he was likely to become unconscious and commit the act, but this situation would have to be presented in the facts.)

1. **Omission as an "Act"**
Failure to act gives rise to liability only if:

   (i) There is a ***specific duty to act*** imposed by law;

   (ii) The ***defendant has knowledge*** of the facts giving rise to the duty to act; and

   (iii) It is ***reasonably possible to perform*** the duty.

   A legal duty to act can arise from a statute, contract, relationship between the defendant and the victim (*e.g.,* a parent has a duty to protect child from harm), voluntary assumption of care by the defendant for the victim, or the creation of peril for the victim by the defendant.

Exam Tip For an omission to be a criminal act, there must be a ***duty*** to act. There is no general Good Samaritan law requiring people to help others in trouble. Thus, a defendant is not liable for the failure to help or rescue another person unless he has a duty to do so—no matter how easy it would have been to render help. Your moral outrage is not enough for a criminal conviction.

C. MENTAL STATE

1. Specific Intent

A crime may require not only the doing of an act, but also the doing of it with a specific intent or objective. The existence of a specific intent cannot be inferred from the doing of the act. The major specific intent crimes and the intents they require are as follows:

a. ***Solicitation***: Intent to have the person solicited commit the crime.

b. ***Attempt***: Intent to complete the crime.

c. ***Conspiracy***: Intent to have the crime completed.

d. ***First degree premeditated murder***: Premeditation.

e. ***Assault***: Intent to commit a battery.

f. ***Larceny and robbery***: Intent to permanently deprive the other of his interest in the property taken.

g. ***Burglary***: Intent to commit a felony in the dwelling.

h. ***Forgery***: Intent to defraud.

i. ***False pretenses***: Intent to defraud.

j. ***Embezzlement***: Intent to defraud.

CMR **Exam Tip** Never forget that attempt is a ***specific intent*** crime—even when the crime attempted is not. Thus, although murder does not require a specific intent to kill (*i.e.,* recklessly disregarding a high risk to human life would be enough), attempted murder requires the specific ***intent to kill***. Without that intent, a defendant is not guilty of attempted murder.

Examples: 1) D intends to kill V but only wounds him. D had the requisite specific intent (*i.e.,* the intent to kill) and is guilty of attempted murder.

2) D intends to scare V by shooting V's hat off his head. If D's shot kills V, D is guilty of murder; but if V is merely wounded, D is not guilty of attempted murder. (D may, of course, be guilty of battery.)

2. Malice—Common Law Murder and Arson

The intent necessary for malice crimes (common law murder and arson) sounds like specific intent, but it is not as restrictive; it requires only a reckless disregard of an obvious or high risk that the particular harmful result will occur. Defenses to specific intent crimes (*e.g.,* voluntary intoxication) do not apply to malice crimes.

3. General Intent—Awareness of Factors Constituting Crime

Almost all crimes require at least "general intent," which is an awareness of all factors constituting the crime; *i.e.*, defendant must be aware that she is acting in the proscribed way and that any required attendant circumstances exist. The defendant need not be certain that all the circumstances exist; it is sufficient that she is aware of a high likelihood that they will occur.

a. Inference of Intent from Act

A jury may infer the required general intent merely from the doing of the act.

b. Transferred Intent

The defendant can be liable under the doctrine of transferred intent where she intends the harm that is actually caused, but to a different victim or object. Defenses and mitigating circumstances may also usually be transferred. The doctrine of transferred intent applies to homicide, battery, and arson. It does not apply to attempt.

CMR Exam Tip A person found guilty of a crime on the basis of transferred intent is usually guilty of two crimes: the completed crime against the actual victim and attempt against the intended victim. Thus, if D intends to shoot and kill X, but instead shoots and kills V, D can be guilty of the murder of V (under the transferred intent doctrine) and the attempted murder of X.

c. Motive Distinguished

Motive is the reason or explanation for the crime; it is different from intent to commit the crime. Motive is immaterial to substantive criminal law.

4. Strict Liability Offenses

A strict liability or public welfare offense is one that does not require awareness of all of the factors constituting the crime; *i.e.,* the defendant can be found guilty from the mere fact that she committed the act. Common strict liability offenses are selling liquor to minors and statutory rape. Certain defenses, such as mistake of fact, are not available.

CMR SUMMARY CHART

REQUISITE INTENT FOR MAJOR CRIMES

Specific Intent	General Intent	Malice	Strict Liability
1. Solicitation	1. Battery	1. Common Law Murder	1. Statutory Rape
2. Attempt	2. Rape	2. Arson	2. Selling Liquor to Minors
3. Conspiracy	3. Kidnapping		3. Bigamy (some jurisdictions)
4. First Degree Premeditated Murder	4. False Imprisonment		
5. Assault (Attempted Battery)			
6. Larceny, Robbery			
7. Burglary			
8. Forgery			
9. False Pretenses			
10. Embezzlement			

5. **Model Penal Code Analysis of Fault**
The M.P.C. eliminates the common law distinctions between general and specific intent and adopts the following categories of intent:

a. **Purposely, Knowingly, or Recklessly**
When a statute requires that the defendant act purposely, knowingly, or recklessly, a ***subjective standard*** is used.

1) **Purposely**
A person acts purposely when his ***conscious object*** is to engage in certain conduct or cause a certain result.

2) **Knowingly**
A person acts knowingly when he is ***aware*** that his conduct is of a particular nature or ***knows*** that his conduct will necessarily or very likely cause a particular result. Knowing conduct satisfies a statute requiring willful conduct.

3) **Recklessly**
A person acts recklessly when he ***knows*** of a ***substantial and unjustifiable risk*** and ***consciously disregards*** it. Mere realization of the risk is not enough. Thus, recklessness involves both objective ("unjustifiable risk") and subjective ("awareness") elements. Unless the statute specifies a different degree of fault or is a strict liability offense, the defendant must have acted at least recklessly to be criminally liable.

CMR **Exam Tip** A criminal law question often asks you to interpret a statute. Check the language of the statute carefully for the mental state required for each material element of the crime, because whether a defendant is guilty often turns on that mental state. For example, if the statute requires that a defendant act "knowingly" (such as "knowingly selling guns to a felon"), the defendant will not be guilty if she did not have that knowledge (*e.g.,* did not know the purchaser was a felon). In interpreting a statute, also keep in mind that "willfully" is equivalent to "knowingly."

b. **Negligence**
A person acts negligently when he ***fails to be aware of a substantial and unjustifiable risk***, where such failure is a substantial deviation from the standard of care. To determine whether a person acted negligently, an ***objective standard*** is used. However, it is not just the reasonable person standard that is used in torts. The defendant must have taken a very unreasonable risk.

6. **Vicarious Liability Offenses**
A vicarious liability offense is one in which a person without personal fault may nevertheless be held liable for the criminal conduct of another (usually an employee). The trend is to limit vicarious liability to regulatory crimes and to limit punishment to fines.

7. **Enterprise Liability—Liability of Corporations and Associations**
At common law, a corporation does not have capacity to commit crimes. Under modern statutes, corporations may be held liable for an act performed by: (i) an agent of the corporation acting within the scope of his office or employment; or (ii) a corporate agent high enough in hierarchy to presume his acts reflect corporate policy.

CMR SUMMARY CHART

STATE OF MIND

Mens Rea	State of Mind Required	Objective or Subjective Test?
	Common Law	
Specific Intent	Intent to engage in proscribed conduct	Subjective
General Intent	Awareness of acting in proscribed manner	Subjective
Malice	Reckless disregard of a known risk	Subjective
Strict Liability	Conscious commission of proscribed act	Objective
	M.P.C. Fault Standards	
Purposely	Conscious object to engage in proscribed conduct	Subjective
Knowingly	Awareness that conduct is of a particular nature or will cause a particular result	Subjective
Recklessly	Consciously disregarding a substantial known risk	Subjective
Negligently	Failure to be aware of a substantial risk	Objective

D. CONCURRENCE OF MENTAL FAULT WITH PHYSICAL ACT

The defendant must have had the intent necessary for the crime at the time he committed the act constituting the crime, and the intent must have actuated the act. For example, if D is driving to V's house to kill him, he will lack the necessary concurrence for murder if he ***accidentally*** runs V over before reaching the house.

E. CAUSATION

Some crimes (*e.g.,* homicide) require result and causation (*see* VII.C.4., *infra*).

III. ACCOMPLICE LIABILITY

A. PARTIES TO A CRIME

1. Common Law

At common law, parties to a crime included the ***principal in the first degree*** (person who actually engaged in the act or omission that constitutes the offense), ***principal in the second degree*** (person who aided, commanded, or encouraged the principal and was present at the crime), ***accessory before the fact*** (person who assisted or encouraged but was ***not present***), and ***accessory after the fact*** (person who, with knowledge that the other committed a felony, assisted him to escape arrest or punishment).

At common law, conviction of the principal was required for conviction of an accessory and the charge must have indicated the correct theory of liability (*i.e.,* as principal or accessory).

2. Modern Statutes

Most jurisdictions have abolished the distinctions between principals in the first degree and principals in the second degree or accessories before the fact. All such "parties to the crime" can be found guilty of the principal offense. For convenience, however, think of the one who actually engages in the act or omission as the principal and the other parties as accomplices.

Note: An accessory after the fact (one who assists another knowing that he has committed a felony in order to help him escape) is still treated separately. Punishment for this crime usually bears no relationship to the principal offense.

CMR SUMMARY CHART

MODERN ACCOMPLICE LIABILITY

Defendant	Conduct	Liability
Principal	Person who commits the illegal act	Liable for principal crime
Accomplice (includes common law accessory before the fact)	Person who aids or encourages principal to commit the illegal conduct	Liable for principal crime if accomplice intended to aid or encourage crime
Accessory After the Fact	Person who aids another to escape knowing that he has committed a felony	Liable for separate, less serious crime of being an accessory after the fact

B. MENTAL STATE—INTENT REQUIRED

To be guilty as an accomplice, most jurisdictions require that the person give aid, counsel, or encouragement to the principal with the ***intent*** to encourage the crime. In the absence of a statute, most courts would hold that ***mere knowledge*** that a crime will result is not enough, at least where the aid given is in the form of the sale of ordinary goods at ordinary prices (*e.g.,* a gas station attendant will not be liable for arson for knowingly selling a gallon of gasoline to an arsonist). However, procuring an illegal item or selling at a higher price because of the buyer's purpose (*e.g.,* charging the arsonist $100 for the gallon of gas) may constitute a sufficient "stake in the venture" to constitute intent.

C. SCOPE OF LIABILITY

An accomplice is responsible for the crimes he did or counseled ***and*** for any other crimes committed in the course of committing the crime contemplated to the same extent as the principal, as long as the other crimes were ***probable or foreseeable***.

1. Inability to Be Principal No Bar to Accomplice Liability

One who may not be convicted of being a principal may be convicted of being an accomplice. *Example:* At common law a woman cannot be convicted of being the principal in a rape but can be found guilty as an accomplice if she aids the principal.

2. Exclusions from Liability

a. Members of the Protected Class

Members of the class protected by a statute are excluded from accomplice liability. *Example:* A woman transported across state lines cannot be an accomplice to the crime of transporting women across state lines for immoral purposes, since she is within the class protected.

b. Necessary Parties Not Provided For

A party necessary to the commission of a crime, by statutory definition, who is not provided for in the statute is excluded from accomplice liability. *Example:* If a statute makes the sale of heroin illegal, but does not provide for punishment of the purchaser, he cannot be found guilty under the statute as an accomplice to the seller.

c. Withdrawal

A person who effectively withdraws from a crime before it is committed cannot be held guilty as an accomplice. Withdrawal must occur ***before*** the crime becomes unstoppable.

(i) ***Repudiation*** is sufficient withdrawal for mere encouragement.

(ii) ***Attempt to neutralize*** assistance is required if participation went beyond mere encouragement.

Notifying the police or taking other action to prevent the crime is also sufficient.

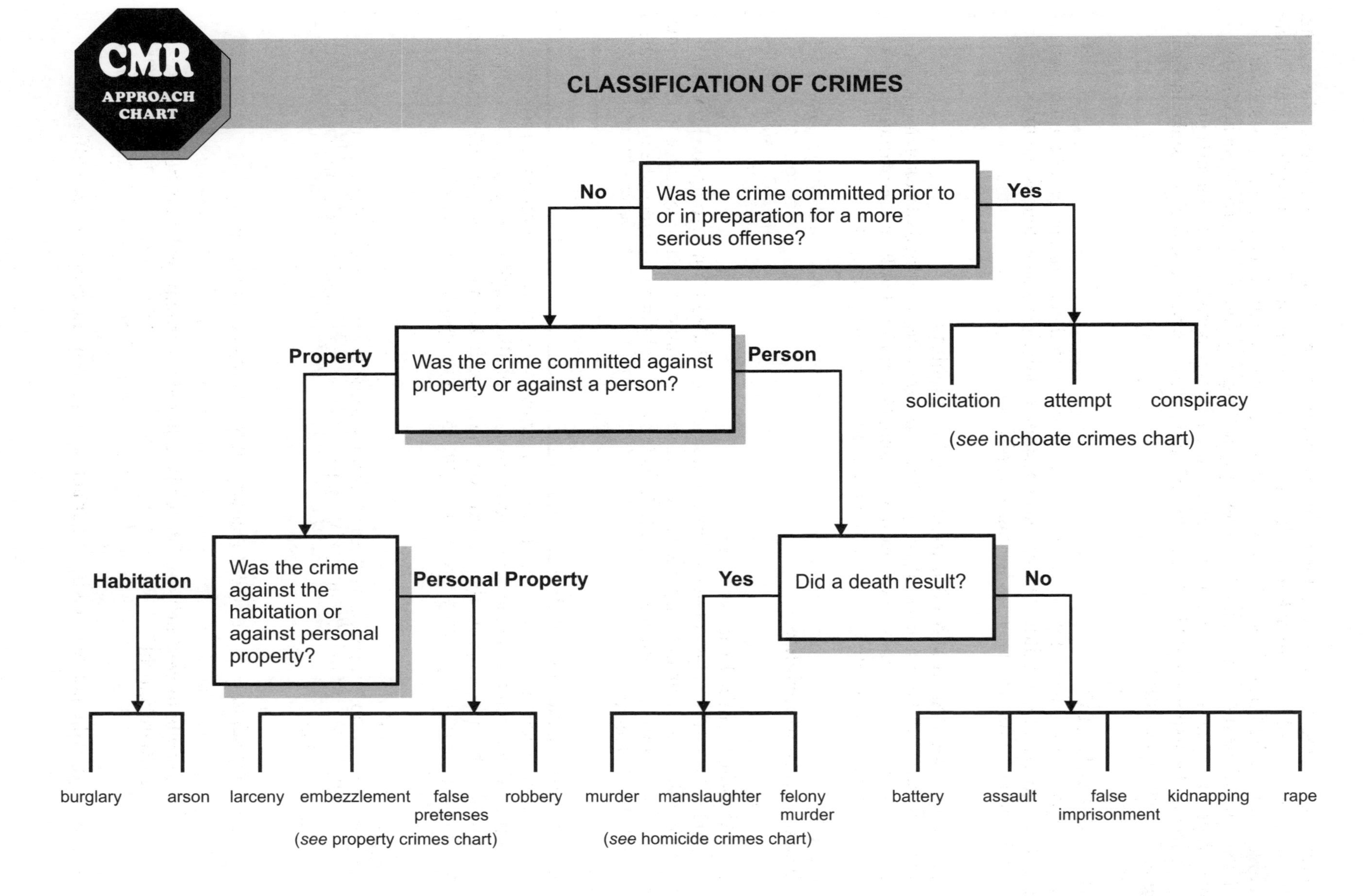
CMR APPROACH CHART
CLASSIFICATION OF CRIMES
Was the crime committed prior to or in preparation for a more serious offense?
No
Yes
solicitation
attempt
conspiracy
(see inchoate crimes chart)
Was the crime committed against property or against a person?
Property
Person
Was the crime against the habitation or against personal property?
Habitation
Personal Property
burglary
arson
larceny
embezzlement
false pretenses
robbery
(see property crimes chart)
Did a death result?
Yes
No
murder
manslaughter
felony murder
(see homicide crimes chart)
battery
assault
false imprisonment
kidnapping
rape

IV. INCHOATE OFFENSES

CMR COMPARISON CHART

INCHOATE CRIMES

	Solicitation	Conspiracy	Attempt
Culpable Conduct	Solicitation of another to commit a felony	Agreement between two or more people to commit a crime	Performance of an act that would be a crime if successful
Mental State	Specific intent that person solicited commit the crime	Specific intent to: (i) enter into agreement; and (ii) achieve objective	Specific intent to commit the particular crime attempted
Overt Act	No act (other than the solicitation)	Act in furtherance of the conspiracy	Act dangerously close to success (M.P.C.—substantial step test)
Merger into Completed Crime?	Yes	No	Yes
Withdrawal a Defense?	Generally no	No, except for further crimes of co-conspirators	Generally no

A. SOLICITATION

1. Elements

Solicitation consists of ***inciting***, ***counseling***, ***advising***, ***urging***, ***or commanding*** another to commit a crime, with the ***intent that the person solicited commit the crime***. It is not necessary that the person solicited respond affirmatively.

2. Defenses

It is not a defense that the person solicited is not convicted, nor that the offense solicited could not in fact have been successful. In most jurisdictions, it is not a defense that the solicitor renounces or withdraws the solicitation. However, it ***is a defense*** that the solicitor could not be found guilty of the completed crime because of a legislative intent to exempt her (*e.g.,* a woman cannot be found guilty of soliciting a man to transport her across state lines for immoral purposes).

3. **Merger**
If the person solicited commits the crime solicited, both that person and the solicitor can be held liable for that crime. If the person solicited commits acts sufficient to be liable for attempt, both parties can be liable for attempt. If the person solicited agrees to commit the crime, but does not even commit acts sufficient for attempt, both parties can be held liable for conspiracy. However, under the doctrine of merger, the solicitor ***cannot be punished for both*** the solicitation and these other offenses.

B. CONSPIRACY

A conspiracy is an agreement between two or more parties to commit a crime.

1. **Elements**
A conspiracy requires (i) an ***agreement*** between two or more persons; (ii) an ***intent to enter into the agreement***; and (iii) an ***intent*** by at least two persons ***to achieve the objective of the agreement***. A majority of states now also require an ***overt act***, but an act of mere preparation will suffice.

CMR **Exam Tip** Conspiracy is probably the most tested inchoate crime. One important thing for you to remember is that it takes two to conspire at common law. Make sure that the facts of a question show at least two "guilty minds"—two people who intend to agree ***and*** intend that the crime be committed. Thus, if the defendant and an undercover police officer "agree" to commit a crime, there is no conspiracy at common law because only the defendant intended that the crime be committed. Similarly, if the defendant and another person "agree" but the facts show that the other person merely pretended to go along and really meant to warn the police, there is no conspiracy.

a. **Agreement Requirement**
The parties must agree to accomplish the same objective by mutual action. However, the agreement need not be express; it may be inferred from joint activity.

1) **Implications of Requirement of Two or More Parties**
A conspiracy at common law must involve a "meeting of minds" between at least two independent persons. This requirement presents the following issues:

a) **Husband and Wife**
At common law, a husband and wife could not conspire together, but this distinction has been abandoned in most states.

b) **Corporation and Agent**
There can be no conspiracy between a corporation and a single agent acting on its behalf. There is a split of authority as to whether the agents of a corporation can be deemed co-conspirators with the corporation.

c) **Wharton Rule**
Under the Wharton Rule, where two or more people are necessary for the commission of the substantive offense (*e.g.*, adultery, dueling), there is no crime of conspiracy unless ***more parties participate*** in the agreement than are necessary for the crime (*e.g.,* because it takes two people to commit adultery, it takes three people to conspire to commit adultery). *Exception:* The Wharton Rule does not apply to agreements with "necessary parties not

provided for" by the substantive offense; both parties may be guilty of conspiracy even though both are necessary for commission of the substantive offense.

d) **Agreement with Person in "Protected Class"**
If members of a conspiracy agree to commit a crime designed to protect persons within a given class, persons within that class cannot be guilty of the crime itself or of conspiracy to commit that crime. Likewise, the nonprotected person cannot be guilty of conspiracy if the agreement was with the protected person only.

e) **Effect of Acquittal of Some Conspirators**
Under the traditional view, the ***acquittal*** of all persons with whom a defendant is alleged to have conspired precludes conviction of the remaining defendant. In some jurisdictions following the traditional view, a conviction for conspiracy against one defendant is allowed to stand when the alleged co-conspirator is acquitted in a ***separate trial***.

CMR Exam Tip Acquittal is the key here. If the defendant and others allegedly conspired and only the defendant is charged and tried (*e.g.,* the other parties are not apprehended or not prosecuted), the defendant can be convicted. But if the defendant is charged and tried and ***all the others have been acquitted***, the defendant cannot be convicted. (The acquittals show that there was no one with whom the defendant could conspire.)

f) **Model Penal Code Unilateral Approach**
Under the M.P.C. "unilateral" approach, the defendant can be convicted of conspiracy regardless of whether the other parties have all been acquitted or were only feigning agreement.

b. **Mental State—Specific Intent**
Conspiracy is a specific intent crime. Parties must have: (i) the intent to ***agree*** and (ii) the intent to ***achieve the objective*** of the conspiracy.

c. **Overt Act**
Most states require that an act in furtherance of the conspiracy be performed. An act of mere preparation is usually sufficient.

2. **Liability for Co-Conspirators' Crimes**
A conspirator may be held liable for crimes committed by other conspirators if the crimes (i) were committed ***in furtherance*** of the objectives of the conspiracy and (ii) were ***foreseeable.***

3. **Termination of Conspiracy**
The point at which a conspiracy terminates is important because acts and statements of co-conspirators are admissible against a conspirator only if they were done or made in furtherance of the conspiracy. A conspiracy usually terminates ***upon completion of the wrongful objective***. Unless agreed to in advance, acts of concealment are ***not*** part of the conspiracy. Note also that the government's defeat of the conspiracy's objective does not automatically terminate the conspiracy.

4. **Defenses**

a. **Impossibility**
Impossibility is ***not*** a defense to conspiracy.

b. **Withdrawal**
Generally, withdrawal from the conspiracy is ***not*** a defense ***to the conspiracy***, because the conspiracy is complete as soon as the agreement is made and an act in furtherance is performed. Withdrawal ***may*** be a defense to ***crimes committed in furtherance*** of the conspiracy, including the substantive target crime of the conspiracy.

1) **When Withdrawal Effective**
To withdraw, a conspirator must perform an affirmative act that notifies all members of the conspiracy of her withdrawal. Notice must be given in time for the members to abandon their plans. If she has also provided assistance as an accomplice, she must try to neutralize the assistance.

CMR **Exam Tip** Withdrawal from a conspiracy is another important test issue. You must be careful here not to let your feelings get in the way of a correct answer. Remember that a conspiracy is complete upon the agreement with the requisite intent and an overt act. Since the overt act can be a preparatory act, the conspiracy is usually complete very soon after the agreement. If the crime is complete, the defendant is ***guilty of conspiracy***—even if the facts show that she had second thoughts, told her co-conspirators that she was backing out, warned the police, hid the weapons, etc. These actions come too late; defendant is guilty of conspiracy. (Such actions may relieve defendant of criminal liability for her co-conspirators' acts after this withdrawal, but they have no effect on the crime of conspiracy.)

5. **Punishment—No Merger**
Conspiracy and the completed crime are distinct offenses; *i.e.*, there is no merger. A defendant may be convicted of and punished for both.

6. **Number of Conspiracies in Multiple Party Situations**
In complex situations, there may be a large conspiracy with a number of subconspiracies. In such situations, it is important to determine whether members of one subconspiracy are liable for the acts of another subconspiracy. The two most common situations are:

a. **Chain Relationship**
A chain relationship is a single, large conspiracy in which all parties to subagreements are interested in the single large scheme. In this case, all members are liable for the acts of the others in furtherance of the conspiracy.

b. **Hub-and-Spoke Relationship**
In a hub-and-spoke relationship a number of independent conspiracies are linked by a common member. Although the common member will be liable for all of the conspiracies, members of the individual conspiracies are not liable for the acts of the other conspirators.

C. ATTEMPT

1. Elements

Attempt is an act, done with ***intent to commit a crime***, that ***falls short of completing*** the crime.

a. Mental State

To be guilty of attempt, the defendant must intend to perform an act and obtain a result that, if achieved, would constitute a crime. Regardless of the intent necessary for the completed offense, an attempt ***always requires a specific intent*** (*i.e.,* the intent to commit the crime). *Example:* To be guilty of attempt to commit murder, defendant must have had the specific ***intent to kill*** another person, even though the mens rea for murder itself does not necessarily require a specific intent to kill.

CMR **Exam Tip** Attempt to commit a crime defined as the negligent production of a result (*e.g.,* negligent homicide) is logically impossible because a person does not intend to be negligent. Thus, there can be no attempted negligent homicide, etc.

b. Overt Act

Defendant must commit an act ***beyond mere preparation*** for the offense. Traditionally, most courts followed the "***proximity***" ***test***, which requires that the act be "dangerously close" to successful completion of the crime (*e.g.,* pointing a loaded gun at an intended victim and pulling the trigger, only to have the gun not fire or the bullet miss its mark is sufficient). However, today most state criminal codes (and the Model Penal Code) require that the act or omission constitute a "***substantial step*** in a course of conduct planned to culminate in the commission of the crime" that strongly corroborates the actor's criminal purpose.

Exam Tip Note that the overt act required for attempt is much more substantial than the overt act required for conspiracy.

2. Defenses

a. Impossibility of Success

1) Factual Impossibility No Defense

Factual impossibility (*i.e.,* that it was factually impossible for defendant to complete the intended crime) is ***not*** a defense to attempt (*e.g.,* it is not a defense to attempted robbery that the intended victim had no money with her). This includes impossibility due to mistake in attendant circumstances (*e.g.,* it is no defense to a charge of ***attempted*** receipt of stolen goods that the goods were no longer stolen because defendant purchased them from an undercover police officer).

2) Legal Impossibility Is a Defense

Legal impossibility (*i.e.,* that it is not a crime to do that which defendant intended to do) is a defense (*e.g.,* defendant going fishing in a lake in which he erroneously believed fishing was prohibited cannot be convicted of attempted violation of the fishing ordinance).

CMR **Exam Tip** On the MBE, when facts give rise to impossibility, it is usually factual impossibility and is no defense to attempt. Thus, if you are unsure how to categorize the impossibility in a particular fact pattern, your best bet is to decide that it is no defense.

b. Abandonment

Abandonment is ***not*** a defense. If defendant had the intent and committed an overt act, she is guilty of attempt despite the fact that she changed only her mind and abandoned the plan before the intended crime was completed.

3. Prosecution for Attempt—Merger

Attempt merges with the completed crime. Thus, a defendant ***cannot be found guilty of both*** attempt and the completed crime. Also, a defendant charged only with a completed crime may be found guilty of attempt, but a defendant charged only with attempt may not be convicted of the completed crime.

V. RESPONSIBILITY AND CRIMINAL CAPACITY

A. INSANITY

There are several formulations of the test to be applied to determine whether, at the time of the crime, the defendant was so mentally ill as to be entitled to acquittal.

1. *M'Naghten* Rule

Under this rule, a defendant is entitled to acquittal only if he had a mental disease or defect that caused him to either: (i) ***not know that his act would be wrong***; or (ii) ***not understand the nature and quality of his actions***. Loss of control because of mental illness is no defense.

2. Irresistible Impulse Test

Under this test, a defendant is entitled to acquittal only if, because of a mental illness, he was ***unable to control his actions or conform his conduct to the law***.

3. *Durham* (or New Hampshire) Test

Under this test, a defendant is entitled to acquittal if the ***crime was the product of his mental illness*** (*i.e.,* crime would not have been committed but for the disease). The *Durham* test is broader than either the *M'Naghten* test or the irresistible impulse test.

4. A.L.I. or Model Penal Code Test

Under the M.P.C. test (which represents the "modern trend"), a defendant is entitled to acquittal if he had a mental disease or defect, and, as a result, he ***lacked the substantial capacity*** to either:

(i) ***Appreciate the criminality*** of his conduct; or

(ii) ***Conform his conduct*** to the requirements of law.

CMR **Exam Tip** It is important to know these separate insanity tests because questions may ask you about a specific test (*e.g.,* "If the jurisdiction has adopted the M.P.C. test for determining insanity, what is defendant's best argument for acquittal on this ground?"). To answer this type of question, you must know the requirements for that particular test. A shorthand way to remember the test is:

M'Naghten—defendant does ***not know right from wrong***;

Irresistible Impulse—(as the name says) an ***impulse*** that defendant ***cannot resist***;

Durham—***but for the mental illness***, defendant would not have done the act;

A.L.I. or M.P.C.—***combination*** of *M'Naghten* and irresistible impulse.

5. Procedural Issues

a. Burdens of Proof

All defendants are presumed sane; the defendant must raise the insanity issue. There is a split among the jurisdictions as to whether the defendant raising the issue bears the burden of proof.

b. When Defense May Be Raised

Although the insanity defense may be raised at the arraignment when the plea is taken, the defendant need not raise it then. A simple "not guilty" at that time does not waive the right to raise the defense at some future time.

c. Pretrial Psychiatric Examination

If the defendant does ***not*** raise the insanity issue, he ***may*** refuse a court-ordered psychiatric examination to determine his competency to stand trial. If the defendant ***raises*** the insanity issue, he may ***not*** refuse to be examined by a psychiatrist appointed to aid the court in the resolution of his insanity plea.

6. Post-Acquittal Commitment to Mental Institution

In most jurisdictions, a defendant acquitted by reason of insanity may be committed to a mental institution until cured. Confinement may exceed the maximum period of incarceration for the offense charged.

7. Mental Condition During Criminal Proceedings

Under the Due Process Clause of the United States Constitution, a defendant may not be tried, convicted, or sentenced if, as a result of a mental disease or defect, he is unable (i) to understand the nature of the proceedings being brought against him; or (ii) to assist his lawyer in the preparation of his defense. A defendant may not be executed if he is incapable of understanding the nature and purpose of the punishment.

8. **Diminished Capacity**
Some states recognize the defense of "diminished capacity" under which defendant may assert that as a result of a mental defect short of insanity, he did not have the mental state required for the crime charged. Most states allowing the diminished capacity defense limit it to specific intent crimes, but a few states allow it for general intent crimes as well.

B. INTOXICATION

Intoxication may be caused by any substance (*e.g.,* drugs, alcohol, medicine). It may be raised whenever intoxication negates one of the elements of the crime. The law usually distinguishes between voluntary and involuntary intoxication.

1. Voluntary Intoxication

Intoxication is voluntary if it is the result of the intentional taking without duress of a substance known to be intoxicating.

a. Defense to Specific Intent Crimes

Evidence of "voluntary" intoxication may be offered by defendant only if the crime requires ***purpose* (*intent*) *or knowledge***, and the intoxication prevented the defendant from formulating the purpose or obtaining the knowledge. Thus, it is often a good defense to ***specific intent*** crimes. The defense is not available if the defendant purposely becomes intoxicated in order to establish the defense.

b. No Defense to Other Crimes

Voluntary intoxication is no defense to crimes involving malice, recklessness, negligence, or strict liability.

2. Involuntary Intoxication

Intoxication is involuntary only if it results from the taking of an intoxicating substance ***without knowledge*** of its nature, ***under direct duress*** imposed by another, or ***pursuant to medical advice*** while unaware of the substance's intoxicating effect. Involuntary intoxication may be treated as a mental illness, and the defendant is entitled to acquittal if she meets the jurisdiction's insanity test.

3. Relationship to Insanity

Continuous, excessive drinking or drug use may bring on actual insanity and thus a defendant may be able to claim both an intoxication defense and an insanity defense.

C. INFANCY

At common law, there could be no liability for an act committed by a child under age seven. For acts committed by a child between ages seven and 14, there was a rebuttable presumption that the child was unable to understand the wrongfulness of his acts. Children age 14 or older were treated as adults. Modern statutes often modify this and provide that no child can be convicted of a crime until a stated age is reached, usually 13 or 14. However, children can be found to be delinquent in special juvenile or family courts.

CMR SUMMARY CHART

DEFENSES NEGATING CRIMINAL CAPACITY

Defense	Elements	Applicable Crimes
Insanity	Meet applicable ***insanity test*** (*M'Naghten*, irresistible impulse, *Durham*, or M.P.C.)	Defense to ***all*** crimes
Intoxication -voluntary	***Voluntary, intentional taking*** of a substance ***known to be*** intoxicating	Defense to ***specific intent*** crime if intoxication prevents formation of required intent
-involuntary	Taking intoxicating substance ***without knowledge*** of its nature, ***under duress***, or pursuant to ***medical advice***	Treated as mental illness (*i.e.,* apply appropriate insanity test); may be a defense to ***all*** crimes
Infancy	Defendant under age 14 ***at common law***; under ***modern statutes***, defendant under age 13 or 14	*Common law:* Under age seven, absolute defense to ***all*** crimes; under 14, rebuttable presumption of defense. *Modern statutes:* Defense to adult crimes but may still be delinquent
Diminished Capacity (some states)	As a result of mental defect ***short of insanity***, defendant did not have the required mental state to commit the crime	Most states with this defense limit it to ***specific intent*** crimes

VI. PRINCIPLES OF EXCULPATION

A. JUSTIFICATION

The justification defenses arise when society has deemed that although the defendant committed a proscribed act, she should not be punished because the circumstances justify the action.

CMR Exam Tip The right to self-defense or other justification defenses depends on the immediacy of the threat; a threat of future harm is not sufficient. Thus, if someone threatens the defendant by saying, "Tomorrow I'm going to kill you," the defendant is ***not justified*** in killing the person to "protect" himself.

CMR Exam Tip It is crucial to determine the level of force that the defendant used in committing the proscribed act. As a rule of thumb, ***nondeadly force*** is justified where it appears necessary to avoid imminent injury or to retain property; ***deadly force*** is justified only to prevent death or serious bodily injury.

1. **Self-Defense**

   a. **Nondeadly Force**
   A person without fault may use such force as ***reasonably appears necessary*** to protect herself from the imminent use of unlawful force upon herself. There is no duty to retreat.

   b. **Deadly Force**
   A person may use deadly force in self-defense if (i) she is without fault; (ii) she is confronted with "unlawful force"; and (iii) she is threatened with imminent death or great bodily harm.

CMR **Exam Tip** If the defendant kills in self-defense but not all three of the requirements for the use of deadly force are met, some states would find the defendant guilty of manslaughter rather than murder under the "imperfect self-defense" doctrine.

   1) **Retreat**
   Generally there is no duty to retreat before using deadly force. The minority view requires retreat before using deadly force if the victim can safely do so, ***unless***: (i) the attack occurs in the victim's home, (ii) the attack occurs while the victim is making a lawful arrest, or (iii) the assailant is in the process of robbing the victim.

   c. **Right of Aggressor to Use Self-Defense**
   If one is the aggressor in the altercation, she may use force in defense of herself only if (i) she ***effectively withdraws*** from the altercation and ***communicates*** to the other her desire to do so, ***or*** (ii) the victim of the initial aggression ***suddenly escalates*** the minor fight into a deadly altercation and the initial aggressor has no chance to withdraw.

2. **Defense of Others**
A defendant has the right to defend others if she reasonably believes that the person assisted has the legal right to use force in his own defense. All that is necessary is the ***reasonable appearance*** of the right to use force. Generally, there need be no special relationship between the defendant and the person in whose defense she acted.

3. **Defense of a Dwelling**
Nondeadly force may be used to prevent or terminate what is reasonably regarded as an unlawful entry into or attack on the defender's dwelling. ***Deadly force*** may be used only to prevent a violent entry made with the intent to commit a personal attack on an inhabitant, or to prevent an entry to commit a felony in the dwelling.

CMR **Exam Tip** As a practical matter, deadly force usually is justified in repelling a home invader but the basis for the right to use such force is ***not*** to protect the dwelling, but to protect the safety of the inhabitants of the dwelling.

4. **Defense of Other Property**

a. **Defending Possession**
Deadly force may never be used in defense of property. ***Nondeadly force*** may be used to defend property in one's possession from unlawful interference, but may not be used if a request to desist or refrain from the activity would suffice.

b. **Regaining Possession**
Force ***cannot*** be used to regain possession of property wrongfully taken unless the person using force is in immediate pursuit of the taker.

5. **Crime Prevention**
Nondeadly force may be used to the extent that it reasonably appears necessary to prevent a felony or serious breach of the peace. ***Deadly force*** may be used only to terminate or prevent a dangerous felony involving risk to human life.

6. **Use of Force to Effectuate Arrest**
Nondeadly force may be used by police officers if it reasonably appears necessary to effectuate an arrest. ***Deadly force*** is reasonable only if it is necessary to prevent a felon's escape ***and*** the felon threatens death or serious bodily harm.

a. **Private Persons**
A private person has a privilege to use ***nondeadly force*** to make an arrest if a ***crime was in fact committed*** and the private person has ***reasonable grounds to believe*** the person arrested has in fact committed the crime. A private person may use ***deadly force only if*** the person harmed was ***actually guilty*** of the offense for which the arrest was made.

7. **Resisting Arrest**
Nondeadly force may be used to resist an improper arrest even if a known officer is making that arrest. ***Deadly force*** may be used, however, only if the person does not know that the person arresting him is a police officer.

8. **Necessity**
It is a defense to a crime that the person ***reasonably believed*** that commission of the crime was necessary to avoid an imminent and greater injury to society than that involved in the crime. The test is objective; a good faith belief is not sufficient.

a. **Limitation—Death**
Causing the death of another person to protect property is ***never justified***.

b. **Limitation—Fault**
The defense of necessity is not available if the defendant is at fault in creating the situation requiring that he choose between two evils.

c. **Duress Distinguished**
Necessity involves pressure from natural or physical forces; duress involves a human threat (*see* B., *infra*).

9. **Public Policy**
A police officer (or one assisting him) is justified in using reasonable force against another, or in taking property, provided the officer acts pursuant to a law, court order, or process requiring or authorizing him to so act.

10. Domestic Authority

The parents of a minor child, or any person "in loco parentis" with respect to that child, may lawfully use reasonable force upon the child for the purpose of promoting the child's welfare.

CMR SUMMARY CHART

JUSTIFICATION DEFENSES

Defense	Amount of Force Allowed: Nondeadly Force	Amount of Force Allowed: Deadly Force
Self-Defense	If reasonably necessary to protect self	Only if threatened with death or great bodily harm
Defense of Others	If reasonably necessary to protect person	Only if threatened with death or great bodily harm
Defense of Dwelling	If reasonably necessary to prevent or end unlawful entry	Only if person inside is threatened or to prevent felony inside
Defense of Other Property	If reasonably necessary to defend property in one's possession (but if request to desist would suffice, force ***not*** allowed)	Never
Crime Prevention	If reasonably necessary to prevent felony or serious breach of peace	Only to prevent or end felony risking human life
Effectuate Arrest		
– Police	If reasonably necessary to arrest	Only to prevent escape of felon who threatens human life
– Private Person	If crime in fact committed and reasonable belief that this person committed it	Only to prevent escape of person who actually committed felony and who threatens human life
Resisting Arrest	If improper arrest	Only if improper arrest and defendant does not know arrester is a police officer
Necessity	If reasonably necessary to avoid greater harm	Never

B. EXCUSE OF DURESS

It is a defense to a crime ***other than a homicide*** that the defendant reasonably believed that another person would imminently inflict death or great bodily harm upon him or a member of his family if he did not commit the crime.

C. OTHER DEFENSES

1. Mistake or Ignorance of Fact

Mistake or ignorance of fact is relevant to criminal liability only if it shows that the defendant ***lacked the state of mind required*** for the crime; thus, it is irrelevant if the crime imposes "strict" liability.

a. Reasonableness

If mistake is offered to "disprove" a ***specific intent***, the mistake ***need not be reasonable***; however, if it is offered to disprove any other state of mind, it ***must have been reasonable*** mistake or ignorance.

CMR **Exam Tip** Don't confuse the defense of mistake of fact with the issue of factual impossibility, discussed earlier. Even though in both situations defendant is mistaken about certain facts, the results are different. ***Mistake*** is usually raised as a defense to a crime that has been completed; mistake of fact may negate the intent required for the crime. ***Impossibility*** arises only when defendant has ***failed*** to complete the crime because of his mistaken belief about the facts, and is being charged with an ***attempt*** to commit the crime; factual impossibility is ***not*** a defense to attempt.

2. Mistake or Ignorance of Law—No Defense

Generally, it is not a defense that the defendant believed that her activity would not be a crime, even if that belief was reasonable and based on the advice of an attorney. However, if the reliance on the attorney negates a necessary mental state element, such reliance can demonstrate that the government has not proved its case beyond a reasonable doubt.

a. Exceptions

The defendant has a defense if: (i) the statute proscribing her conduct was not published or made reasonably available prior to the conduct; (ii) there was reasonable reliance on a statute or judicial decision; or (iii) in some jurisdictions, there was reasonable reliance on official interpretation or advice.

b. Ignorance of Law May Negate Intent

If the defendant's mistake or ignorance as to a collateral legal matter proves that she lacked the state of mind required for the crime, she is entitled to acquittal. This rule applies only to those crimes in which the state of mind required involves some knowledge of the law.
Example: A defendant cannot be found guilty of selling a gun to a known felon if she thought that the crime the buyer had been found guilty of was only a misdemeanor.

3. Consent

Unless the crime requires the lack of consent of the victim (*e.g.,* rape), consent is usually ***not*** a defense. Consent is a defense to minor assaults or batteries if there is no danger of serious bodily injury. Whenever consent may be a defense, it must be established that: (i) the consent was ***voluntarily and freely given***; (ii) the party was ***legally capable*** of consenting; and (iii) ***no fraud*** was involved in obtaining the consent.

EXCULPATORY DEFENSES

Defense	Applicable To	When Available
Justification (self-defense, defense of others, defense of property, necessity, etc.)	Usually crimes of force (*e.g.,* battery, homicide)	***Nondeadly force*** may usually be used if reasonably necessary to avoid imminent injury or to retain property; ***deadly force*** may be used only to prevent serious bodily harm
Duress	All crimes ***except*** homicide	Defendant reasonably believed that another would ***imminently*** harm him or a family member if he did not commit the crime
Mistake of Fact	Crimes with a mental state element (*i.e.,* all crimes ***except*** strict liability)	For ***specific intent*** crimes, any mistake that negates intent; for other crimes, ***only reasonable mistakes***
Mistake of Law	Crimes with a mental state element and statutory crimes	Mistake must ***negate awareness of some aspect of law that the crime requires or must be due to***: statute not being reasonably available, reasonable reliance on statute or judicial interpretation, or (in some states) reasonable reliance on official advice; reliance on advice of counsel may negate mental state element
Consent	Crimes requiring lack of consent (*e.g.,* rape) and minor assaults and batteries	Applicable ***only*** if: consent is freely given, the party is capable of consenting, and no fraud was used to obtain consent
Entrapment	Most crimes, but ***not*** available if the police merely provide the opportunity to commit the crime	Criminal design ***originated with the police*** and the defendant was ***not predisposed*** to commit the crime before contact with police

4. **Condonation or Criminality of Victim—No Defense**
Forgiveness by the victim is no defense. Likewise, the nearly universal rule is that illegal conduct by the victim of a crime is no defense.

5. **Entrapment**
Entrapment exists only if (i) the ***criminal design originated with law enforcement officers*** and (ii) the defendant was ***not predisposed*** to commit the crime prior to contact by the government. Merely providing the opportunity for a predisposed person to commit a crime is not entrapment.

a. **Unavailable—If Private Inducement or If Material for Crime Provided by Government Agent**
A person cannot be entrapped by a private citizen. Under federal law, an entrapment defense cannot be based on the fact that a government agent provided an ingredient for commission of the crime (*e.g.*, ingredients for drugs), even if the material provided was contraband.

CMR **Exam Tip** Entrapment is a difficult defense to establish in court and so too on the MBE. In fact, on the exam, the defendant is usually predisposed to commit the crime and thus entrapment usually is a wrong choice.

VII. OFFENSES AGAINST THE PERSON

A. ASSAULT AND BATTERY

1. **Battery**
Battery is an ***unlawful application of force*** to the person of another resulting in either ***bodily injury or an offensive touching***. Simple battery is a misdemeanor. A battery need not be intentional, and the force need not be applied directly (*e.g.*, causing a dog to attack the victim is a battery). Some jurisdictions recognize consent as a defense to simple battery and/or certain specified batteries.

a. **Aggravated Battery**
Most jurisdictions treat the following as aggravated batteries and punish them as felonies: (i) battery with a deadly weapon; (ii) battery resulting in serious bodily harm; and (iii) battery of a child, woman, or police officer.

2. **Assault**
Assault is ***either*** (i) an ***attempt to commit a battery*** or (ii) the ***intentional creation***—other than by mere words—***of a reasonable apprehension*** in the mind of the victim of ***imminent bodily harm***. If there has been an actual touching of the victim, the crime can only be battery, not assault.

a. **Aggravated Assault**
Aggravated assault (*e.g.*, with a deadly weapon or with intent to rape or maim) is treated more severely than simple assault.

CMR **Exam Tip** Think of assault as two separate crimes: (i) attempted battery assault—a ***specific intent*** crime (*i.e.,* defendant must intend to commit a battery), and (ii) creation of reasonable apprehension assault. Be sure to consider both types of assault in answering a question, because one may apply even though the other does not. For example, if D stops V at knifepoint and demands V's money, but was merely trying to scare V by posing as a robber and feigning a holdup (*e.g.,* as a practical joke), D has committed creation of reasonable apprehension assault but ***not*** attempted battery assault. You would not want to decide that D is not guilty of assault because you thought only about attempted battery assault.

B. MAYHEM

At common law, the felony of mayhem required either dismemberment or disablement of a bodily part. The recent trend is to abolish mayhem as a separate offense and to treat it instead as a form of aggravated battery.

C. HOMICIDE

1. Common Law Criminal Homicides

At common law, criminal homicide is divided into three categories:

a. Murder

Murder is the unlawful killing of a human being with ***malice aforethought***. Malice aforethought exists if there are no facts reducing the killing to voluntary manslaughter or excusing it (*i.e.,* giving rise to a defense) and it was committed with one of the following states of mind:

(i) Intent ***to kill***;

(ii) Intent ***to inflict great bodily injury***;

(iii) ***Reckless indifference to an unjustifiably high risk to human life*** ("abandoned and malignant heart"); or

(iv) Intent ***to commit a felony*** (felony murder).

Intentional use of a deadly weapon authorizes a permissive inference of intent to kill.

CMR **Exam Tip** Homicides are emotionally charged crimes, so you must be careful not to let your emotions lead you to an incorrect answer. If a defendant killed with one of the states of mind above, he is guilty of murder; if he did not, he is not guilty of murder (although he could be guilty of other crimes). Thus, even where the facts go out of their way to paint the defendant as a completely despicable human being (*e.g.,* a mass murderer), you cannot convict him of murder when he drives into a schoolyard, killing three children, if the incident was due to defendant's fiddling with a cigarette lighter. More troublesome is the mercy killing case. If defendant intends to kill, even as an act of love, he ***is*** guilty of murder. Society does not accept compassion as a sufficient justification for the killing of a human being.

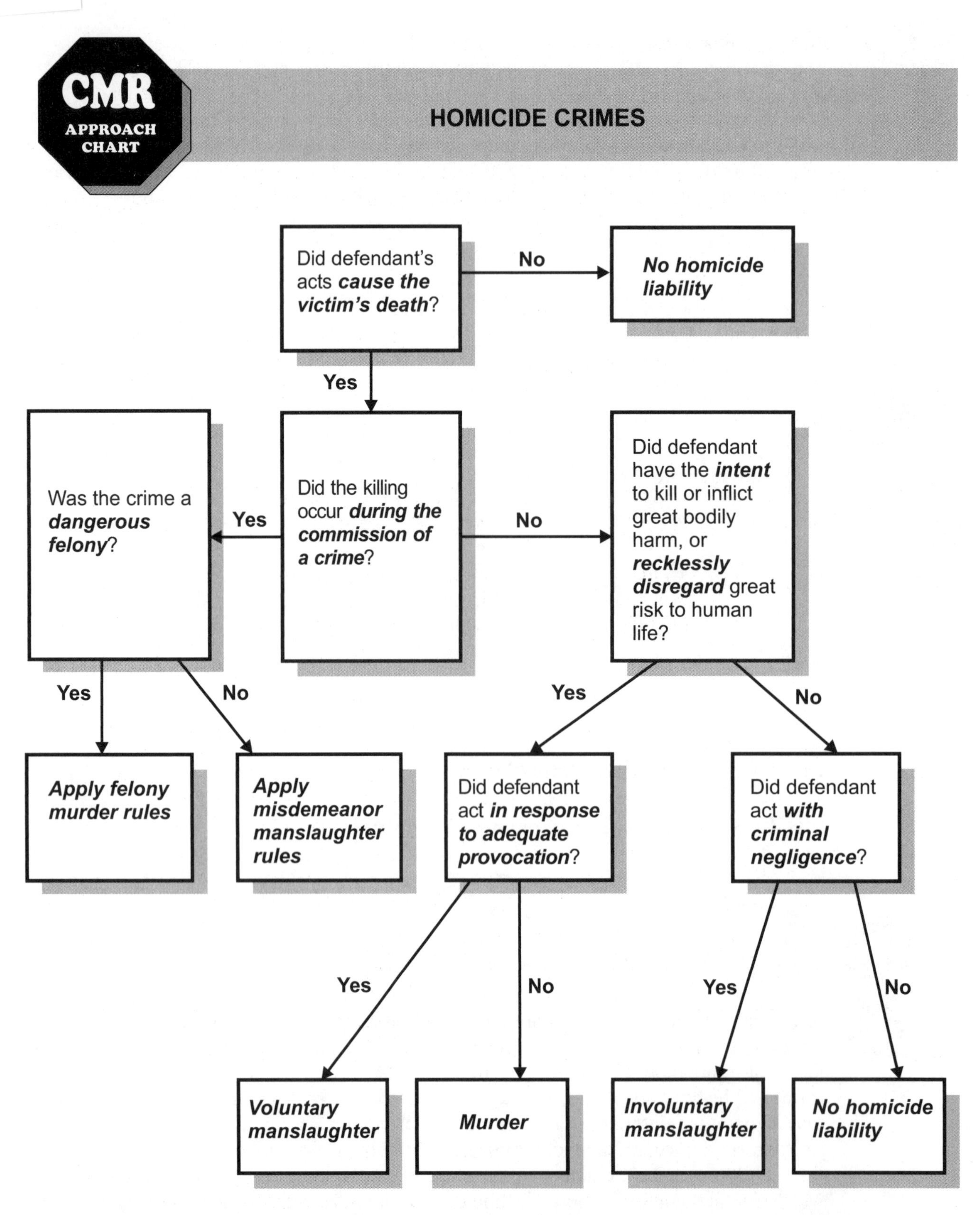

Note: This chart will lead you to the prima facie homicide that defendant committed. You must then decide whether any defenses apply.

b. Voluntary Manslaughter

Voluntary manslaughter is a killing that would be ***murder but for the existence of adequate provocation***. Provocation is adequate ***only if***:

(i) It was a provocation that would arouse ***sudden and intense passion*** in the mind of an ordinary person, causing him to lose self-control (*e.g.*, exposure to a ***threat of deadly force*** or finding your ***spouse in bed with another*** are adequate);

(ii) The defendant was ***in fact provoked***;

(iii) There was ***not sufficient time*** between provocation (or provocations) and killing for passions of a reasonable person to cool; and

(iv) The defendant ***in fact did not cool off*** between the provocation and the killing.

CMR **Exam Tip** The adequacy of provocation is a key issue in homicide questions. Be sure to consider carefully the four factors for adequate provocation and not just jump to the conclusion that there was adequate provocation because you see some signs of provocation in the fact pattern. Also note the interplay between the reasonable person standard and what actually happened to defendant. Consider:

(i) ***Sudden and intense passion*** that would cause a ***reasonable person to*** lose control—passion must be reasonable under the circumstances; defendant cannot have been set off by something that would not bother most others.

(ii) ***Defendant lost control***—even if a reasonable person would have been provoked, if defendant was not, there is no reduction to manslaughter.

(iii) ***Not enough time*** for ***reasonable person*** to cool off—this is tricky because it is hard to say how much time is needed to cool off; a lot depends on the situation, but the more time that has passed, the more likely it is that a reasonable person would have cooled off.

(iv) ***Defendant did not cool off***—this is a little easier to judge; if the facts show that defendant calmed down, there is no reduction to manslaughter.

CMR **Exam Tip** Remember that "heat of passion" is no defense to a killing, although it may ***reduce*** the killing from murder to manslaughter. Often a question will set up facts showing sufficient provocation and then ask about defendant's criminal liability. Don't be fooled by a choice "Not guilty because defendant acted in the heat of passion." The correct choice will be something like "Guilty of manslaughter, but not murder, because defendant acted in the heat of passion."

1) Imperfect Self-Defense

Some states recognize an "imperfect self-defense" doctrine under which murder may be reduced to manslaughter even though (i) the defendant was at fault in starting the altercation; or (ii) the defendant ***unreasonably*** but honestly believed in the necessity of responding with deadly force (*i.e.*, defendant's actions do not qualify for self-defense).

c. **Involuntary Manslaughter**
A killing is involuntary manslaughter if it was committed ***with criminal negligence*** (defendant was grossly negligent) or ***during the commission of an unlawful act*** (misdemeanor or felony not included within felony murder rule).

CMR **Exam Tip** Some questions refer specifically to the type of manslaughter (voluntary or involuntary), while others just say "manslaughter." If the question does not specify the type, be sure to consider both, although on the MBE, voluntary manslaughter is more often involved.

2. **Statutory Modification of Common Law Classification**
In some jurisdictions, murder is divided into degrees by statute. A murder will be second degree murder unless it comes under the following circumstances, which would make it first degree murder:

a. **Deliberate and Premeditated**
If defendant made the decision to kill in a cool and dispassionate manner and actually reflected on the idea of killing, even if only for a very brief period, it is first degree murder.

CMR **Exam Tip** First degree murder based on premeditation requires a specific intent, which may be negated by the defense of ***voluntary intoxication***. If the defendant was so intoxicated that he was unable to premeditate, he can be convicted only of second degree or common law murder, which requires only reckless indifference to human life (and for which voluntary intoxication is ***not*** a defense).

b. **Felony Murder**
If a murder is committed during the perpetration of an enumerated felony, it is first degree murder. The felonies most commonly listed include arson, robbery, burglary, rape, mayhem, and kidnapping. In these jurisdictions, other felony murders are second degree murder.

c. **Others**
Some statutes make killings performed in certain ways (*e.g.*, by torture) first degree murder.

3. **Felony Murder**
Any death caused in the ***commission of, or in an attempt to commit, a felony*** is murder. Malice is implied from the intent to commit the underlying felony.

a. **Felonies Included**
At common law, there are only a handful of felonies (*e.g.*, burglary, arson, rape, sodomy, etc.). Statutes today have created many more felonies, but the felony murder doctrine is limited to felonies that are ***inherently dangerous***.

b. **Limitations on Liability**
There are several limitations on this rule:

(i) The ***defendant must be guilty*** of the underlying felony.

(ii) The ***felony must be distinct*** from the killing itself (*e.g.*, commission of aggravated battery that causes a victim's death does not qualify as an underlying felony for felony murder liability).

(iii) ***Death must have been a foreseeable result*** of the felony (a minority of courts require only that the felony be malum in se).

(iv) The ***death must have been caused before the defendant's "immediate flight"*** from the felony ended; once the felon has reached a place of "temporary safety," subsequent deaths are not felony murder.

(v) In most jurisdictions, the defendant is ***not*** liable for felony murder when a ***co-felon*** is killed as a result of resistance from the felony victim or the police.

(vi) Under the "agency theory," the defendant is not liable for felony murder when an ***innocent party*** is killed ***unless*** the death is caused by the defendant or his "agent" (*i.e.*, an accomplice). (Under the "proximate cause" theory, the defendant may be liable when an innocent party is killed by the victim or police.)

1) Misdemeanor Manslaughter

Note that there are similar limitations on misdemeanor manslaughter. Generally, the misdemeanor must be "malum in se," or, if the misdemeanor involved is not malum in se, the death must have been a foreseeable result of the commission of the misdemeanor.

4. Causation

The defendant's conduct must be both the cause-in-fact and the proximate cause of the victim's death.

a. Cause-in-Fact

A defendant's conduct is the cause-in-fact of the result if the result would not have occurred "***but for***" the defendant's conduct.

b. Proximate Causation

A defendant's conduct is the proximate cause of the result if the result is ***a natural and probable consequence*** of the conduct, even if the defendant did not anticipate the precise manner in which the result occurred. Superseding factors break the chain of proximate causation.

c. Rules of Causation

An act that ***hastens an inevitable result*** is still the legal cause of that result. Also, ***simultaneous acts*** of two or more persons may be independently sufficient causes of a single result. A victim's preexisting weakness or fragility, even if unforeseeable, does not break the chain of causation.

d. Limitations

1) Year and a Day Rule

Traditionally, for a defendant to be liable for homicide, the death of the victim must occur within one year and one day from infliction of the injury or wound. Most states that have recently reviewed this rule have abolished it.

2) Intervening Acts

Generally, an intervening act shields the defendant from liability if the act is a coincidence or is outside the foreseeable sphere of risk created by the defendant. Note that a third party's negligent medical care and the victim's refusal of medical treatment for religious reasons are both foreseeable risks, so the defendant would be liable.

D. FALSE IMPRISONMENT

False imprisonment consists of the ***unlawful confinement*** of a person ***without his valid consent***. It is not confinement to simply prevent a person from going where she desires to go, as long as alternative routes are available to her. Note also that consent is invalidated by coercion, threats, deception, or incapacity due to mental illness, retardation, or youth.

E. KIDNAPPING

Modern statutes often define kidnapping as unlawful confinement of a person that involves either (i) some ***movement*** of the victim, or (ii) ***concealment*** of the victim in a "secret" place.

1. Aggravated Kidnapping

Aggravated kidnapping includes kidnapping for ransom, kidnapping for the purpose of committing other crimes, kidnapping for offensive purposes, and child stealing (the consent of a child to her detention or movement is not of importance because a child is incapable of giving valid consent).

VIII. SEX OFFENSES

A. RAPE

Rape is the unlawful carnal knowledge of a woman by a man, not her husband, without her effective consent. The slightest penetration is sufficient.

1. Absence of Marital Relationship

Under the traditional rule, a husband cannot rape his wife, but most states today either reject this rule entirely or reject it where the parties are estranged or separated.

2. Lack of Effective Consent

To be rape, the intercourse must be without effective consent. Lack of effective consent exists where:

(i) Intercourse is accomplished by ***actual force***;

(ii) Intercourse is accomplished by ***threats of great and immediate bodily harm***;

(iii) The victim is ***incapable of consenting*** due to unconsciousness, intoxication, or mental condition; or

(iv) The victim is ***fraudulently caused to believe that the act is not intercourse***.

Note that consent due to other types of fraud (*e.g.,* perpetrator persuading victim that he is her husband or that he will marry her) ***is*** effective.

B. STATUTORY RAPE

This is carnal knowledge of a female under the age of consent; it is not necessary to show lack of consent. A showing of reasonable mistake as to age or a showing of voluntary consent is irrelevant since statutory rape is a ***strict liability crime***.

C. ADULTERY AND FORNICATION

Adultery is committed by both parties to sexual intercourse if either is validly married to someone else. It is often required that the behavior be open and notorious. Fornication is sexual intercourse or open and notorious cohabitation by unmarried persons.

D. INCEST

Incest consists of marriage or a sexual act between closely related persons.

E. SEDUCTION

Seduction consists of inducing, by promise of marriage, an unmarried woman to engage in intercourse. The M.P.C. does not require chastity or that the female be unmarried.

F. BIGAMY

Bigamy is the common law strict liability offense of marrying someone while having another living spouse.

IX. PROPERTY OFFENSES

A. LARCENY

Larceny consists of:

(i) ***A taking*** (obtaining control);

(ii) ***And carrying away*** (asportation);

(iii) ***Of tangible personal property*** (excluding realty, services, and intangibles, but including written instruments embodying intangible rights such as stock certificates);

(iv) ***Of another*** with possession;

(v) ***By trespass*** (without consent or by consent induced by fraud);

(vi) ***With intent to permanently deprive*** that person of her interest in the property.

1. Possession

The property must be taken from the possession of another. If the ***defendant*** had possession of the property at the time of the taking, the crime is not larceny, but may be embezzlement.

a. Custody vs. Possession

Possession involves a greater scope of authority to deal with the property than does custody. Ordinarily, low level employees have only custody of an employer's property and so are guilty of larceny for taking it. A bailee, on the other hand, has a greater scope of authority over an owner's property and so is not guilty of larceny for taking it, but may be guilty of embezzlement.

2. Intent to Permanently Deprive

Generally, larceny requires that ***at the time of the taking*** defendant intended to permanently deprive a person of her property.

a. Sufficient Intent

An intent to create a substantial risk of loss, or an intent to sell or pledge the goods to the owner, is sufficient for larceny.

b. Insufficient Intent

Where the defendant believes that the property she is taking is hers or where she intends only to borrow the property or to keep it as repayment of a debt, there is no larceny.

c. Possibly Sufficient Intent

There ***may be*** larceny where the defendant intends to pay for the goods (***if*** the goods were not for sale) or intends to collect a reward from the owner (***if*** there is no intent to return the goods absent a reward).

CMR **Exam Tip** For a larceny question, be sure that the defendant had the intent to permanently deprive ***when she took the property***. If not, there is no larceny (unless it is a continuing trespass situation (*see* 4., *infra*)). Many questions turn on this one small point.

3. Abandoned, Lost, or Mislaid Property

Larceny can be committed with lost or mislaid property or property that has been delivered by mistake, but not with abandoned property.

4. "Continuing Trespass" Situation

If the defendant ***wrongfully*** takes property ***without*** the intent to permanently deprive (*e.g.,* without permission borrows an umbrella), and later decides to keep the property, she is guilty of larceny when she decides to keep it. However, if the original taking was ***not wrongful*** (*e.g.,* she took the umbrella thinking it was hers) and she later decides to keep it, it is not larceny.

B. EMBEZZLEMENT

Embezzlement is:

(i) The ***fraudulent***;

(ii) ***Conversion*** (*i.e.,* dealing with the property in a manner inconsistent with the arrangement by which defendant has possession);

(iii) Of ***personal property***;

(iv) Of ***another***;

(v) By a person ***in lawful possession*** of that property.

1. Distinguish from Larceny
Embezzlement differs from larceny because in embezzlement the defendant misappropriates property while it is in his rightful possession, while in larceny the defendant misappropriates property not in his possession.

2. Fraudulent Intent
Defendant must intend to defraud.

a. Intent to Restore
If the defendant intends to restore the ***exact*** property taken, it is ***not*** embezzlement. However, if the defendant intends to restore similar or substantially identical property, it is embezzlement, even if it was money that was initially taken and other money—of identical value—that he intended to return.

b. Claim of Right
As in larceny, embezzlement is not committed if the conversion is pursuant to a claim of right to the property. Whether defendant took the property openly is an important factor.

C. FALSE PRETENSES
The offense of false pretenses is:

(i) Obtaining ***title***;

(ii) To ***personal property of another***;

(iii) By an ***intentional false statement*** of past or existing ***fact***;

(iv) With ***intent to defraud*** the other.

1. "Larceny by Trick" Distinguished
If the victim is tricked—by a misrepresentation of fact—into giving up mere ***possession*** of property, the crime is larceny by trick. If the victim is tricked into giving up ***title*** to property, the crime is false pretenses.

2. The Misrepresentation Required
The victim must actually be deceived by, or act in reliance on, the misrepresentation, and this must be a major factor (or the sole cause) of the victim passing title to the defendant. A misrepresentation as to what will occur in the future is not sufficient. A false promise, even if made without the present intent to perform, is also not sufficient.

D. ROBBERY
Robbery consists of:

(i) A ***taking***;

(ii) Of ***personal property of another***;

(iii) ***From the other's person or presence*** (including anywhere in his vicinity);

(iv) ***By force or threats of immediate death or physical injury*** to the victim, a member of his family, or some person in the victim's presence;

(v) With the ***intent to permanently deprive*** him of it.

CMR **Exam Tip** For a defendant to be guilty of robbery, the victim must give up her property because she feels threatened. If she gives up her property for another reason (*e.g.*, she feels sorry for the defendant, or she wants the defendant to go away), the defendant will not be guilty of robbery. He may, however, be guilty of attempted robbery.

1. Distinguish Larceny

Robbery differs from larceny because robbery requires that the defendant use ***force or threats*** to obtain or retain the victim's property. Thus, pickpocketing generally would be larceny, but if the victim notices the attempt and resists, the taking would be robbery.

CMR COMPARISON CHART

PROPERTY CRIMES

Crime	Activity	Method	Intent	Title
Larceny	Taking and asportation of property from possession of another person	Without consent or with consent obtained by fraud	With intent to steal	Title does not pass
Embezzlement	Conversion of property held pursuant to a trust agreement	Use of property in a way inconsistent with terms of trust	With intent to defraud	Title does not pass
False Pretenses	Obtaining title to property	By consent induced by fraudulent misrepresentation	With intent to defraud	Title passes
Robbery	Taking of property from another's presence	By force or threat of force	With intent to steal	Title does not pass

E. EXTORTION

Common law extortion consists of the corrupt collection of an unlawful fee by an officer under color of office. Under modern statutes, extortion (blackmail) often consists of obtaining property ***by means of threats*** to do harm or to expose information. Under some statutes, the crime is complete when threats are made with the intent to obtain property; *i.e.,* the property need not be obtained.

1. **Distinguish Robbery**
Extortion differs from robbery because in extortion the threats may be of future harm and the taking does not have to be in the presence of the victim.

F. **RECEIPT OF STOLEN PROPERTY**
Receipt of stolen property consists of:

(i) Receiving ***possession and control***;

(ii) Of ***"stolen" personal property***;

(iii) ***Known*** to have been obtained in a manner constituting a criminal offense;

(iv) ***By another person***;

(v) With the ***intent to permanently deprive*** the owner of his interest in it.

1. **"Possession"**
Manual possession is not necessary. The defendant possesses the property when it is put in a location designated by her or she arranges a sale for the thief to a third person (*i.e.,* "fencing").

2. **"Stolen" Property**
The property must be stolen property ***at the time the defendant receives it***.

Exam Tip In analyzing receipt of stolen property questions, carefully check the property's status at the time defendant receives it. If the police have already recovered the property and use it ***with the owner's permission***, it is no longer stolen, and the defendant cannot be convicted of receipt of stolen property. Note, however, that the defendant ***can*** be convicted of ***attempted*** receipt of stolen property if she intended to receive the property believing it to be stolen.

G. **THEFT**
Under many modern statutes, some or all of the above property offenses are combined and defined as the crime of "theft."

H. **FORGERY**
Forgery consists of the following:

(i) ***Making or altering*** (by drafting, adding, or deleting);

(ii) A ***writing*** with apparent legal significance (*e.g.,* a contract, not a painting);

(iii) So that it is ***false***; *i.e.,* representing that it is something that it is not, not merely containing a misrepresentation (*e.g.,* a ***fake*** warehouse receipt, but not an ***inaccurate*** real warehouse receipt);

(iv) With ***intent to defraud*** (although no one need actually have been defrauded).

1. Fraudulently Obtaining Signature of Another
If the defendant fraudulently causes a third person to sign a document that the third person does not realize he is signing, forgery has been committed. But if the third person realizes he is signing the document, forgery has not been committed even if the third person was induced by fraud to sign it.

2. Uttering a Forged Instrument
Uttering a forged instrument consists of: (i) ***offering as genuine***; (ii) an ***instrument*** that may be the subject of forgery and is ***false***; (iii) with ***intent to defraud***.

I. MALICIOUS MISCHIEF
Malicious mischief consists of:

(i) The ***malicious***;

(ii) ***Destruction*** of or damage to;

(iii) The ***property of another***.

Malice requires no ill will or hatred. It does, however, require that the damage or destruction have been ***intended or contemplated*** by the defendant.

X. OFFENSES AGAINST THE HABITATION

A. BURGLARY
Common law burglary consists of:

(i) A ***breaking*** (creating or enlarging an opening by at least minimal force, fraud, or intimidation; if defendant had the resident's consent to enter, the entry is not a breaking);

(ii) And ***entry*** (placing any portion of the body or any instrument used to commit the crime into the structure);

(iii) ***Of a dwelling*** (a structure used with regularity for sleeping purposes, even if used for other purposes such as conducting a business);

(iv) ***Of another*** (ownership is irrelevant; occupancy by someone other than defendant is all that is required);

(v) ***At nighttime***;

(vi) ***With the intent to commit a felony in the structure*** (felony need not be carried out to constitute burglary).

Modern statutes often eliminate many of the "technicalities" of common law burglary, including the requirements of a breaking, that the structure be a dwelling, that the act occur at nighttime, and that the intent be to commit a felony (*i.e.,* intent to commit misdemeanor theft is often enough).

CMR **Exam Tip** The intent to commit a felony within must be present ***at the time of entry***; a later-acquired intent is not sufficient. This technicality is tested; remember it.

B. ARSON

Arson at common law consists of:

(i) The ***malicious*** (*i.e.*, intentional or with reckless disregard of an obvious risk);

(ii) ***Burning*** (requiring some damage to the structure caused by fire);

(iii) ***Of the dwelling***;

(iv) ***Of another.***

CMR **Exam Tip** Although common law arson requires a burning of a ***dwelling***, MBE questions testing on other arson issues often assume, without specifically stating, that arson extends to structures other than dwellings. Many statutes so provide.

1. Damage Required

Destruction of the structure, or even significant damage to it, is not required to complete the crime of arson. Mere blackening by smoke or discoloration by heat (scorching) is not sufficient, but mere ***charring is sufficient***.

CMR **Exam Tip** For arson, the damage must be caused by fire. An explosion is not enough unless it causes a fire.

2. Related Offense—Houseburning

The common law misdemeanor of houseburning consisted of: (i) a malicious; (ii) burning; (iii) of one's own dwelling; (iv) if the structure is situated either in a city or town, or so near to other houses as to create a danger to them.

XI. OFFENSES INVOLVING JUDICIAL PROCEDURE

A. PERJURY

Perjury is the ***intentional*** taking of a false oath (lying) in regard to a ***material matter*** (*i.e.,* one that might affect the outcome of the proceeding) in a judicial proceeding.

B. SUBORNATION OF PERJURY

Subornation of perjury consists of ***procuring or inducing*** another to commit perjury.

C. BRIBERY

Bribery at common law was the corrupt payment or receipt of anything of value for official action. Under modern statutes, it may be extended to nonpublic officials, and either the offering of a bribe or the taking of a bribe may constitute the crime.

D. COMPOUNDING A CRIME

Compounding consists of agreeing, for valuable consideration, not to prosecute another for a felony or to conceal the commission of a felony or the whereabouts of a felon. Under modern statutes, the definition refers to any crime.

E. MISPRISION OF A FELONY

At common law, misprision of a felony consisted of the failure to disclose knowledge of the commission of a felony or to prevent the commission of a felony. Under modern statutes, misprision is no longer a crime, or if it remains a crime, it requires some affirmative action in aid of the felon.

CRIMINAL PROCEDURE

TABLE OF CONTENTS

CRIMINAL PROCEDURE - 13 questions

I. CONSTITUTIONAL RESTRAINTS ON CRIMINAL PROCEDURE

A. CONSTITUTIONAL REQUIREMENTS BINDING ON STATES

The first eight amendments to the U.S. Constitution apply to the federal government. Most of these rights are applicable to the states through the Due Process Clause of the Fourteenth Amendment. The following rights are binding on the states (as well as the federal government):

1. The Fourth Amendment ***prohibition against unreasonable searches and seizures***, and the ***exclusionary rule***;
2. The Fifth Amendment ***privilege against compulsory self-incrimination***;
3. The Fifth Amendment ***prohibition against double jeopardy***;
4. The Sixth Amendment right to ***speedy trial***;
5. The Sixth Amendment right to a ***public trial***;
6. The Sixth Amendment right to ***trial by jury***;
7. The Sixth Amendment right to ***confront witnesses***;
8. The Sixth Amendment right to ***compulsory process*** for obtaining witnesses;
9. The Sixth Amendment right to ***assistance of counsel*** in felony cases and in misdemeanor cases in which imprisonment is imposed; and
10. The Eighth Amendment ***prohibition against cruel and unusual punishment***.

B. CONSTITUTIONAL RIGHTS NOT BINDING ON STATES

The right to indictment by a grand jury for capital and infamous crimes has been held not to be binding on the states. It has not yet been determined whether the Eighth Amendment prohibition against excessive bail creates a right to bail. However, most state constitutions create a right to bail and prohibit excessive bail.

II. EXCLUSIONARY RULE

A. IN GENERAL—SCOPE OF RULE

The exclusionary rule is a judge-made doctrine that prohibits introduction of evidence obtained in violation of a defendant's Fourth, Fifth, and Sixth Amendment rights. Under the rule, illegally obtained evidence is inadmissible at trial, and all "fruit of the poisonous tree" (*i.e.,* evidence obtained from exploitation of the illegally obtained evidence) must also be excluded. ***Exceptions to fruit of the poisonous tree doctrine:***

(i) Evidence obtained from a ***source independent*** of the original illegality;

(ii) An ***intervening act of free will*** by the defendant (*e.g.,* defendant is illegally arrested but is released and later returns to the station to confess);

(iii) ***Inevitable discovery; i.e.,*** the prosecution can show that the police would have discovered the evidence whether or not the police acted unconstitutionally; and

(iv) ***Violations of the knock and announce rule*** (*see* III.C.3.e., *infra*).

Note: It is difficult to have live witness testimony excluded on exclusionary rule grounds. Also, a defendant may not exclude a witness's in-court identification on the ground that it is the fruit of an unlawful detention.

B. LIMITATIONS ON THE RULE

1. Inapplicable to Grand Juries, Civil Proceedings, Internal Agency Rules, and Parole Revocation Proceedings

The exclusionary rule is inapplicable to grand juries unless evidence was obtained in violation of the federal wiretapping statute. The rule is also inapplicable at parole revocation proceedings, in civil proceedings, or where evidence was obtained contrary only to agency rules.

2. Good Faith Reliance on Law, Defective Search Warrant, or Clerical Error

The exclusionary rule does not apply when police act in good faith based on (i) case law, (ii) a facially valid statute or ordinance, or (iii) a computer report containing clerical errors not made by the police. Neither does the rule apply when the police act in good faith reliance on a defective search warrant ***unless*** (i) the underlying affidavit was so lacking in probable cause that it could not reasonably be relied on, (ii) the warrant was defective on its face, (iii) the affiant lied to or misled the magistrate, or (iv) the magistrate has "wholly abandoned his judicial role."

Exceptions to good faith D

3. Use of Excluded Evidence for Impeachment Purposes

Some illegally obtained evidence may still be used to impeach defendant's credibility if he takes the stand at trial. Specifically, an otherwise ***voluntary confession*** taken in violation of the *Miranda* requirements is admissible for impeachment purposes, and ***evidence obtained from an illegal search*** may be used by the prosecution to impeach defendant's, but not others', statements.

4. *Miranda* Violations

The fruits derived from statements obtained in violation of *Miranda* may be admissible despite the exclusionary rule. (*See, e.g.,* IV.D.4.c., *infra.*)

C. HARMLESS ERROR TEST

If illegal evidence is admitted, a resulting conviction should be overturned ***on appeal*** unless the government can show beyond reasonable doubt that the error was ***harmless***. In a habeas proceeding where the petitioner claims constitutional error, he should be released if he can show that the error had a ***substantial and injurious effect or influence*** in determining the jury's verdict; if the judge is in grave doubt as to the harm, the petition must be granted.

CMR **Exam Tip** The harmless error standard never applies to the denial of the right to counsel ***at trial***; *i.e.,* this error is never harmless.

D. ENFORCING THE EXCLUSIONARY RULE

A defendant is entitled to have the admissibility of evidence or a confession decided as a matter of law by a judge out of the hearing of the jury. The government bears the burden of establishing the admissibility by a preponderance of the evidence. The defendant has the right to testify at a suppression hearing without his testimony being admitted against him at trial on the issue of guilt.

III. FOURTH AMENDMENT

A. IN GENERAL

The Fourth Amendment provides that people should be free from unreasonable searches and seizures.

B. ARRESTS AND OTHER DETENTIONS

Governmental seizures of persons, including arrests, are seizures within the scope of the Fourth Amendment and so must be reasonable.

1. What Constitutes a Seizure?

A seizure occurs when a reasonable person would believe that she is not free to leave or terminate an encounter with the government.

2. Arrests

An arrest occurs when the police take a person into custody against her will for purposes of criminal prosecution or interrogation.

a. Probable Cause Requirement

An arrest must be based on probable cause—*i.e.,* trustworthy facts or knowledge sufficient for a reasonable person to believe that the suspect has committed or is committing a crime.

b. Warrant Generally Not Required Except for Home Arrests

A warrant generally is not required before arresting a person ***in a public place***. However, police generally must have a warrant to effect a nonemergency arrest of a person in his home.

3. Other Detentions

a. Investigatory Detentions (Stop and Frisk)

If the police have a ***reasonable suspicion*** of criminal activity or involvement in a completed crime, supported by ***articulable facts*** (*i.e.,* not merely a hunch), they may detain a person for investigative purposes. If the police also have reasonable suspicion that the detainee is armed and dangerous, they may frisk the detainee for weapons.

1) Duration and Scope

The detention must be no longer than necessary to conduct a limited investigation to verify the suspicion. The police may ask the detained person to identify himself (*i.e.,* state his name) and generally may arrest the detainee for failure to comply with such a request. The detention will also turn into an arrest if during the detention other probable cause for arrest arises.

2) Property Seizures

Brief property seizures are similarly valid if based on reasonable suspicion.

b. Automobile Stops

Generally, police may not stop a car unless they have at least reasonable suspicion to believe that a law has been violated. However, if ***special law enforcement needs*** are involved, the Supreme Court allows police to set up roadblocks to stop cars without individualized suspicion that the driver violated some law. To be valid, the roadblock must: (i) stop cars on the basis of some neutral, articulable standard (*e.g.,* every car); and (ii) be designed to serve purposes closely related to a particular problem pertaining to automobiles and their mobility (*e.g.,* a roadblock to test for drunk drivers is valid because of the pervasiveness of the drunk driving problem, but a roadblock to search cars for illegal drugs is not valid because the purpose of such a checkpoint is only to detect evidence of ordinary criminal wrongdoing).

1) **Police May Order Occupants Out**
After lawfully stopping a vehicle, in the interest of officer safety, the officer may order the occupants of the vehicle to get out. Moreover, if the officer reasonably believes the detainees to be armed, he may frisk the occupants and search the passenger compartment for weapons, even after he has ordered the occupants out.

2) **Pretextual Stops**
If the police reasonably believe a driver violated a traffic law, they may stop the car, even if their ulterior motive is to investigate whether some other law—for which the police lack reasonable suspicion—has been violated.

c. **Detention to Obtain a Warrant**
If the police have probable cause to believe that a suspect has hidden drugs in his home, they may, for a reasonable time, prevent him from going into the home unaccompanied so that they can prevent him from destroying the drugs while they obtain a search warrant.

d. **Occupants of the Premises**
A valid warrant to search for contraband allows the police to detain occupants of the premises during a proper search.

e. **Station House Detentions**
Police must have full probable cause for arrest to bring a suspect to the station for questioning or fingerprinting.

4. **Grand Jury Appearance**
Seizure of a person (by subpoena) for a grand jury appearance is not within the Fourth Amendment's protection.

5. **Deadly Force**
A police officer may not use deadly force to apprehend a suspect unless the officer has probable cause to believe that the suspect poses a significant threat of death or serious physical injury. On the other hand, a mere attempt to arrest that results in the death of a suspect is not necessarily a seizure governed by the Fourth Amendment.

C. EVIDENTIARY SEARCH AND SEIZURE

Like arrests, evidentiary searches and seizures must be reasonable to be valid under the Fourth Amendment, but here reasonableness requires a warrant except in six circumstances (*see* 4., *infra*). Evidentiary search and seizure issues should be approached using the following analytical model:

(i) Does defendant have a ***Fourth Amendment right*** (seizure by the ***government*** concerning a place or thing in which defendant had a ***reasonable expectation of privacy***)?

(ii) Did the government have a ***valid warrant*** (issued by a neutral and detached magistrate on a showing of ***probable cause*** and ***reasonably precise*** as to the place to be searched and items to be seized)?

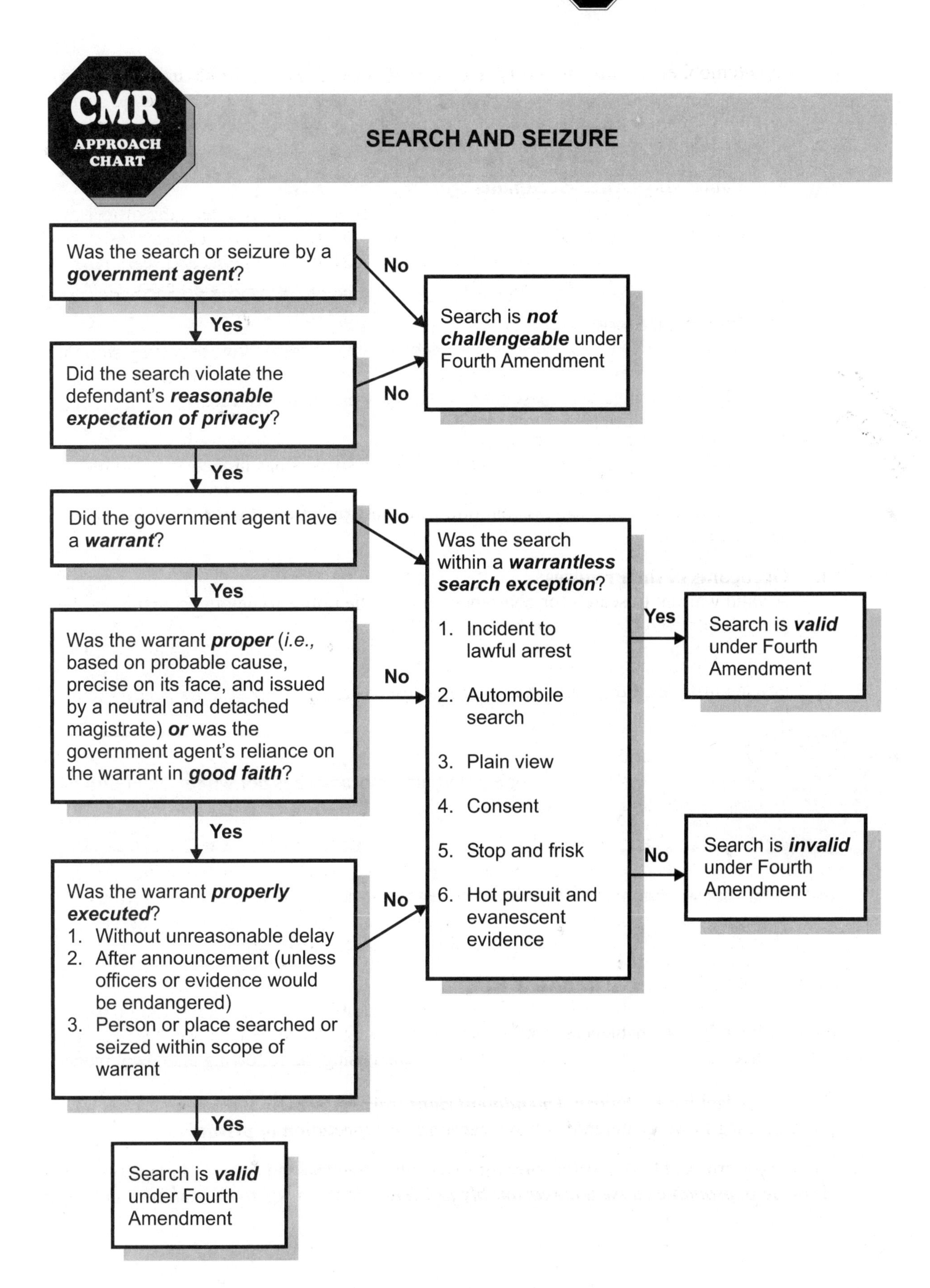
CMR
APPROACH CHART
SEARCH AND SEIZURE
Was the search or seizure by a *government agent*?
No
Search is *not challengeable* under Fourth Amendment
Yes
Did the search violate the defendant's *reasonable expectation of privacy*?
No
Yes
Did the government agent have a *warrant*?
No
Was the search within a *warrantless search exception*?
1. Incident to lawful arrest
2. Automobile search
3. Plain view
4. Consent
5. Stop and frisk
6. Hot pursuit and evanescent evidence
Yes
Search is *valid* under Fourth Amendment
No
Search is *invalid* under Fourth Amendment
Yes
Was the warrant *proper* (*i.e.*, based on probable cause, precise on its face, and issued by a neutral and detached magistrate) *or* was the government agent's reliance on the warrant in *good faith*?
No
Yes
Was the warrant *properly executed*?
1. Without unreasonable delay
2. After announcement (unless officers or evidence would be endangered)
3. Person or place searched or seized within scope of warrant
No
Yes
Search is *valid* under Fourth Amendment

(iii) If the police did not have a valid warrant, did they make a ***valid warrantless search and seizure***?

1. Governmental Conduct Required

The Fourth Amendment generally protects only against governmental conduct (*i.e.,* police or other government agents), and not against searches by private persons—including private security guards—unless deputized as officers of the public police.

2. Reasonable Expectation of Privacy

a. Standing

To have a Fourth Amendment right, a person must have his own reasonable expectation of privacy with respect to the place searched or the item seized. The determination is made on the totality of the circumstances, but a person has a legitimate expectation of privacy any time:

1) He owned or had a ***right to possession*** of the place searched;

2) The place searched was in fact ***his home***, whether or not he owned or had a right to possession of it; or

3) He was an ***overnight guest*** of the owner of the place searched.

b. Things Held Out to the Public

One does not have a reasonable expectation of privacy in objects held out to the public.

Note: Use of sense-enhancing technology that is not in general public use (*e.g.,* a thermal imager as opposed to a telephoto camera lens) to obtain information from inside a suspect's home that could not otherwise be obtained without physical intrusion violates the suspect's reasonable expectation of privacy.

CMR EXAMPLE CHART

NO REASONABLE EXPECTATION OF PRIVACY

One has ***no reasonable expectation of privacy in:***

1. The sound of one's voice
2. One's handwriting
3. Paint on the outside of one's vehicle
4. Account records held by a bank
5. The location of one's vehicle on public roads or its arrival at a private residence
6. Areas outside the home and related buildings ("curtilage"), such as a barn
7. Garbage left for collection
8. Land visible from a public place, even from a plane or helicopter
9. The smell of one's car or luggage ("sniff-test")

3. Searches Conducted Pursuant to a Warrant

Generally, the police must have a warrant to conduct a search unless it falls within one of the six exceptions to the warrant requirement (*see* 4., *infra*).

a. Showing of Probable Cause

A warrant will be issued only if there is probable cause to believe that seizable evidence will be found on the person or premises at the time the warrant is executed. Officers must submit to a magistrate an affidavit setting forth circumstances enabling the magistrate to make a determination of probable cause independent of the officers' conclusions.

1) Use of Informers

An affidavit based on an informer's tip must meet the "totality of the circumstances" test. Under this test, the affidavit may be sufficient even though the reliability and credibility of the informer or his basis for knowledge are not established. Note that the informer's identity generally need not be revealed.

2) Going "Behind the Face" of the Affidavit

A search warrant issued on the basis of an affidavit will be held invalid if the defendant establishes ***all three*** of the following:

(i) A ***false statement*** was included in the affidavit by the affiant (the officer applying for the warrant);

(ii) The affiant ***intentionally or recklessly*** included the false statement; ***and***

(iii) The false statement was ***material to the finding of probable cause***.

CMR **Exam Tip** This test for invalidating the affidavit is very restrictive—all three requirements for invalidity (falsehood, intentionally or recklessly included, and material to probable cause) must be met. Thus, if the affiant believed the lie, or if he intentionally included the lie but it was not material to the finding of probable cause (because there was sufficient other evidence), the affidavit is valid. Therefore, a defendant is rarely successful in challenging the affidavit.

a) Police May Reasonably Rely on Validity of Warrant

Evidence obtained by the police in reasonable reliance on a facially valid warrant may be used by the prosecution, despite an ultimate finding that the warrant was not supported by probable cause. (*See* II.B.2., *supra*.)

CMR **Exam Tip** This good faith exception applies ***only if the police obtained a warrant*** and it is invalid. The exception does not apply if the police failed to obtain a warrant.

b. Warrant Must Be Precise on Its Face

A warrant must describe with reasonable precision the place to be searched and items to be seized. If it does not, the warrant is unconstitutional, even if the underlying affidavit gives such detail.

c. **Search of Third-Party Premises Permissible**
A warrant may be obtained to search premises belonging to nonsuspects, as long as there is probable cause to believe that evidence will be found there.

d. **Neutral and Detached Magistrate Requirement**
The magistrate who issues the warrant must be neutral and detached (*e.g.,* state attorney general is not neutral).

e. **Execution of Warrant**
Only the police (and not private citizens) may execute a warrant, and it must be executed without unreasonable delay. Police must knock, announce their purpose, and wait a reasonable time for admittance (unless the officer has reasonable suspicion, based on facts, that announcing would be dangerous or futile or would inhibit the investigation). Police may seize any contraband or fruits or instrumentalities of crime that they discover, whether or not specified in the warrant. In any case, remember that violations of the knock and announce rule ***will not*** result in the suppression of evidence otherwise properly obtained—the exclusionary rule does not apply here.

1) **Search of Persons Found on Searched Premises**
A warrant founded on probable cause to search for contraband authorizes the police to ***detain*** occupants of the premises during a proper search, but a search warrant does ***not*** authorize the police to ***search*** persons found on the premises who were not named in the warrant.

4. **Exceptions to Warrant Requirement**
All warrantless searches are unconstitutional unless they fit into one of six recognized exceptions to the warrant requirement.

a. **Search Incident to Lawful Arrest**
Incident to a ***lawful*** arrest, the police may search the person and areas into which he might reach to obtain weapons or destroy evidence (including the entire passenger compartment of a car). The police may also make a protective sweep of the area if they believe accomplices may be present. The search must be contemporaneous in time and place with the arrest.

1) **Lawful Arrest Requirement**
If an arrest is unlawful, any search incident to that arrest is also unlawful.

2) **Search Incident to Incarceration**
At the police station, the police may make an inventory search of the arrestee's belongings. Similarly, the police may make an inventory search of an impounded vehicle.

b. **"Automobile" Exception**
If the police have probable cause to believe that a vehicle contains fruits, instrumentalities, or evidence of a crime, they may search the whole vehicle and any container that might reasonably contain the item for which they had probable cause to search. If a warrantless search of a vehicle is valid, the police may tow the vehicle to the station and search it later.

Note: If the police have probable cause to believe that an automobile itself is contraband, they may seize it from a public place without a warrant.

VALID WARRANTLESS SEARCHES

Type of Search	Need Probable Cause?	Contemporaneousness Requirement?	Other Limitations?
Search Incident to Lawful Arrest	Yes (for arrest)	Yes	Lawful arrest
Search Incident to Incarceration (Inventory Search)	No	No	Established routine
"Automobile" Exception	Yes	No	Containers—limited to those that could contain evidence sought
Plain View	Yes (to believe item is evidence, contraband, etc.)	Yes	Lawfully on premises; evidence in plain view
Consent	No	Yes	Voluntary and intelligent consent; apparent authority to consent; cannot be against wishes of a co-occupant who is present and objecting to the search
Stop and Frisk			
Stop	No	Yes	Reasonable and articulable suspicion of criminal activity
Frisk	No	Yes	Reasonable belief that person is armed; limited to patdown of outer clothing
Hot Pursuit, Emergencies	No	Yes	Emergency situation—No time to get warrant

CMR **Exam Tip** Note that the police have fairly broad authority to search a vehicle depending on what they are looking for. If there is probable cause to search the vehicle, the police can search the entire car and anything in it that ***might contain the evidence***. Thus, if they are looking for evidence of illegal drugs, they can look in almost anything in the car, but if they are looking for undocumented aliens, they cannot look inside a small suitcase.

1) **Passenger's Belongings**
The search may extend to packages belonging to a passenger; it is not limited to the driver's belongings.

2) **Containers Placed in Vehicle**
If the police have probable cause only to search a container in a vehicle (*e.g.*, luggage recently placed in the trunk), they may search only the container, not other parts of the vehicle.

c. **Plain View**
The police may make a warrantless seizure when they:

(i) Are ***legitimately on the premises***;

(ii) Discover ***evidence, fruits or instrumentalities*** of crime, or ***contraband***;

(iii) See such evidence in ***plain view***; and

(iv) ***Have probable cause*** to believe (*i.e.,* it must be immediately apparent) that the item is evidence, contraband, or a fruit or instrumentality of crime.

CMR **Exam Tip** For this exception, be sure the police officer is legitimately on the premises (*i.e.,* where she has a lawful right to be), such as on a public sidewalk or in a home executing a warrant. If she is, anything the officer sees (or smells, hears, etc.) in plain view is admissible. Thus, if while executing a search warrant for a handgun, the officer opens a small drawer where the gun could be and sees heroin, the heroin is admissible since it was in plain view of an officer who had a right to look there.

d. **Consent**
A warrantless search is valid if the police have a ***voluntary and intelligent*** consent. Knowledge of the right to withhold consent is ***not*** a prerequisite to establishing a voluntary and intelligent consent. The scope of the search may be limited by the scope of the consent, but generally extends to all areas to which a reasonable person under the circumstances would believe it extends.

1) **Authority to Consent**
Any person with an apparent equal right to use or occupy the property may consent to a search, and any evidence found may be used against the other owners or occupants. However, an occupant cannot give valid consent to a search when a co-occupant is present and objects to the search and the search is directed against the co-occupant.

CMR **Exam Tip** Exam questions on the validity of warrantless searches often suggest consent as a choice, especially the consent of someone other than the defendant. Be careful to check whether the person has reasonably apparent authority to consent. For example, a homeowner parent can certainly consent to a search of the home's kitchen, and probably to a search of her son's room ***unless*** the facts strongly indicate that the parent does not have a right to go in the room (*e.g.,* always locked, only defendant has key, etc.). *Note:* The Supreme Court has not yet decided whether a parent may consent over the objection of his child.

e. **Stop and Frisk**

1) **Standards**
As noted above, a police officer may stop a person without probable cause for arrest if she has an ***articulable and reasonable suspicion*** of criminal activity. The officer may require the detainee to state his name, and if the officer also reasonably believes that the person may be armed and presently dangerous, she may conduct a protective frisk.

CMR **Exam Tip** Remember that a ***stop*** is not an arrest, and thus an officer need not have probable cause. However, he must have a reason to believe that criminal activity is afoot. Thus, seeing a person pace in front of a jewelry store might justify a stop. A ***frisk*** will be justified only if the officer reasonably thinks that the suspect has a weapon.

2) **Scope of Intrusion**
The scope of the frisk is generally limited to a patdown of outer clothing, unless the officer has specific information that a weapon is hidden in a particular area of the suspect's clothing. An officer may also order occupants out of a stopped vehicle and frisk them and search the passenger compartment of the vehicle if the officer has a reasonable belief that an occupant is dangerous.

3) **Admissibility of Evidence**
During a patdown, an officer may reach into the suspect's clothing and seize any item that the officer reasonably believes, based on its "plain feel," is a ***weapon or contraband***, and such items are admissible as evidence.

f. **Hot Pursuit, Evanescent Evidence, and Other Emergencies**
There is no general "emergency" exception (*e.g.*, no need to investigate a fire after it has been extinguished and its cause determined). However, (i) police in hot pursuit of a fleeing felon may make a warrantless search and seizure and may even pursue the suspect into a private dwelling; (ii) police may seize without a warrant evidence likely to disappear before a warrant can be obtained; and (iii) contaminated food or drugs, persons injured or threatened with injury, and burning fires justify warrantless searches and seizures.

5. **Administrative Inspections and Searches**
Inspectors must have a warrant for searches of private residences and commercial buildings, but the probable cause required to obtain a warrant is more lenient than for other searches: A showing of a general and neutral enforcement plan will justify issuance of a warrant.

a. Exceptions Permitting Warrantless Searches

The following warrantless searches have been upheld:

1) Administrative searches to ***seize spoiled or contaminated food***;

2) Administrative searches of a ***business within a highly regulated industry***;

3) ***Inventory searches of arrestees***;

4) Searches of ***airline passengers*** prior to boarding;

5) Searches of ***probationers and their homes***—even without reasonable grounds for the search, at least as long as there is a statute authorizing such searches;

6) Searches of ***government employees' desks and file cabinets*** where the scope is reasonable and there is a work-related need or reasonable suspicion of work-related misconduct;

7) ***Drug tests of railroad employees involved in an accident***;

8) ***Drug tests of persons seeking customs employment in positions connected to drug interdiction***; and

9) ***Drug tests of public school students who participate in extracurricular activities.***

6. Searches in Foreign Countries and at the Border

a. Searches in Foreign Countries

The Fourth Amendment does not apply to searches and seizures by United States officials in foreign countries and involving an alien, at least where the alien does not have a substantial connection to the United States. Thus, for example, the Fourth Amendment was held not to bar the use of evidence obtained in a warrantless search of an alien's home in Mexico.

b. Searches at the Border or Its Equivalent

No warrant is necessary for border searches. Neither citizens nor noncitizens have any Fourth Amendment rights at the border. Roving patrols inside the U.S. border may stop a vehicle for questioning of occupants if an officer ***reasonably suspects*** that the vehicle contains illegal aliens. Border officials may stop a vehicle at a fixed checkpoint inside the border for questioning of occupants and may disassemble the vehicle, even without reasonable suspicion.

c. Opening International Mail

Permissible border searches include opening of international mail when postal authorities have reasonable cause to suspect that the mail contains contraband.

d. Immigration Enforcement Actions
The Immigration Services Division may do a "factory survey" of the work force in a factory to determine citizenship of each employee. Moreover, even illegally obtained evidence (*i.e.*, evidence obtained in violation of the Fourth Amendment) may be used in a ***civil*** deportation hearing.

e. Detentions
Officials with "reasonable suspicion" that a traveler is smuggling contraband in her stomach may detain the traveler.

7. Wiretapping and Eavesdropping – requires a warrant
Wiretapping (and other forms of electronic surveillance violating a reasonable expectation of privacy) constitutes a search under the Fourth Amendment. A valid warrant authorizing a wiretap may be issued if (i) there is showing of probable cause, (ii) the suspected persons involved in the conversations to be overheard are named, (iii) the warrant describes with particularity the conversations that can be overheard, (iv) the wiretap is limited to a short period of time, (v) the wiretap is terminated when the desired information has been obtained, and (vi) return is made to the court, showing what conversations have been intercepted.

a. Exceptions
A speaker assumes the risk that the person to whom he is talking is an informer wired for sound or taping the conversation. A speaker has no Fourth Amendment claim if he makes no attempt to keep a conversation private.

b. Pen Registers
Although pen registers (devices that record only phone numbers that are dialed from a phone) are not controlled by the Fourth Amendment, by statute judicial approval is required before a pen register may be used.

D. METHOD OF OBTAINING EVIDENCE THAT SHOCKS THE CONSCIENCE
Evidence obtained in a manner offending a "sense of justice" is inadmissible under the Due Process Clause. The reasonableness of searches within a person's body is determined by balancing society's need against the magnitude of the intrusion. Taking of a blood sample is usually upheld, but surgery (*e.g.*, to remove a bullet) requires great need.

IV. CONFESSIONS

A. INTRODUCTION
The admissibility of a defendant's confession (or other incriminating admission) involves analysis under the Fourth, Fifth, Sixth, and Fourteenth Amendments.

B. FOURTEENTH AMENDMENT—VOLUNTARINESS
For a self-incriminating statement to be admissible under the Due Process Clause, it must be voluntary, as determined by the totality of the circumstances. A statement will be involuntary only if there is some official compulsion (*e.g.*, a confession is not involuntary merely because it is a product of mental illness).

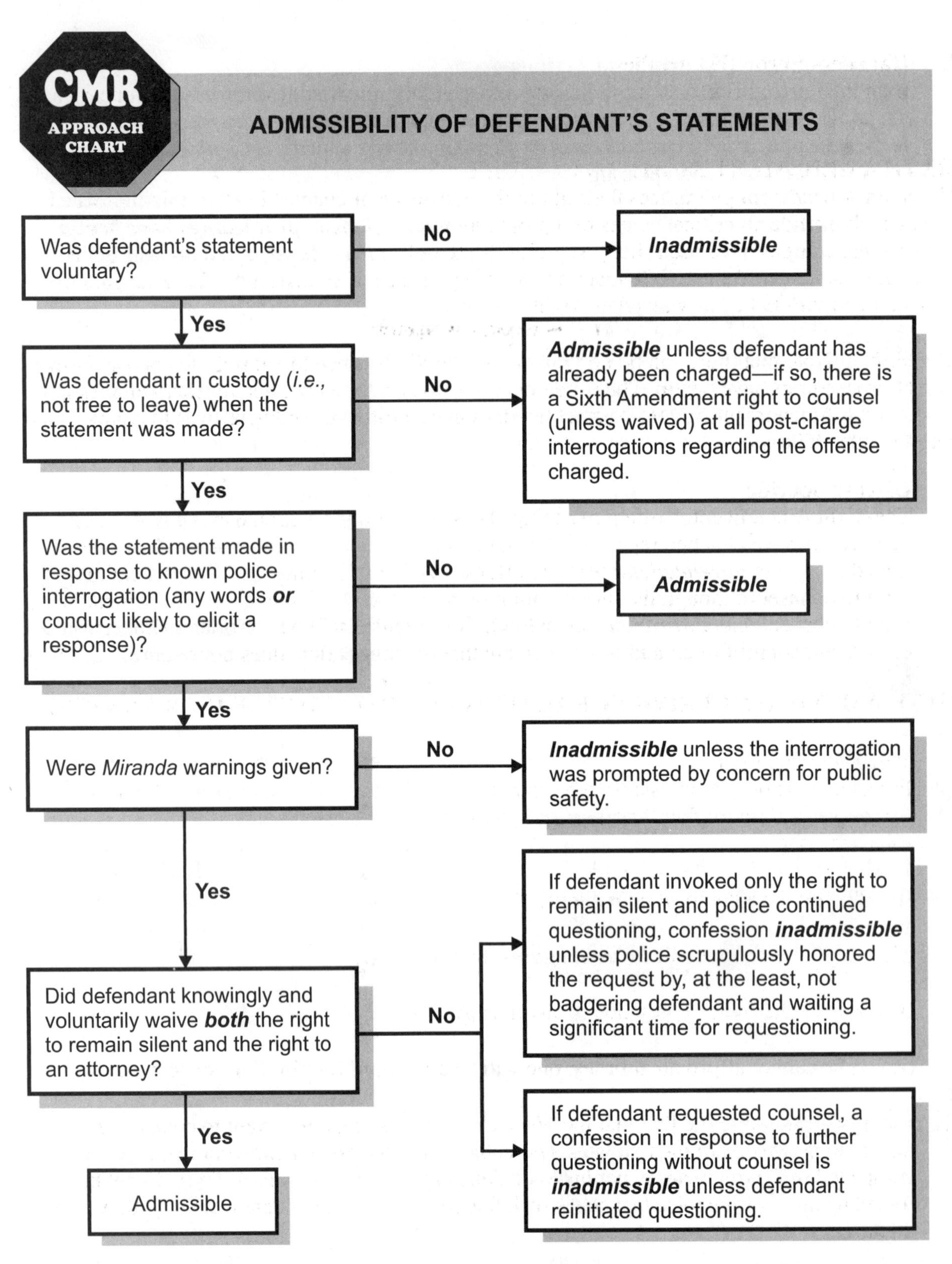

Note: Confessions obtained in violation of *Miranda* are admissible to ***impeach*** defendant's trial testimony.

And note: If inadmissible confessions are erroneously admitted into evidence, a resulting conviction need not be reversed if there is other overwhelming evidence of guilt (the "harmless error" test).

1. **Harmless Error Test Applies**
If an involuntary confession is admitted into evidence, the harmless error test applies; *i.e.*, the conviction need not be overturned if there is other overwhelming evidence of guilt.

C. **SIXTH AMENDMENT RIGHT TO COUNSEL**
The Sixth Amendment guarantees the right to the assistance of counsel in all criminal proceedings, which include all critical stages of a prosecution ***after judicial proceedings have begun*** (*e.g.*, formal charges have been filed). It prohibits the police from deliberately eliciting an incriminating statement from a defendant outside the presence of counsel after the defendant has been charged ***unless*** he has waived his right to counsel.

CMR **Exam Tip** Note that there can be no violation of the Sixth Amendment right to counsel before formal proceedings have begun. Thus, a defendant who is arrested but not yet charged does not have a Sixth Amendment right to counsel but does have a Fifth Amendment right to counsel (*see* below) under *Miranda.*

1. **Offense Specific**
The Sixth Amendment is offense specific. Thus, even though a defendant's Sixth Amendment rights have attached regarding the charge for which he is being held, he may be questioned regarding ***unrelated***, ***uncharged*** offenses without violating the Sixth Amendment right to counsel (although the interrogation might violate the defendant's Fifth Amendment right to counsel under *Miranda; see* below). Two offenses will be considered different if each requires proof of an additional element that the other crime does not require.

D. **FIFTH AMENDMENT PRIVILEGE AGAINST COMPELLED SELF-INCRIMINATION**

1. ***Miranda*** **Warnings**
For an admission or confession to be admissible under the Fifth Amendment privilege against self-incrimination, a person in custody must, prior to interrogation, be informed, in substance, that:

(i) He has the right to ***remain silent***;

(ii) Anything he says ***can be used against*** him in court;

(iii) He has the right to presence of an ***attorney***; and

(iv) If he cannot afford an attorney, one will be ***appointed*** for him if he so desires.

CMR **Exam Tip** Despite the fact that the *Miranda* warnings mention a right to counsel, the failure to give the warnings violates a defendant's ***Fifth Amendment*** right to be free from compelled self-incrimination, not his Sixth Amendment right to counsel. Thus, do not be fooled by an answer choice that states such failure is a violation of defendant's Sixth Amendment rights.

2. **When Required**
Anyone in the custody of the government and accused of a crime must be given *Miranda* warnings ***prior*** to interrogation by the police.

a. **Governmental Conduct**
Generally, *Miranda* warnings are necessary only if the defendant ***knows*** that he is being interrogated by a ***government agent***.

b. **Custody Requirement**
Whether a person is in custody depends on whether the person's freedom of action is denied in a significant way based on the ***objective*** circumstances (*e.g.*, an arrest constitutes custody; a routine traffic stop does not constitute custody).

c. **Interrogation Requirement**
"Interrogation" includes any words or conduct by the police that they should know would ***likely elicit a response*** from the defendant. Thus, *Miranda* warnings are not required before spontaneous statements are made by a defendant. Note that routine booking questions do not constitute interrogation.

d. **Waiver**
A suspect can waive his *Miranda* rights, but the prosecution must prove that the waiver was knowing, voluntary, and intelligent.

e. **Types of Statements**
Miranda applies to both inculpatory statements and exculpatory statements (*e.g.*, "I didn't shoot V, you did").

f. **Inapplicable at Grand Jury Hearing**
The *Miranda* requirements do not apply to a witness testifying before a grand jury, even if the witness was compelled by subpoena to be there.

3. **Right to Terminate Interrogation**
The accused may terminate police interrogation any time prior to or during the interrogation by invoking either the right to remain silent or the right to counsel.

a. **Right to Remain Silent**
If the accused indicates that he wishes to remain silent, the police must scrupulously honor this request by not badgering the accused, although the Supreme Court has allowed later questioning to occur on an unrelated crime.

b. **Right to Counsel**
If the accused ***unambiguously*** indicates that he wishes to speak to counsel, ***all questioning must cease*** until counsel has been provided unless the accused then waives his right to counsel (*e.g.*, by reinitiating questioning). The request must be specific (*i.e.*, indicate that the defendant desires assistance in dealing with interrogation). Allowing defendant to consult with counsel and then resuming interrogation after counsel has left generally does not satisfy the right to counsel—counsel must be present during the interrogation unless defendant has waived the right.

Exam Tip Note the difference here depending on what the defendant asks: If the defendant indicates that he wishes to remain silent, the police probably may requestion him about a different crime after a break if fresh warnings are administered. If the defendant requests counsel, the police may not resume interrogating defendant until counsel is provided or the defendant initiates the questioning.

4. Effect of Violation

Generally, evidence obtained in violation of the *Miranda* rules is inadmissible at trial under the exclusionary rule.

a. Use of Confession for Impeachment

Statements obtained in violation of the *Miranda* rules may be used to impeach the ***defendant's*** trial testimony, but may not be used as evidence of guilt.

b. Warnings After Questioning and Confession

If the police obtain a confession from a defendant without giving him *Miranda* warnings and then give the defendant *Miranda* warnings and obtain a subsequent confession, the subsequent confession will be inadmissible if the "question first, warn later" nature of the questioning was intentional (*i.e.*, the facts make it seem like the police used this as a scheme to get around the *Miranda* requirements). However, a subsequent valid confession may be admissible if the original unwarned questioning seemed unplanned and the failure to give *Miranda* warnings seemed inadvertent.

c. Nontestimonial Fruits of an Unwarned Confession

If the police fail to give *Miranda* warnings and during interrogation a suspect gives the police information that leads to nontestimonial evidence, it is unclear whether the nontestimonial evidence must be suppressed as the fruit of an unlawful interrogation. In a case where there was no majority opinion, five justices held that suppression was not necessary.

5. Public Safety Exception

The Supreme Court has allowed interrogation without *Miranda* warnings where it was reasonably prompted by a concern for public safety (*e.g.*, to locate a hidden gun that could have caused injury to innocent persons).

V. PRETRIAL IDENTIFICATION

A. SUBSTANTIVE BASES FOR ATTACK

1. Sixth Amendment Right to Counsel

A suspect has a right to the presence of an attorney at any ***post-charge*** lineup or showup. An accused does ***not*** have a right to counsel at photo identifications or when police take physical evidence, such as handwriting exemplars or fingerprints, from him.

CMR **Exam Tip** Recall that the right to counsel ***before*** trial is very limited and does not cover procedures where defendant is not personally confronted by the witness against him (as in photo identification).

2. Due Process Standard

A defendant can attack an identification as denying due process if the identification is ***unnecessarily suggestive*** and there is a ***substantial likelihood of misidentification***.

Exam Tip Since a lineup does not involve compulsion to give "testimonial" evidence, a suspect's Fifth Amendment right against compelled self-incrimination does not apply. Thus, the defendant may not refuse to participate in a lineup on this basis.

B. THE REMEDY

The remedy for unconstitutional identifications is exclusion of the in-court identification and is rarely granted.

1. Independent Source

A witness may make an in-court identification despite the existence of an unconstitutional pretrial identification if the in-court identification has an independent source. The most common independent source is opportunity to observe at the time of the crime (*e.g.,* the witness viewed the defendant close up for 40 minutes during commission of the crime).

2. Hearing

Admissibility of identification evidence should be determined at a suppression hearing in the absence of the jury, but exclusion of the jury is not constitutionally required. The government bears the burden of proving that: (i) counsel was present; (ii) the accused waived counsel; or (iii) there is an independent source for the in-court identification. The defendant must prove an alleged due process violation.

VI. PRETRIAL PROCEDURES

A. PRELIMINARY HEARING TO DETERMINE PROBABLE CAUSE TO DETAIN

A defendant's liberty can be restricted only on a finding of probable cause. If probable cause has already been determined (*e.g.,* the arrest was pursuant to a warrant or a grand jury indictment), no preliminary hearing to determine probable cause need be held. If probable cause has not already been determined and there are ***significant constraints on an arrestee's liberty*** (*e.g.*, jail or bail, but not release on recognizance), a preliminary hearing to determine probable cause must be held within a reasonable time (*e.g.*, 48 hours). The hearing is an informal, nonadversarial proceeding. There is no real remedy for a denial of the hearing, but evidence discovered as a result of the unlawful detention can be excluded under the exclusionary rule.

B. PRETRIAL DETENTION—BAIL

Most state constitutions create a right to be released on bail unless the charge is a capital one. Generally, bail can be set no higher than is necessary to assure the defendant's appearance at trial. Refusal to grant bail or the setting of excessive bail may be appealed immediately; however, the Supreme Court has upheld portions of the federal Bail Reform Act that allow arrestees to be held without bail if they pose a danger or would fail to appear at trial.

Exam Tip Since the Supreme Court has never held that the Eighth Amendment provision for bail applies to the states, the Eighth Amendment is not a very strong argument against a state's denial of bail. If, however, a state provides for bail (and most states do), arbitrary denials of bail will violate ***due process***—detainees must be given the opportunity to prove eligibility.

1. Defendant Incompetent to Stand Trial

Standards for commitment and subsequent release of defendants incompetent to stand trial must be essentially identical with those for commitment of persons not charged with a crime; otherwise there is a denial of equal protection.

C. GRAND JURIES

1. Use of Grand Jury

The Fifth Amendment right to indictment by grand jury has not been incorporated into the Fourteenth Amendment, but some state constitutions require grand jury indictment. Most states east of the Mississippi and the federal system use the grand jury as a regular part of the charging process. Western states generally charge by filing an information—a written accusation of the crime prepared and presented by the prosecutor.

2. Grand Jury Proceedings

a. Secrecy and Defendant's Lack of Access

Grand jury proceedings are conducted in secret. The defendant has ***no right*** to notice that the grand jury is considering an indictment against him, to be present and confront witnesses at the proceeding, or to introduce evidence before the grand jury.

b. No Right to Counsel or to *Miranda* Warnings

A witness subpoenaed to testify before the grand jury does not have the right to receive *Miranda* warnings, nor is he entitled to a warning that he is a "potential defendant" when called to testify before the grand jury. Witnesses have no right to have an attorney present.

c. No Right to Have Evidence Excluded

A grand jury may base its indictment on evidence that would be inadmissible at trial, and an indicted defendant may not have the indictment quashed on the ground that it is based on illegally obtained evidence.

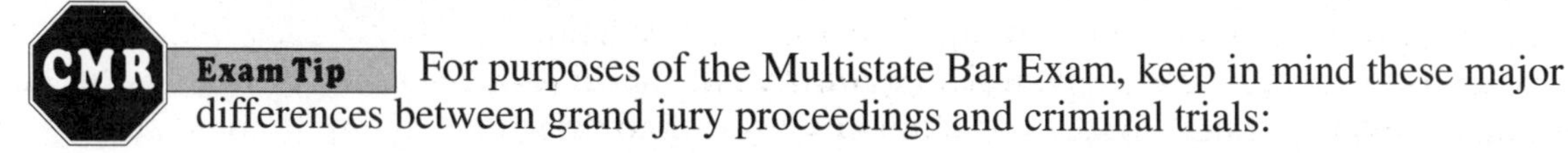

CMR Exam Tip For purposes of the Multistate Bar Exam, keep in mind these major differences between grand jury proceedings and criminal trials:

- The "defendant" (grand jury witness) has no right to have counsel present during his grand jury testimony;
- The grand jury may consider evidence that would be excluded at the criminal trial (*e.g.,* illegally obtained evidence or hearsay); and
- The "defendant" (grand jury witness) must appear if called, although he can refuse to answer specific questions on the grounds that they may incriminate him.

d. No Right to Challenge Subpoena

There is no right to challenge a subpoena on the Fourth Amendment grounds that the grand jury lacked "probable cause"—or any reason at all—to call a witness for questioning.

e. Exclusion of Minorities

A conviction resulting from an indictment issued by a grand jury from which members of a minority group have been excluded will be reversed ***without regard*** to harmlessness of error.

CMR **Exam Tip** For purposes of the Multistate Bar Exam, exclusion of minorities is about the only defect sufficient to quash a grand jury indictment.

D. SPEEDY TRIAL

1. Standards

A determination of whether a defendant's Sixth Amendment right to a speedy trial has been violated is made by an evaluation of the ***totality of the circumstances.*** Factors considered are the length of delay, reason for delay, whether defendant asserted his right, and prejudice to defendant. The remedy for a violation of the right to speedy trial is dismissal with prejudice.

2. When Right Attaches

The right to speedy trial does not attach until the defendant has been ***arrested or charged***. If the defendant is charged and is incarcerated in another jurisdiction, reasonable efforts must be used to obtain the presence of the defendant. Also, it is a violation of the right to speedy trial to permit the prosecution to indefinitely suspend charges.

Note: The defendant does not need to know of the charges for the speedy trial rights to attach.

CMR **Exam Tip** When a speedy trial issue is raised in a question, first check the timing—has the defendant been arrested or charged? If not, there is no right to a speedy trial.

E. PROSECUTORIAL DUTY TO DISCLOSE EXCULPATORY INFORMATION AND NOTICE OF DEFENSES

1. Prosecutor's Duty to Disclose Exculpatory Evidence

The government has a duty to disclose material, exculpatory evidence to the defendant. Failure to disclose such evidence—whether willful or inadvertent—violates the Due Process Clause and is grounds for reversing a conviction if the defendant can prove that: (i) the evidence is ***favorable*** to him because it either impeaches or is exculpatory; and (ii) ***prejudice has resulted*** (*i.e.,* there is a ***reasonable probability*** that the result of the case would have been different if the undisclosed evidence had been presented at trial).

2. Notice of Alibi and Intent to Present Insanity Defense

If the defendant is going to use an alibi or insanity defense, he must notify the prosecution. If an alibi is to be used, the defendant must give the prosecution a list of his witnesses. The prosecution must give the defendant a list of the witnesses it will use to rebut the defense. The prosecutor may not comment at trial on defendant's failure to produce a witness named as supporting the alibi or on failure to present the alibi itself.

F. COMPETENCY TO STAND TRIAL

1. Competency and Insanity Distinguished

Insanity is a defense to a criminal charge based on the defendant's ***mental condition at the time he committed the charged crime***. A defendant acquitted by reason of insanity may not be retried and convicted, although he may be hospitalized under some circumstances. ***Incompetency*** to stand trial, on the other hand, is not a defense to the charge, but rather is a bar to trial. It is based on the defendant's ***mental condition at the time of trial***. If defendant later regains his competency, he can then be tried and convicted.

2. **Due Process Standard**
A defendant is incompetent to stand trial if he either (i) lacks a rational as well as factual understanding of the charges and proceedings, or (ii) lacks sufficient present ability to consult with his lawyer with a reasonable degree of understanding. The state may place on the defendant the burden of proving incompetency by a preponderance of the evidence, but requiring the defendant to show incompetency by "clear and convincing" evidence is unconstitutional.

3. **Detention of Defendant**
A defendant who has successfully asserted the insanity defense may be confined to a mental hospital for a term longer than the maximum period of incarceration for the offense. However, the defendant cannot be indefinitely committed after regaining sanity merely because he is unable to prove himself not dangerous to others.

G. **PRETRIAL PUBLICITY**
Excessive pretrial publicity prejudicial to the defendant may require change of venue or retrial.

VII. TRIAL

A. **BASIC RIGHT TO A FAIR TRIAL**

1. **Right to Public Trial**
The Sixth and Fourteenth Amendments guarantee the right to a public trial, but the right varies with the stage of the proceeding involved.

a. **Pretrial Proceedings**
Preliminary probable cause hearings are presumptively open to the public and press, as are ***pretrial*** suppression hearings, although the latter may be closed to the public under limited circumstances (*e.g.*, the party seeking closure has an overriding interest likely to be prejudiced by disclosure and there is no reasonable alternative besides closure).

b. **Trial**
The press and public have a First Amendment right to attend the ***trial itself***, even when the defense and prosecution agree to close it. The state may constitutionally permit televising criminal proceedings over the defendant's objection.

2. **Right to Unbiased Judge**
Due process is violated if the judge is shown to have ***actual malice*** against the defendant or to have had a ***financial interest*** in having the trial result in a guilty verdict.

3. **Must Judge Be Lawyer?**
A defendant in a minor misdemeanor prosecution has no right to have the trial judge be a lawyer if upon conviction the defendant has a right to trial de novo in a court with a lawyer-judge, but for serious crimes, the judge probably must be law-trained.

4. **Other Due Process Rights**
Due process is violated if:

(i) The trial is conducted in a manner making it ***unlikely that the jury gave the evidence reasonable consideration***;

(ii) The state compels the defendant to stand trial in ***prison clothing***;

(iii) The state compels the defendant to stand trial or appear at penalty phase proceedings ***visibly shackled***, unless the court finds the shackling justified by concerns about courtroom security or escape; or

(iv) The jury is exposed to ***influence favorable to the prosecution***.

Due process does not require the police to preserve all items that might be used as exculpatory evidence at trial, but does prohibit bad faith destruction.

B. RIGHT TO TRIAL BY JURY

1. Right to Jury Trial Only for "Serious" Offenses

There is no constitutional right to jury trial for petty offenses, but only for serious offenses. An offense is serious if imprisonment for ***more than six months*** is authorized. Also, there is no right to jury trial in juvenile delinquency proceedings.

a. Contempt

For civil contempt proceedings, there is no jury trial right. For criminal contempt proceedings, cumulative penalties totaling more than six months cannot be imposed without affording the defendant the right to a jury trial. If a judge summarily imposes punishment for contempt ***during trial***, penalties may aggregate more than six months without a jury trial.

1) Probation

A judge may place a contemnor on probation for up to five years without affording him the right to a jury trial, as long as revocation of probation would not result in imprisonment for more than six months.

2. Number and Unanimity of Jurors

There is no constitutional right to a jury of 12, but there must be at least six jurors to satisfy the right to a jury trial. The Supreme Court has upheld convictions that were less than unanimous, but probably would not approve an 8-4 vote for conviction. Six-person juries must be unanimous.

3. Right to Venire Selected from Representative Cross-Section of Community

A defendant has a right to have the jury selected from a representative cross-section of the community. He need only show the underrepresentation of a distinct and numerically significant group in the venire to show his jury trial right was violated. Note that a defendant does not have the right to proportional representation of all groups on his ***particular jury***.

a. Use of Peremptory Challenges for Racial and Gender-Based Discrimination

Although generally a prosecutor may exercise peremptory challenges for any reason, the Equal Protection Clause forbids the use of peremptory challenges to exclude potential jurors solely on account of their race or gender. An equal protection-based attack on peremptory strikes involves three steps: (i) The defendant must show ***facts or circumstances that raise an inference*** that the exclusion was based on race or gender. (ii) Upon such a showing, the prosecutor must come forward with a ***race-neutral explanation*** for the strike (even an unreasonable explanation is sufficient, as long as it is race-neutral). (iii) The judge then determines whether the prosecutor's explanation was the genuine reason for striking the juror, or merely a pretext for purposeful discrimination. If the judge believes that the ***prosecutor was sincere***, the strike may be upheld.

4. Right to Impartial Jury

a. Right to Questioning on Racial Bias
A defendant is entitled to questioning on voir dire specifically directed to racial prejudice whenever race is bound up in the case or he is accused of an interracial ***capital*** crime.

b. Juror Opposition to Death Penalty
In capital punishment cases, a state may not automatically exclude for cause all those who express a doubt or scruple about the death penalty; it must be determined whether the juror's views would prevent or substantially impair performance of his duties in accordance with his instructions and oath. A death sentence imposed by a jury from which a juror was improperly excluded is subject to automatic reversal.

c. Juror Favoring Death Penalty
If a jury is to decide whether a defendant is to be sentenced to death, on voir dire the defendant must be allowed to ask potential jurors if they would automatically give the death penalty upon a guilty verdict. A juror who answers affirmatively must be excluded for cause because such a juror cannot perform his duties in accordance with instructions as to mitigating circumstances.

d. Use of Peremptory Challenge to Maintain Impartial Jury
If a trial court refuses to exclude for cause a juror whom the court should exclude, and the defendant uses a peremptory challenge to exclude the juror, there is no constitutional violation.

5. Inconsistent Verdicts
Inconsistent verdicts (*e.g.,* finding defendant guilty and co-defendant not guilty on the same evidence) are ***not*** reviewable.

6. Sentence Enhancement
If substantive law provides that a sentence may be increased beyond the statutory maximum for a crime if additional facts (other than prior conviction) are proved, proof of the facts must be ***submitted to the jury*** and proved beyond reasonable doubt; the defendant's right to jury trial is violated if the judge makes the determination. The same general rule applies to sentencing enhancements after guilty pleas. In deciding whether to overturn a sentence for failure to submit a sentencing factor to the jury, the harmless error test is applied.

C. RIGHT TO COUNSEL
A defendant has a right to counsel. Violation of this right ***at trial***, including erroneous disqualification of defendant's privately retained counsel, requires reversal. For nontrial denials, the harmless error test is applied.

1. Stages at Which Applicable
A defendant has a right to be represented by privately retained counsel, or to have counsel appointed for him by the state if he is indigent, at the following stages: (i) custodial police interrogation; (ii) post-indictment interrogation, whether or not custodial; (iii) preliminary hearings to determine probable cause to prosecute; (iv) arraignment; (v) post-charge lineups;

(vi) guilty plea and sentencing; (vii) felony trials; (viii) misdemeanor trials when imprisonment is actually imposed or when a suspended jail sentence is imposed; (ix) overnight recesses during trial; (x) appeals as a matter of right; and (xi) appeals of guilty pleas.

CMR **Exam Tip** Remember that the right to counsel is available in misdemeanor cases only if imprisonment is actually imposed. Thus, if an exam question involves a nonfelony and defendant asks for counsel, is denied, and is convicted, whether the right to counsel has been violated depends on defendant's sentence: if he receives no imprisonment, his right has not been violated; if he receives prison time, his right has been violated.

2. Stages at Which Not Applicable

(i) Blood sampling; (ii) taking of handwriting or voice exemplars; (iii) precharge or investigative lineups; (iv) photo identifications; (v) preliminary hearings to determine probable cause to detain; (vi) brief recesses during the defendant's testimony at trial; (vii) discretionary appeals; (viii) parole and probation revocation proceedings; and (ix) post-conviction proceedings.

3. Waiver of Right to Counsel and Right to Defend Oneself

A defendant has a right to defend himself ***at trial*** if, in the judgment of the judge, his waiver is knowing and intelligent; he need not be found capable of representing himself effectively. Note that a defendant does not have a right to self-representation on appeal.

4. Indigence and Recoupment of Cost

The state generally provides counsel in close cases of indigence, but may then seek reimbursement from those convicted defendants who later become able to pay.

5. Effective Assistance of Counsel

The Sixth Amendment right to counsel includes the right to ***effective*** counsel. This right extends to the first appeal. Effective assistance of counsel is ***generally presumed***.

a. Circumstances Constituting Ineffective Assistance

An ineffective assistance claimant must show:

(i) ***Deficient performance*** by counsel; and

(ii) But for the deficiency, the ***result of the proceeding would have been different*** (*e.g.*, defendant would not have been convicted or his sentence would have been shorter).

The defendant must point out specific deficiencies and cannot base the claim on inexperience, lack of time to prepare, the gravity of the charges, the complexity of defenses, or accessibility of witnesses to counsel.

b. Circumstances Not Constituting Ineffective Assistance

Circumstances ***not*** constituting ***ineffective*** assistance include trial tactics and the failure to raise a constitutional defense that is later invalidated.

6. Conflicts of Interest

Joint representation is not per se invalid. However, if an attorney advises the trial court of a resulting conflict of interest at or before trial, and the court refuses to appoint separate counsel, the defendant is entitled to automatic reversal.

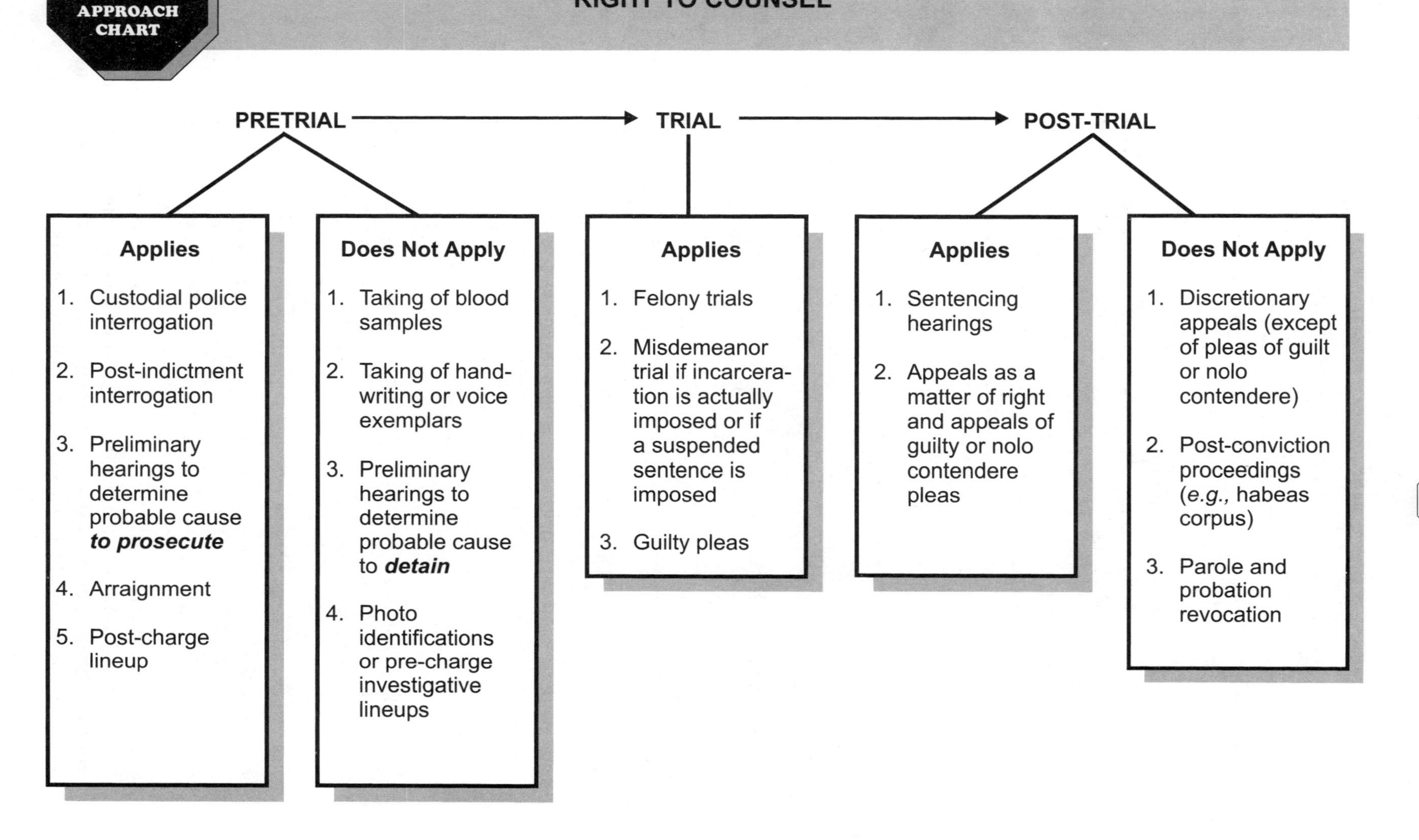
CMR
APPROACH CHART
RIGHT TO COUNSEL
PRETRIAL
TRIAL
POST-TRIAL
Applies
1. Custodial police interrogation
2. Post-indictment interrogation
3. Preliminary hearings to determine probable cause *to prosecute*
4. Arraignment
5. Post-charge lineup
Does Not Apply
1. Taking of blood samples
2. Taking of handwriting or voice exemplars
3. Preliminary hearings to determine probable cause to *detain*
4. Photo identifications or pre-charge investigative lineups
Applies
1. Felony trials
2. Misdemeanor trial if incarceration is actually imposed or if a suspended sentence is imposed
3. Guilty pleas
Applies
1. Sentencing hearings
2. Appeals as a matter of right and appeals of guilty or nolo contendere pleas
Does Not Apply
1. Discretionary appeals (except of pleas of guilt or nolo contendere)
2. Post-conviction proceedings (*e.g.,* habeas corpus)
3. Parole and probation revocation

a. **Conflict with Attorney**
A defendant's conflict of interest with his attorney is rarely a ground for relief.

b. **No Right to Joint Representation**
A defendant has no right to be jointly represented with his co-defendants if the government can show a potential conflict of interest.

7. **Right to Support Services for Defense**
Where a defendant has made a preliminary showing that he is likely to be able to use the insanity defense, the state must provide a psychiatrist for the preparation of the defense.

8. **Seizure of Funds Constitutional**
The right to counsel does not forbid the seizure of drug money and property obtained with drug money, even where defendant was going to use such money or property to pay an attorney.

9. **Right Limited While Testifying**
A defendant has no right to consult with her attorney while testifying, and may be sequestered from her attorney during short breaks (*e.g.,* 15 minutes as opposed to overnight).

D. RIGHT TO CONFRONT WITNESSES

The Sixth Amendment grants to a defendant in a criminal prosecution the right to confront adverse witnesses. The right is not absolute: Face to face confrontation is not required when preventing such confrontation serves an important public purpose (*e.g.,* protecting child witnesses from trauma). Also, a judge may remove a disruptive defendant, and a defendant may voluntarily leave the courtroom during trial.

1. **Introduction of Co-Defendant's Confession**
If two persons are tried together and one has given a confession that implicates the other, the right of confrontation prohibits use of that statement, even where the confession interlocks with the defendant's own confession, which is admitted. However, such a statement may be admitted if:

a. All portions referring to the other defendant can be ***eliminated***;

b. The ***confessing defendant takes the stand*** and subjects himself to cross-examination with respect to truth or falsity of what the statement asserts; or

c. The confession of the nontestifying co-defendant is being used ***to rebut the defendant's claim that his confession was obtained coercively***.

2. **Hearsay**
"Hearsay," if admitted, could deny a defendant the right to confront the declarant. Nevertheless, for a time, the Supreme Court admitted hearsay statements made at a prior judicial proceeding if the declarant was unavailable to testify in court and the statement was supported by indicia of reliability. But in 2004, the Court found that this standard was too lax under the Confrontation Clause. Now a prior testimonial statement of an unavailable witness will be admitted only if the defendant had an opportunity to cross-examine the declarant at the time the statement was made. The Court has not provided a comprehensive definition of

the term "testimonial," but has held that it includes, at a minimum, statements from a preliminary hearing, a grand jury hearing, a former trial, or police interrogation conducted to establish or prove ***past acts***. However, statements from police interrogations intended to aid the police in responding to an ***ongoing emergency***—such as answering a 911 operator's question while reporting a crime in progress—are not testimonial.

Note: The right to confront witnesses can be waived through wrongdoing (*e.g.,* through intimidating a witness). The states are free to decide the standard of proof needed to show waiver; federal courts require the government to show waiver by a preponderance of the evidence.

E. BURDEN OF PROOF AND SUFFICIENCY OF EVIDENCE

The Due Process Clause requires in all criminal cases that the ***state*** prove guilt beyond a reasonable doubt. The presumption of innocence is a basic component of a fair trial. However, the state may generally impose the burden of proof upon the defendant in regard to an affirmative defense, such as insanity or self-defense.

1. Presumptions

A mandatory presumption or a presumption that shifts the burden of proof to the defendant violates the Fourteenth Amendment's requirement that the state prove every element of the crime beyond a reasonable doubt.

VIII. GUILTY PLEAS AND PLEA BARGAINING

A. TAKING THE PLEA

1. Advising Defendant of the Charge, the Potential Penalty, and His Rights

The judge must determine that the plea is ***voluntary and intelligent.*** This must be done by addressing the defendant personally in open court ***on the record***. Specifically, the judge must be sure that the defendant knows and understands things like:

(i) ***The nature of the charge*** to which the plea is offered and the ***crucial elements*** of the crime charged;

(ii) The ***maximum possible penalty*** and any ***mandatory minimum***; and

(iii) That he has a ***right not to plead guilty*** and that if he does plead guilty, he ***waives the right to trial***.

a. Attorney May Inform Defendant

The judge need not personally explain the elements of each charge to the defendant on the record; it is sufficient that the record reflects that the nature of the charge and the elements of the crime were explained to the defendant by his own counsel.

2. Remedy

The remedy for a failure to meet the standards for taking a plea is withdrawal of the plea and pleading anew.

B. COLLATERAL ATTACKS ON GUILTY PLEAS AFTER SENTENCE

Those pleas that are seen as an intelligent choice among a defendant's alternatives are immune from collateral attack. But a plea can be set aside for (i) involuntariness (failure to meet standards for taking a plea), (ii) lack of jurisdiction, (iii) ineffective assistance of counsel, or (iv) failure to keep the plea bargain.

C. PLEA BARGAINING

A plea bargain will be enforced against the prosecutor and the defendant, but not against the judge, who does not have to accept the plea. A guilty plea is not involuntary merely because it was entered in response to the prosecution's threat to charge defendant with a more serious crime if he does not plead guilty. There is no prosecutorial vindictiveness in charging a more serious offense when defendant demands a jury trial.

D. COLLATERAL EFFECTS OF GUILTY PLEAS

A guilty plea conviction may be used as a conviction in other proceedings when relevant (*e.g.*, as the basis for sentence enhancement). However, a guilty plea neither admits the legality of incriminating evidence nor waives Fourth Amendment claims in a subsequent civil damages action.

IX. CONSTITUTIONAL RIGHTS IN RELATION TO SENTENCING AND PUNISHMENT

A. PROCEDURAL RIGHTS IN SENTENCING

A defendant has a ***right to counsel*** during sentencing. The usual sentence may be based on hearsay and uncross-examined reports (*i.e.,* defendant has ***no right to confrontation or cross-examination***). However, where a magnified sentence is based on a statute that requires new findings of fact to be made (*e.g.*, defendant is mentally ill), those facts must be found in a context that grants a right to confrontation and cross-examination.

1. Capital Sentencing

A defendant in a death penalty case must have more opportunity for confrontation than need be given a defendant in other sentencing proceedings.

B. RESENTENCING AFTER SUCCESSFUL APPEAL AND RECONVICTION

If a greater punishment is imposed on a defendant who has been reconvicted after a successful appeal than was imposed at the first trial, the judge must set forth in the record the reasons for the harsher sentence. This ensures that the defendant is not vindictively penalized for exercising his right to appeal.

1. Exceptions

A judge need not give reasons if the greater sentence was imposed upon a de novo trial or in a state that uses jury sentencing, unless the second jury was told of the first jury's sentence.

C. SUBSTANTIVE RIGHTS IN REGARD TO PUNISHMENT

The Eighth Amendment prohibits ***cruel and unusual punishment***. A penalty that is grossly disproportionate to the seriousness of the offense committed is cruel and unusual. State appellate courts do not have to compare the death sentence imposed in a case under appeal with other penalties imposed in similar cases.

1. **Death Penalty**

Any death penalty statute that does NOT give Δ a chance to present mitigating circumstances is unconstitutional.

a. **For Murder**
The death penalty can be imposed only under a statutory scheme that gives the judge or jury reasonable discretion, full information concerning defendants, and guidance in making the decision. The statute cannot be vague. Moreover, it must allow the sentencing body to consider all mitigating evidence.

1) **Based on Prior Convictions**
If the death sentence is partly based on the aggravating factor of defendant's prior conviction, the sentence must be reversed if the prior conviction is invalidated.

2) **Standard of Review**
A death sentence that has been affected by a vague or otherwise unconstitutional factor can still be upheld, but only if all aggravating and mitigating factors involved are reweighed and death is still found to be appropriate.

b. **For Rape or Felony Murder**
The Eighth Amendment prohibits imposition of the death penalty for the crime of raping an adult woman, because the penalty is disproportionate to the offense. Also, the same logic precludes the death penalty for felony murder unless the felony murderer's participation was major and he acted with reckless indifference to the value of human life.

c. **Sanity Requirement**
The Eighth Amendment prohibits executing a prisoner who is insane at the time of execution, even if he was sane at the time the crime was committed.

d. **Mental Retardation**
It is cruel and unusual punishment to impose the death penalty on a person who is mentally retarded.

e. **For Minors**
Execution of persons who were under 18 years old at the time they committed their offense (including murder) violates the Eighth Amendment.

2. **Status Crimes**
A statute that makes it a crime to have a given "status" violates the Eighth Amendment because it punishes a mere propensity to engage in dangerous behavior. However, it is permissible to make criminal specific activity related to a certain status (*e.g.,* driving while intoxicated).

3. **Considering Defendant's Perjury**
In determining the sentence, the trial judge may take into account a belief that the defendant committed perjury while testifying at trial on his own behalf.

4. **Imprisonment of Indigents for Nonpayment**
Where aggregate imprisonment exceeds the maximum period fixed by statute and results directly from involuntary nonpayment of a fine or court costs, there is an impermissible discrimination and violation of the Equal Protection Clause.

X. CONSTITUTIONAL PROBLEMS ON APPEAL

A. NO RIGHT TO APPEAL

There is no federal constitutional right to an appeal.

B. EQUAL PROTECTION AND RIGHT TO COUNSEL ON APPEAL

If an avenue of post-conviction review is provided, conditions that make the review less accessible to the poor than to the rich violate equal protection. Thus, indigents must be given counsel at state expense during a first appeal granted to all ***as a matter of right*** and for appeals of guilty pleas and pleas of nolo contendere.

In a jurisdiction using a two-tier system of appellate courts with discretionary review by the highest court, an indigent defendant need not be provided with counsel during the second, discretionary appeal.

C. RETROACTIVITY

If the Supreme Court announces a new rule of criminal procedure (*e.g.*, one not dictated by precedent) in a case on direct review, the rule must be applied to all other cases on direct review.

XI. COLLATERAL ATTACK UPON CONVICTION

A. AVAILABILITY OF COLLATERAL ATTACK

After appeal is no longer available or has proven unsuccessful, defendants may generally still attack their convictions collaterally.

B. HABEAS CORPUS PROCEEDING

An indigent has no right to appointed counsel at a habeas corpus proceeding. Petitioner has the burden of proof by ***preponderance of evidence*** to show an unlawful detention. The state may appeal the grant of a writ of habeas corpus. A defendant generally may bring a habeas petition only if the defendant is in custody. Generally, this includes anyone who has not fully served the sentence about which he wishes to complain.

XII. RIGHTS DURING PUNISHMENT

A. RIGHT TO COUNSEL AT PAROLE AND PROBATION REVOCATION

If revocation of probation also involves imposition of a new sentence, the defendant is entitled to representation by counsel in all cases in which she is entitled to counsel at trial. If, after probation revocation, an already imposed sentence of imprisonment springs into application, or if the case involves parole revocation, the right to counsel is available ***only if representation is necessary*** to a fair hearing (*e.g.*, defendant denies commission of alleged acts, or issues are otherwise difficult to present and develop).

B. PRISONERS' RIGHTS

Prisoners' rights issues rarely appear on the Multistate Bar Exam, and when they do appear they usually involve the same constitutional analysis as set out in the general constitutional law outline. The most important rules peculiar to criminal procedure are:

1. **Due Process**
   Prison regulations impinge on due process rights only if the regulations impose "***atypical and significant hardship***" in relation to the ordinary incidents of prison life.

2. **No Fourth Amendment Protection in Cells**
   Prisoners have no reasonable expectation of privacy in their cells and so have no Fourth Amendment protection with respect to searches of their cells.

3. **Right of Access to Courts**
   Prisoners must be given reasonable access to the courts.

4. **First Amendment Rights**
   Prisoners' First Amendment rights of freedom of speech, association, and religion may be burdened by regulations ***reasonably related to penological interests*** (*e.g.*, running a safe and secure prison). Note that ***incoming*** mail can be broadly regulated, but outgoing mail generally cannot be regulated. Note also that a federal statute prohibits states from interfering with a prisoner's religious practices absent a compelling interest.

5. **Right to Adequate Medical Care**
   Prisoners have a right to adequate medical care under the Eighth Amendment prohibition against cruel and unusual punishment.

C. NO RIGHT TO BE FREE FROM DISABILITIES UPON COMPLETION OF SENTENCE
A person convicted of a felony may be unable to vote in state elections, and this disability can constitutionally continue beyond the term of her sentence.

XIII. DOUBLE JEOPARDY

A. WHEN JEOPARDY ATTACHES
Under the Fifth Amendment, a person may not be retried for the same offense once jeopardy has attached. Jeopardy attaches in a jury trial at the empaneling and swearing of the jury. In bench trials jeopardy attaches when the first witness is sworn. Commencement of a juvenile proceeding bars a subsequent criminal trial for the same offense. Jeopardy generally does not attach in civil proceedings other than juvenile proceedings.

B. EXCEPTIONS PERMITTING RETRIAL
Certain exceptions permit retrial of a defendant even if jeopardy has attached:

1. A state may retry a defendant whose first trial ends in a ***hung jury***.

2. A trial may be discontinued and the defendant reprosecuted for the same offense when there is ***manifest necessity*** to abort the original trial or when termination occurs at the behest of the defendant on any ground not constituting acquittal on the merits.

3. A state may retry a defendant who has ***successfully appealed*** a conviction unless the ground for reversal was insufficient evidence to support a guilty verdict. Retrial is permitted when reversal is based on the ***weight*** (rather than sufficiency) of the evidence. However, on retrial,

a defendant ***may not be tried for a greater offense*** than that for which he was convicted. A harsher sentence may be imposed for reasons other than vindictiveness for taking an appeal, but if the jury found that the death penalty was not appropriate in the first trial, a death sentence may not be imposed at the second trial.

4. Charges may be reinstated after a defendant ***breaches*** her ***plea bargain***.

C. SAME OFFENSE

1. General Rule—When Two Crimes Not the Same Offense

Two crimes are the same offense unless ***each crime requires proof of an additional element*** that the other does not require, even though some of the same facts may be necessary to prove both crimes.

2. Cumulative Punishments for Offenses Constituting the Same Crime

Even if two crimes constitute the same offense under this test, multiple punishments are permissible if there was a ***legislative intent*** to have the cumulative punishments (*e.g.*, a defendant can be sentenced both for robbery and using a weapon during the commission of a crime if statutes so provide).

3. Lesser Included Offenses

Attachment of jeopardy for a greater offense bars retrial for lesser included offenses. Attachment of jeopardy for a lesser included offense bars retrial for a greater offense, except that retrial for murder is permitted if the victim dies after attachment of jeopardy for battery. A state may continue to prosecute a charged offense despite defendant's guilty plea to a lesser included or "allied" offense stemming from the same incident.

a. Exception—New Evidence

An exception to the double jeopardy bar exists if unlawful conduct that is subsequently used to prove the greater offense (i) has not occurred at the time of prosecution for the lesser offense or (ii) has not been discovered despite due diligence.

4. Conduct Used as a Sentence Enhancer

The Double Jeopardy Clause is not violated when a person is indicted for a crime the conduct of which was already used to enhance the defendant's sentence for another crime.

5. Subsequent Civil Actions

The Double Jeopardy Clause prohibits only repetitive ***criminal*** prosecutions. Thus, a state generally is free to bring a civil action against a defendant even if the defendant has already been criminally tried for the conduct out of which the civil action arises. Similarly, the government may bring a criminal action even though the defendant has already faced civil trial for the same conduct unless it is clear from the statutory scheme that the purpose or effect of the statute is to impose a criminal penalty.

D. SEPARATE SOVEREIGNS

The constitutional prohibition against double jeopardy does not apply to trials by separate sovereigns. Thus, a person may be tried for the same conduct by both the state and federal governments or by two states, but not by a state and its municipalities.

CMR **Exam Tip** Double jeopardy questions on the MBE occasionally raise the separate sovereign issue. The rule is simple: Separate sovereigns ***can*** try a defendant for the same offense. Beware of facts that try to divert you from this easy issue (*e.g.,* statements about juries being empaneled or witnesses sworn in—things that go to attachment). Attachment does not matter if there are two separate sovereigns.

On the other hand, remember that municipalities are considered part of the state, and so both a state and its municipality ***cannot*** validly try a defendant for the same offense.

E. APPEALS BY PROSECUTION

Even after jeopardy has attached, the prosecution may appeal any dismissal on defendant's motion that does not constitute an acquittal on the merits. Also, the Double Jeopardy Clause does not bar appeals by the prosecution if a successful appeal would not require a retrial. There is no bar to a government appeal of a ***sentence*** pursuant to statute permitting such review. However, if the jury fails to impose the death penalty, the prosecution may not seek the death penalty on retrial after successful appeal.

F. COLLATERAL ESTOPPEL

Under the doctrine of collateral estoppel, a defendant may not be tried or convicted of a crime if a prior prosecution by that sovereignty resulted in a factual determination inconsistent with one required for conviction.

XIV. PRIVILEGE AGAINST COMPELLED SELF-INCRIMINATION

A. WHO MAY ASSERT THE PRIVILEGE

Only natural persons may assert the privilege, not corporations or partnerships. The privilege is personal and so may be asserted by a defendant, witness, or party only if the answer to the question might tend to incriminate him.

B. WHEN PRIVILEGE MAY BE ASSERTED

A person may refuse to answer a question whenever his response might furnish a link in the chain of evidence needed to prosecute him. The privilege must be claimed in civil proceedings to prevent the privilege from being waived for a later criminal prosecution. Thus, if an individual responds to questions instead of claiming the privilege during a civil proceeding, he cannot later bar that evidence from a criminal prosecution on compelled self-incrimination grounds.

C. METHOD FOR INVOKING PRIVILEGE

A ***criminal defendant*** has a right not to take the witness stand at trial and not to be asked to do so. In any other situation, the privilege does not permit a person to avoid being sworn as a witness or being asked questions. Rather, the person must listen to the questions and specifically invoke the privilege rather than answer the questions. *Note:* Merely being required to furnish one's name after a *Terry* stop (*see* III.B.3.a.1), *supra*) generally does not violate the Fifth Amendment because disclosure of one's name generally poses no danger of incrimination.

D. SCOPE OF PROTECTION

1. **Testimonial but Not Physical Evidence**
The Fifth Amendment privilege protects only testimonial or communicative evidence and not real or physical evidence. For a suspect's communication to be considered testimonial, it must relate a factual assertion or disclose information.

2. **Compulsory Production of Documents**
A person served with a subpoena requiring production of documents tending to incriminate him generally has no basis in the privilege to refuse to comply, because the act of producing the documents does not involve testimonial self-incrimination.

3. **Seizure of Incriminating Documents**
The Fifth Amendment does not prohibit law enforcement officers from searching for and seizing documents tending to incriminate a person.

4. **When Does Violation Occur?**
A violation of the Self-Incrimination Clause does not occur until a person's compelled statements are used against him in a criminal case.

CMR Exam Tip For purposes of the Multistate Bar Exam, two of the most important things to remember about the Fifth Amendment self-incrimination privilege are:

- Only ***testimonial*** evidence is protected. Thus, a defendant has no self-incrimination basis to object to a lineup or other identification procedure—even if he is asked to say certain words (*e.g.*, "Your money or your life!"). This procedure does not involve testimonial evidence; the words are used for identification purposes and not as testimony.

- Likewise, only ***compelled*** testimonial evidence is privileged. Thus, if the defendant produced a writing of his own free will (*e.g.*, took incriminating notes of a meeting), the police may seize this writing, or the defendant may be compelled to produce it by subpoena, because he was not compelled to make the statement originally.

E. PROHIBITION AGAINST BURDENS ON ASSERTION OF PRIVILEGE

1. **Comments on Defendant's Silence**
A prosecutor may not comment on a defendant's silence after being arrested and receiving *Miranda* warnings. Neither may the prosecutor comment on a defendant's failure to testify at trial. However, a defendant, upon timely motion, is entitled to have the judge instruct the jury that they may not draw an adverse inference from the defendant's failure to testify. Moreover, the judge may offer this instruction sua sponte, even over the defendant's objection.

   a. **Exception**
   A prosecutor can comment on a defendant's failure to take the stand when the comment is in response to defense counsel's assertion that the defendant was not allowed to explain his side of the story.

   b. **Harmless Error Test Applies**
   When a prosecutor impermissibly comments on a defendant's silence, the harmless error test applies.

2. **Penalties for Failure to Testify**
The state may not chill exercise of the Fifth Amendment privilege against compelled self-incrimination by imposing penalties for failure to testify.

F. ELIMINATION OF PRIVILEGE

1. **Grant of Immunity**
A witness may be compelled to answer questions if granted adequate immunity from prosecution.

a. **"Use and Derivative Use" Immunity Sufficient**
"Use and derivative use" immunity guarantees that the witness's testimony and evidence located by means of the testimony will not be used against the witness. However, the witness may still be prosecuted if the prosecutor shows that the evidence to be used against the witness was derived from a source independent of the immunized testimony.

b. **Immunized Testimony Involuntary**
Testimony obtained by a promise of immunity is coerced and therefore involuntary. Thus, immunized testimony may not be used for impeachment of a defendant's testimony at trial. However, any immunized statements, whether true or untrue, can be used in a trial for perjury.

c. **Use of Testimony by Another Sovereign Prohibited**
Federal prosecutors may not use evidence obtained as a result of a state grant of immunity, and vice versa.

2. **No Possibility of Incrimination**
A person has no privilege against compelled self-incrimination if there is no possibility of incrimination (*e.g.*, statute of limitations has run).

3. **Scope of Immunity**
Immunity extends only to the offenses to which the question relates and does not protect against perjury committed during the immunized testimony.

G. WAIVER OF PRIVILEGE
A criminal defendant, by taking the witness stand, waives the privilege to the extent necessary to subject him to any cross-examination. A witness waives the privilege only if he discloses incriminating information.

XV. JUVENILE COURT PROCEEDINGS

A. RIGHTS THAT MUST BE AFFORDED
The following rights must be given to a child during trial of a delinquency proceeding: (i) written ***notice*** of charges, (ii) ***assistance of counsel***, (iii) ***opportunity to confront*** and cross-examine witnesses, (iv) the ***right not to testify***, and (v) the right to have "***guilt***" ***established by proof beyond reasonable doubt***.

The Supreme Court has held that there is ***no*** right to trial by jury in delinquency proceedings. Pretrial detention of a juvenile is allowed where it is found that the juvenile is a "serious risk" to society, as long as the detention is for a strictly limited time before trial may be held.

B. DOUBLE JEOPARDY

If the juvenile court adjudicates a child a delinquent, jeopardy has attached and the prohibition against double jeopardy prevents him from being tried as an adult for the same behavior.

XVI. FORFEITURE ACTIONS

A. INTRODUCTION

Actions for forfeiture are brought directly against property and are generally regarded as quasi-criminal in nature. Certain constitutional rights may exist for those persons whose interest in property would be lost by forfeiture.

B. RIGHT TO PRE-SEIZURE NOTICE AND HEARING

The owner of ***personal*** property (and others with an interest in it) is not constitutionally entitled to notice and a hearing before the property is seized for purposes of a forfeiture proceeding. A hearing is, however, required before final forfeiture of the property. Where ***real property*** is seized, notice and an opportunity to be heard is required before the seizure of the real property unless the government can prove that exigent circumstances justify immediate seizure.

C. MAY BE SUBJECT TO EIGHTH AMENDMENT

1. General Rule

The Supreme Court has held that the Excessive Fines Clause of the Eighth Amendment applies only to fines imposed as punishment; it does not apply to civil fines. Thus, ***penal*** forfeitures are subject to the Clause, but ***civil*** forfeitures are not. Even if the Clause applies, the forfeiture will not be "excessive" unless ***grossly disproportionate*** to the gravity of the offense.

2. Compare—Nonpunitive Forfeiture

a. Civil In Rem Forfeitures

Civil in rem forfeitures generally are ***not*** subject to the Excessive Fines Clause.

b. Monetary Forfeitures

Monetary forfeitures (*e.g.*, forfeiture of twice the value of illegally imported goods) brought in civil actions generally are ***not*** subject to the Eighth Amendment.

D. PROTECTION FOR "INNOCENT OWNER" NOT REQUIRED

The Due Process Clause does ***not*** require forfeiture statutes to provide an "innocent owner" defense (*e.g.*, a defense that the owner took all reasonable steps to avoid having the property used by another for illegal purposes), at least where the innocent owner ***voluntarily entrusted*** the property to the wrongdoer.

EVIDENCE

TABLE OF CONTENTS

EVIDENCE

I. GENERAL CONSIDERATIONS

A. SOURCES OF EVIDENCE LAW

There are three sources of evidence law: (i) state common law and miscellaneous state statutes, (ii) comprehensive state evidence codes, and (iii) the Federal Rules of Evidence.

CMR **Exam Tip** The Federal Rules govern on the Multistate Bar Examination ("MBE"). Beware of answer choices stating the correct common law rule, rather than the Federal Rule.

B. THRESHOLD ADMISSIBILITY ISSUES

Generally, relevant evidence is admissible if it is competent. Under the Federal Rules, "relevant evidence" tends to prove (probativeness) any fact of consequence to the action (materiality). Evidence is competent if it does not violate any exclusionary rule (*e.g.,* the hearsay rule).

C. DIRECT AND CIRCUMSTANTIAL EVIDENCE

Direct evidence involves no inferences. It is testimony or real evidence that speaks directly to a material issue in the case. Circumstantial evidence is indirect and relies on inference. It is evidence of a subsidiary or collateral fact from which, alone or in conjunction with other facts, the existence of the material issue can be inferred.

D. LIMITED ADMISSIBILITY

Evidence may be admissible for one purpose but not another, or admissible against one party but not another. In these situations, the court must, upon request, restrict the evidence to its proper scope and instruct the jury accordingly.

II. RELEVANCE

CMR **Exam Tip** Relevance questions should be approached in two steps. ***Step 1***: Determine whether the evidence is relevant (*i.e.,* tends to prove or disprove a material fact). ***Step 2***: If relevant, determine whether the evidence should nonetheless be excluded based on: (i) judicial discretion (*i.e.,* probative value outweighed by prejudice, etc.), or (ii) public policy (*e.g.,* insurance, subsequent repairs).

A. DETERMINING RELEVANCE

Evidence is relevant if it tends to make the existence of any fact of consequence to the outcome of the action more probable than it would be without the evidence.

1. General Rule—Must Relate to Time, Event, or Person in Controversy

Generally, the evidence must relate to the time, event, or person involved in the ***present*** litigation; otherwise, it is not relevant.

When considering the relevance of evidence relating to a time, event, or person other than the one at issue, an important factor is its proximity in time to the current events.

2. Exceptions—Certain Similar Occurrences Are Relevant

Previous similar occurrences may be relevant if they are probative of a material issue and that probativeness outweighs the risk of confusion or unfair prejudice. The following are examples of relevant similar occurrences:

CMR APPROACH CHART

DETERMINING ADMISSIBILITY OF EVIDENCE

STEP 1
Is the evidence ***relevant*** ?

STEP 2
Is there a proper ***foundation*** (*e.g.,* has the competency of the witness, the authenticity of the evidence, or the reliability of the scientific test been established)?

STEP 3
Is the evidence in the proper ***form*** (*e.g.,* questions are properly phrased, answers are within the requirements for lay and expert opinion, and documents comply with the best evidence rule)?

STEP 4
Is the evidence beyond the application of, or within an exception to, one of the following ***exclusionary rules*** ?

- Discretionary exclusion for prejudice (Rule 403)
- Policy-based exclusions (*i.e.,* subsequent remedial measures, settlement negotiations)
- Privilege
- Hearsay
- Parol evidence

ADMISSIBLE

a. **Causation**
Complicated issues of causation may be established by evidence concerning other times, events, or persons (*e.g.,* damage to nearby homes caused by D's blasting is relevant to prove D's blasting damaged P's home).

b. **Prior False Claims or Same Bodily Injury**
Evidence that a person has previously filed similar tort claims or has been involved in prior accidents is generally inadmissible to show the invalidity of the present claim. But evidence that the party has made previous similar false claims or claims involving the same bodily injury is usually relevant to prove that: (i) the present claim is likely to be false, or (ii) the plaintiff's condition is attributable in whole or in part to the prior injury.

c. **Similar Accidents or Injuries Caused by Same Event or Condition**
Evidence of prior accidents or injuries caused by the same event or condition is admissible to prove: (i) the ***existence*** of a dangerous condition, (ii) that the defendant had ***knowledge*** of the dangerous condition, and (iii) that the dangerous condition was the ***cause*** of the present injury.

1) **Absence of Similar Accidents**
Many courts are reluctant to admit evidence of the ***absence*** of similar accidents to show absence of negligence or lack of a defect. However, evidence of the absence of complaints is admissible to show the defendant's lack of knowledge of the danger.

d. **Previous Similar Acts Admissible to Prove Intent**
Similar conduct previously committed by a party may be introduced to prove the party's present motive or intent when such elements are relevant (*e.g.,* history of school segregation admissible to show motive for current exclusion of minorities).

e. **Rebutting Claim of Impossibility**
The requirement that prior occurrences be similar to the litigated act may be relaxed when used to rebut a claim of impossibility (*e.g.,* defendant's claim that car will not go above 50 m.p.h. can be rebutted by showing occasions when car went more than 50 m.p.h.).

f. **Sales of Similar Property**
Evidence of sales of similar personal or real property that are not too remote in time is admissible to prove value. Prices quoted in mere offers to purchase are not admissible. However, evidence of unaccepted offers by a party to the action to buy or sell the property may be used against him as an admission.

g. **Habit**
Habit describes a person's ***regular response*** to a specific set of circumstances. In contrast, character describes one's disposition in respect to general traits. Under Federal Rule 406, evidence of the habit of a person is relevant to prove that the conduct of the person on a particular occasion was in conformity with the habit.

CMR **Exam Tip** Watch for words such as ***"instinctively"*** and ***"automatically"*** in a question's fact pattern. These words indicate habit.

CHARACTER EVIDENCE VS. HABIT EVIDENCE

Character Evidence	Habit Evidence
"Sally is always in a hurry."	"Sally always takes the stairs two at a time."
"Bart is a drunk."	"Bart stops at Charlie's tavern every night after work and has exactly four beers."
"Jeff is a careless driver."	"Jeff never slows down for the YIELD sign at the end of the street."
"Lara is very conscientious about the maintenance of her car."	"Lara checks the brakes on her car every Sunday before church."

h. **Industrial or Business Routine**
Evidence that a particular business had an established business routine is relevant as tending to show that a particular event occurred.

i. **Industry Custom as Evidence of Standard of Care**
Industry custom may be offered to show adherence to or deviance from an industry-wide standard of care. However, industry custom is not conclusive on this point; *e.g.*, an entire industry may be acting negligently.

B. DISCRETIONARY EXCLUSION OF RELEVANT EVIDENCE

A trial judge has broad discretion to exclude relevant evidence if its ***probative value is substantially outweighed*** by the danger of unfair prejudice, confusion of issues, misleading the jury, undue delay, or waste of time.

CMR **Exam Tip** Under the Federal Rules, ***unfair surprise*** is ***not*** a valid ground upon which to exclude relevant evidence.

C. EXCLUSION OF RELEVANT EVIDENCE FOR PUBLIC POLICY REASONS

Certain evidence of questionable relevance is excluded by the Federal Rules because public policy favors the behavior involved. Subsequent repairs, for example, are not admissible to show negligence because society wishes to encourage the immediate repair of dangerous conditions. Evidence excluded for public policy reasons includes the following:

1. **Liability Insurance**
Evidence of insurance against liability is ***not admissible to show negligence or ability to pay*** a substantial judgment. However, it may be admissible: (i) to prove ownership or control, (ii) to impeach, or (iii) as part of an admission.

ADMISSIBILITY OF RELEVANT EVIDENCE

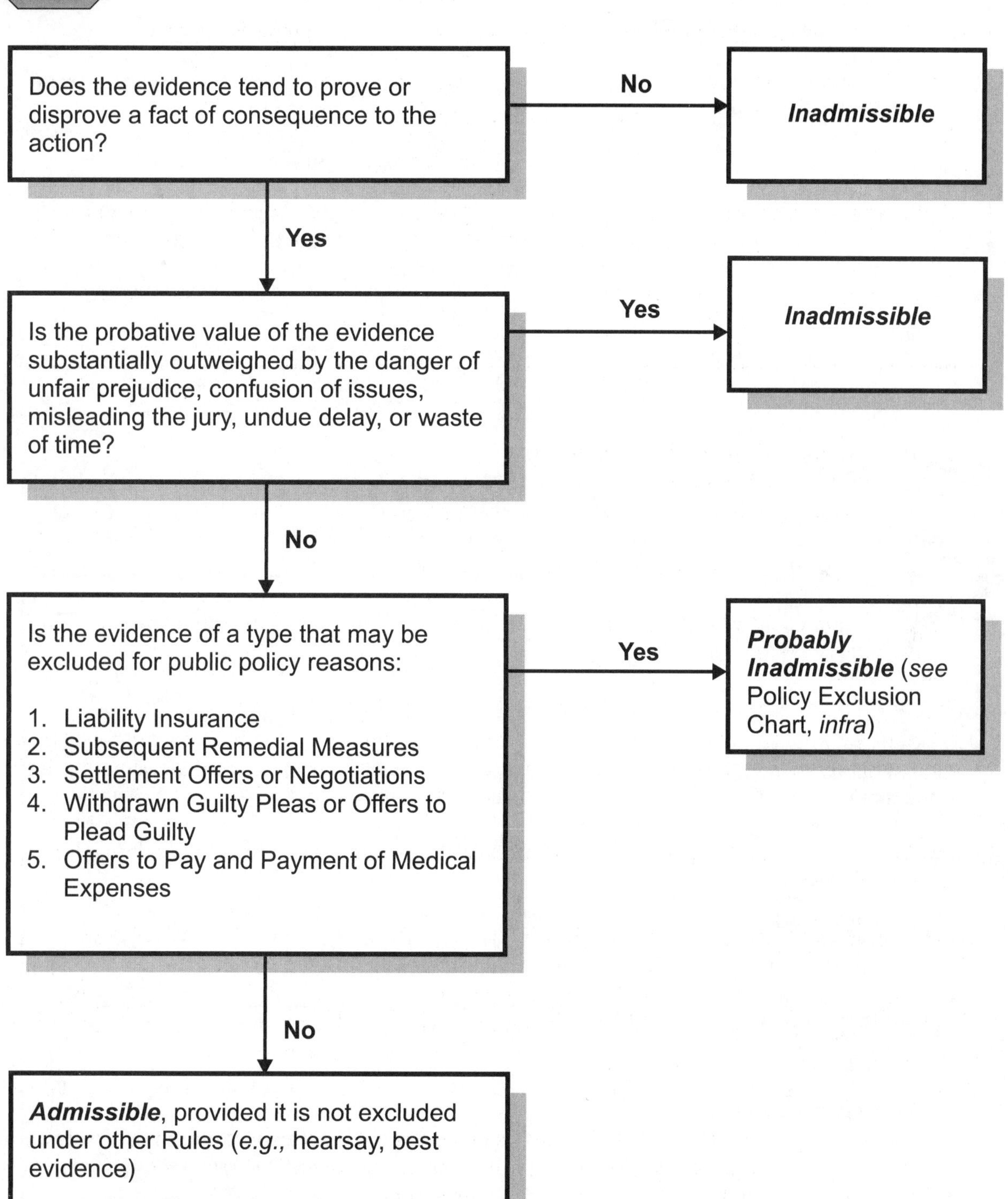

2. **Subsequent Remedial Measures**
Evidence of repairs or other precautionary measures made following an injury is ***not admissible*** to prove negligence, culpable conduct, a defect in a product or its design, or a need for a warning or instruction. However, it may be admissible to: (i) prove ownership or control, (ii) rebut a claim that the precaution was not feasible, or (iii) prove that the opposing party has destroyed evidence.

3. **Settlement Offers and Withdrawn Guilty Pleas**
Evidence of compromises or offers to compromise is ***not admissible to prove liability for, or invalidity of, a claim that is disputed as to validity or amount***. Not even direct admissions of liability during compromise negotiations are admissible. Likewise, withdrawn guilty pleas and offers to plead guilty are inadmissible.

CMR **Exam Tip** For the exclusionary rule to apply to settlement negotiations, there must be some indication that a party is going to ***make a claim*** (although the party need not have actually filed suit). Furthermore, the claim must be ***in dispute*** as to liability or amount.

4. **Offers to Pay Medical Expenses**
Payment of or offers to pay the injured party's medical expenses are inadmissible. However, unlike the situation with compromise negotiations, admissions of fact accompanying offers to pay medical expenses are admissible.

CMR SUMMARY CHART

EVIDENCE THAT MAY BE EXCLUDED FOR POLICY REASONS

Evidence	Inadmissible	Admissible
Liability Insurance	To prove negligence or ability to pay	To prove ownership or control, as impeachment, or as part of an admission
Subsequent Remedial Measures	To prove negligence, culpable conduct, a defect in a product or its design, or a need for a warning or instruction	To prove ownership or control, to rebut a claim that precautions were impossible, or to prove destruction of evidence
Settlement Offers or Negotiations	To prove liability or invalidity of a claim that is disputed as to validity or amount	For all other purposes
Withdrawn Guilty Pleas and Offers to Plead Guilty	For nearly all purposes	Not admissible
Offers to Pay and Payment of Medical Expenses	To prove culpable conduct	For all other purposes (Admissions of fact accompanying an offer to pay medical expenses are admissible)

D. CHARACTER EVIDENCE—A SPECIAL RELEVANCE PROBLEM

Character evidence may be offered as substantive, rather than impeachment, evidence to: (i) prove character when it is the ***ultimate issue*** in the case, or (ii) serve as ***circumstantial evidence*** of how a person probably acted. The latter is more heavily tested and is the focus of the following discussion.

1. Means of Proving Character

Depending on the jurisdiction, the purpose of the offer, and the nature of the case, one or all of the following methods of proving character may be available:

a. Evidence of ***specific acts***;

b. ***Opinion testimony*** of a witness who knows the person; and

c. Testimony as to the person's general ***reputation*** in the community.

2. Generally Not Admissible in Civil Cases

Unless character is directly in issue (*e.g.,* defamation), evidence of character offered by either party to prove the conduct of a person in the litigated event is generally not admissible in a civil case. For example, a plaintiff in a suit involving a car accident may not introduce evidence that the defendant is usually a reckless driver to prove that she was negligent at the time in question, nor may the defendant introduce evidence that she is generally a cautious driver.

3. Accused in Criminal Case—Generally Only Accused Can Initiate

The prosecution cannot initiate evidence of bad character of the defendant merely to show that she is more likely to have committed the crime. (Although the prosecution may introduce evidence of prior misconduct for reasons other than propensity to commit the crime. *See* 5., below.) The accused, however, may introduce evidence of her good character to show her innocence of the alleged crime.

a. How Defendant Proves Character

Under the Federal Rules, a witness for the defendant may testify as to the defendant's good ***reputation*** for the trait in question and may give his personal ***opinion*** concerning that trait of the defendant.

CMR **Exam Tip** Remember that a defendant does not put his character in issue merely by testifying. Taking the stand places the defendant's ***credibility*** (as opposed to character) in issue; *i.e.,* the prosecution is limited to impeachment evidence rather than substantive character evidence.

b. How Prosecution Rebuts Defendant's Character Evidence

Once the defendant opens the door by introducing character evidence, the prosecution may rebut it by:

1) ***Cross-examining the character witness*** regarding the basis for his testimony, including whether he knows or has heard of specific instances of the defendant's misconduct.

CMR **Exam Tip** ***Any*** misconduct, including prior arrests, may be inquired about while cross-examining a defendant's character witness. Remember, however, that the prosecutor is limited to inquiry of the witness; she ***may not introduce any extrinsic evidence*** of the misconduct. Be careful to distinguish asking a ***character*** witness whether he is aware of the ***defendant's*** prior arrests, which is proper, and impeaching a witness with the ***witness's*** arrests, which is improper. (*See* VI. E. 3.d., *infra.*)

2) ***Calling qualified witnesses*** to testify to the defendant's bad reputation or give their opinions of the defendant's character.

4. Victim in Criminal Case

Except in rape cases, the defendant may introduce reputation or opinion evidence of a bad character trait of the alleged crime victim when it is relevant to show the defendant's innocence. Once the defendant has introduced evidence of a bad character trait of the victim, the prosecution may counter with reputation or opinion evidence of (i) the victim's ***good*** character, or (ii) the ***defendant's*** bad character for the ***same trait***.

a. Rape Victim's Past Behavior Generally Inadmissible

In any civil or criminal proceeding involving alleged sexual misconduct, evidence offered to prove the sexual behavior or sexual disposition of the victim is generally inadmissible.

1) Exceptions in Criminal Cases

In a criminal case, a victim's sexual behavior is admissible to prove that someone other than the defendant is the source of semen, injury, or other physical evidence. Also, specific instances of sexual behavior between the victim and the accused are admissible by the prosecution for any reason and by the defense to prove consent.

2) Exceptions in Civil Cases

In a civil case, evidence of the alleged victim's sexual behavior is admissible if it is not excluded by any other rule and its probative value substantially outweighs the danger of harm to the victim and of unfair prejudice to any party. Evidence of an alleged victim's reputation is admissible only if it has been placed in controversy by the victim.

5. Specific Acts of Misconduct

Evidence of a person's other crimes or misconduct is inadmissible if offered solely to establish a criminal disposition or bad character.

a. Admissible If Independently Relevant

Evidence of other crimes or misconduct is admissible if these acts are ***relevant to some issue other than the defendant's character or disposition*** to commit the crime or act charged. Such issues include motive (*e.g.,* burn building to hide embezzlement), intent (*i.e.,* guilty knowledge, lack of good faith), absence of mistake or accident, identity (*e.g.,* stolen gun used or "signature" crimes), or common plan or scheme. In a criminal case, the prosecution must, upon request, provide reasonable notice prior to trial of the general nature of any of this type of evidence it intends to introduce.

CMR **Exam Tip** A convenient way to remember the issues for which evidence of prior acts of misconduct is admissible is through the mnemonic device "MIMIC":

Motive
Intent
Mistake (absence of)
Identity
Common plan or scheme

1) **Requirements for Admissibility**
To be admissible: (i) there must be sufficient evidence to support a jury finding that the defendant committed the prior act, ***and*** (ii) its probative value must not be substantially outweighed by the danger of unfair prejudice (or the judge, in her discretion, may exclude it).

b. **Prior Acts of Sexual Assault or Child Molestation**
Evidence of a defendant's prior acts of sexual assault or child molestation is admissible in a case where the defendant is accused of committing an act of sexual assault or child molestation. The party intending to offer this evidence must disclose it to the defendant 15 days before trial (or later with good cause).

III. JUDICIAL NOTICE

A. JUDICIAL NOTICE OF FACT

Judicial notice is the recognition of a fact as true without formal presentation of evidence.

1. **Facts Appropriate for Judicial Notice**
Courts take judicial notice of ***indisputable facts*** that are either matters of ***common knowledge*** in the community (notorious facts) or ***capable of verification*** by resort to easily accessible sources of unquestionable accuracy (manifest facts). Courts have increasingly taken judicial notice of scientific principles as a type of manifest fact. Judicial notice of such facts may be taken at any time, whether or not requested.

2. **Procedural Aspects of Judicial Notice**
If a court does not take judicial notice of a fact on its own accord, a party must formally request that notice be taken of the particular fact. Judicial notice may be taken for the first time on appeal. The Federal Rules provide that a judicially noticed fact is conclusive in a civil case but not in a criminal case. In a criminal case, the jury is instructed that it may, but is not required to, accept as conclusive any judicially noticed fact.

3. **"Adjudicative" and "Legislative" Facts**
The Federal Rules, and thus their requirements, govern only judicial notice of "adjudicative" facts (*i.e.,* those that relate to the particular case). "Legislative" facts (*i.e.,* those relating to legal reasoning and lawmaking), such as the rationale behind the spousal privilege, need not be of common knowledge nor capable of indisputable verification to be judicially noticed.

B. JUDICIAL NOTICE OF LAW—MANDATORY OR PERMISSIVE

Courts ***must*** take judicial notice of federal and state law and the official regulations of the forum state and the federal government. Courts ***may*** take judicial notice of municipal ordinances and private acts or resolutions of Congress or of the local state legislature. Laws of foreign countries may also be judicially noticed.

IV. REAL EVIDENCE

A. IN GENERAL

Real or demonstrative evidence is actual physical evidence addressed directly to the trier of fact. Real evidence may be direct, circumstantial, original, or prepared (demonstrative).

B. GENERAL CONDITIONS OF ADMISSIBILITY

Real evidence must be relevant and meet the following legal requirements:

1. Authentication

The object must be identified as what the proponent claims it to be, either by:

a. ***Testimony*** of a witness that she ***recognizes*** the object as what the proponent claims it is (*e.g.,* witness testifies that a gun is the one found at the crime scene); or

b. Evidence that the object has been held in a ***substantially unbroken chain of possession*** (*e.g.,* blood taken for blood-alcohol test).

2. Condition of Object

If the condition of the object is significant, it must be shown to be in substantially the same condition at trial.

3. Balancing Test—Legal Relevance

Some auxiliary policy or principle may outweigh the need to admit the real evidence. Such policies include physical inconvenience of bringing the object into the courtroom, indecency or impropriety, or undue prejudice.

C. PARTICULAR TYPES OF REAL PROOF

1. Reproductions and Explanatory Real Evidence

Relevant photographs, diagrams, maps, or other reproductions are admissible if their value is not outweighed by the danger of unfair prejudice. However, items used entirely for explanatory purposes are permitted at a trial, but are usually not admitted into evidence (*i.e.,* they are not given to the jury during its deliberations).

2. Maps, Charts, Models, Etc.

Maps, charts, models, etc., are usually admissible for the purpose of illustrating testimony, but must be authenticated (testimonial evidence that they are faithful reproductions of the object or thing depicted).

3. Exhibition of Child in Paternity Suits

In paternity suits, almost all courts permit exhibition of the child to show whether she is the race of the putative father. The courts are divided with respect to the propriety of exhibition for the purpose of proving physical resemblance to the putative father.

4. Exhibition of Injuries
Exhibition of injuries in a personal injury or criminal case is generally permitted, but the court has discretion to exclude this evidence if unfair prejudice would result.

5. Jury View of the Scene
The trial court has discretion to permit the jury to view places at issue in a civil or criminal case. The need for the view and changes in the condition of the premises are relevant considerations here.

6. Demonstrations
The court, in its discretion, may permit experiments or demonstrations to be performed in the courtroom. Demonstrations of bodily injury may not be allowed where the demonstrations would unduly dramatize the injury.

V. DOCUMENTARY EVIDENCE

A. IN GENERAL

Documentary evidence must be relevant in order to be admissible. In the case of writings, the authenticity of the document is one aspect of its relevancy.

B. AUTHENTICATION

As a general rule, a writing or any secondary evidence of its content will not be received in evidence unless the writing is authenticated by proof that shows that the writing is what the proponent claims it is. The proof must be ***sufficient to support a jury finding*** of genuineness.

1. Authentication by Pleadings or Stipulation
The genuineness of a document may be admitted by the pleadings or by stipulation.

2. Evidence of Authenticity
The following are examples of proper authentication:

a. Admissions
A writing may be authenticated by evidence that the party against whom it is offered has either admitted its authenticity or acted upon it as authentic.

b. Eyewitness Testimony
A writing can be authenticated by testimony of one who sees it executed or hears it acknowledged. The testimony need not be given by a subscribing witness.

c. Handwriting Verifications
A writing may be authenticated by evidence of the genuineness of the handwriting of the maker. This evidence may be the opinion of a ***nonexpert with personal knowledge*** of the alleged writer's handwriting or the opinion of an ***expert who has compared*** the writing to samples of the maker's handwriting. Genuineness may also be determined by the ***trier of fact through comparison of samples***.

CMR **Exam Tip** Remember that a nonexpert without personal knowledge of the handwriting cannot become familiar with it for purposes of testifying.

d. Ancient Documents

A document may be authenticated by evidence that it:

1) Is at least ***20 years old***;

2) Is in such ***condition*** as to be free from suspicion as to authenticity; and

3) Was found in a ***place*** where such a writing would likely be kept.

Exam Tip In contrast to the rule in many jurisdictions, the ancient document provision of the Federal Rules applies to all writings, not just dispositive instruments.

e. Reply Letter Doctrine

A writing may be authenticated by evidence that it was written in response to a communication sent to the claimed author.

f. Photographs

Generally, photographs are admissible only if identified by a witness as a portrayal of certain facts relevant to the issue and verified by the witness as a correct representation of those facts. Ordinarily, it is not necessary to call the photographer to authenticate the photograph; a witness familiar with the scene is sufficient.

1) Unattended Camera—Proper Operation of Camera

If a photograph is taken when no person who could authenticate the scene is present, the photograph may be admitted upon a showing that the camera was properly operating at the relevant time and that the photograph was developed from film obtained from that camera.

g. X-Ray Pictures, Electrocardiograms, Etc.

Unlike photographs, an X-ray cannot be authenticated by testimony of a witness that it is a correct representation of the facts. It must be shown that the process used is accurate, the machine was in working order, and the operator was qualified to operate it. Finally, a custodial chain must be established to assure that the X-ray has not been tampered with.

3. Compare—Authentication of Oral Statements

When a statement is admissible only if said by a particular person (*e.g.,* admission by a party), authentication as to the ***identity of the speaker*** is required.

a. Voice Identification

A voice may be identified by the opinion of anyone who has heard the voice at ***any time***, including after litigation has begun for the sole purpose of testifying.

b. Telephone Conversations

Statements made during a telephone conversation may be authenticated by one of the parties to the call who testifies that: (i) he recognized the other party's voice; (ii) the speaker had knowledge of certain facts that only a particular person would have; (iii) he called a particular person's number and a voice answered as that person or that person's residence; or (iv) he called a business and talked with the person answering the phone about matters relevant to the business.

4. Self-Authenticating Documents

Certain writings are said to "prove themselves." Extrinsic evidence of authenticity is not required for the following: (i) certified copies of public records, (ii) official publications, (iii) newspapers and periodicals, (iv) trade inscriptions, (v) acknowledged documents, (vi) commercial paper and related documents, and (vii) certified business records.

C. BEST EVIDENCE RULE

This rule is more accurately called the "***original document rule***." To ***prove the terms*** of a writing (including a recording, photograph, or X-ray), the original writing must be produced if the terms of the writing are material. Secondary evidence of the writing (*e.g.,* oral testimony) is admissible only if the original is unavailable.

1. Applicability of the Rule

The rule applies to two classes of situations, namely where: (i) the writing is a ***legally operative or dispositive instrument***; or (ii) the ***knowledge of a witness*** concerning a fact results from having read it in the document.

2. Nonapplicability of the Rule

The best evidence rule does not apply in the following circumstances:

a. Fact to Be Proved Exists Independently of Writing

The rule does not apply where the fact to be proved has an existence independent of any writing. Many writings record details of essentially nonwritten transactions. Oral testimony of these facts may be given without the original writings recording the event.

b. Writing Is Collateral to Litigated Issue

The rule does not apply where the writing is of minor importance (*i.e.,* collateral) to the matter in controversy.

c. Summaries of Voluminous Records

The rule does not apply to summaries of voluminous records. It would be inconvenient to examine a voluminous collection of writings in court, and so the proponent may present their contents in the form of a chart or summary.

d. Public Records

The rule does not apply to copies of public records that are certified as correct or testified to as correct.

3. Definitions of "Writings," "Original," and "Duplicate"

The Federal Rules govern ***writings***, ***recordings***, ***and photographs***, and they are broadly defined. An original is the writing itself or any duplicate that is intended by the person executing it to have the same effect as an original. A duplicate is an ***exact copy*** of an original, such as a carbon copy. Duplicates are admissible in federal courts unless the authenticity of the original is challenged or unfairness would result.

BEST EVIDENCE RULE

Best Evidence Rule Applies	Best Evidence Rule Does Not Apply
Party seeks to prove the contents of a deed through witness testimony or other secondary evidence.	If D denies having made a contract with P, P may introduce secondary evidence to prove that a contract exists—but not its contents.
Party seeks to prove the contents of a contract through witness testimony or other secondary evidence.	Witness may testify that he is 30 years old and married, without producing the respective certificates.
Party seeks to prove the contents of a will through witness testimony or other secondary evidence.	Witness may testify to testimony he heard at a prior proceeding, without producing a transcript.
In breach of warranty case, a witness seeks to testify to the contents of the written warranty, which she read.	Witness may testify that he is a real estate broker without producing his license (if not material to the case).
Nurse seeks to testify regarding the content of a medical record that she read.	Nurse who took vital signs may testify to them without producing medical record.
In an obscenity or copyright trial for a book, movie, photograph, etc., party seeks to introduce a newspaper review or witness testimony.	Party may introduce chart summarizing the personnel records of 500 employees.
In a case where P claimed D defrauded her by selling her a gown she claimed was an original "Halvenchy," P seeks to testify that she found a label in the arm of the gown stating that it was made by L-Mart.	Party may introduce a certified copy of a certificate of incorporation, the original of which is on file with the secretary of state.
Radiologist seeks to testify regarding the extent of P's injuries he found in X-rays he took, without producing the X-rays.	W may testify about a plane crash she witnessed, despite the fact that the crash was captured on home video.
	P may testify that D delivered a deed to her by handing it to her.

CMR **Exam Tip** It is important to distinguish photocopies and copies made by hand. Photocopies are duplicates and, thus, are treated the same as originals. In contrast, handwritten copies are considered secondary evidence and are admissible only if the original or a duplicate is unavailable.

4. **Admissibility of Secondary Evidence of Contents**
If the proponent cannot produce the original writing in court, he may offer secondary evidence of its contents (handwritten copies, notes, oral testimony) if a satisfactory explanation is given for the nonproduction of the original.

   a. **Satisfactory Foundation**
   Valid excuses justifying the admissibility of secondary evidence include:

      1) ***Loss or destruction*** of the original.

      2) The original is in possession of a third party ***outside the jurisdiction*** and is ***unobtainable***.

      3) The original is ***in the possession of an adversary*** who, after due notice, fails to produce the original.

   b. **No Degrees of Secondary Evidence**
   Upon satisfactory foundation, the Federal Rules permit a party to prove the contents of a writing by any kind of secondary evidence, thus abolishing degrees of secondary evidence.

   c. **Testimony or Written Admission of Party**
   A proponent may prove the contents of a writing, recording, or photograph through the testimony, deposition, or written admission of the party against whom it is offered, and need not account for the nonproduction of the original.

5. **Functions of Court and Jury**
Ordinarily, it is for the ***court*** to make determinations of fact regarding ***admissibility*** of duplicates, other copies, and oral testimony as to the contents of an original. However, the Federal Rules reserve the following questions of preliminary fact for the jury:

   a. Whether the original ever existed;

   b. Whether a writing, recording, or photograph produced at trial is an original; and

   c. Whether the evidence offered correctly reflects the contents of the original.

D. **PAROL EVIDENCE RULE**
If an agreement is reduced to writing, that writing is the agreement and hence constitutes the only evidence of it. Prior or contemporaneous negotiations or agreements are merged into the written agreement, and they are inadmissible to vary the terms of the writing.

1. **When the Rule Does Not Apply**
The parol evidence rule does not apply to exclude evidence of prior or contemporaneous agreements in the following circumstances:

a. **Incomplete or Ambiguous Contract**
Parol evidence is admissible to complete an incomplete contract or explain an ambiguous term.

b. **Reformation of Contract**
The parol evidence rule does not apply where a party alleges facts (*e.g.,* mistake) entitling him to reformation.

c. **Challenge to Validity of Contract**
Parol evidence is admissible to show that the contract is ***void or voidable***, or was made subject to a valid ***condition precedent*** that has not been satisfied.

2. **Subsequent Modifications**
The rule applies only to negotiations prior to, or at the time of, the execution of the contract. Parol evidence is admissible to show subsequent modification or discharge of the written contract.

VI. TESTIMONIAL EVIDENCE

A. COMPETENCY OF WITNESSES

Witnesses must pass tests of basic reliability to establish their competency to give testimony, but they are generally presumed to be competent until the contrary is established. Witnesses must possess to some degree four basic testimonial attributes: the capacity to observe, to recollect, to communicate, and to appreciate the obligation to speak truthfully.

1. **Federal Rules of Competency**
The Rules do not specify any mental or moral qualifications for witness testimony beyond these two limitations:

(i) The witness must have ***personal knowledge*** of the matter about which he is to testify; and

(ii) The witness must ***declare he will testify truthfully***.

If a witness requires an interpreter, the interpreter must be qualified and take an oath to make a true translation.

2. **Modern Modifications of the Common Law Disqualifications**
Most jurisdictions and the Federal Rules have removed the common law witness disqualifications for lack of religious belief, conviction of a crime, and interest in the lawsuit.

a. **Infancy**
The competency of an infant depends on the capacity and intelligence of the particular child as determined by the trial judge.

b. **Insanity**
An insane person may testify, provided he understands the obligation to speak truthfully and has the capacity to testify accurately.

c. **Judge and Jurors**
The presiding judge may not testify as a witness. Likewise, jurors are incompetent to testify before the jury in which they are sitting.

3. **Dead Man Acts**
Most states have Dead Man Acts, which provide that a party or person interested in the event is incompetent to testify to a personal transaction or communication with a deceased, when such testimony is offered against the representative or successors in interest of the deceased. A person is "interested" if he stands to gain or lose by the judgment or the judgment may be used for or against him in a subsequent action. A predecessor in interest of the interested party is also disqualified.

CMR **Exam Tip** There is no Dead Man Act in the Federal Rules, but a state Act will apply in federal cases where state law, under the *Erie* doctrine, provides the rule of decision (*e.g.,* diversity cases).

B. **FORM OF EXAMINATION OF WITNESS**
The judge may exercise reasonable control over the examination of witnesses in order to aid the ascertainment of truth, to avoid wasting time, and to protect witnesses from harassment.

1. **Leading Questions**
Leading questions (*i.e.,* questions that suggest the answer desired) are ***generally improper on direct*** examination. However, they are permitted:

a. On cross-examination;

b. To elicit preliminary or introductory matter;

c. When the witness needs aid to respond because of loss of memory, immaturity, or physical or mental weakness; or

d. When the witness is hostile.

2. **Improper Questions and Answers**
Questions that are misleading (cannot be answered without making an unintended admission), compound (requiring a single answer to more than one question), argumentative, conclusionary, cumulative, unduly harassing or embarrassing, call for a narrative answer or speculation, or assume facts not in evidence are improper and are not permitted. Answers that lack foundation (the witness has insufficient personal knowledge) and answers that are nonresponsive (do not answer the specific question asked) may be stricken.

3. **Use of Memoranda by Witness**
A witness ***cannot read her testimony*** from a prepared memorandum. However, a memorandum may be used in certain circumstances.

CMR **Exam Tip** Any time you encounter an exam question in which a witness consults a writing, keep in mind the differences between refreshing and recorded recollection. The fact patterns are very similar and could be confusing if you have not thoroughly memorized the distinguishing features.

a. **Present Recollection Revived—Refreshing Recollection**
A witness may use any writing or thing for the purpose of refreshing her present

recollection. She usually may not read from the writing while she actually testifies because the writing is not authenticated and not in evidence.

b. Past Recollection Recorded—Recorded Recollection

Where a witness states that she has insufficient recollection of an event to enable her to testify fully and accurately, even after she has consulted a writing given to her on the stand, the writing itself may be ***read into evidence*** if a proper foundation is laid. The foundation must include proof that:

1) The witness at one time had ***personal knowledge*** of the facts in the writing;

2) The writing was ***made by the witness*** or under her direction, or it was ***adopted*** by the witness;

3) The writing was ***timely made*** when the matter was fresh in the witness's mind;

4) The writing is ***accurate***; and

5) The witness has ***insufficient recollection*** to testify fully and accurately.

c. Inspection and Use on Cross-Examination

Whenever a witness has used a writing to refresh her memory on the stand, an adverse party is entitled to have the writing produced at trial, to cross-examine the witness thereon, and to introduce portions relating to the witness's testimony into evidence.

PRESENT RECOLLECTION REFRESHED VS. PAST RECOLLECTION RECORDED

Present Recollection Refreshed	Past Recollection Recorded
Any writing may be used to refresh a witness's memory. (Things other than a writing may also be used, *e.g.,* a photograph.)	Only a ***writing*** that meets several ***foundational requirements*** (*e.g.,* timely made by witness; witness cannot remember the events after reading the writing) may be used.
The witness cannot read from the writing while testifying.	The writing itself is read into evidence.
There is ***no hearsay problem***, because the writing is not offered into evidence.	This is ***hearsay***, but it falls within a specific ***exception*** to the hearsay rule.

C. OPINION TESTIMONY

The general policy of the law is to prohibit admissibility of opinion evidence except in cases where the courts are sure that it will be necessary or at least helpful.

1. Opinion Testimony by Lay Witnesses

a. General Rule of Inadmissibility

Opinions by lay witnesses are generally inadmissible. However, there are many cases where no better evidence can be obtained. In most jurisdictions and under the Federal Rules, opinion testimony by a lay witness is admissible when it is: (i) rationally based on the witness's perception, (ii) helpful to a clear understanding of his testimony or helpful to the determination of a fact in issue, and (iii) not based on scientific, technical, or other specialized knowledge.

b. Situations Where Opinions of Lay Witnesses Are Admissible

An opinion of a lay witness is generally admissible with respect to:

1) The ***general appearance or condition*** of a person;

2) The ***state of emotion*** of a person;

3) Matters involving ***sense recognition***;

4) ***Voice or handwriting identification***;

5) The ***speed*** of a moving object;

6) The ***value of his own services***;

7) The ***rational or irrational nature*** of another's conduct; and

8) ***Intoxication*** of another.

c. Situations Where Opinions of Lay Witnesses Are Not Admissible

Opinions of lay witnesses are not admissible with regard to whether one acted as an agent or whether an agreement was made.

2. Opinion Testimony by Expert Witnesses

An expert may state an opinion or conclusion, provided:

(i) The ***subject matter*** is one where scientific, technical, or other specialized knowledge would ***assist the trier of fact*** (an opinion will assist the trier of fact if it is relevant and reliable);

(ii) The ***witness is qualified*** as an expert (*i.e.,* possesses special knowledge, skill, experience, training, or education);

ADMISSIBLE OPINIONS OF LAY WITNESSES

1. ***General Appearance or Condition of a Person***	"He was about 80 years old." ***or*** "She seemed ill."
2. ***State of Emotion***	"She was angry." ***or*** "He was distraught."
3. ***Matters Involving Sense Recognition***	"The suitcase was heavy." ***or*** "He smelled of garlic."
4. ***Voice or Handwriting Identification*** (Foundation required)	"It sounded like Mark." ***or*** "That's Fran's handwriting."
5. ***Speed of Moving Object***	"The truck was going very fast" or (if experienced in estimating rates of speed), "The truck was going at least 60 miles per hour."
6. ***Value of Own Services***	"My time is worth $50 per hour."
7. ***Rational or Irrational Nature of Another's Conduct***	"He was acting crazy."
8. ***Intoxication*** (Foundation may be required)	"She was slurring her words and smelled of gin. She was drunk."

(iii) The expert possesses ***reasonable probability regarding his opinion***; and

(iv) The opinion is supported by a ***proper factual basis***. The expert's opinion may be based on one or more of three possible sources of information: (i) personal observation, (ii) facts made known to the expert at trial, or (iii) facts not known personally but supplied to him outside the courtroom and of a ***type reasonably relied upon by experts*** in the particular field.

a. Opinion on Ultimate Issues

Under the Federal Rules, an expert may render an opinion as to the ultimate issue in the case. However, in a criminal case in which the defendant's mental state constitutes an element of the crime or defense, an expert may not, under the Federal Rules, state an opinion as to whether the accused did or did not have the mental state in issue.

b. Authoritative Texts and Treatises

An expert may be cross-examined concerning statements contained in any publication established as reliable authority either by the testimony of this expert or another expert, or by judicial notice. Under the Federal Rules, these texts and treatises can be used not only to impeach experts, but also as substantive evidence, subject to the following limitations:

1) An ***expert must be on the stand*** when an excerpt is read from a treatise; and

2) The relevant portion is ***read into evidence*** but is not received as an exhibit.

D. CROSS-EXAMINATION

Cross-examination of adverse witnesses is a matter of right in every trial of a disputed issue of fact, but the scope of cross-examination is frequently a matter of judicial discretion.

1. Restrictions on Scope

Cross-examination is generally limited to: (i) the scope of direct examination, including all reasonable inferences that may be drawn from it, and (ii) testing the credibility of the witness.

2. Collateral Matters

The cross-examiner is generally bound by the answers of the witness to questions concerning collateral matters. Thus, the response may not be refuted by extrinsic evidence. However, certain recognized matters of impeachment, such as bias, interest, or a conviction, may be developed by extrinsic evidence because they are sufficiently important. The trial court has considerable discretion in this area.

E. CREDIBILITY—IMPEACHMENT

Impeachment means the casting of an adverse reflection on the veracity of the witness.

1. Accrediting or Bolstering

Generally, a party may not bolster or accredit the testimony of his witness (*e.g.,* by introducing a prior consistent statement) until the witness has been impeached. However, in certain cases, a party may prove the witness made a timely complaint or a prior statement of identification. The prior identification may also serve as substantive evidence that the identification was correct.

2. Any Party May Impeach

Under the Federal Rules, a witness may be impeached by any party, including the party calling him.

CMR **Exam Tip** When a question involves a party impeaching his own witness, be sure to avoid the following ***wrong answer choices*** reflecting the traditional rule, which prohibits impeaching your own witness unless the witness:

(i) Is an ***adverse party*** or identified with an adverse party;

(ii) Is ***hostile*** and affirmatively uncooperative;

(iii) Is one whom the party is ***required by law*** to call; or

(iv) Gives ***surprise testimony*** that is affirmatively harmful to the party calling him.

3. Impeachment Methods—Cross-Examination and Extrinsic Evidence

A witness may be impeached either by cross-examination (by eliciting facts from the witness that discredit his own testimony) or by extrinsic evidence (by putting other witnesses on the stand who will introduce facts discrediting his testimony). Certain grounds for impeachment require that a foundation be laid during cross-examination before extrinsic evidence can be introduced. Other grounds allow impeachment to be accomplished only by cross-examination and not by extrinsic evidence. (*Note:* The term "cross-examination" is used for convenience because it is usually an adverse witness who is impeached. But remember that a party may impeach his own witness, which would be on direct or redirect examination.) The traditional impeachment devices follow.

a. Prior Inconsistent Statements

A party may show, by cross-examination or extrinsic evidence, that the witness has, on another occasion, made statements inconsistent with his present testimony. To prove the statement by extrinsic evidence, a proper foundation must be laid and the statement must be relevant to some issue in the case.

1) Foundation for Extrinsic Evidence

Extrinsic evidence can be introduced to prove a prior inconsistent statement only if the witness is, at some point, given an opportunity to explain or deny the statement. The exception to the rule is that inconsistent statements by hearsay declarants may be used to impeach despite the lack of a foundation. Under the Federal Rules, foundation requirements may be dispensed with where the interests of justice require (*e.g.,* witness unavailable when inconsistent statement is discovered).

CMR **Exam Tip** Remember the MBE follows the Federal Rules. Under the Rules, the opportunity to explain or deny need not come before introduction of a prior inconsistent statement.

2) Evidentiary Effect of Prior Inconsistent Statements
Usually, prior inconsistent statements are hearsay, admissible only for impeachment purposes. If, however, the statement was made under oath at a prior proceeding, it is admissible nonhearsay and may be admitted as substantive evidence of the facts stated.

b. Bias or Interest
Evidence that a witness is biased or has an interest in the outcome of a suit tends to show that the witness has a motive to lie.

1) Foundation for Extrinsic Evidence
Before a witness can be impeached by extrinsic evidence of bias or interest, he must first be asked about the facts that show bias or interest on cross-examination.

CMR **Exam Tip** Watch for facts indicating that the foundation requirement for extrinsic evidence of bias or interest has been fulfilled. Evidence that is otherwise inadmissible (*e.g.*, arrests, liability insurance) may be introduced if relevant for these impeachment purposes, provided the proper foundation is laid.

c. Conviction of Crime
A witness may be impeached by proof of a ***conviction*** (arrest or indictment is not sufficient) for certain crimes. A pending review or appeal does not affect the use of a conviction for impeachment.

1) Type of Crime

a) Any Crime Involving Dishonesty
A witness may be impeached by any crime, felony or misdemeanor, requiring an act of dishonesty or false statement. The court has ***no discretion*** to bar impeachment by these crimes.

b) Felony Not Involving Dishonesty
A witness may also be impeached by a felony that does not involve dishonesty, but the court has ***discretion to exclude*** it if:

(1) The witness being impeached is a ***criminal defendant***, and the ***prosecution has not shown*** that the conviction's probative value outweighs its prejudicial effect; or

(2) In the case of all other witnesses, the ***court determines*** that the conviction's probative value is substantially outweighed by its prejudicial effect.

2) Remote, Juvenile, and Constitutionally Defective Convictions Not Admissible
Generally, if more than 10 years have elapsed since the date of conviction or the

date of release from confinement (whichever is later), the conviction is inadmissible. Juvenile convictions are similarly inadmissible. A conviction obtained in violation of the defendant's constitutional rights is invalid for all purposes, including impeachment.

3) Effect of Pardon

A conviction may not be used to impeach a witness if the witness has been pardoned and: (i) the pardon is based on innocence, or (ii) the person pardoned has not been convicted of a subsequent felony.

4) No Foundation Required for Extrinsic Evidence

A prior conviction may be shown either by cross-examination of the witness or by introducing a record of the judgment. No foundation is necessary.

d. Specific Instances of Misconduct—Bad Acts

Under the Federal Rules, subject to discretionary control of the trial judge, a witness may be interrogated upon cross-examination with respect to an act of misconduct only if the act is ***probative of truthfulness*** (*i.e.,* is an act of deceit or lying). However, the cross-examiner must inquire in good faith.

1) Extrinsic Evidence Not Permitted

Extrinsic evidence of "bad acts" to prove misconduct is not permitted. A specific act of misconduct, offered to attack the witness's character for truthfulness, can be elicited only on cross-examination of the witness.

CMR **Exam Tip** Keep in mind that asking about specific instances of misconduct does not include inquiring about arrests. An arrest itself is not a bad act. Thus, it is permissible to ask a witness whether he embezzled money from his employer. It is not permissible to ask him whether he was ***arrested*** for embezzlement.

e. Opinion or Reputation Evidence for Truth

A witness may be impeached by showing that he has a poor reputation for truthfulness. This may include evidence of reputation in business circles as well as in the community in which the witness resides. Under the Federal Rules, an impeaching witness may state his own opinion as to the character of a witness for truth.

f. Sensory Deficiencies

A witness may be impeached by showing, either on cross-examination or by extrinsic evidence, that his faculties of perception and recollection were so impaired as to make it doubtful that he could have perceived those facts. A witness may also be impeached by showing that he had no knowledge of the facts to which he testified.

4. Impeachment on Collateral Matter

Where a witness makes a statement not directly relevant to the issue in the case, the rule against impeachment on a collateral matter applies to bar his opponent from proving the statement untrue either by extrinsic evidence or by a prior inconsistent statement.

5. Impeachment of Hearsay Declarant

Under the Federal Rules, the credibility of someone who does not testify but whose out-of-court statement is introduced at trial may be attacked (and if attacked, may be supported) by evidence that would be admissible if the declarant had testified as a witness. The declarant need not be given the opportunity to explain or deny a prior inconsistent statement. In addition, the party against whom the out-of-court statement was offered may call the declarant as a witness and cross-examine him about the statement.

CMR SUMMARY CHART

METHODS OF IMPEACHMENT

Impeachment Method	Means of Proof	Foundation
Prior Inconsistent Statements	• Cross-examination • Extrinsic evidence (if not a collateral matter)	Witness must be given opportunity to explain or deny the inconsistent statement. (Exception for hearsay declarants)
Bias or Interest	• Cross-examination • Extrinsic evidence	Witness must be asked on cross-examination about facts showing bias or interest before extrinsic evidence is allowed. If these facts are admitted on cross-examination, admissibility of extrinsic evidence is within court's discretion.
Conviction of Crime—Must be a ***felony*** or crime involving ***dishonesty***	• Cross-examination • Record of judgment	None required
Specific Instances of Misconduct (Bad Acts)	• Cross-examination only	Not applicable
Opinion or Reputation for Truthfulness	• Calling other witnesses	None required
Sensory Deficiencies	• Cross-examination • Extrinsic evidence	None required

6. **Rehabilitation**

A witness who has been impeached may be rehabilitated by the following methods:

a. **Explanation on Redirect**

The witness on redirect may explain or clarify facts brought out on cross-examination.

b. Good Reputation for Truth

When the witness's character for truth and veracity has been attacked, other witnesses may be called to testify to the good reputation for truth of the impeached witness or to give their opinions as to the truthfulness of the impeached witness.

c. Prior Consistent Statement

A party may not ordinarily rehabilitate a witness by showing a prior consistent statement. This is true even when the witness has been impeached by showing a prior inconsistent statement. But if the testimony of the witness has been attacked by an express or implied charge that the witness is ***lying or exaggerating*** because of some motive, a previous consistent statement is admissible to rebut this evidence. This previous statement also is substantive evidence of the truth of its contents.

F. OBJECTIONS, EXCEPTIONS, AND OFFERS OF PROOF

1. Objections

Objections at trial should be made after the question, but before the answer, if the question calls for inadmissible matter. Otherwise, a motion to strike must be made as soon as an answer emerges as inadmissible. At a deposition, objections to the form of a question, or to a testimonial privilege, should be made when the question is asked or it may be waived. Objections based on the substance of a question or answer may be postponed until the deposition is offered in evidence.

CMR **Exam Tip** Failure to object is deemed a waiver of any ground for objection. Thus, if no objection is made, otherwise inadmissible evidence will be admitted.

a. Specificity of Objections

1) General Objections

A sustained general objection (one that does not state the grounds of the objection) will be upheld on appeal if there was any ground for the objection. An overruled general objection will be upheld on appeal unless the evidence was not admissible under any circumstances for any purpose.

2) Specific Objections

A sustained specific objection, which states the reason for the objection, will be upheld on appeal only if the ground stated was correct or if the evidence excluded was not competent and could not be made so.

b. "Opening the Door"

One who introduces evidence on a particular subject thereby asserts its relevance and cannot complain if his adversary thereafter offers evidence on the same subject.

c. Introducing Part of Transaction

Where part of a conversation, act, or writing is introduced into evidence, the adverse party may require the proponent of the evidence to introduce any other part that ought in fairness to be considered.

d. Motion to Strike—Unresponsive Answers

Examining counsel may move to strike an unresponsive answer, but opposing counsel may not.

2. **Exceptions**
It is not necessary for a party to "except" from a trial ruling in order to preserve the issue for appeal in most states.

3. **Offers of Proof**
An offer of proof may be made, disclosing the nature, purpose, and admissibility of rejected evidence, to persuade the trial court to hear the evidence and to preserve the evidence for review on appeal. It may be made by witness testimony, a lawyer's narration, or tangible evidence marked and offered.

G. TESTIMONIAL PRIVILEGES

Testimonial privileges permit one to refuse to disclose, and prohibit others from disclosing, certain confidential information in judicial proceedings.

1. **Federal Rules—No Specific Privilege Provisions**
The Federal Rules have no specific privilege provisions; privilege in federal courts is governed by common law principles as interpreted by the courts. The federal courts currently recognize the attorney-client privilege, the privilege for spousal communications, and the psychotherapist/social worker-client privilege. In ***diversity*** cases, the state law of privilege applies.

2. **General Considerations**

a. **Persons Who May Assert Privilege**
A privilege is personal to the holder; *i.e.,* it generally may be asserted only by the holder. Sometimes the person with whom the confidence was shared (*e.g.,* an attorney) may assert the privilege on the holder's behalf.

b. **Confidentiality**
To be privileged, a communication must be shown or presumed to have been made in confidence.

c. **Comment on Privilege Forbidden**
Neither counsel for the parties nor the judge may comment on a claim of privilege.

d. **Waiver**
Any privilege is waived by: (i) failure to claim the privilege; (ii) voluntary disclosure of the privileged matter by the privilege holder; or (iii) a contractual provision waiving in advance the right to claim a privilege.

CMR **Exam Tip** A privilege is not waived when someone wrongfully discloses information without the privilege holder's consent. Similarly, a waiver by one joint holder does not affect the right of the other holder to assert the privilege.

e. **Eavesdroppers**
A privilege based on confidential communications is not abrogated because it was overheard by someone whose presence is unknown to the parties. Under the modern view, in the absence of negligence by the one claiming privilege, even the eavesdropper would be prohibited from testifying.

3. Attorney-Client Privilege

Communications between an attorney and client, made during professional consultation, are privileged from disclosure. The important elements of this privilege are:

a. Attorney-Client Relationship

The client must be seeking the professional services of the attorney at the time of the communication. Disclosures made before the attorney accepts or declines the case are covered by the privilege.

1) Corporate Clients

Corporations are "clients" within the meaning of the privilege, and statements made by corporate officials or employees to an attorney are protected if the employees were authorized by the corporation to make such statements.

b. Confidential Communication

To be protected, the communication must be confidential (*i.e.,* not intended to be disclosed to third parties), but representatives of the attorney or client may be present without destroying the privilege; otherwise, communications made in the known presence and hearing of a stranger are not privileged.

1) Communications Through Agents

Communications made to third persons (*e.g.,* secretaries, messengers, accountants) are confidential and covered by the privilege if necessary to transmit information between the attorney and client.

CMR Exam Tip A favorite exam topic involves communications between a client and a doctor during an examination made at the attorney's request. Be careful—the physician-patient privilege (*infra*) does not apply because no treatment is contemplated. The attorney-client privilege will apply, however, as long as the doctor is not called as an expert witness.

2) No Privilege Where Attorney Acts for Both Parties

Where an attorney acts for both parties to a transaction, no privilege can be invoked in a lawsuit between the two parties, but the privilege can be claimed in a suit between either or both of the two parties and third persons.

c. Client Holds Privilege

The client holds the privilege, and she alone may waive it. The attorney's authority to claim the privilege on behalf of the client is presumed in the absence of contrary evidence.

d. Privilege Applies Indefinitely

The attorney-client privilege applies indefinitely. The privilege even continues to apply after the client's death.

e. When the Privilege Does Not Apply

There are three significant exceptions to the attorney-client privilege. There is no privilege:

1) If the attorney's services were sought to aid in the planning or commission of something the ***client should have known was a crime or fraud***;

2) Regarding a communication relevant to an issue between ***parties claiming through the same deceased client***; and

3) For a communication relevant to an issue of breach of duty in a ***dispute between the attorney and client***.

f. Attorney's Work Product
Although documents prepared by an attorney for his own use in a case are not protected by the privilege, they are not subject to discovery except in cases of necessity.

4. Physician-Patient Privilege
The physician-patient privilege belongs to the patient, and he may decide to claim or waive it. Confidential communications between a patient and his physician are privileged, provided that:

(i) A ***professional relationship*** exists;

(ii) The information is acquired while attending the patient in the ***course of treatment***; and

(iii) The information is ***necessary for treatment***. (Nonmedical information is not privileged.)

a. When the Privilege Does Not Apply
The physician-patient privilege does not apply (or is impliedly waived) if:

1) The ***patient puts his physical condition in issue*** (*e.g.*, personal injury suit);

2) The physician's assistance was sought to ***aid wrongdoing*** (*e.g.*, commission of crime or tort);

3) The communication is relevant to an issue of breach of duty in a ***dispute between the physician and patient***;

4) The patient ***agreed*** by contract (*e.g.*, insurance policy) to waive the privilege; or

5) It is a ***federal case applying the federal law of privilege***.

b. Criminal Proceedings
In some states, the privilege applies in both civil and criminal cases. In a number of others, it cannot be invoked in criminal cases generally. In still other states, the privilege is denied in felony cases, and in a few states, it is denied only in homicide cases.

CMR **Exam Tip** Remember that when a psychiatrist is the doctor involved, the applicable privilege is the psychotherapist-client privilege (below), which is more widely accepted in all proceedings than is the physician-patient privilege.

5. Psychotherapist/Social Worker-Client Privilege
The United States Supreme Court recognizes a federal privilege for communications between a psychotherapist (psychiatrist or psychologist) or licensed social worker and his client. Thus, the federal courts and virtually all of the states recognize a privilege for this type of confidential communication. In most particulars, this privilege operates in the same manner as the attorney-client privilege (*supra*).

6. **Husband-Wife Privilege**
There are two distinct spousal privileges.

a. **Spousal Immunity**
A married person whose spouse is a defendant in a ***criminal*** case may not be called as a witness by the prosecution. Moreover, a married person may not be compelled to ***testify*** against his spouse in ***any criminal proceeding***, regardless of whether the spouse is the defendant. There must be a valid marriage for the privilege to apply, and the privilege lasts only during the marriage.

1) **Who Holds the Privilege**
In federal court, the privilege belongs to the witness-spouse. Thus, the witness-spouse cannot be compelled to testify, but may choose to do so. (In most state courts, however, the privilege belongs to the party-spouse.)

b. **Privilege for Confidential Marital Communications**
In any civil or criminal case, confidential communications between a husband and wife during a valid marriage are privileged. For this privilege to apply, the ***marital relationship must exist*** when the communication is made. Divorce will not terminate the privilege, but communications after divorce are not privileged. In addition, the communication must be ***made in reliance upon the intimacy*** of the marital relationship (confidential).

c. **When Neither Marital Privilege Applies**
Neither privilege applies in actions between the spouses or in cases involving crimes against the testifying spouse or either spouse's children.

HUSBAND-WIFE PRIVILEGE

Spousal Immunity	Confidential Marital Communications
One spouse ***cannot be compelled to testify*** against the other spouse in any ***criminal*** proceeding.	***Communications*** made in reliance upon the intimacy of the marital relationship are privileged. The privilege applies in both ***civil and criminal*** proceedings.
Only the ***witness-spouse*** may invoke spousal immunity (*i.e.*, the party-spouse cannot prevent the witness-spouse from testifying).	***Both spouses*** have the privilege not to disclose, and to prevent the other from disclosing, a confidential marital communication.
The privilege can be claimed ***only during marriage***, but covers information learned before and during the marriage.	The privilege ***survives the marriage***, but covers only statements ***made during marriage***.

7. **Privilege Against Self-Incrimination**
Under the Fifth Amendment to the Constitution, a witness cannot be compelled to testify against himself. Any witness compelled to appear in a civil or criminal proceeding may refuse to give an answer that ties the witness to the commission of a crime.

8. **Clergy or Accountant Privilege**
A privilege exists for statements made to a member of the clergy or an accountant, the elements of which are very similar to the attorney-client privilege.

9. **Professional Journalist Privilege**
There is no constitutional right for a professional journalist to protect his source of information, so any privilege in this area is limited to individual state statutes on the subject.

10. **Governmental Privileges**
Official information not otherwise open to the public or the identity of an informer may be protected by a privilege for the government. No privilege exists if the identity of the informer is voluntarily disclosed by a holder of the privilege.

H. EXCLUSION AND SEQUESTRATION OF WITNESSES
Upon a party's request, the trial judge will order witnesses excluded from the courtroom. The judge may also do this on his own motion. The judge, however, may not exclude: (i) a party or a designated officer or employee of a party, (ii) a person whose presence is essential to the presentation of a party's case, or (iii) a person statutorily authorized to be present.

VII. THE HEARSAY RULE

A. STATEMENT OF THE RULE
The Federal Rules define hearsay as "a statement, other than one made by the declarant while testifying at the trial or hearing, offered in evidence to prove the truth of the matter asserted." If a statement is hearsay, and no exception to the rule applies, the evidence must be excluded upon appropriate objection. The reason for excluding hearsay is that the adverse party was denied the opportunity to cross-examine the declarant.

CMR **Exam Tip** An out-of-court statement that incorporates other hearsay ("hearsay on hearsay" or "double hearsay") is admissible only if each part of the statement falls within an exception to the rule. If any part is inadmissible, the entire statement is inadmissible.

1. **"Statement"**
For purposes of the hearsay rule, a "statement" is: (i) an oral or written assertion, or (ii) nonverbal conduct intended as an assertion (*e.g.,* nod of the head).

2. **"Offered to Prove the Truth of the Matter"**
If the out-of-court statement is introduced for any purpose other than to prove the truth of the matter asserted, there is no need to cross-examine the declarant; so the statement is not hearsay. The following out-of-court statements are ***not hearsay***:

a. ***Verbal acts or legally operative facts*** (*e.g.,* words of contract; defamatory words);

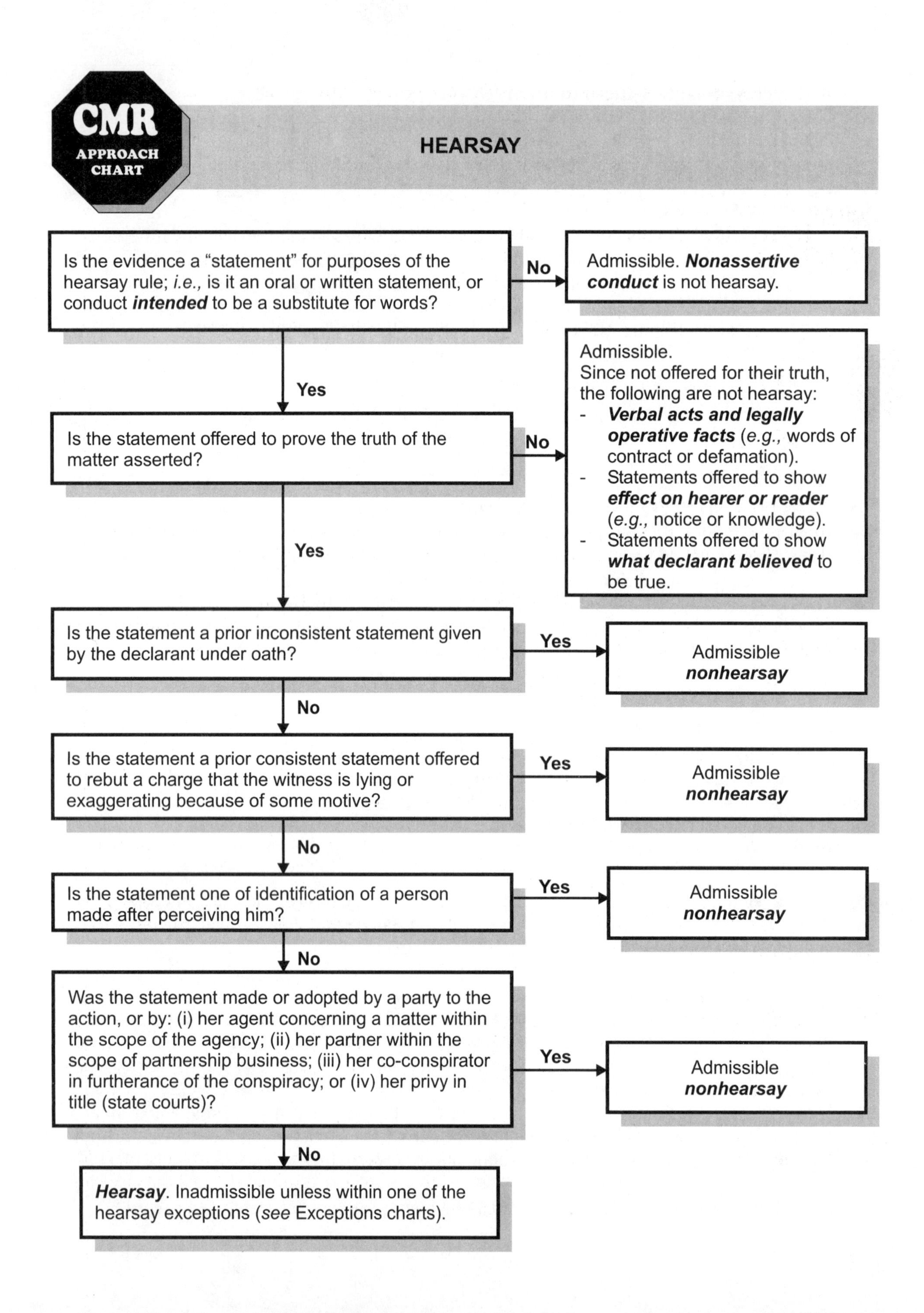
CMR
APPROACH CHART
HEARSAY
Is the evidence a "statement" for purposes of the hearsay rule; *i.e.,* is it an oral or written statement, or conduct ***intended*** to be a substitute for words?
No
Admissible. ***Nonassertive conduct*** is not hearsay.
Yes
Is the statement offered to prove the truth of the matter asserted?
No
Admissible.
Since not offered for their truth, the following are not hearsay:
- ***Verbal acts and legally operative facts*** (*e.g.,* words of contract or defamation).
- Statements offered to show ***effect on hearer or reader*** (*e.g.,* notice or knowledge).
- Statements offered to show ***what declarant believed*** to be true.
Yes
Is the statement a prior inconsistent statement given by the declarant under oath?
Yes
Admissible ***nonhearsay***
No
Is the statement a prior consistent statement offered to rebut a charge that the witness is lying or exaggerating because of some motive?
Yes
Admissible ***nonhearsay***
No
Is the statement one of identification of a person made after perceiving him?
Yes
Admissible ***nonhearsay***
No
Was the statement made or adopted by a party to the action, or by: (i) her agent concerning a matter within the scope of the agency; (ii) her partner within the scope of partnership business; (iii) her co-conspirator in furtherance of the conspiracy; or (iv) her privy in title (state courts)?
Yes
Admissible ***nonhearsay***
No
Hearsay. Inadmissible unless within one of the hearsay exceptions (*see* Exceptions charts).

b. Statements offered to show their ***effect on the hearer or reader*** (*e.g.*, to prove notice in negligence case); and

c. Statements offered as ***circumstantial evidence of declarant's state of mind*** (*e.g.*, evidence of insanity or knowledge).

CMR **Exam Tip** Do not confuse statements offered as circumstantial evidence of declarant's state of mind, which are almost always offered as evidence of insanity or knowledge, with statements that reflect directly on declarant's state of mind, which are usually offered to establish intent. The former is not hearsay, while the latter is hearsay subject to a specific exception.

CMR **Exam Tip** In deciding whether evidence is hearsay, ask yourself whether we are relying on the declarant's credibility; *i.e.*, does it matter whether the declarant is telling the truth? If not, the evidence is not hearsay.

3. **Nonhuman Declarations**
There is no such thing as ***animal*** or ***machine*** hearsay; there must be an out-of-court statement by a ***person***. Thus, testimony about what a radar gun "said" or what a drug-sniffing dog did is not hearsay (but still must be relevant and authenticated to be admitted).

B. STATEMENTS THAT ARE NONHEARSAY UNDER THE FEDERAL RULES

Despite meeting the common law definition of hearsay, the following statements are not hearsay under the Federal Rules and are, therefore, admissible as substantive evidence:

1. **Prior Statements by Witness**
Under the Federal Rules, a prior statement by a witness is not hearsay if:

a. The prior statement is ***inconsistent*** with the declarant's in-court testimony and was ***given under oath*** at a prior proceeding;

b. The prior statement is ***consistent*** with the declarant's in-court testimony and is ***offered to rebut*** a charge that the witness is ***lying or exaggerating*** because of some motive (and the statement was made before any motive to lie or exaggerate arose); or

c. The prior statement is one of ***identification*** of a person made after perceiving him.

2. **Admissions by Party-Opponent**
An admission is a statement made or act that amounts to a prior acknowledgment by one of the parties of one of the relevant facts. Admissions of a party-opponent are not hearsay under the Federal Rules. To be an admission, the statement need not have been against the declarant's interest when made, and may even be in the form of an opinion. Personal knowledge is not required; the admission may be predicated on hearsay. The following types of admissions merit special attention.

a. **Judicial and Extrajudicial Admissions**
Formal judicial admissions (*e.g.*, in pleadings, stipulations, etc.) are conclusive. ***Informal*** judicial admissions made during testimony and ***extrajudicial*** (evidentiary) admissions are not conclusive and can be explained.

b. Adoptive Admissions

A party may make an admission by expressly or impliedly adopting or acquiescing in the statement of another.

1) Silence

If a reasonable person would have responded, and a party remains silent in the face of accusatory statements, his silence may be considered an implied admission. Silence is treated as an admission only if:

(i) The party ***heard and understood*** the statement;

(ii) The party was physically and mentally ***capable of denying*** the statement; and

(iii) A ***reasonable person would have denied*** the accusation.

Note that silence in the face of accusations by police in a ***criminal case*** is almost never considered an admission of a crime.

c. Vicarious Admissions

1) Co-Parties

Admissions of a party are not receivable against her co-parties merely because they happen to be joined as parties.

2) Principal-Agent

Under the Federal Rules, an agent's statements concerning any matter within the scope of her agency, made while the employment relationship exists, are not hearsay and are admissible against the principal.

3) Partners

After a partnership is shown to exist, an admission of one partner relating to matters within the scope of the partnership business is binding upon her co-partners.

4) Co-Conspirators

Admissions of one conspirator, made to a third party in furtherance of a conspiracy to commit a crime or civil wrong at a time when the declarant was participating in the conspiracy, are admissible against co-conspirators. However, testimonial admissions of a conspirator are admissible against another conspirator only if there was an opportunity to cross-examine the hearsay declarant.

5) Privies in Title and Joint Tenants—State Courts Only

In most state courts, admissions of each joint owner are admissible against the other, and admissions of a former owner of real property made at the time she held title are admissible against those claiming under her (grantees, heirs, etc.). These statements are not considered admissions under the Federal Rules, but may be admissible under one of the hearsay exceptions (*e.g.*, statement against interest).

6) Preliminary Determinations

Before admitting a hearsay statement as a vicarious admission, the court must make a preliminary determination of the declarant's relationship with the party against whom the statement is offered. In making such a determination, the court

must consider the contents of the statement, but the statement alone is not sufficient to establish the required relationship.

C. HEARSAY EXCEPTIONS—DECLARANT UNAVAILABLE

There are five important exceptions to the hearsay rule that condition admissibility of the hearsay statement on the present unavailability of the declarant to testify.

1. "Unavailability"

A declarant is unavailable if he:

a. Is exempt from testifying because of ***privilege***;

b. ***Refuses to testify*** concerning the statement despite a court order;

c. Testifies to ***lack of memory*** of the subject matter of the statement;

d. Is unable to testify due to ***death or physical or mental illness***; or

e. Is ***absent*** (beyond the reach of the court's subpoena), and the proponent is unable to procure his attendance by reasonable means.

2. Former Testimony

The testimony of a now-unavailable witness, given at another hearing or deposition, is admissible if:

a. The party against whom the testimony is offered was a ***party or in privity*** (*e.g.,* grantor-grantee, life tenant-remainderman) ***with a party in the former action***;

b. The former action involved the ***same subject matter*** (causes of action need not be identical);

c. The testimony was given ***under oath***; and

d. The party against whom the testimony is offered had an ***opportunity at the prior proceeding to develop the declarant's testimony*** (*i.e.,* by direct, cross, or redirect examination).

CMR **Exam Tip** Because grand jury proceedings do not provide an opportunity for cross-examination, the ***grand jury testimony*** of an unavailable declarant is not admissible against a defendant under the former testimony exception to the hearsay rule. Be careful not to confuse this with a prior inconsistent statement given under oath by a witness currently testifying. Grand jury testimony is admissible in that case, both as impeachment and substantive evidence.

3. Statements Against Interest

The statement of a person, now unavailable as a witness, against that person's pecuniary, proprietary, or penal interest ***when made***, as well as collateral facts contained in the statement, is admissible under the statement against interest exception to the hearsay rule. The declarant must also have had personal knowledge of the facts, and must have been aware that the statement was against her interest when she made it.

a. Risk of Criminal Liability

Note that when a criminal defendant wishes to show her innocence by introducing another's statements admitting the crime, ***corroborating circumstances*** indicating the trustworthiness of the statements are required.

b. "Statement" Means Single Remark

If a person makes a declaration containing statements that are against his interest (*e.g.*, "I sold the drugs") and statements that are not (*e.g.*, "X runs the drug ring"), the exception covers only those remarks that inculpate the declarant, not the entire extended declaration.

ADMISSIONS VS. STATEMENTS AGAINST INTEREST

Admissions by Party-Opponent	Statements Against Interest
Statement need not have been against interest when made.	Statement must have been against interest when made.
Declarant need not have personal knowledge of facts.	Declarant must have personal knowledge of facts.
Declarant need not be unavailable.	Declarant must be unavailable.
Declarant must be a party.	

4. Dying Declarations—Statements Under Belief of Impending Death

In a ***homicide prosecution or a civil action***, a statement made by a now unavailable declarant is admissible if:

a. The declarant ***believed his death was imminent*** (he need not actually die); and

b. The statement concerned the ***cause or circumstances*** of what he believed to be his impending death.

CMR **Exam Tip** The bar exam will likely require you to distinguish the Federal Rule on dying declarations from the traditional rule. Beware of answer choices reflecting the traditional rule, which required that the declarant ultimately die of the injury and restricted the statement's use to homicide prosecutions.

5. Statements of Personal or Family History

Statements by a now unavailable declarant concerning births, marriages, divorces, relationship, genealogical status, etc., are admissible provided that:

a. The declarant is a ***member of the family*** in question or intimately associated with it; and

b. The statements are based on the declarant's ***personal knowledge*** of the facts or her knowledge of family reputation.

6. Statements Offered Against Party Procuring Declarant's Unavailability

The statement of a person (now unavailable as a witness) is admissible when offered against a party who has engaged or acquiesced in wrongdoing that ***intentionally procured the declarant's unavailability***.

CMR SUMMARY CHART

HEARSAY EXCEPTIONS—UNAVAILABILITY REQUIRED

Former Testimony	Statement made ***under oath*** at same or at other proceeding at which the party against whom it is offered had ***motive and opportunity to develop testimony***.
Statement Against Interest	Statement against declarant's ***pecuniary, proprietary, or penal interest when made***.
Dying Declaration	Statement made while declarant ***believed death was imminent, concerning the cause*** or circumstances of the impending death.
Statement of Personal or Family History	Statement of personal or family history (*e.g.*, birth, death, marriage) ***made by family member*** or one intimately associated with the family.
Statement Offered Against Party Procuring Declarant's Unavailability	Statement of unavailable declarant ***offered against party who procured*** declarant's unavailability.

D. HEARSAY EXCEPTIONS—DECLARANT'S AVAILABILITY IMMATERIAL

The following exceptions to the hearsay rule do not require that the declarant be unavailable.

1. Present State of Mind

A statement of a declarant's then-existing state of mind, emotion, sensation, or physical condition is admissible. It is usually offered to establish a person's intent or as circumstantial evidence that the intent was carried out. Except as to certain facts concerning the declarant's will, however, a statement of memory or belief is not admissible to prove the truth of the fact remembered or believed.

2. **Excited Utterances**
An out-of-court statement ***relating to a startling event***, made while under the stress of the excitement from the event (*i.e.*, ***before the declarant had time to reflect*** upon it), is admissible.

3. **Present Sense Impressions**
Comments made concurrently with the sense impression of an event that is not necessarily exciting may be admissible. There is little time for a calculated misstatement, and the contemporaneous nature of the statement makes it reliable.

4. **Declarations of Physical Condition**

   a. **Present Bodily Condition—Admissible**
   A spontaneous declaration of present bodily condition is admissible as an exception to the hearsay rule even though not made to a physician.

   b. **Past Bodily Condition—Admissible If to Assist Diagnosis or Treatment**
   Generally, declarations of past physical condition are inadmissible hearsay. Under the Federal Rules, however, these declarations are admissible if made to medical personnel to assist in diagnosing or treating the condition. Even declarations about the cause or source of the condition are admissible if pertinent to diagnosis or treatment.

CMR **Exam Tip** Remember that, contrary to the majority state view, declarations of past physical condition made to a doctor employed to testify are ***admissible*** under the Federal Rules.

5. **Business Records**
Any writing or record made as a memorandum of any act or transaction is admissible in evidence as proof of that act or transaction. Under the Federal Rules and modern statutes, the main requirements for admissibility are as follows:

   a. **"Business"**
   "Business" includes every association, profession, occupation, or calling of any kind, whether or not conducted for profit.

   b. **Entry Made in Regular Course of Business**
   To be admissible, it must appear that the record was made in the course of a regularly conducted business activity, and that it was customary to make the type of entry involved (*i.e.*, the entrant had a duty to make the entry). Self-serving accident reports prepared primarily for litigation usually are inadmissible.

   c. **Personal Knowledge**
   The business record must consist of matters within the personal knowledge of the entrant or within the knowledge of someone with a ***duty*** to transmit such matters to the entrant.

Exam Tip Watch for fact patterns involving police reports containing the statements of witnesses. While police reports may qualify as business records under some circumstances, remember that generally witnesses, or even parties, are not under a business duty to convey information to the police. Therefore, a report containing their statements cannot qualify as a business record, although it may be admissible under another exception (*see* 7., *infra*) or as an admission.

d. **Entry Made Near Time of Event**
The entry must be made at or near the time of the transaction.

e. **Authentication**
The authenticity of the record must be established. This can be accomplished by the custodian (i) ***testifying*** that the record is a business record, or (ii) ***certifying in writing*** that the record is a business record.

CMR **Exam Tip** Business records may be used to prove the nonoccurrence or nonexistence of a matter if it was the regular practice of the business to record all such matters.

6. **Past Recollection Recorded**
If the witness's memory cannot be revived, a party may introduce a memorandum that the witness made at or near the time of the event. For admissibility requirements, *see* VI.B.3.b., *supra*. The writing itself is not admissible; it must be read to the jury.

7. **Official Records and Other Official Writings**

a. **Public Records and Reports**
The following are admissible: records setting forth the activities of the office or agency; recordings of matters observed pursuant to a duty imposed by law (except police observations in criminal cases); or in civil actions and ***against the government in criminal cases***, records of factual findings resulting from an investigation authorized by law. The writing must have been made by and within the scope of the duty of the public employee, and it must have been made at or near the time of the event.

CMR **Exam Tip** Police reports that do not qualify as business records may be admitted under the public records and reports exception. Even the officer's opinions and factual (not legal) conclusions would be admissible under this exception. Be careful, however, to test the statements of others contained in the report to make sure they are admissible under a hearsay exception; otherwise, those statements will be excluded even if the report is admitted.

CMR **Exam Tip** Remember that public records and reports generally are ***not admissible against the defendant in a criminal case***. This means that investigative reports by the police, FBI, and other agencies are inadmissible in this situation.

b. **Records of Vital Statistics**
Records of vital statistics are admissible if the report was made to a public officer pursuant to requirements of law.

c. **Statement of Absence of Public Record**
Evidence in the form of a certification or testimony from the custodian of public records that she has diligently searched and failed to find a record is admissible to prove that the matter was not recorded, or inferentially that the matter did not occur.

d. Judgments

A certified copy of a judgment is always admissible proof that such judgment has been entered.

1) Prior Criminal Conviction—Felony Conviction Admissible

Under the Federal Rules, judgments of felony convictions are admissible in criminal and civil actions to prove any fact essential to the judgment. In a criminal case, however, the government may use the judgment for this purpose only against the accused; it may be used only for impeachment purposes against others.

2) Prior Criminal Acquittal—Excluded

The exclusionary rule is still applied to records of prior acquittals.

3) Judgment in Former Civil Case

A civil judgment is clearly inadmissible in a subsequent criminal proceeding and generally inadmissible in subsequent civil proceedings.

8. Ancient Documents and Documents Affecting Property Interests

Under the Federal Rules, statements in any authenticated document ***20 years old or more*** are admissible, as are statements in ***any document affecting an interest in property***, regardless of age.

9. Learned Treatises

Treatises are admissible as substantive proof under the Federal Rules if:

a. Called to the attention of, or relied upon by, an expert witness; and

b. Established as reliable authority by the testimony of that witness, other expert testimony, or judicial notice.

10. Reputation

Reputation evidence is admissible, under several exceptions to the hearsay rule, as evidence of the following: (i) character; (ii) personal or family history; (iii) land boundaries; and (iv) a community's general history.

11. Family Records

Statements of fact concerning personal or family history contained in family Bibles, jewelry engravings, genealogies, tombstone engravings, etc., are admissible.

12. Market Reports

Market reports and other published compilations are admissible if generally used and relied upon by the public or by persons in a particular occupation.

HEARSAY EXCEPTIONS—AVAILABILITY IMMATERIAL

State of Mind	Statement of ***then-existing state of mind, emotion, sensation, or physical condition***. (Usually introduced to establish ***intent***. Admissible when state of mind is a material issue or to show subsequent acts of declarant.)
Excited Utterance	Statement made while ***under stress of excitement of startling event***.
Present Sense Impression	Statement made ***concurrently with perception*** of event described.
Medical Diagnosis or Treatment	Statement made to ***medical personnel*** for the purpose of diagnosis or treatment.
Recorded Recollection	***Writing by witness who cannot now remember*** the facts, made while the facts were fresh in her mind.
Business Records or Absence Thereof	Writing made in the ***regular course of business***, consisting of matters within the ***personal knowledge*** of one with a ***business duty*** to transmit. Lack of such writing may be used to show nonoccurrence of event.
Public Records and Reports or Absence Thereof; Records of Vital Statistics	Records and reports of ***public agencies*** regarding their activities, and records of ***births, deaths, marriages,*** etc. Absence of public record is admissible to show nonexistence of matter.
Judgments	A copy of a judgment of a ***prior felony conviction*** is admissible to prove any fact essential to the judgment. In a criminal case, it may be used for this purpose only against the accused.
Ancient Documents	Documents ***20 years old*** or more.
Documents Affecting Property Interests	Statements in a document affecting an interest in a property (*e.g.,* ***deed, will***).
Learned Treatises	Statements from ***authoritative works*** admitted if called to attention of expert witness and ***established as reliable*** authority.
Reputation	Reputation evidence concerning a person's ***character***, a person's ***personal or family history***, land ***boundaries***, or a community's ***general history***.
Family Records	Statements of fact found in ***family Bibles, jewelry engravings, tombstones,*** etc.
Market Reports	Market reports and public compilations ***generally relied on by the public*** or persons of a particular occupation.

ADMISSIBLE OUT-OF-COURT STATEMENTS

NONHEARSAY	HEARSAY EXCEPTIONS: Unavailability Required	HEARSAY EXCEPTIONS: Availability Immaterial	
1. Nonassertive Conduct	1. Former Testimony	1. State of Mind	9. Judgments of Prior Convictions
2. Statement Not Offered for Its Truth	2. Dying Declaration	2. Excited Utterance	10. Ancient Documents
3. Prior Inconsistent Statement Made Under Oath	3. Statement Against Interest	3. Present Sense Impression	11. Documents Affecting a Property Interest
4. Prior Consistent Statement Offered to Rebut Charge that Witness Is Lying or Exaggerating	4. Statement of Personal or Family History	4. Physical Condition (Medical Diagnosis or Treatment)	12. Learned Treatises
5. Prior Statement of Identification	5. Statement Offered Against Party Procuring Declarant's Unavailability	5. Recorded Recollection	13. Reputation
6. Admission of Party-Opponent (including vicarious admission)		6. Business Records or Absence Thereof	14. Family Records
		7. Public Records and Reports	15. Market Reports
		8. Records of Vital Statistics	

E. RESIDUAL "CATCH-ALL" EXCEPTION OF FEDERAL RULES

For a hearsay statement that is not covered by a specific exception to be admitted, the Federal Rules provide a catch-all exception, which requires:

1. That the hearsay statement possess circumstantial guarantees of ***trustworthiness***;
2. That the statement be strictly ***necessary***; and
3. That ***notice*** be given to the adversary as to the nature of the statement.

F. CONSTITUTIONAL ISSUES

Because the use of hearsay evidence in a criminal case may violate the Confrontation Clause, prior testimonial evidence is inadmissible against a criminal defendant unless the hearsay declarant is unavailable, and the defendant had an opportunity to cross-examine the hearsay declarant at the time the statement was made. In addition, hearsay rules and other exclusionary rules cannot be applied where such application would deprive the accused of her right to a fair trial or deny her right to compulsory process.

VIII. PROCEDURAL CONSIDERATIONS

A. BURDENS OF PROOF

The burden of proof encompasses the burden of producing or going forward with the evidence, and the burden of persuasion.

1. Burden of Producing Evidence

The party who has the burden of pleading usually has the burden of producing or going forward with evidence sufficient to make out a prima facie case (*i.e.,* create a fact question of the issue for the trier of fact). Once the party has satisfied the burden of going forward with evidence, it is incumbent upon the other side to come forward with evidence to rebut the accepted evidence.

2. Burden of Persuasion (Proof)

After the parties have sustained their burden of production of evidence, the question is whether the party with the burden of persuasion has satisfied it. The burden of persuasion for civil cases is usually by a preponderance of the evidence (more probably true than not true), although some civil cases require proof of clear and convincing evidence (high probability). The burden of persuasion for criminal cases is beyond a reasonable doubt.

B. PRESUMPTIONS

A presumption is a rule that requires that a particular inference be drawn from an ascertained set of facts. It is a form of substitute proof in that proof of the presumed fact is rendered unnecessary once evidence has been introduced of the basic fact that gives rise to the presumption.

1. Effect—Shift Burden of Production

A presumption operates, until rebutted, to shift the burden of production to the party against whom the presumption operates.

Exam Tip Remember that a presumption ***does not shift the burden of persuasion***. The burden of persuasion remains on the same party throughout a trial.

2. **Rebutting a Presumption**

A presumption is overcome or destroyed when the adversary produces some evidence contradicting the presumed fact. Once sufficient contrary evidence is admitted, the presumption is of no force or effect.

3. **Distinguish True Presumptions from Inferences and Substantive Law**

True presumptions are the rebuttable type discussed above. Be careful not to confuse them with inferences and rules of substantive law.

a. **Permissible Inferences**

A permissible inference may allow the party to meet his burden of production (*e.g.,* establish a prima facie case), but does not shift the burden to the adversary. Examples include the inference of negligence arising from res ipsa loquitur, the inference that destroyed evidence was unfavorable to the spoliator, and the inference of undue influence when a will's drafter is also the principal beneficiary.

b. **"Presumptions" in Criminal Cases**

The presumption of innocence in criminal cases is merely a permissible inference. The burden of production never shifts to the accused.

CMR **Exam Tip** Special considerations apply when true presumptions arise in the criminal context. The judge cannot instruct the jury that it ***must*** find a presumed fact against the accused; he must instruct them that they ***may*** regard the basic facts as sufficient evidence of the presumed fact.

CMR **Exam Tip** If, in a criminal case, a presumed fact establishes guilt, is an element of the offense, or negates a defense, it must be proved beyond a reasonable doubt.

c. **Conclusive Presumptions**

Because it cannot be rebutted, a conclusive presumption (*e.g.,* that a child under age seven cannot commit a crime) is really a rule of substantive law.

4. **Specific Presumptions**

The following are common rebuttable presumptions:

a. **Legitimacy**

Every person is presumed to be legitimate.

b. **Against Suicide**

When cause of death is in dispute, there is a presumption in civil cases that it was not suicide.

c. **Sanity**

Every person is presumed sane in civil and criminal cases until the contrary is shown.

d. **Death from Absence**
If a person is unexplainably absent for a continuous period of seven years and he has not been heard from, he is presumed dead.

e. **Ownership of Car—Agent Driver**
Proof of ownership of a motor vehicle creates the presumption that the owner was the driver or that the driver was the owner's agent.

f. **Chastity**
Every person is presumed chaste and virtuous.

g. **Regularity**
It is presumed that persons acting in an official office are properly performing their duties.

h. **Continuance**
Proof of the existence of a person or condition at a given time raises a presumption that it continued for as long as it is usual with things of that nature.

i. **Mail Delivery**
A letter, properly addressed, stamped, and mailed, is presumed to have been delivered.

j. **Solvency**
A person is presumed solvent, and every debt is presumed collectible.

k. **Bailee's Negligence**
Proof of delivery of goods in good condition to a bailee and failure of the bailee to return the goods in the same condition create the presumption that the bailee was negligent.

l. **Marriage**
Upon proof of a marriage ceremony, a marriage is presumed valid.

5. **Conflicting Presumptions**
When two or more conflicting presumptions arise, the judge should apply the presumption founded on the weightier considerations of policy and logic.

6. **Choice of Law Regarding Presumptions in Civil Actions**
Under the Federal Rules, state law governs the effect of a presumption concerning a fact that is an element of a claim or defense to which, under the *Erie* doctrine, the rule of decision is supplied by state law.

C. RELATIONSHIP OF PARTIES, JUDGE, AND JURY

1. **Allocation of Responsibilities**
In our adversarial adjudicative process, the focus is on the party's responsibility to frame the issues in a litigation and to assume the burden of proving the issues he has raised. The trial judge's primary responsibility is to superintend the trial fairly. As a general rule, questions of law are for the trial judge to determine and questions of fact are for the jury.

2. Preliminary Determination of Admissibility

In most cases, the existence of some preliminary or foundational fact is an essential condition to the admissibility of proffered evidence. The Federal Rules distinguish preliminary facts to be decided by the jury from those to be decided by the judge on the ground that the former questions involve the relevancy of the proffered evidence, while the latter questions involve the competency of evidence that is relevant.

a. Preliminary Facts Decided by Jury

Examples of preliminary facts to be decided by the jury include agency, authenticity of a document, credibility of a witness, and personal knowledge.

b. Preliminary Facts Decided by Judge

Facts affecting the competency of the evidence must be determined by the trial judge. Requirements for hearsay exceptions, privileges, and expert testimony, as well as mental competence, must also be decided by the judge.

1) What Evidence May Be Considered

The Federal Rules permit the trial judge to consider any relevant evidence even though not otherwise admissible under the rules of evidence. Most state courts, however, hold that the rules of evidence apply in preliminary fact determinations as much as in any other phase of the trial; thus, only admissible evidence may be considered.

2) Presence of Jury

Whether the jury should be excused during the preliminary fact determination is generally within the discretion of the trial judge.

c. Testimony by Accused Does Not Waive Privilege Against Self-Incrimination

An accused may testify on any preliminary matter (*e.g.,* circumstances surrounding an allegedly illegal search) without subjecting herself to testifying at trial.

d. Judicial Power to Comment upon Evidence

A judge may comment on the weight of the evidence in federal courts, but generally not in state courts.

e. Power to Call Witnesses

A judge may call and interrogate witnesses on her own initiative.

f. Rulings

A trial judge has an obligation to rule promptly on counsel's evidentiary objections and, upon request, to state the grounds for her rulings.

g. Instructions on Limited Admissibility of Evidence

A judge will restrict evidence to its proper scope and instruct the jury accordingly.

REAL PROPERTY

TABLE OF CONTENTS

REAL PROPERTY

I. ESTATES IN LAND

A. PRESENT POSSESSORY ESTATES

A present possessory estate is an interest that gives the holder the right to present possession.

1. Fee Simple Absolute

A fee simple absolute is the largest estate recognized by law. It can be sold, divided, devised, or inherited and has an indefinite or potentially ***infinite duration***. Today, a fee simple is presumed in the absence of express contrary intent (words of inheritance are no longer necessary).

2. Defeasible Fees

Defeasible fees are fee simple estates (*i.e.,* of uncertain or potentially infinite duration) that can be terminated upon the happening of a stated event.

a. Fee Simple Determinable (and Possibility of Reverter)

A fee simple determinable terminates upon the happening of a stated event and ***automatically reverts*** to the grantor. It is created by durational language, such as "for so long as," "while," "during," or "until." A fee simple determinable can be conveyed, but the grantee takes subject to the estate's being terminated by the specified event.

CMR **Exam Tip** Remember that statements of motive or purpose do not create a determinable fee. To create a fee simple determinable, words limiting the ***duration*** of the estate must be used. Watch for grants such as "for the purpose of" and "to be used for"; they are merely expressions of motive.

1) Correlative Future Interest in Grantor—Possibility of Reverter

Whenever a grantor conveys a fee simple determinable he ***automatically*** retains a possibility of reverter, which is a reversionary future interest. A possibility of reverter is transferable, descendible, and devisable.

b. Fee Simple Subject to Condition Subsequent (and Right of Entry)

A fee simple subject to a condition subsequent is an estate in which the grantor ***reserves the right to terminate*** the estate upon the happening of a stated event; *i.e.,* the estate does not automatically terminate—the grantor must take some action. The estate is created by use of conditional words, such as "upon condition that," "provided that," "but if," and "if it happens that."

1) Correlative Future Interest in Grantor—Right of Entry

The right to terminate, reserved by the grantor, is called a right of entry. It must be ***expressly reserved***; in contrast with a possibility of reverter, it does not arise automatically. Some courts hold that rights of entry are not transferable inter vivos, but most states agree they are devisable and all states agree they are descendible.

PRESENT POSSESSORY ESTATES

Present Estate	Examples	Duration	Correlative Future Interest in Grantor	Correlative Future Interest in Third Party
Fee Simple Absolute	"To A & his heirs"	Forever	None	None
Fee Simple Determinable	"To A & his heirs for so long as . . ." until . . ." while . . ." during . . ."	As long as condition is met, then ***automatically*** to grantor	Possibility of Reverter	(*See* Fee Simple Subject to an Executory Interest, below)
Fee Simple Subject to Condition Subsequent	"To A & his heirs, but if . . ." upon condition that . . ." provided that . . ."	Until happening of named event ***and*** reentry by grantor	Right of Entry	(*See* Fee Simple Subject to an Executory Interest, below)
Fee Simple Subject to an Executory Interest	"To A & his heirs for so long as . . ., and if not . . ., to B"	As long as condition is met, then to third party	(*See* Fee Simple Determinable, above)	Executory Interest
	"To A & his heirs, but if . . ., to B"	Until happening of event	(*See* Fee Simple Subject to Condition Subsequent, above)	Executory Interest
Fee Tail	"To A & the heirs of his body"	Until A and his line die out	Reversion	None (but remainder is possible)
Life Estate (may be defeasible)	"To A for life," ***or*** "To A for the life of B"	Until the end of the measuring life	Reversion	None (but see below)
	"To A for life, then to B"	Until the end of the measuring life	None	Remainder
	"To A for life, but if . . ., to B"	Until the end of the measuring life ***or*** the happening of the named event	Reversion	Executory Interest

c. **Fee Simple Subject to an Executory Interest**
If a fee simple estate terminates upon the happening of a stated event (because it is determinable or subject to a condition subsequent) and then passes to a third party rather than reverting to the grantor or giving the grantor a right to terminate, the third party has an executory interest.
Examples: 1) "To A and his heirs for so long as liquor is not sold on the premises; in that event, to B." B has an executory interest.

2) "Blackacre to XYZ Church, but if it is used for anything other than church purposes, then to B." B has an executory interest.

3. **Fee Tail**
The fee tail is an estate where ***inheritability is limited to lineal heirs***. It is created by the words "to B and the heirs of his body." Most jurisdictions have abolished the fee tail, and an attempt to create one results in a ***fee simple.***

4. **Life Estate**
A life estate is one ***measured by the life*** or lives of one or more persons. It may be created by operation of law (*e.g.,* dower) or by conveyance.

a. **Life Estates by Marital Right (Legal Life Estates)**
Dower and curtesy were the common law interests of a spouse in the real property of the other spouse. These interests could not be defeated by conveyance or by creditors. Most states have abolished dower and curtesy in favor of a statutory right to a portion of a spouse's estate.

b. **Conventional Life Estates**

1) **For Life of Grantee**
The usual life estate is measured by the life of the grantee (*e.g.,* "to B for life"). This type of life estate may be implied from language such as "to C after the life of B."

2) **Life Estate Pur Autre Vie (Life of Another)**
A life estate "pur autre vie" is measured by a life ***other than the grantee's*** (*e.g.,* "to B for the life of C"). A life estate pur autre vie also results when the ***life tenant conveys*** his life estate to another (*e.g.,* if B, the holder of a life estate, conveys his interest to D, D has a life estate for the life of B).

CMR **Exam Tip** Although a life estate is usually indefeasible (*i.e.,* it ends only when the life tenant dies), it is possible to create life estates that are defeasible in the same ways that fee estates can be defeasible. A life estate can be determinable, subject to a condition subsequent, and subject to an executory interest (*e.g.,* "to A for life so long as alcohol is not used on the premises" or "to A for life, but if A is divorced, to B").

c. **Rights and Duties of Life Tenant—Doctrine of Waste**
A life tenant is entitled to any ***ordinary*** uses and profits of the land, but cannot do anything that injures the interests of a remainderman or reversioner. A future interest holder may sue for damages or to enjoin such acts.

1) **Affirmative (Voluntary) Waste—Natural Resources**
Exploitation of natural resources (*e.g.*, minerals) by a life tenant is generally limited to situations when: (i) necessary for ***repair or maintenance*** of the land; (ii) the land is ***suitable only for such use***; or (iii) it is expressly or impliedly ***permitted by the grantor***. Under the open mines doctrine, if mining was done on the land prior to the life estate, the life tenant can continue mining—but is limited to the mines already open.

2) **Permissive Waste**
Permissive waste occurs when a life tenant fails to protect or preserve the land. A life tenant is obligated to: (i) preserve the ***land and structures in a reasonable state of repair***; (ii) pay ***interest*** on mortgages (not principal); (iii) pay ***ordinary taxes*** on the land; and (iv) pay ***special assessments*** for public improvements ***of short duration*** (improvements of long duration are apportioned between the life tenant and future interest holder). A life tenant is ***not*** obliged to insure the premises for the benefit of remaindermen and is not responsible for damages caused by a third-party tortfeasor.

3) **Ameliorative Waste**
Ameliorative waste is a change that ***benefits*** the property economically. This waste was actionable at common law, but now a life tenant may alter or even demolish existing buildings if:

(i) The market value of the future interests is not diminished; and ***either***

(ii) The remaindermen do not object; ***or***

(iii) A substantial and permanent change in the neighborhood conditions (*e.g.*, change from residential to 90% industrial) has deprived the property in its current form of reasonable productivity or usefulness.

a) **Compare—Leasehold Tenant**
Leasehold tenants remain liable for ameliorative waste even if the neighborhood has changed and the market value of the premises was increased.

b) **Compare—Worthless Property**
If the land is practically worthless in its present state, the life tenant may seek a partition sale, the proceeds of which are put in trust with income paid to the life tenant.

d. **Renunciation of Life Estate**
If a life tenant who receives the estate by will or intestacy renounces his interest, the future interest following the life estate is generally accelerated so that it becomes immediately possessory.

5. **Estate for Years, Periodic Estate, Estate at Will, Tenancy at Sufferance**
These present estates are considered in the next chapter, which concerns the landlord-tenant relationship.

B. FUTURE INTERESTS

A future interest gives its holder the right or possibility of ***future*** possession of an estate. It is a ***present***, legally protected right in property.

1. Reversionary Interests—Future Interests in Transferor

a. Possibilities of Reverter and Rights of Entry

These interests are discussed *supra* in connection with defeasible fees.

CMR COMPARISON CHART

POSSIBILITY OF REVERTER VS. RIGHT OF ENTRY

	Possibility of Reverter	Right of Entry
Correlative Present Interest	Fee Simple Determinable	Fee Simple Subject to Condition Subsequent
Example	"To A so long as alcohol is not used on the premises"	"To A on condition that if alcohol is used on the premises, O shall have the right to reenter and retake the premises"
Rights of Grantor	Estate ***automatically*** reverts to grantor upon the occurrence of the stated event	Estate does not revert automatically; ***grantor must exercise his right of entry***
Alienability	Transferable, descendible, and devisable	Descendible and devisable, but some courts hold not transferable inter vivos

b. Reversions

A reversion is the estate left in a grantor who conveys less than she owns (*e.g.*, A conveys "to B for life"; A has a reversion). It arises by operation of law; it does not have to be expressly reserved. A reversion is alienable, devisable, and inheritable. Its holder can sue for waste and for tortious damage to the reversionary interest.

CMR **Exam Tip** All reversionary interests are ***vested*** and, thus, not subject to the Rule Against Perpetuities.

2. Remainders

A remainder is a future interest ***in a third person*** that can become possessory on the ***natural expiration*** of the preceding estate. It cannot divest a prior estate, and it cannot follow a time gap after the preceding estate. A remainder must be ***expressly created*** in the instrument creating the preceding possessory estate.

Examples: 1) A conveys "to B for life, then to C and his heirs"; C has a remainder.

2) A conveys "to B for life, then to C and his heirs one day after B's death"; C does ***not*** have a remainder (because there is a gap).

CMR **Exam Tip** Because a remainder cannot "cut short" a preceding estate, it can ***never follow a fee simple*** estate, which is of potentially infinite duration. Executory interests are the future interests that cut short preceding estates or follow a gap after them.

a. Indefeasibly Vested Remainder

A vested remainder is one created in an ***existing and ascertained*** person, and ***not subject to a condition precedent***. The remainderman has a right to immediate possession upon normal termination of the preceding estate. An ***indefeasibly*** vested remainder is a vested remainder that is not subject to divestment or diminution.

b. Vested Remainder Subject to Open

This is a vested remainder created in a class of persons (*e.g.,* "children") that is certain to become possessory, but is ***subject to diminution***—by the birth of additional persons who will share in the remainder as a class.

Example: A conveys "to B for life, then to the children of C." B and C are living and C has one child, D. D has a vested remainder subject to open.

c. Vested Remainder Subject to Total Divestment

This is a vested remainder that is subject to a ***condition subsequent***.

Example: A conveys "to B for life, then to C and his heirs; but if C dies unmarried, then to D and his heirs." C has a vested remainder subject to complete divestment by D's executory interest.

d. Contingent Remainder

Contingent remainders are those created in ***unborn or unascertained*** persons, or ***subject to a condition precedent***.

1) Subject to Condition Precedent

A condition is precedent if it must be satisfied before the remainderman has a right to possession.

Examples: 1) A conveys "to B for life, then to C and his heirs ***if*** C marries D." C's remainder is contingent because he must marry D before he can take possession.

2) A conveys "to B for life, then to C and his heirs if C marries D, otherwise to E and his heirs." C and E have ***alternative contingent remainders***.

Compare: A conveys "to B for life, then to C and his heirs; but if C marries D, then to E and his heirs." C has a vested remainder (because no condition precedent) subject to divestment by E's executory interest.

2) **Unborn or Unascertained Persons**
A remainder created in unborn or unascertained persons is contingent because until the remainderman is ascertained, no one is ready to take possession if the preceding estate ends.
Example: A conveys "to B for life, then to the children of C." If C is childless at the time, the remainder is contingent.

3) **Destructibility of Contingent Remainders**
At common law, a contingent remainder was destroyed if it failed to vest before or upon the termination of the preceding freehold estate.
Example: A conveys "to B for life, then to C if she reaches age 21." If B dies before C reaches age 21, C's remainder is destroyed.

Most states have abolished the destructibility rule. In those states, C's interest in the above example would be converted to an executory interest upon B's death because it will divest A's reversionary estate when C turns 21.

a) **Related Doctrine of Merger**
When one person acquires all of the present and future interests in land except a contingent remainder, under the common law, the contingent remainder is destroyed.
Example: X conveys "to Y for life, then to Z's children." If, before Z has any children, X purchases Y's life estate, X will have a life estate pur autre vie and a reversion. These interests merge, and the contingent remainder in Z's unborn children is destroyed.

CMR **Exam Tip** When considering whether estates merge to destroy a contingent remainder, remember that if the life estate and the next vested interest were ***created by the same instrument***, there is no merger. (This would defeat the grantor's obvious intent.) Merger ***may*** occur only as in the example above, when one person later acquires immediately successive estates.

e. **Rule in Shelley's Case (Rule Against Remainders in Grantee's Heirs)**
At common law, if the same instrument created a life estate in A and gave the remainder only to A's heirs, the remainder was not recognized, and A took the life estate ***and*** the remainder.
Example: A conveys "to B for life, then to C for life, then to the heirs of B." The Rule transforms the remainder in B's heirs into a remainder in B. (No merger, however, because the remainder for life in C is ***vested***.)

The Rule in Shelley's Case has been abolished in most states.

f. **Doctrine of Worthier Title (Rule Against Remainders in Grantor's Heirs)**
Under the Doctrine of Worthier Title ("DOWT"), a remainder in the grantor's heirs is invalid and becomes a reversion in the grantor. For example, if A grants Blackacre "to B for life, then to the heirs of A," B has a life estate, and A has a reversion. DOWT is generally treated as a rule of construction (*i.e.,* it does not apply if an intent to create a remainder in heirs has been clearly manifested). DOWT applies only to inter vivos transfers (not wills), and only if the word "heirs" is used.

TECHNICAL RULES OF THE COMMON LAW

	Destruction of Contingent Remainders	Rule in Shelley's Case	Doctrine of Worthier Title
Rule	Contingent remainders are destroyed if not vested at time of termination of preceding estate.	A remainder in a life tenant-grantee's heirs is deemed to be in the life tenant herself.	A remainder in the grantor's heirs is ineffective, so grantor has a reversion.
Example	"To A for life, remainder to A's children who reach 21."	"To B for life, then to B's heirs."	"To B for life, then to my heirs at law."
Result	If A has no children who are at least 21 at time of her death, property reverts to grantor.	B has a fee simple.	B has a life estate; grantor has a reversion.
Modern Status	Abolished in most jurisdictions.	Abolished in most jurisdictions.	Generally treated as rule of construction only.
Modern Result	Property reverts to grantor; A's children have a springing executory interest.	B's heirs have a contingent remainder.	Grantor's heirs have a contingent remainder.

3. Executory Interests

Executory interests are future interests in third parties that either ***divest*** a transferee's preceding freehold estate ("shifting interests"), or ***follow a gap*** in possession or ***cut short*** a grantor's estate ("springing interests").

Examples: 1) In a grant from A "to B and his heirs when B marries C," B has a ***springing*** executory interest because it divests the grantor's estate.

2) In a grant from A "to B for life, then to C and his heirs; but if C predeceases B, then to D and his heirs," D has a ***shifting*** executory interest because it divests a transferee's preceding estate.

Executory interests are not considered vested and thus are subject to the Rule Against Perpetuities, but executory interests are not destructible.

CMR **Exam Tip** Remember that if the future interest does not follow the natural termination of the preceding estate, it must be an executory interest; only an executory interest can follow a fee simple estate.

CMR **Exam Tip** Where language is ambiguous, the preference is for vested remainders subject to divestment rather than contingent remainders or executory interests. Policy favors early vesting of estates.

4. Transferability of Remainders and Executory Interests

Vested remainders are fully transferable, descendible, and devisable. At common law, contingent remainders and executory interests were not transferable inter vivos, but most courts today hold that they are freely transferable. Contingent remainders and executory interests are descendible and devisable, provided survival is not a condition to the interest's taking.

CMR **Exam Tip** Any future interest that is transferable is subject to involuntary transfer; *i.e.,* it is reachable by creditors.

5. Class Gifts

A "class" is a group of persons having a common characteristic (*e.g.,* children, nephews). The share of each member is determined by the number of persons in the class. A class gift of a remainder may be vested subject to open (where at least one group member exists) or contingent (where all group members are unascertained).

a. When the Class Closes—The Rule of Convenience

Under the rule of convenience, in the absence of express contrary intent, a class closes (*i.e.,* no one born after that time may share in the gift) ***when some member of the class can call for distribution*** of her share of the class gift.

Examples: 1) T's will devises property to W for life, then to A's children. At the time the will is executed, A has two children, B and C. A then has another child, D. T dies. A has child E, then W dies. After W's death, A has another child, F. The class closed at W's death because it was time to make the distribution. Thus, B, C, D, and E share the property, and F is excluded.

2) T's will devises the residue of his estate "to those of A's children who attain age 21." If any of A's children is 21 at T's death, the class closes at that time. Otherwise it closes when one of A's children reaches age 21. But remember, if it had been a future gift (*i.e.,* "to A for life, then to such of A's children who attain age 21"), the class would remain open until the life tenant's death even if some of the class members had reached the stated age at T's death.

Exam Tip Recall that persons in gestation at the time the class closes are included in the class.

b. Survivorship

Survivorship of a class member to the time of closing is usually unnecessary to share in a future gift—unless survival was made an express condition (*e.g.*, "to B for life and then to his ***surviving*** children"). However, certain terms are construed to create ***implied*** survivorship conditions (*e.g.*, widow, issue, heirs, next of kin).

CMR Exam Tip Generally, when the instrument creating a gift of a future interest in an open class becomes effective, existing class members have a vested remainder subject to open. But watch for a condition precedent, which will prevent the remainder from vesting. For example, "to A for life, remainder to those of B's children who survive A" creates a contingent remainder in B's children even if they are in existence—and even if B is dead—because the remainder is contingent on surviving A.

C. TRUSTS

A trust is a fiduciary relationship with respect to specific property (***res***) wherein the ***trustee*** holds legal title to the property subject to enforceable equitable rights in a ***beneficiary***. The creator of a trust is the ***settlor***, who must own the property at the time of trust creation and must have had the ***intent*** to create the trust.

1. Application of Rule Against Perpetuities

The Rule Against Perpetuities applies to the equitable future interests of the beneficiaries in a private trust just as it does to "legal" future interests.

2. Creation of Trusts

A trust can be created by will (testamentary trust), inter vivos transfer of the trust res, or inter vivos declaration that the settlor is holding property in trust. All trusts of real property must be in writing. Note that a settlor may bequeath (by will) property to a trust created during his lifetime—*i.e.*, he may "pour it over" into the trust.

3. Charitable Trusts

A charitable trust must have a charitable purpose. The rules governing charitable trusts differ from those applicable to private trusts in three important ways: (i) a charitable trust must have ***indefinite beneficiaries***; (ii) it may be ***perpetual*** (*i.e.*, the Rule Against Perpetuities does not apply); and (iii) the ***cy pres doctrine***, which allows a court to select an alternative charity when the purpose of the settlor becomes impractical or impossible, applies. Charitable trusts may be enforced by an action of the attorney general of the state.

CMR Exam Tip Remember that the Rule Against Perpetuities does apply to a shift from a private to charitable use or a charitable to private use.

D. THE RULE AGAINST PERPETUITIES

No interest in property is valid unless it must vest, if at all, not later than ***21 years after some life in being*** ("measuring life") at the creation of the interest. If there is ***any possibility*** that the interest might vest more than 21 years after a life in being, the interest is void. The Rule applies to contingent remainders, executory interests, vested remainders subject to open (class gifts), options to purchase (not attached to a leasehold), rights of first refusal, and powers of appointment.

FUTURE INTERESTS IN TRANSFEREES

Future Interests	Example	Alienability	Subject to Rule Against Perpetuities?
Indefeasibly Vested Remainder	"To A for life, then to B."	Transferable, descendible, and devisable	No
Vested Remainder Subject to Total Divestment	"To A for life, and on A's death, to B; but if B predeceases A, then to C."	Transferable, descendible, and devisable	No
Vested Remainder Subject to Open	"To A for life, then to A's children in equal shares."	Transferable, descendible, and devisable	Yes—As long as the class remains open
Contingent Remainder	"To A for life, then to B if B marries C." ***or*** "To X for life, then to X's surviving children."	Transferable in most states (not at common law), descendible, and devisable	Yes
Shifting Executory Interest	"To A for life, remainder to B and her heirs; but if B predeceases A, then to C and his heirs."	Transferable in most states (not at common law), descendible, and devisable	Yes
Springing Executory Interest	"To X when and if he becomes a doctor." ***or*** "To X for life, then two years after X's death, to Y."	Transferable in most states (not at common law), descendible, and devisable	Yes

1. When Perpetuities Period Begins to Run

The time the interest is created and the perpetuities period begins to run depends on the instrument and the interest created: For interests granted by ***will***, it runs from the date of the ***testator's death***; for ***deeds***, it is the date of ***delivery***. The period runs on an ***irrevocable trust*** from the date it is ***created***; it runs on a ***revocable trust*** from the date it ***becomes irrevocable***.

2. "Must Vest"

An interest vests for purposes of the Rule when it becomes: (i) possessory, or (ii) an indefeasibly vested remainder or a vested remainder subject to total divestment.

CMR **Exam Tip** In analyzing Rule Against Perpetuities problems, keep in mind that the key is when the interest ***could possibly vest***—not when it is likely to vest or even when it did. You must examine the grant as of the time of its ***creation*** and be sure that if the interest vests it will be within the period of the Rule (*i.e.*, life in being plus 21 years). If there is any possibility that it could vest beyond the period, it is void.

CMR **Exam Tip** Remember that the Rule Against Perpetuities applies ***only*** to ***contingent*** remainders, ***executory interests***, vested remainders ***subject to open***, and in most states, ***options to purchase***. Thus, the ***grantor's interests*** (reversions, possibilities of reverter, rights of entry) are safe from the Rule; you don't need to consider them.

3. "Lives in Being"

Unless other measuring lives are specified, one connected with the vesting of the interest is used. Any lives may be denominated measuring lives, provided they are ***human*** and of reasonable number.

4. Interests Exempt from Rule

Except for vested remainders subject to open, the Rule Against Perpetuities does not apply to vested interests. Thus, other vested remainders, reversions, possibilities of reverter, and rights of entry are not subject to the Rule. Moreover, there is a ***charity-to-charity*** exception to the Rule (*i.e.*, the Rule does not apply to any disposition over from one charity to another), and an exception for options to purchase ***held by a current tenant***.

5. Effect of Violating Rule—Offensive Interest Stricken

Violation of the Rule destroys only the offending interest. The exception is the rare case of "infectious invalidity" where the testator would probably have preferred the entire gift to fail.

6. The Rule in Operation—Common Pitfall Cases

a. Executory Interest Following Defeasible Fee

Generally, an executory interest that follows a defeasible fee (*e.g.*, "to A for so long as no liquor is consumed on the premises, then to B") violates the Rule Against Perpetuities, and the executory interest is stricken. (An executory interest following a defeasible fee is valid only if the condition is specific to the fee holder or expressly limited to the perpetuities period.)

CMR **Exam Tip** When a void interest is stricken, the interests are classified as if the void interest were never there. For example, if G conveys "to A for as long as no liquor is consumed on the premises, then to B," B's interest would be stricken, A would have a fee simple determinable, and G would have a possibility of reverter. In contrast, if G conveys "to A, but if liquor is ever consumed on the premises, then to B," B's interest and the condition are stricken, and A has a fee simple absolute.

b. Age Contingency Beyond Age Twenty-One in Open Class

A gift to an open class conditioned on members surviving beyond age 21 violates the Rule.

Example: "To X for life, then to those of X's children who attain the age of 25." The remainder in X's children violates the Rule and is void.

Some states have enacted perpetuities reform legislation that reduces such age contingencies to 21.

c. Fertile Octogenarian

A woman is conclusively presumed to be capable of bearing children, regardless of her age or medical condition. Thus, a disposition "to A for life, then to A's children for life, then to A's grandchildren in fee" is invalid as to A's grandchildren despite the fact that A is 80 years old. Some states have enacted perpetuities reform statutes that raise a presumption that women over a certain age (*e.g.,* 55) cannot bear children. Also, medical testimony regarding a woman's childbearing capacity is admissible in these states.

d. Unborn Widow or Widower

Because a person's widow (or widower) is not determined until his death, it may turn out to be someone who was not in being at the time of the disposition.

Example: O conveys "to A for life, then to A's widow for life, then to A's surviving ***issue*** in fee." In the absence of a statute to the contrary, the gift to A's issue is invalid, because A's widow might be a spouse who was not in being when the interest was created.

Compare: A remainder "to A's ***children***" would be valid because, unlike issue, they would be determined at A's death.

Where necessary to sustain a gift, some state statutes raise a presumption that any reference to a person's spouse, widow, or widower is to a person in being at the time of the transfer.

e. Administrative Contingency

A gift conditioned on an administrative contingency (*e.g.,* admission of will to probate) violates the Rule. For example, a gift "to my issue surviving at the distribution of my estate" is invalid because the estate might be administered beyond the period of the Rule. Some state reform statutes eliminate this problem by raising a presumption that the transferor intended that the contingency should occur, if at all, within 21 years.

f. Options and Rights of First Refusal

Generally, an option to purchase or right of first refusal that is structured so that it might be exercised later than the end of the perpetuities period is void. *Exception:* The Rule Against Perpetuities does not apply to options to purchase held by the current lessee.

Example: When A conveys Blackacre to B, he includes a clause in the deed that states, "B, his heirs, and assigns promise that upon finding a ready, willing, and able buyer for Blackacre, Blackacre will be offered to A, his heirs, or assigns on the same terms." This right of first refusal can be exercised well beyond a life in being plus 21 years, and thus violates the Rule.

Exam Tip Watch for a fact pattern on the exam where a tenant has an option to purchase beyond the perpetuities period. Remember that the Rule does not apply to such an option held by a ***current*** tenant, but it does apply to a former tenant and to any party to whom the current tenant might transfer the option separately from the lease (in jurisdictions permitting such a transfer).

7. Application of the Rule to Class Gifts

a. "Bad-as-to-One, Bad-as-to-All" Rule

If the interest of any class member may vest too remotely, the whole class gift fails. For the class gift to vest, the ***class must be closed*** and ***all conditions precedent must be satisfied*** for every member.

b. "Gift to Subclass" Exception

Each gift to a subclass may be treated as a separate gift under the Rule.

Example: "Income to A for life, then to A's children for their lives. Upon the death of each of A's children, the corpus is to be distributed to that child's issue, per stirpes." The gifts to each of A's children's issue are considered separately. Thus, the gifts to issue of A's children living at the time of the disposition are good, but the gifts to the issue of afterborn children of A violate the Rule and are void.

c. Per Capita Gift Exception

A gift of a fixed amount to each member of a class is not treated as a class gift under the Rule.

Example: "$1,000 to each of my great-grandchildren, whether born before or after my death." This creates gifts to individuals, each of whom is judged separately under the Rule.

8. Statutory Reforms

In a number of states, statutes modify the Rule Against Perpetuities. "Wait and see" statutes determine an interest's validity upon the termination of the preceding life estate—if the interest ***actually*** vests or fails within the perpetuities period, it is good; if it does not, it is void. Some states have statutes dealing with the common pitfall cases (*see supra*). Other statutes provide alternative vesting periods (*e.g.,* 90 years), and some allow court reformation of invalid interests to carry out the donor's general intent (*e.g.*, cy pres). These reforms are irrelevant for bar exam purposes unless referred to in the question.

INTERESTS UNDER THE RULE AGAINST PERPETUITIES

Valid Interests	Void Interests
"To A for life, then to A's children for their lives; and upon the death of the last survivor, to B." (B's interest is vested.)	"To A for life, then to A's children for their lives; and upon the death of the last survivor, to A's grandchildren." (A may have a child after this interest is created, so she could have grandchildren beyond the perpetuities period.)
"To B for life, remainder to those of B's siblings who reach age 21." (B's parents can be used as measuring lives.)	"To A for life, then to such of A's children who attain age 25." (Age contingency beyond age 21 in an open class.)
"To XYZ Orphanage for so long as it is used to house orphans; if it ceases to be so used, then to the American Red Cross." (This falls within the charity-to-charity exception.)	"To Amnesty International for so long as the premises are used for Amnesty International purposes; when they cease to be so used, then to Jane Webb." (This gift passes from a charity to a private person and so does not fall within the charity-to-charity exception.)
"To A for life, and on his death to his wife, W, for life; upon W's death to A's children then living." (No unborn widow problem because the gift is to W, a life in being.)	"To A for life, then to his widow for life, then to A's surviving descendants." (Unborn widow problem.)
"To X for life, then to Y; but if at her death Y is not survived by children, then to Z." (Y is the measuring life.)	"To M for life, then to M's children for their lives, then to M's grandchildren in fee." M is 80 years old and has had a complete hysterectomy. (Fertile octogenarian problem.)
"To A, but if alcohol is served on the premises during Z's lifetime or within 21 years of Z's death, to B." (B's interest will vest, if at all, within a life in being plus 21 years.)	"To X, but if alcohol is ever served on the premises, then to Y." (Future interest following a defeasible fee.)
"Trust income to Polo Club. At the death of the survivor of A, B, C, D, and E (all babies born on this date at Obie Hospital), the trust will terminate and the corpus will be distributed to Z, his heirs, successors, or assigns." (Saving clause.)	"The residue of my estate to my descendants who are living when my estate is distributed." (Administrative contingency problem.)
"To A for life, then to A's children for their lives, then to B if B is then living, and if B is not then living, to C." (B is the measuring life. B's and C's interests will vest or fail within B's lifetime.)	"To B for life, then to such of B's children who become lawyers." (B may have a child born after the disposition who becomes a lawyer more than 21 years after B's death.)

E. THE RULE AGAINST RESTRAINTS ON ALIENATION

Generally, any restriction on the transferability of a legal (as opposed to equitable) interest is void.

1. Types of Restraints on Alienation

There are three types of restraints on alienation: (i) ***disabling*** restraints, under which attempted transfers are ineffective; (ii) ***forfeiture*** restraints, under which an attempted transfer forfeits the interest; and (iii) ***promissory*** restraints, under which an attempted transfer breaches a covenant.

a. Disabling Restraints on Legal Interests Are Void

All disabling restraints on ***any*** type of legal interest (*e.g.,* fee simple, life estate) are void.

b. Absolute Restraints on Fee Simple Are Void

All absolute restraints on fee simple estates are void; thus, the grantee may freely transfer the property. However, restraints on fee simple estates for a ***limited time*** and ***reasonable purpose*** are likely to be upheld (*e.g.*, a restraint limited to the joint lifetimes of co-owners as a reasonable way to ensure that neither will have to reside with a stranger).

2. Valid Restraints on Alienation

The following are valid restraints on alienation:

a. Forfeiture and promissory restraints on life estates;

b. Forfeiture restraints on transferability of future interests;

c. Reasonable restrictions in commercial transactions;

d. Rights of first refusal; and

e. Restrictions on assignment and sublease of leaseholds (*e.g.,* requiring landlord's consent).

Exam Tip Remember that the Rule Against Restraints on Alienation applies only to legal interests. Restraints on the alienation of ***equitable*** interests (*e.g.,* spendthrift clauses in trust instruments) are valid.

F. CONCURRENT ESTATES

An estate in land can be held concurrently by several persons, all of whom have the right to enjoyment and possession of the land.

1. Joint Tenancy

A joint tenancy's distinguishing feature is the ***right of survivorship***. When one joint tenant dies, the property is ***freed*** from her concurrent interest (her survivors do not succeed to it).

a. Creation

The common law requires four unities—***time, title, interest, possession***—to create a joint tenancy; *i.e.,* the interests of joint tenants must be ***equal*** in every way. They must take ***identical*** interests, at the ***same time***, by the ***same instrument***, with the ***same right***

to possession. Thus, all interests in a joint tenancy must be equal shares. If there are three joint tenants, they each own an undivided one-third interest. In a tenancy in common, by contrast, equal shares are presumed, but are not required. In a tenancy in common held by three parties, one tenant may own a two-thirds undivided interest while each of the other two tenants holds an undivided one-sixth share. In addition, modern law requires a clear expression of a right of survivorship; otherwise a conveyance to two or more persons is ***presumed to be a tenancy in common***.

CMR **Exam Tip** If the bar examiners tell you in the question that the parties are joint tenants, take it as given that they are joint tenants with right of survivorship. In this situation, ***do not*** apply the presumption that any conveyance to two or more persons is a tenancy in common. The bar examiners are not testing your knowledge of that presumption unless the fact pattern actually gives you the quoted language of the grant creating the concurrent estate and asks you about the type of tenancy involved.

b. Severance

Under certain circumstances, the right of survivorship is severed (*i.e.,* terminated) and a tenancy in common results.

1) Inter Vivos Conveyance

A voluntary or involuntary conveyance by a joint tenant of her undivided interest destroys the joint tenancy. The transferee takes as a tenant in common. When there are more than two joint tenants, conveyance by one destroys the joint tenancy only to the extent of the conveyor's interest. Severance may not occur where one joint tenant does not transfer her entire interest.

a) Judgment Liens

Usually when a plaintiff obtains a money judgment against a defendant, that judgment becomes a lien on the defendant's real property in the county where the judgment is docketed. The lien runs with the land, burdening it until the judgment is paid or the lien expires (usually 10 years). If such a lien is acquired against a joint tenant, it does not sever the joint tenancy until it is actually sold at a foreclosure sale.

b) Mortgages

In most states, a mortgage is a lien on title and does not sever a joint tenancy. Severance occurs only if the mortgage is foreclosed and the property is sold. The execution of a mortgage in title theory states, however, does sever a joint tenancy.

c) Leases

States are split as to whether one joint tenant's lease of her interest causes a severance.

2) Contract to Convey

Severance results if one joint tenant contracts to convey her interest, but the courts are split on whether an executory contract by ***all*** joint tenants works a severance.

CONCURRENT OWNERSHIP

Type of Tenancy	Definition	Creation	Termination
Joint Tenancy	Each tenant has an undivided interest in the whole estate, and the surviving co-tenant has a right to the whole estate (***right of survivorship***).	"To A and B as joint tenants with the right of survivorship." (Without survivorship language, it may be construed as a tenancy in common.) Joint tenants must take: (i) identical interests; (ii) from the same instrument; (iii) at the same time; (iv) with an equal right to possess (the four unities).	The right of survivorship may be severed, and the estate converted to a tenancy in common, by: a conveyance by one joint tenant, agreement of joint tenants, murder of one co-tenant by another, or simultaneous deaths of co-tenants. A joint tenancy can be terminated by partition (voluntary or involuntary).
Tenancy by the Entirety	Husband and wife each has an undivided interest in the whole estate and a ***right of survivorship***.	"To H and W." Most states presume a tenancy by the entirety in any joint conveyance to husband and wife where the four unities (above) are present.	The right of survivorship may be severed by death, divorce, mutual agreement, or execution by a joint creditor. Tenancy by the entirety cannot be terminated by involuntary partition.
Tenancy in Common	Each tenant has a distinct, proportionate, undivided interest in the property. There is ***no right of survivorship***.	"To A and B" or, sometimes, "To A and B as joint tenants." Only unity required is possession.	May be terminated by partition.

3) **Testamentary Disposition Has No Effect**
A will is ineffective to work a severance because at death the testator's interest vanishes.

4) **Effect of One Joint Tenant's Murdering Another**
Conceptually, a joint tenant who murders the other joint tenant should not lose her right of survivorship. In some jurisdictions, statutes change this result; in others, a constructive trust is imposed for the decedent's estate.

2. **Tenancy by the Entirety**
A tenancy by the entirety is a ***marital*** estate akin to joint tenancy. In common law jurisdictions it arises presumptively in any conveyance to a husband and wife. Only death, divorce, ***mutual*** agreement, or execution by a joint creditor of ***both*** the husband and wife can sever a tenancy by the entirety. An individual spouse cannot convey or encumber tenancy by the entirety property. A deed or mortgage executed by only one spouse is ineffective.

3. **Tenancy in Common**
A tenancy in common is a concurrent estate with no right of survivorship. Tenants can hold different interests in the property, but each is entitled to possession of the whole. Interests are alienable, devisable, and inheritable. Today, multiple grantees are ***presumed*** to take as tenants in common, not as joint tenants.

4. **Rights and Duties of Co-Tenants**

a. **Possession**
Each co-tenant has the right to possess all portions of the property but has no right to exclusive possession of any part. A co-tenant out of possession cannot bring a possessory action unless she is "ousted" (*e.g.,* another co-tenant claims right to exclusive possession).

b. **Rents and Profits**
In most states, a co-tenant in possession has the right to retain profits from her own use of the property; *i.e.*, she need not share profits with other co-tenants absent ouster or an agreement to the contrary. She must, however, share net rents from third parties and net profits gained from exploitations of land, such as mining.

c. **Effect of One Concurrent Owner's Encumbering the Property**
A joint tenant or tenant in common may encumber her interest (*e.g.,* by mortgage or judgment lien), but may not encumber the interests of other co-tenants. If, *e.g.,* one tenant in common mortgages her interest, the mortgagee can foreclose only on the mortgaging co-tenant's interest. If a joint tenancy is involved, a mortgage (in a lien theory state) or lien does not sever the joint tenancy, but a foreclosure sale will. Note, however, that in the case of a joint tenancy, a mortgagee or lienor runs the risk that the obligated co-tenant will die before foreclosure, extinguishing the mortgagee's or lienor's interest.

d. **Remedy of Partition**
Any co-tenant has a right to judicial partition, either in kind (physical division of land among co-tenants) or by sale and division of proceeds. Although generally this right

may be exercised at any time, restraints on partition by co-tenants are valid, provided they are limited to a ***reasonable time***.

e. Expenses for Preservation of Property—Contribution

1) Repairs
A co-tenant who pays more than her pro rata share of ***necessary*** repairs is entitled to contribution from the other co-tenants, provided she has notified the other co-tenants of the need for repairs.

2) Improvements
There is no right of contribution for the cost of improvements unless there is a partition.

3) Taxes and Mortgages
Contribution can be demanded for taxes or mortgage payments paid on the entire property. However, reimbursement to a co-tenant in sole possession is limited to the extent that expenditures exceed the rental value of her use.

f. Duty of Fair Dealing
A confidential relationship exists among co-tenants; *e.g.*, one co-tenant's acquisition of an outstanding title or lien that may affect the estate is deemed to be on behalf of other co-tenants. It is difficult for one co-tenant to adversely possess against other co-tenants.

II. LANDLORD AND TENANT

A. NATURE OF LEASEHOLD
A leasehold is an ***estate in land***, under which the tenant has a present possessory interest in the leased premises and the landlord has a future interest (reversion).

1. Tenancies for Years
A tenancy for years continues for a ***fixed*** period of time (*e.g.,* A rents to B for two years).

a. Creation
Tenancies for years are usually created by written leases. Under the Statute of Frauds, a writing is required if the lease is for more than one year.

b. Termination
A tenancy for years ends ***automatically*** at its termination date.

1) Breach of Covenants
In most leases, the landlord reserves a right of entry, which allows him to terminate the lease if the tenant breaches any of the lease's covenants.

a) Failure to Pay Rent
In many jurisdictions, a landlord may, by statute, terminate the lease upon the tenant's failure to pay the promised rent—even in the absence of a reserved right of entry.

2) **Surrender**
A tenancy for years may also terminate if the tenant surrenders the tenancy and the landlord accepts. The same formalities required for creation of the leasehold are required for surrender (*e.g.,* if unexpired term exceeds one year, surrender must be in writing).

2. **Periodic Tenancies**
A periodic tenancy continues for successive periods (*e.g.,* month to month) until terminated by proper notice by either party.

a. **Creation**
A periodic tenancy can be created by:

(i) ***Express agreement*** (*e.g.,* L leases to T from month to month);

(ii) ***Implication*** (*e.g.,* L leases to T at a rent of $100 payable monthly); or

(iii) ***Operation of law*** (*e.g.,* T remains in possession after the lease expires, and L treats it as a periodic tenancy; or the lease is invalid, but T goes into possession).

b. **Termination**
A periodic tenancy is automatically renewed until proper notice of termination is given. Usually, the notice must be one full period in advance (*e.g.,* one month's notice for a month-to-month tenancy) and timed to terminate the lease at the end of a period (*e.g.,* the usual month-to-month tenancy can end only on the 30th or 31st, not the 15th). For a year-to-year lease, six months' notice is required.

3. **Tenancies at Will**
A tenancy at will is terminable at the will of either the landlord or the tenant.

a. **Creation**
Generally, a tenancy at will must be created by an express agreement that the lease can be terminated at any time. Absent such an agreement, periodic rent payments will cause a court to treat it as a periodic tenancy. If the lease gives only the landlord the right to terminate, a similar right will be implied in favor of the tenant. However, if only the tenant has a right to terminate, a similar right will not be implied in favor of the landlord.

b. **Termination**
A tenancy at will may be terminated without notice by any party with the power to do so, or it may be terminated by operation of law (*e.g.,* death, commission of waste, etc.).

4. **Tenancies at Sufferance**

a. **Creation**
A tenancy at sufferance arises when a tenant wrongfully remains in possession after the expiration of a lawful tenancy.

b. **Termination**
A tenancy at sufferance lasts only until the landlord takes steps to evict the tenant. No notice of termination is required.

LEASEHOLD ESTATES

Type of Leasehold	Definition	Creation	Termination
Tenancy for Years	Tenancy that lasts for some fixed period of time.	"To A for 10 years."	Terminates at the end of the stated period without either party giving notice.
Periodic Tenancy	Tenancy for some fixed period that continues for succeeding periods until either party gives notice of termination.	"To A from month to month." ***or*** "To A, with rent payable on the first day of every month." ***or*** Landlord elects to bind hold-over tenant for an additional term.	Terminates by notice from one party at least equal to the length of the time period (*e.g.,* one full month for a month-to-month tenancy). *Exception:* Only six months' notice is required to terminate a year-to-year tenancy.
Tenancy at Will	Tenancy of no stated duration that lasts as long as both parties desire.	"To T for and during the pleasure of L." (Even though the language gives only L the right to terminate, L or T may terminate at any time.) ***or*** "To T for as many years as T desires." (Only T may terminate.)	Usually terminates after one party displays an intention that the tenancy should come to an end. May also end by operation of law (*e.g.,* death of a party, attempt to transfer interest).
Tenancy at Sufferance	Tenant wrongfully holds over after termination of the tenancy.	B's lease expires, but B continues to occupy the premises.	Terminates when landlord evicts tenant or elects to hold tenant to another term.

5. **The Hold-Over Doctrine**
If a tenant continues in possession after his right to possession has ended, the landlord may: (i) ***evict*** him, or (ii) bind him to a ***new periodic tenancy***. Generally, the terms and conditions of the expired tenancy govern the new one. However, if the landlord notifies the tenant before the lease expires that occupancy after the termination will be at increased rent, the tenant, by holding over, is held to have acquiesced to the new terms (even if the tenant actually objected to the new terms).

CMR **Exam Tip** There are exceptions to the hold-over doctrine. Watch for situations where: (i) the tenant remains in possession for ***only a few hours*** after termination or leaves a few articles of personal property, (ii) the delay is ***not the tenant's fault*** (*e.g.,* severe illness), or (iii) it is a ***seasonal lease***. In these cases, the landlord cannot bind the tenant to a new tenancy.

B. LEASES

A lease is a contract that governs the landlord-tenant relationship. Covenants in the lease are generally independent; *i.e.,* if one party breaches a covenant, the other party can recover damages but must still perform his promises and cannot terminate the landlord-tenant relationship. The doctrines of actual and constructive eviction and the implied warranty of habitability are exceptions to this rule. Also, many states have created a statutory exception allowing the landlord to terminate the lease for the nonpayment of rent.

C. TENANT DUTIES AND LANDLORD REMEDIES

1. **Tenant's Duty to Repair (Doctrine of Waste)**
A tenant cannot damage (*i.e.,* commit waste on) the leased premises. The rules governing waste in the leasehold context are much like those governing waste in the life estate context.

a. **Types of Waste**
There are three types of waste:

1) ***Voluntary (affirmative) waste*** results when the tenant intentionally or negligently damages the premises or exploits minerals on the property.

2) ***Permissive waste*** occurs when the tenant fails to take reasonable steps to protect the premises from damage from the elements. The tenant is liable for all ordinary repairs, excluding ordinary wear and tear. If the duty is shifted to the landlord (by lease or statute), the tenant has a duty to report deficiencies promptly.

3) ***Ameliorative waste*** occurs when the tenant alters the leased property, thereby increasing its value. Generally, the tenant is liable for the cost of restoration. There is a modern exception to this rule, however, which permits a tenant to make this type of change if he is a long-term tenant and the change reflects changes in the neighborhood.

b. **Destruction of Premises Without Fault**
If the leased premises are destroyed without the fault of either the landlord or the tenant, no waste is involved. In the absence of lease language or a statute to the contrary, neither party has a duty to restore the premises, but the tenant has a duty to continue paying rent. In most states, statutes or case law now give the tenant the option to terminate the lease in this situation, even in the presence of an explicit covenant to repair.

c. **Tenant's Liability for Covenants to Repair**
If the tenant ***specifically covenants to make repairs***, his duty will be higher than the duty implied by the law of waste. The tenant has a duty to repair even ordinary wear and tear unless ***expressly excluded***, but has no duty to repair structural failures or damage from fire or other casualty unless ***expressly included***. A tenant with a duty to repair is liable under such a covenant for all other defects, including reconstruction if the premises are destroyed.

2. **Duty to Not Use Premises for Illegal Purpose**
If the tenant uses the premises for an illegal purpose, the landlord may terminate the lease or obtain damages and injunctive relief. Occasional unlawful conduct by the tenant does not breach this duty.

3. **Duty to Pay Rent**
At common law, rent was due at the end of the leasehold term. However, leases usually contain a provision making rent payable at some other time (*e.g.,* "monthly in advance"). Most states today have statutes providing that if the leasehold terminates before the time originally agreed upon, the tenant must pay a ***proportionate amount*** of the agreed rent.

a. **Rent Deposits**
The landlord is not permitted to retain a ***security deposit*** beyond the damages actually suffered. If a rent deposit is denominated a ***"bonus,"*** the landlord can retain it after the tenant is evicted.

b. **Termination of Rent Liability—Surrender**
If a tenant effectively conveys (surrenders) his leasehold interest back to the landlord, his duty to pay rent ends.

4. **Landlord Remedies**

a. **Tenant on Premises But Fails to Pay Rent—Evict or Sue for Rent**
At common law, a breach of the lease, such as failure to pay rent, resulted only in a cause of action for money damages; a breach did not give rise to a right to terminate the lease. Most modern leases, however, give the nonbreaching party the right to terminate. Thus, if a tenant is on the premises and fails to pay rent, the landlord may bring suit for rent due or may evict the tenant under the state's ***unlawful detainer*** statute. The ***only*** issue in an unlawful detainer proceeding is whether the tenant has the right to possession; the tenant cannot raise counterclaims.

b. **Tenant Abandons—Do Nothing or Repossess**
If the tenant ***unjustifiably*** abandons the property, the majority view is that the landlord has a duty to mitigate damages by seeking to relet the premises. If the landlord repossesses and/or relets, the tenant's liability depends on whether the landlord has ***accepted the surrender***. If surrender is not found, the tenant is liable for the difference between the promised rent and the fair rental value of the property (in cases of reletting, between the promised rent and the rent received from the reletting). If surrender is found, the tenant is free from any rent liability accruing after abandonment. Note that the landlord's resumption of possession for himself constitutes acceptance of surrender.

D. LANDLORD DUTIES AND TENANT REMEDIES

Subject to modification by the lease, a statute, or the implied warranty of habitability, the general rule is that a landlord has ***no duty to repair or maintain*** the premises.

1. Duty to Deliver Possession of Premises

Statutes in most states require the landlord to put the tenant in ***actual*** possession of the premises at the beginning of the leasehold term; *i.e.,* the landlord is in breach if he has not evicted a hold-over tenant by the beginning of the lease term.

2. Quiet Enjoyment

Every lease has an implied covenant that neither the landlord nor a paramount title holder (*e.g.*, a prior mortgagee who forecloses) will interfere with the tenant's quiet enjoyment and possession of the premises. This covenant may be breached in the following ways:

a. Actual Eviction

Actual eviction occurs when the landlord or a paramount title holder excludes the tenant from the ***entire*** leased premises. Actual eviction terminates the tenant's obligation to pay rent.

b. Partial Eviction

Partial actual eviction occurs when the tenant is physically excluded from only part of the leased premises. Partial eviction ***by the landlord*** relieves the tenant of the obligation to pay rent for the ***entire*** premises, even though the tenant continues in possession of the remainder. Partial eviction by a third person with paramount title results in an apportionment of rent; *i.e.,* the tenant is liable for the reasonable rental value of the portion she continues to possess.

c. Constructive Eviction

If the landlord does something (or, more often, fails to provide a service he has a legal duty to provide) that renders the property ***uninhabitable***, the tenant may terminate the lease and seek damages. The conditions must be the result of the ***landlord's actions*** (not a neighbor's or other third party's), and the tenant ***must vacate*** the premises within a reasonable time.

3. Implied Warranty of Habitability

Most jurisdictions imply a covenant of habitability into ***residential leases***. This warranty is ***nonwaivable***. The landlord's duty is tied to standards of local housing codes. In the event of a breach, the tenant may: (i) ***terminate*** the lease; (ii) ***make repairs and offset*** the cost against future rent; (iii) ***abate the rent*** to an amount equal to the fair rental value in view of the defects; or (iv) remain in possession, pay full rent, and ***sue for damages.***

CMR **Exam Tip** Keep in mind that the implied warranty of habitability does ***not*** apply to commercial tenants—only to residential tenants.

4. Retaliatory Eviction

In many states, a landlord may not terminate a lease or otherwise penalize a tenant in retaliation for the tenant's exercise of her legal rights, including reporting housing or building code violations. Many statutes presume a retaliatory motive if the landlord acts within, *e.g.,* 90 to 180 days after the tenant exercises her rights. To overcome the presumption, the landlord must show a valid, nonretaliatory reason for his actions.

E. ASSIGNMENTS AND SUBLEASES

Absent an express restriction in the lease, a tenant may freely transfer her leasehold interest, in whole or in part. A ***complete*** transfer of the entire remaining term is an ***assignment***. If the tenant retains any part of the remaining term (other than a right to reenter upon breach), the transfer is a ***sublease***.

Exam Tip For bar exam purposes, a transfer will be considered a sublease, rather than an assignment, only when the original tenant reserves time for herself (*e.g.,* the last month of the lease).

1. Consequences of Assignment

An assignee stands in the shoes of the original tenant in a direct relationship with the landlord; *i.e.,* the assignee and the landlord are in ***"privity of estate,"*** and each is liable to the other on all covenants in the lease that "run with the land."

a. Covenants that Run with the Land

A covenant runs with the land if the original parties to the lease so intend and if the covenant "touches and concerns" the land (*i.e.,* benefits the landlord and burdens the tenant (or vice versa) with respect to their interests in the property).

b. Rent Covenants

Because a covenant to pay rent runs with the land, the assignee owes rent ***directly*** to the landlord. After assignment, the original tenant is no longer in privity of estate with the landlord but remains liable on the ***original contractual obligation*** to pay rent (privity of contract). If the assignee reassigns the leasehold interest, his privity of estate with the landlord ends, and he has no liability for the subsequent assignee's failure to pay rent.

2. Consequences of Sublease—Sublessee Not in Privity with Landlord

A sublessee is the tenant of the original lessee and usually pays rent to the original lessee, who then pays the landlord. A sublessee is not personally liable to the landlord for rent or for the performance of any of the covenants in the main lease unless the sublessee expressly assumes the covenants.

a. Landlord's Remedies

The landlord may terminate the main lease for nonpayment of rent or breach of other covenants if the lease so states or the power is given by statute. The sublease automatically terminates with the main lease. Also, many states allow a landlord who does not receive rent to assert a lien on personal property found on the premises; this applies to a sublessee's property as well as that of the original tenant.

b. Rights of Sublessee

A sublessee cannot enforce any covenants made by the landlord in the main lease, except a residential sublessee may be able to enforce the implied warranty of habitability against the landlord.

3. Covenants Against Assignment or Sublease

Lease covenants restricting assignment and sublease are strictly ***construed against the landlord***. (Thus, a covenant prohibiting assignment does not prohibit subleasing and vice versa.)

ASSIGNMENT VS. SUBLEASE

	Assignment by Landlord	Assignment by Tenant	Sublease by Tenant
Consent	Tenant's consent not required.	Landlord's consent may be required by lease.	Landlord's consent may be required by lease.
Privity of Estate	Assignee and tenant are in privity of estate.	Assignee and landlord are in privity of estate.	Sublessee and landlord are not in privity of estate. Original tenant remains in privity of estate with landlord.
Privity of Contract	Assignee and tenant are not in privity of contract. Original landlord and tenant remain in privity of contract.	Assignee and landlord are not in privity of contract. Original tenant and landlord remain in privity of contract.	Sublessee and landlord are not in privity of contract. Original tenant and landlord remain in privity of contract.
Liability for Covenants in Lease	Assignee liable to tenant on all covenants that run with the land.	Assignee liable to landlord on all covenants that run with the land.	Sublessee is not personally liable on any covenants in the original lease and cannot enforce the landlord's covenants.
	Original landlord remains liable on ***all*** covenants in the lease.	Original tenant remains liable for rent and ***all*** other covenants in the lease.	Original tenant remains liable for rent and ***all*** other covenants in the lease and can enforce the landlord's covenants.

a. **Waiver**

A valid covenant against assignment is considered waived if the landlord was aware of the assignment and did not object (*e.g.,* by knowingly accepting rent from the assignee). Once the landlord consents to one transfer, he waives the covenant as to future transfers unless he expressly reserves it.

b. **Transfer in Violation of Lease**

If a tenant assigns or sublets in violation of a lease provision, the transfer is not void. The landlord, however, usually may terminate the lease or sue for damages.

4. **Assignments by Landlords**

A landlord may assign the rents and reversion interest he owns. This is usually done by deed when the landlord conveys a building to a new owner. The tenants' consent is ***not*** required.

a. **Rights of Assignee Against Tenants—Attornment**

Once tenants are given reasonable notice of the assignment, they must recognize and pay rent to the new owner as their landlord. The benefit of all tenant covenants that touch and concern the land runs with the landlord's estate to the new owner.

b. **Liabilities of Assignee to Tenants**

The burden of the landlord's covenants that touch and concern the land runs with the landlord's estate to the assignee; thus, the assignee is liable for the performance of those covenants. ***The original landlord also remains liable on all of the covenants he made in the lease.***

F. CONDEMNATION OF LEASEHOLDS

If the ***entire leasehold*** is taken by eminent domain, the tenant's liability for rent is extinguished because both the leasehold and reversion have merged in the condemnor and there is no longer a leasehold estate. The lessee is entitled to compensation. However, if the taking is ***temporary*** or ***partial***, the tenant is ***not*** discharged from the rent obligation, but is entitled to compensation (*i.e.,* a share of the condemnation award) for the taking.

G. TORT LIABILITY OF LANDLORD AND TENANT

1. **Landlord's Liability**

At common law, a landlord had no duty to make the premises safe. Today, there are several exceptions.

a. **Concealed Dangerous Condition (Latent Defect)**

If, at the time the lease is entered into, the landlord knows (or should know) of a dangerous condition that the tenant could not discover by reasonable inspection, the landlord must ***disclose*** (not repair) it. Otherwise, the landlord will be liable for any injuries resulting from the condition. If the tenant accepts the premises after disclosure, she assumes the risk for herself and others; the landlord is no longer liable.

b. **Public Use**

A landlord is liable for injuries to members of the public if, at the time of the lease, he:

1) Knows (or should know) of a ***dangerous condition***;

2) Has reason to believe the tenant ***may admit the public before repairing*** the condition; and

3) ***Fails to repair*** the condition.

c. **Repairs**
Although the landlord is not liable for injuries from dangerous conditions arising after the tenant takes possession, if ***the landlord undertakes such repairs***, he owes a duty of reasonable care. The landlord also has a duty of reasonable care in maintaining common areas (*e.g.,* halls, elevators). If the landlord covenants to repair or has a statutory duty to repair (*e.g.,* housing codes), he is liable for injuries resulting from failure to repair or negligent repair.

d. **Furnished Short-Term Residence**
A landlord who rents a fully furnished premises for a short period (*e.g.,* summer cottage) is under a stricter duty. He is liable for injuries resulting from ***any*** defect whether or not he knew of the defect.

e. **Modern Trend—General Duty of Reasonable Care**
Many courts are now holding that a landlord owes a general duty of reasonable care toward residential tenants, and will be held liable for injuries resulting from ordinary negligence if he had notice of a defect and an opportunity to repair it.

2. **Tenant's Liability**
The duty of care owed by a tenant, as an occupier of land, to third persons is discussed in the Torts outline.

III. FIXTURES

A. IN GENERAL
A fixture is a chattel that has been so affixed to land that it has ceased being personal property and has become part of the realty. A fixture passes with the ownership of the land.

B. CHATTELS INCORPORATED INTO STRUCTURE
When items are incorporated into the realty so that they lose their identity (*e.g.,* bricks, concrete), they are fixtures, as are items that are identifiable but whose removal would cause considerable damage (*e.g.,* plumbing, heating ducts).

C. COMMON OWNERSHIP CASES
A common ownership case is one in which the person who brings the chattel to the land owns both the chattel and the land (*e.g.*, X installs a furnace in his home). An item is a "fixture" if the ***objective intention*** of the party who made the "annexation" was to make the item part of the realty. This intention is determined by: the ***nature of the article***; the ***manner of attachment***; the ***amount of damage*** that would be caused by its removal; and the ***adaptation*** of the item to the use of the realty.

1. **Constructive Annexation**
An article of personal property that is so uniquely adapted to the real estate that it makes no sense to separate it (*e.g.,* keys to doors, custom curtain rods) may be considered a fixture even if it is not physically annexed to the property.

D. DIVIDED OWNERSHIP CASES
In divided ownership cases, the chattel is owned and brought to the realty by someone other than the landowner (*e.g.*, tenant, licensee, or trespasser).

1. **Landlord-Tenant**
An agreement between the landlord and tenant is controlling on whether an annexed chattel is a fixture. Absent an agreement, a tenant is deemed to lack the intent to permanently improve the property, and thus may remove his annexed chattels if removal would not damage the premises or destroy the chattel. Annexed chattels must be removed by the end of the lease term (or within a reasonable time after the termination of an indefinite tenancy), and the tenant is responsible for repairing any damage caused by the removal.

2. **Life Tenant and Remainderman**
The same rules apply in the life tenant-remainderman context as in landlord-tenant situations, except that the life tenant must remove annexations before the end of his tenancy.

3. **Licensee or Trespasser and Landowner**
Licensees are treated much like tenants, whereas trespassers normally lose their annexations. Thus, absent a statute, an adverse possessor or good faith trespasser cannot remove fixtures (*e.g.*, house erroneously constructed on a parcel that possessor believed she owned). Some courts, however, allow a good faith trespasser recovery measured by the value added to the land (not construction costs).

E. THIRD-PARTY CASES

1. **Third-Party Lien on Land to Which Chattel Affixed**
Generally, the mortgagee has no greater rights than the mortgagor. Thus, chattels annexed by the mortgagor's tenant are generally not within the lien of the mortgagee ***except*** where the mortgage is made after the lease and the mortgagee is without notice of the tenant's rights.

2. **Third-Party Lien on Chattel Affixed to Land**
Suppose a landowner affixes a chattel to the land. The seller of the chattel retains a security interest in the chattel, and the landowner mortgages the land. If the landowner then defaults on both chattel and mortgage payments, as between the seller and the mortgagee, the general rule is that the first to record his interest wins. However, under the U.C.C., a seller wins if the "fixture filing" is recorded within 20 days after the chattel is affixed to the land. The seller must compensate the mortgagee for damage or repair caused by removal.

IV. RIGHTS IN THE LAND OF ANOTHER—EASEMENTS, PROFITS, COVENANTS, AND SERVITUDES

A. IN GENERAL
Easements, profits, covenants, and servitudes are ***nonpossessory*** interests in land, creating a right to ***use land possessed by someone else***.

NONPOSSESSORY INTERESTS

	Easement	License	Profit	Real Covenant/ Equitable Servitude
Definition	A grant of an interest in land that allows someone to use another's land	Permission to go onto another's land	Right to take resources from another's land	Promise to do or not to do something on the land
Example	Owner of parcel A grants owner of parcel B the right to drive across parcel A	O allows the electrician to come onto his land to fix an outlet	O allows A to come onto O's land to cut and remove timber	O conveys an adjoining parcel to A. A promises not to build a swimming pool on the property
Writing	Generally required. *Exceptions:* Less than one year Implication Necessity Prescription	Not required. *Note:* An invalid oral easement is a license	Required	Required. *Exception:* Equitable servitude may be implied from common scheme of development of residential subdivision
Termination	Stated conditions Release Merger Abandonment Estoppel Prescription End of necessity	Usually revocable at will. May be irrevocable if coupled with an interest or if licensor estopped by licensee's expenditures	Same as easement	Release Merger Condemnation Also equitable defenses may apply to enforcement of servitude

B. EASEMENTS

1. Introduction

An easement holder has the right to use another's tract of land for a special purpose (*e.g.*, to lay pipe, to access a road or lake), but has no right to possess or enjoy that land. An easement is presumed to be of ***perpetual duration*** unless the grant specifically limits the interest.

a. **Types of Easements**

Most easements are ***affirmative***, which means the holder is entitled to make affirmative use of the servient tenement. ***Negative*** easements, which entitle the holder to compel the possessor of the servient tenement to refrain from engaging in an activity on the servient estate (*e.g.,* building a structure in excess of three stories), are generally confined to only four types of easements: (i) for ***light***, (ii) for ***air***, (iii) for lateral and subjacent ***support***, and (iv) for ***flow*** of an artificial stream.

CMR **Exam Tip** Negative easements are really restrictive covenants. Thus, for exam purposes, a restriction relating to light, air, support, or flow of an artificial stream can be either a negative easement or a restrictive covenant. Restrictions relating to anything else, however, are considered restrictive covenants.

b. **Easement Appurtenant**

An easement is appurtenant when it benefits the holder in his physical use or enjoyment of another tract of land. Thus, for an easement to be appurtenant, there must be ***two tracts***: the ***dominant*** tenement (the estate benefited by the easement), and the ***servient*** tenement (the estate subject to the easement right). An easement appurtenant passes with the transfer of the benefited land, regardless of whether it is mentioned in the conveyance. The burden of the easement also passes automatically with the servient estate unless the new owner is a bona fide purchaser with no actual or constructive notice of the easement.

CMR **Exam Tip** It is important to remember that the easement appurtenant ***passes with the benefited land***. Don't be fooled by questions that make you think it must be specifically mentioned in the deed. Similarly, recall that an easement appurtenant cannot be conveyed apart from the dominant tenement (unless it is conveyed to the owner of the servient tenement to ***extinguish*** the easement).

c. **Easement in Gross**

The holder of an easement in gross acquires a right to use the servient tenement independent of his possession of another tract of land; *i.e.,* the easement benefits the holder rather than another parcel. An easement in gross for the holder's personal pleasure (*e.g.,* right to swim in the pond on Blackacre) is not transferable, but one that serves an economic or commercial interest (*e.g.,* right to erect billboards on Blackacre) is transferable.

2. **Creation of Easements**

The basic methods of creating an easement are: express grant or reservation, implication, and prescription.

a. **Express Grant**

Any easement must be in writing and signed by the holder of the servient tenement unless its duration is brief enough (commonly one year or less) to be outside a particular state's Statute of Frauds' coverage. A grant of easement must comply with all the formal requisites of a deed (*see* VI.B.1., *infra*).

b. **Express Reservation**

An easement by reservation arises when a grantor conveys title to land, but reserves the right to continue to use the tract for a special purpose.

CMR **Exam Tip** Watch for fact patterns in which a grantor reserves an easement for someone else. Under the majority view, an easement can be reserved only for the ***grantor***. An attempt to reserve an easement for anyone else is ***void***.

c. **Implication**

An easement by implication is created by operation of law; it is an exception to the Statute of Frauds. Aside from the easement automatically implied with any grant of a profit (*see* C., *infra*), there are two types of easements by implication:

1) **Easement Implied from Existing Use ("Quasi-Easement")**

An easement may be implied if:

(i) ***Prior to the division*** of a single tract,

(ii) An ***apparent and continuous*** use exists on the "servient" part,

(iii) That is ***reasonably necessary*** for the enjoyment of the "dominant" part, and

(iv) The court determines that the parties ***intended*** the use to continue after division of the land.

a) **Easement Implied Without Any Existing Use**

In two limited situations, easements may be implied without preexisting use.

(1) **Subdivision Plat**

When lots are sold in a subdivision with reference to a recorded plat or map that also shows streets leading to the lots, buyers of the lots have implied easements to use the streets to access their lots.

(2) **Profit a Prendre**

The holder of the profit a prendre (*see* C., *infra*) has an implied easement to pass over the surface of the land and to use it as reasonably necessary to extract the product.

2) **Easement by Necessity**

An easement by necessity arises when a landowner sells a portion of his tract and by this division deprives one lot of access to a public road or utility line. The owner of the servient parcel has the right to locate the easement.

d. **Prescription**

Acquiring an easement by prescription is analogous to acquiring property by adverse possession. To acquire a prescriptive easement, the use must be:

(i) ***Open and notorious*** (*i.e.,* discoverable upon inspection);

(ii) ***Adverse*** (*i.e.,* without the owner's permission); and

(iii) ***Continuous and uninterrupted***;

(iv) For the ***statutory period***.

Generally, prescriptive easements cannot be acquired in public land.

3. Scope

In the absence of specific limitations in the grant, courts assume that the easement was intended to meet both present and future needs of the dominant tenement (*e.g.,* easement may widen to accommodate new, wider cars). If, however, the dominant parcel is subdivided, the lot owners will not succeed to the easement if to do so would unreasonably overburden the servient estate.

CMR **Exam Tip** When confronted with an exam question involving overuse or misuse of an easement, remember that such use ***does not terminate*** the easement. The appropriate remedy for the servient owner is an injunction against the misuse.

a. Use of Servient Estate—Repairs

The servient owner generally may use her land in any way she wishes so long as her conduct does not interfere with performance of the easement. The easement holder has the duty to make repairs to the easement if he is the sole user; but if both parties are using the easement, the court will apportion the repair costs.

4. Termination of Easements

An easement can be terminated in the following ways:

a. Stated Conditions

The original easement grant may specify when or under what conditions the easement will terminate.

b. Unity of Ownership (Merger)

If the same person acquires ownership of both the easement and the servient estate, the dominant and servient estates merge and the easement is destroyed. Even though there may be later separation, the easement will not be automatically revived. The unity must be complete (*e.g.,* the holder of the easement must acquire an interest in the servient tenement of equal or greater duration than the duration of the easement privilege).

c. Release

An easement (including an easement in gross, which is otherwise inalienable) can be terminated by a deed of release from the owner of the easement to the owner of the servient tenement.

d. Abandonment

An easement is extinguished when its holder demonstrates by physical action (*e.g.,* building a structure that blocks access to easement on adjoining lot) an intent to permanently abandon the easement. Merely expressing a wish to abandon does not extinguish the easement; neither does mere nonuse.

e. Estoppel

Oral expressions of an intent to abandon do not terminate an easement unless committed to writing (release) or accompanied by action (abandonment). But if the owner of the servient estate changes his position in reasonable reliance on the representations made or conduct by the owner of the easement, the easement terminates through estoppel.

f. Prescription

To terminate an easement by prescription there must be an adverse, continuous interruption of the use for the prescriptive period (typically 20 years).

g. **Necessity**
Easements created by necessity expire as soon as the necessity ends.

h. **Condemnation and Destruction**
Condemnation of the servient estate extinguishes all easements. Courts are split as to whether easement holders are entitled to compensation. Involuntary destruction of a structure in which there is an easement extinguishes the easement; voluntary destruction of such a structure does not.

5. **Compare—Licenses**
Licenses privilege their holders to go upon the land of another. But unlike an easement, a license is not an interest in land; it is merely a privilege, ***revocable*** at the will of the licensor. A license is personal to the licensee and, thus, inalienable. Any attempt to transfer a license results in revocation by operation of law.

CMR **Exam Tip** A failed attempt to create an easement results in a license. Thus, if a grantor orally grants an easement for more than one year, it is unenforceable because it is not in writing. The grantee does not have a valid easement but does have a license.

a. **Irrevocable Licenses**
A license becomes irrevocable in the following circumstances:

1) **Estoppel**
If a licensee invests substantial amounts of money or labor in reliance on the license, the licensor is estopped to revoke. The license becomes an easement by estoppel, which lasts until the holder receives sufficient benefit to reimburse him for his expenditures.

2) **License Coupled with an Interest**
A license coupled with an interest is irrevocable as long as the interest lasts. For example, the vendee of a chattel may enter the seller's land to remove the chattel, and a future interest holder may enter and inspect the land for waste.

C. PROFITS

Profits entitle the holder of the benefit to take some resources (*e.g.*, soil, timber, materials, fish) from the servient estate. Implied in every profit is an easement entitling the benefit holder to enter the servient estate to remove the resources. All of the rules governing creation, alienation, and termination of easements are applicable to profits. In addition, a profit may be extinguished through ***surcharge*** (misuse that overly burdens the servient estate).

D. COVENANTS RUNNING WITH THE LAND AT LAW (REAL COVENANTS)

A real covenant, normally found in a deed, is a ***written promise*** to do something on the land (*e.g.*, maintain a fence) or a promise not to do something on the land (*e.g.*, not build a multi-family dwelling). Real covenants run with the land at law, which means that subsequent owners may enforce or be burdened by the covenants.

1. **Requirements for Burden to Run**
If the following requirements are met, any successor in interest to the burdened estate will be bound by the covenant as if she had herself expressly agreed to it.

a. **Intent**
The covenanting parties must have ***intended*** that successors in interest to the covenantor be bound by the terms of the covenant. This intent may be inferred from circumstances surrounding the creation of the covenant, but is usually found in the language of the conveyance itself.

b. **Notice**
Under modern recording acts (*see* VI.E., *infra*), to be bound by a covenant, a subsequent purchaser for value must have had actual, inquiry, or record notice of the arrangement at the time of purchase.

CMR **Exam Tip** Because the notice requirement arises under the recording acts, remember that it will protect ***only purchasers for value***. Someone who does not give value may be bound by a covenant at law (not equity) even if he has no actual or constructive notice of the covenant.

c. **Horizontal Privity**
At the time the promisor entered into the covenant with the promisee, the two must have shared ***some interest*** in the land independent of the covenant (*e.g.,* grantor-grantee, landlord-tenant, mortgagee-mortgagor).

CMR **Exam Tip** Horizontal privity concerns only the ***original*** parties. Even if successors in interest are trying to enforce the covenant, you must look only to the original covenanting parties to determine horizontal privity.

d. **Vertical Privity**
To be bound, the successor in interest to the covenanting party must hold the ***entire durational interest*** held by the covenantor at the time he made the covenant.

e. **Touch and Concern**
Negative covenants touch and concern the land if they restrict the holder of the servient estate in his ***use of that parcel*** of land. Affirmative covenants touch and concern the land if they require the holder of the servient estate to ***do something***, which increases his obligations in connection with his enjoyment of the land.

2. **Requirements for Benefit to Run**
If the following three requirements are met, the promisee's successor in interest may enforce the covenant:

a. **Intent**
The covenanting parties must have ***intended*** that the successors in interest to the covenantee be able to enforce the covenant.

b. **Vertical Privity**
The benefits of a covenant run to the assignees of the ***original estate or any lesser estate***; *i.e.,* ***any*** succeeding possessory estate may enforce the benefit.

CMR **Exam Tip** Horizontal privity is not required for the benefit to run. Thus, where horizontal privity is lacking, the promisee's successors can enforce the covenant against the promisor, but not against the promisor's successors.

c. **Touch and Concern**
The benefit of a covenant touches and concerns the land if the promised performance benefits the covenantee and her successors in their use and enjoyment of the benefited land.

3. **Specific Situations Involving Real Covenants**
Generally, promises to ***pay money*** to be used in connection with the land (*e.g.*, homeowners' association fees) and covenants ***not to compete*** run with the land. Racially restrictive covenants are unenforceable.

4. **Remedy—Damages Only**
A breach of a real covenant is remedied by an award of money damages, collectible from the defendant's general assets. If an injunction is sought, the promise must be enforced as an equitable servitude (*see* below) rather than a real covenant.

5. **Termination**
As with all other nonpossessory interests, a covenant may be terminated by: (i) a written ***release***, (ii) the ***merger*** of the benefited and burdened estates, or (iii) the ***condemnation*** of the burdened property.

CMR COMPARISON CHART

DISTINGUISHING CHARACTERISTICS OF REAL COVENANTS AND EQUITABLE SERVITUDES

	Real Covenants	Equitable Servitudes
Creation	Writing is ***always*** required	Writing is ***usually*** required but may arise by ***implication*** from common scheme of development of a residential subdivision
Running of Burden	Horizontal privity (shared interest in land, apart from the covenant, by ***original*** covenanting parties; *e.g.*, mortgagor-mortgagee, landlord-tenant) ***and*** vertical privity (successor holds entire interest held by covenanting party) required	No privity required
Running of Benefit	Vertical privity required	No privity required
Remedy	Damages	Injunction

E. EQUITABLE SERVITUDES

An equitable servitude is a covenant that, regardless of whether it runs with the land at law, equity will enforce against the assignees of the burdened land who have ***notice*** of the covenant. The usual remedy is an injunction.

CMR **Exam Tip** The crucial difference between real covenants and equitable servitudes is the remedy sought. If money damages are sought, you must use the real covenant analysis. If a party seeks an injunction, you must consider whether the requirements for enforcement as an equitable servitude have been met. A single promise can create both a real covenant and an equitable servitude.

1. Creation

Generally, as with real covenants, equitable servitudes are created by ***covenants*** contained in a ***writing*** that satisfies the Statute of Frauds. There is one exception: Negative equitable servitudes may be implied from a common scheme for development of a residential subdivision. Thus, if a developer subdivides land, and some deeds contain negative covenants while others do not, the negative covenants will be binding on all parcels provided there was a common scheme of development and notice of the covenants.

a. Common Scheme

Reciprocal negative servitudes will be implied only if, at the time that sales in the subdivision began, the developer had a plan that all parcels would be subject to the restriction. The scheme may be evidenced by: (i) a recorded plat, (ii) a general pattern of restrictions, or (iii) oral representations to early buyers.

CMR **Exam Tip** If the scheme arises after some lots are sold, no implied servitude can arise with respect to the lots already sold without express covenants. So remember, if Lots 1 through 5 are sold without a restrictive covenant and the deeds to Lots 6 through 50 contain one, the covenant cannot be enforced as a servitude against the owners of Lots 1 through 5.

b. Notice

To be bound by a covenant not in her deed, a grantee must have had notice of the covenants in the deeds of others in the subdivision. Notice may be ***actual*** (direct knowledge of covenants), ***inquiry*** (neighborhood appears to conform to common restrictions), or ***record*** (prior deed with covenant in grantee's chain of title).

2. Requirements for Burden to Run

A successor of the promisor is bound if:

a. The covenanting parties ***intended*** that the servitude be enforceable by and against assignees;

b. The successor of the promisor has ***actual***, ***inquiry***, ***or record*** notice of the servitude; and

c. The covenant ***touches and concerns*** the land (*i.e.,* it restricts the holder of the servient estate in his use of that parcel).

3. **Requirements for Benefit to Run**
The benefit of an equitable servitude runs with the land, and thus is enforceable by the promisee's successors if: (i) the original parties so ***intended***, and (ii) the servitude ***touches and concerns*** the benefited property.

CMR **Exam Tip** In contrast to real covenants, which require vertical and horizontal privity of estate for burdens to run, and vertical privity for benefits to run, ***no privity of estate is required*** for an equitable servitude to be enforceable by and against assignees.

4. **Equitable Defenses to Enforcement**
A court will not enforce an equitable servitude if:

a. The person seeking enforcement is violating a similar restriction on his own land (***unclean hands***);

b. A benefited party ***acquiesced*** in a violation of the servitude by one burdened party;

c. A benefited party acted in such a way that a reasonable person would believe the covenant was abandoned (***estoppel***);

d. The benefited party fails to bring suit against the violator within a reasonable time (***laches***); or

e. The ***neighborhood has changed*** so significantly that enforcement would be inequitable.

5. **Termination**
Like other nonpossessory interests, an equitable servitude may be extinguished by: (i) ***written release*** from the benefit holders, (ii) ***merger*** of the benefited and burdened estates, or (iii) ***condemnation*** of the burdened property.

CMR SUMMARY CHART

CHECKLIST OF REQUIREMENTS FOR THE RUNNING OF BENEFITS AND BURDENS

	Covenants		Equitable Servitudes	
	Benefit	Burden	Benefit	Burden
Intent	✓	✓	✓	✓
Notice		✓*		✓
Touch & Concern	✓	✓	✓	✓
Horizontal Privity		✓		
Vertical Privity	✓	✓		

* Under recording acts

F. PARTY WALLS AND COMMON DRIVEWAYS

Courts will treat a wall erected partly on the property of each of two adjoining landowners as belonging to each owner to the extent it rests upon her land. Courts will also imply mutual cross-easements of support, with the result that each party can use the wall or driveway and neither party can unilaterally destroy it.

1. Creation

A ***written agreement*** is required by the Statute of Frauds for the express creation of a party wall or common driveway agreement, but an "irrevocable license" can arise from detrimental reliance on a parol agreement. Party walls and common driveways can also result from ***implication or prescription***.

2. Running of Covenants

If party wall or common driveway owners agree to be mutually responsible for maintaining the wall or driveway, the burdens and benefits of these covenants run to the successive owners of each parcel.

V. ADVERSE POSSESSION

A. IN GENERAL

Title to real property may be acquired by adverse possession. Title by adverse possession results from the operation of the statute of limitations for trespass. If an owner does not, within the statutory period, take action to eject a possessor who claims adversely to the owner, the title vests in the possessor.

B. REQUIREMENTS

1. Running of Statute

The statute of limitations begins to run when the true owner can first bring suit. Filing a suit will not stop the period from running, however; the suit must be pursued to judgment.

2. Open and Notorious Possession

Possession is open and notorious when it is the kind of use the owner would make of the land. The adverse possessor's occupation must be ***sufficiently apparent*** to put the true owner on ***notice*** that a trespass is occurring.

3. Actual and Exclusive Possession

An adverse possessor will gain title only to land she actually occupies. In some cases, actual possession of the entire parcel claimed is not necessary. If an adverse possessor actually occupies a reasonable portion of the parcel, and her occupation is under ***color of title*** to the entire parcel, then she will be deemed to have constructively possessed the ***entire*** parcel, with the same result as if she had actually occupied the entire parcel. "Exclusive" means that the possessor is not sharing with the true owner or the public. Two or more people may obtain title by adverse possession; they take title as tenants in common.

4. Continuous Possession

An adverse claimant's possession must be continuous throughout the statutory period. Intermittent periods of occupancy are ***not*** sufficient. However, constant use by the claimant is not required as long as possession is of a type that the usual owner would make. Also, there need ***not*** be continuous possession by the same person; an adverse possessor can ***tack*** her own possession onto the periods of adverse possession of her predecessors, but privity is required.

5. **Hostile**
The hostility requirement is satisfied if the possessor enters ***without the owner's permission***. The adverse possessor's state of mind is irrelevant; *i.e.*, it does not matter whether she believes the land to be her own or knows she is trespassing. When possession starts permissively (*e.g.*, by lease), possession does not become adverse until the possessor makes clear to the true owner the fact that she is claiming "hostilely."

   a. **Co-Tenants—Ouster Required**
   Possession by one co-tenant is usually not adverse to his co-tenants because each co-tenant has the right to possession of all the property. A co-tenant must oust others or make an explicit declaration that he is claiming exclusive dominion to create adverse possession.

   b. **Grantor Stays in Possession—Permission Presumed**
   Where a grantor stays in possession of land after her conveyance, she is presumed to be there with permission of the grantee. (Likewise, if a tenant remains in possession after the expiration of the lease, he is presumed to have permission of the landlord.)

6. **Payment of Property Taxes Generally Not Required**
Most states do ***not*** require the adverse possessor to pay taxes on the property, but consider such payment good evidence of a claim of right.

C. DISABILITY
The statute of limitations does not begin to run if the true owner was under some disability to sue ***when the cause of action first accrued***. (Typical disabilities: minority, imprisonment, insanity.) Only the disability of the ***owner*** existing at the time the cause of action arose is considered.

D. ADVERSE POSSESSION AND FUTURE INTERESTS
The statute of limitations does not run against a holder of a future interest until the interest becomes possessory.

CMR **Exam Tip** The event or condition giving rise to a grantor's right of entry (*e.g.*, "To Grantee on condition that if alcohol is ever used on the premises, Grantor shall have the right to reenter and retake the premises") does not trigger the statute of limitations for purposes of adverse possession. The statute does not begin to run until the right is ***asserted by the grantor*** because, until that time, the grantee's continued possession of the land is proper.

E. EFFECT OF COVENANTS IN TRUE OWNER'S DEED
If an adverse possessor uses the land in violation of a restrictive covenant in the owner's deed for the limitations period, she takes free of the restriction. If, however, the possessor's use complies with such a covenant, she takes title subject to the restriction.

F. LAND THAT CANNOT BE ADVERSELY POSSESSED
Title to government-owned land and land registered under a Torrens system cannot be acquired by adverse possession.

VI. CONVEYANCING

A. LAND SALE CONTRACTS

Contracts of sale precede most transfers of land.

1. Statute of Frauds Applicable

A contract must be in writing and contain the signature of the party to be charged and the essential terms (*e.g.*, parties, description of land, price). Part performance (*e.g.*, possession, substantial improvements, payment of purchase price) can take a contract out of the statute.

2. Doctrine of Equitable Conversion

Under this doctrine, once a contract is signed, equity regards the buyer as the owner of the real property. The seller's interest (the right to the proceeds of sale) is considered personal property. The bare legal title that remains in the seller is considered to be held in trust for the buyer. The right to possession follows the bare legal title, however; thus, the seller is entitled to possession until closing.

a. Risk of Loss

If property is destroyed (without fault of either party) before closing, the majority rule places the risk on the buyer. Some states, however, have enacted the Uniform Vendor and Purchaser Risk Act, which places the risk on the seller unless the buyer has title or possession at the time of loss.

CMR **Exam Tip** Even though the risk of loss is on the buyer, if the property is damaged or destroyed, the seller must credit any fire or casualty insurance proceeds he receives against the purchase price the buyer is required to pay.

b. Passage of Title on Death

Under the doctrine of equitable conversion, if a party to a land sale contract dies before the contract is completed, the seller's interest passes as personal property and the buyer's interest passes as real property. Thus, if the seller dies, bare legal title passes to his heirs or devisees, but they must give up title to the buyer at closing. If the buyer dies, his heirs or devisees can demand conveyance of the land at closing.

CMR **Exam Tip** If the property is specifically devised by will, check to see whether the ademption rules (*see* F.1., *infra*) change the result of the equitable conversion doctrine.

3. Marketable Title

Every contract contains an implied warranty that the seller will provide marketable title (*i.e.*, title reasonably free from doubt) at closing. It need not be perfect title, but must be free of questions that present an unreasonable risk of litigation.

a. Defects in Record Chain of Title

Title may be unmarketable because of a defect in the chain of title (*e.g.*, variation in land description in deeds, defectively executed deed, evidence that a prior grantor lacked capacity to convey).

1) Adverse Possession

On the Multistate Bar Exam, title acquired by adverse possession is ***unmarketable***, despite the fact that most modern cases are contra.

2) **Future Interests Held by Unborn or Unascertained Parties**
While most states consider all types of future interests transferable, when a holder of a future interest is unborn or unascertained it is impossible to convey marketable title. Courts will not appoint a guardian ad litem to represent the unborn or unascertained parties for the purposes of conveying land.

b. **Encumbrances**
Generally, mortgages, liens, restrictive covenants, easements, and ***significant*** encroachments render title unmarketable. A beneficial easement, however, if visible or known to the buyer, does not impair the marketability of title.

CMR **Exam Tip** Remember that a seller has the right to satisfy a mortgage or lien at closing, with the proceeds of the sale. Thus, the buyer cannot claim that title is unmarketable because it is subject to a mortgage prior to closing, if the closing will result in marketable title.

c. **Zoning Restrictions**
Zoning restrictions do not affect marketability, but an ***existing violation*** of a zoning ordinance does render title unmarketable.

d. **Time of Marketability**
If the seller has agreed to furnish title at the date of closing, the buyer cannot rescind prior to that date on grounds that the seller's title is not marketable. Note that in an installment land contract, the seller need not provide marketable title until the buyer has made his last payment.

CMR **Exam Tip** Avoid answer choices referring to the implied warranty of marketability of title if the closing has already occurred. Once the closing occurs and the deed changes hands, the seller is ***no longer liable*** on this contractual warranty. The seller is then liable only for promises made ***in the deed***.

e. **Remedy If Title Not Marketable**
The buyer must notify the seller that his title is unmarketable and give him reasonable time to cure the defects. If the seller fails to cure the defects, the buyer's remedies include rescission, damages, specific performance with abatement, and a quiet title suit. But if closing occurs, the contract and deed merge, and the seller's liability on the implied contractual warranty ends.

CMR **Exam Tip** Don't be fooled into choosing the answer that lets the seller off the hook for title defects because the contract calls for a quitclaim deed. A quitclaim deed does not in any way affect the warranty to provide marketable title.

4. **Time of Performance**
Courts presume that time is not "of the essence" in real estate contracts. Thus, the closing date is not absolutely binding, and a party late in tendering her own performance can still enforce the contract if she tenders within a reasonable time (*e.g.,* two months) after the closing date.

THE SALE OF LAND

This chart represents the chronological progression from contract through recording.

Parties Enter into Land Sale Contract →	Time Between Contract and Closing →	Closing →	Recordation →
1. Contract must be in writing (Statute of Frauds). 2. Presumption that time is not of the essence unless so stated. 3. Implied warranty of marketability arises.	1. Buyer investigates Seller's title. If defective, Buyer must notify Seller and give him an opportunity to cure. 2. During this time, the risk of loss is on Buyer.	1. Title passes if deed is validly executed and delivered. Valid execution requires a writing signed by the grantor containing an adequate description of the parcel. Valid delivery requires intent by the grantor to immediately part with legal control. 2. When title passes, the land sale contract is extinguished (along with the implied warranty of marketability). 3. The only basis for a suit by Buyer after title passes is an express covenant, if any, in the deed. There are six possible covenants: Seisin Right to Convey Encumbrances Quiet Enjoyment Warranty Further Assurances	Buyer records deed to protect her title against a subsequent purchaser for value.

a. **When Presumption Overcome**
Time is of the essence if: (i) the ***contract*** so states, (ii) the circumstances indicate that was the parties' ***intent***, or (iii) one party gives the other ***notice*** that time is of the essence.

b. **Liability**
If time is of the essence, a party who fails to tender performance on the closing date is in breach and may not enforce the contract. Even if time is not of the essence, a party who is late in tendering performance is liable for incidental losses.

5. **Tender of Performance**
The buyer's obligation to pay and the seller's obligation to convey are ***concurrent conditions***. Thus, neither party is in breach until the other tenders performance (even if the closing date passes). If neither party tenders performance, the closing date is extended until one of them does so.

a. **When Party's Tender Excused**
A party need not tender performance if the other party has repudiated the contract or it is impossible (*e.g.,* unmarketable title that cannot be cured) for the other party to perform.

6. **Remedies for Breach of Sales Contract**
The nonbreaching party is entitled to ***damages*** (difference between contract price and market value on date of breach, plus incidental costs) or, because land is unique, ***specific performance***. Note that if the buyer wishes to proceed despite unmarketable title, she can usually get specific performance with an abatement of the purchase price.

a. **Liquidated Damages**
Sales contracts usually require the buyer to deposit "earnest money" with the seller, and provide that if the buyer defaults in performance, the seller may retain this money as liquidated damages. Courts routinely uphold the seller's retention of earnest money if the amount appears to be reasonable in light of the seller's anticipated and actual damages.

7. **Seller's Liabilities for Defective Property**

a. **Warranty of Fitness or Quality—New Construction Only**
Contracts of sale and deeds of real property carry no implied warranty of quality or fitness for purpose. However, a majority of courts now recognize a warranty of fitness or quality in the sale of a new house.

b. **Negligence of Builder**
A person may sue a builder for negligence in performing a building contract. Some courts permit the ultimate vendee to sue the builder despite lack of privity.

c. **Sale of Existing Land and Buildings—Liability for Defects**
The seller of existing buildings (not new construction) may be liable to the purchaser for defects such as a leaky roof, flooding basement, or termite infestation, on any of several different theories:

1) **Misrepresentation (Fraud)**
The seller is liable for defects about which he knowingly ***or negligently*** made a false statement of fact to the buyer if the ***buyer relied*** on the statement and it ***materially affected*** the value of the property.

2) **Active Concealment**
The seller will be liable for defects, even ***without making any statements***, if he took steps to ***conceal the defects*** (*e.g.,* wallpapering over water damage).

3) **Failure to Disclose**
Most states hold a seller liable for failure to disclose defects if: (i) he ***knows*** or has reason to know of the defect; (ii) the defect is ***not apparent***, and the seller knows that the buyer is unlikely to discover it upon ordinary inspection; and (iii) the defect is ***serious*** and would probably cause the buyer to reconsider the purchase if known. Factors increasing the likelihood that liability will be imposed in these cases include whether the property is a personal residence, whether the defect is dangerous, and whether the seller created the defect or made a failed attempt to repair it.

d. **Disclaimers of Liability**
A general disclaimer in the sales contract (*e.g.,* "property sold as is" or "with all defects") is ***not*** sufficient to overcome a seller's liability for fraud, concealment, or (in the states that recognize it) failure to disclose. If the disclaimer identifies specific types of defects (*e.g.,* "seller is not liable for any defects in the roof"), it will likely be upheld.

8. **Real Estate Brokers**
Real estate brokers are the seller's agents, but should disclose material information about the property if they have actual knowledge of it. Traditionally, agents earned their commissions when they produced a buyer who was ready, willing, and able to purchase the property. Therefore, the commission was owed regardless of whether the deal actually closed. The growing trend, however, is to award the commission only if the sale actually closes or if it fails to close because of the fault of the seller.

B. DEEDS—FORM AND CONTENT

Deeds transfer title to an interest in real property.

1. **Formalities**
A deed must be ***in writing***, be ***signed by the grantor***, and ***reasonably identify the parties and land***. Most other formalities (*e.g.,* seal, consideration, attestation, and acknowledgment) are generally unnecessary.

CMR **Exam Tip** Note that if a deed is delivered with the ***name of the grantee*** left blank, the court presumes that the person taking delivery has authority to fill in the name of the grantee. If the person fills in a name, the deed is valid. If, however, the ***land description*** is left blank, the deed is void unless the grantee was explicitly given authority to fill in the description.

2. **Defective Deeds**
A ***void*** deed will be set aside by the court even if the property has passed to a bona fide purchaser, but a ***voidable*** deed will be set aside only if the property has ***not*** passed to a bona fide purchaser. Void deeds include those that are forged, were never delivered, or were obtained by fraud in the factum (*i.e.,* the grantor was deceived and did not realize that she

was executing a deed). Voidable deeds include those executed by minors or incapacitated persons, and those obtained through fraud in the inducement, duress, undue influence, mistake, and breach of fiduciary duty.

CMR **Exam Tip** Watch for a situation in which a joint owner attempts to convey property by forging the signature(s) of the other owner(s). Such a conveyance would be valid as to the interest of the owner whose signature is genuine but void as to the other owner(s). Thus, if one joint tenant executes a deed for the entire property with his own signature and the forged signature of the other joint tenant, the conveyance works a severance; the buyer would hold as a tenant in common with the joint tenant whose signature was forged.

3. **Fraudulent Conveyances**

Even when a deed complies with the required formalities, it may be set aside by the grantor's creditors if it was made: (i) with actual intent to hinder, delay, or defraud any creditor of the grantor; or (ii) without receiving a reasonably equivalent value in exchange for the transfer, and the debtor was insolvent or became insolvent as a result of the transfer. However, the deed will not be set aside as against any grantee who took in good faith and paid reasonably equivalent value.

4. **Description of Land Conveyed**

A description is sufficient if it provides a ***good lead*** to the identity of the property (*e.g.,* "all my land in Stockton"). If it is too indefinite, the grantor retains title (but reformation of the deed is a possible remedy). Parol evidence is generally admissible to resolve patent or latent ambiguities if the description gives a good lead, but may not be admissible where the description is inadequate.

a. **Rules of Construction**

Where descriptions are inconsistent or conflicting, these methods of description are given the following order of priority: natural monuments (*e.g.,* oak tree); artificial monuments (*e.g.,* stakes, buildings); courses (*e.g.,* angles); distances (*e.g.,* feet, yards); name (*e.g.,* Blackacre); and quantity (*e.g.,* 300 acres).

b. **Boundary Cases**

Presumptively, title to land passes to the center of a right-of-way or water boundary. This presumption can be rebutted by language in the deed. In variable boundary line cases (*i.e.,* water boundary) the ***slow and imperceptible change*** in the course of a river or stream operates to change the legal boundary; ***accretion*** (slow deposit of soil on land abutting water) belongs to the abutting owner. ***Avulsion*** (sudden change of watercourse) does not change ownership rights. Fixed boundaries are not changed by encroachment of water.

c. **Reformation of Deeds**

A deed will be reformed if it does not represent the parties' agreement because of: (i) mutual mistake; (ii) a scrivener's error; or (iii) a unilateral mistake caused by misrepresentation or other inequitable conduct.

C. DELIVERY AND ACCEPTANCE

A deed is not effective unless it has been delivered and accepted.

Exam Tip Remember that a deed to a dead person is void and conveys no title. The fact that the grantor was unaware of the grantee's death is irrelevant. Title remains in the grantor.

1. **Delivery—In General**
Delivery refers to the grantor's ***intention*** to make a deed ***presently*** effective even if possession is postponed. Delivery may be satisfied by manual delivery, notarized acknowledgment by the grantor, recording, or anything else showing the grantor's intent to deliver. Parol evidence is admissible on the issue of intent to deliver, but not to show that delivery was conditional.

Exam Tip Title passes upon delivery. It cannot be canceled or taken back. Thus, if a fact pattern has the grantee returning a deed to the grantor, this has no effect; it is not a cancellation or a reconveyance. To return title to the grantor, the grantee must draw up a new deed and deliver it to the grantor.

2. **Retention of Interest by Grantor or Conditional Delivery**
Retention of control or interest by the grantor (*e.g.,* right to revoke) indicates a lack of intent to pass title. Thus, if a grantor executes a deed but does not deliver it during his lifetime, no title passes. Failure to record a delivered deed does not affect the passage of title even if the parties believe that the deed is ineffective until recording.

    a. **Express Condition of Grantor's Death**
    A properly executed and delivered deed that provides that title will not pass until the grantor's death is valid and creates a future interest in the grantee.

    b. **Conditions Not Contained in Deed**
    If a deed is absolute on its face but delivered with an oral condition, the condition is disregarded and the delivery is absolute.

3. **Where Grantor Gives Deed to Third Party**
Here, conditional delivery is permissible.

    a. **Transfer to Third Party with No Conditions**
    If the grantor gives a deed to a third party with instructions to give it to the grantee, there is a valid delivery. If the grantor fails to give instructions, the validity of the delivery depends on whether the third party could be considered the grantor's agent. If so, there is no delivery.

    b. **Transfer to Third Party with Conditions (Commercial Transaction)**
    A valid conditional delivery occurs when a grantor gives a deed to a third party with instructions to give it to the grantee when certain conditions occur (*e.g.,* if grantee pays purchase price before a certain date). Parol evidence is admissible to show that delivery is conditional. (Remember that the rule is contra where the grantor gives the deed ***directly*** to the grantee; *see* 1., *supra.*)

        1) **Grantor's Right to Recover Deed**
        A grantor can revoke only if: (i) the condition has not yet occurred, and (ii) there is no enforceable written contract to convey.

        2) **Breach of Escrow Conditions**
        If a grantee wrongfully acquires the deed from the escrow holder prior to

performance of the condition, title does not pass and the grantee cannot give good title to a subsequent purchaser.

3) **"Relation Back" Doctrine**
Title usually passes when the condition occurs, but if justice requires it (*e.g.*, grantor dies or becomes incompetent) and there is an enforceable contract to convey, title may "relate back" to the time when the grantor gave the deed to the third party. Rights of intervening bona fide purchasers are protected.

c. **Transfer to Third Party with Conditions (Donative Transaction)**
When a grantor gives a deed to a third party to give to a ***donee*** when a condition occurs, the main issue is whether the grantor can revoke the deed before the condition occurs. Where the condition is not the grantor's death, delivery is irrevocable and creates a springing executory interest in the donee. Where the condition is the grantor's death, most courts follow the same reasoning, but some hold deeds revocable unless there is an enforceable contract to convey (*i.e.,* same as true escrow cases, above).

4. **Acceptance**
Acceptance by the grantee is required in order to complete a conveyance. Most states ***pre-sume*** acceptance. Acceptance relates back to the date the deed was delivered into escrow (unless this would defeat the rights of intervening third parties).

5. **Dedication**
Land may be transferred to a public body (*e.g.,* city, county) by dedication. An offer may be made by written or oral statement, submission of a map or plat showing the dedication, or opening the land for public use. To be effective, a dedication must be accepted, which may be done by formal resolution, approval of map or plat, or actual assumption of maintenance or improvements.

D. **COVENANTS FOR TITLE AND ESTOPPEL BY DEED**
There are three types of deeds used to convey property interests other than leaseholds: the general warranty deed, the special warranty deed, and the quitclaim deed. The difference among these deeds is the scope of title assurance (*i.e.,* covenants for title).

Exam Tip Be careful not to confuse covenants for title with real covenants (written promises to do or not do something on the land). They are completely different. Real covenants do not relate to title.

1. **Covenants in General Warranty Deed**

a. **Usual Covenants**
The following are the usual covenants for title contained in a general warranty deed.

1) **Covenant of Seisin**
The grantor covenants that she has the estate she purports to convey. She must have both title and possession at the time of the grant.

2) **Covenant of Right to Convey**
The grantor covenants that she has the authority to make the grant. Title alone will satisfy this covenant.

3) **Covenant Against Encumbrances**
The grantor covenants against the existence of physical (*e.g.,* encroachments) or title (*e.g.,* mortgages) encumbrances.

4) **Covenant for Quiet Enjoyment**
The grantor covenants that the grantee will not be disturbed in possession by a third party's ***lawful*** claim of title.

5) **Covenant of Warranty**
The grantor agrees to defend against reasonable claims of title by a third party, and to compensate the grantee for any loss sustained by the claim of superior title.

Exam Tip The covenant for quiet enjoyment and the covenant of warranty are generally considered to be identical covenants for title.

6) **Covenant for Further Assurances**
The grantor promises to perform acts reasonably necessary to perfect title conveyed. (This covenant is ***not*** one of the usual covenants, but is frequently given.)

b. **Breach of the Covenants**
Three of the covenants (seisin, right to convey, encumbrances) are breached, if at all, at the time of conveyance. Quiet enjoyment, warranty, and further assurances are future covenants and are breached only upon disturbance of the grantee's possession.

c. **Damages and Remote Grantees**
If there are successive conveyances by general warranty deed and the last grantee is evicted by lawful claim of title, he may sue ***anyone*** up the line. Some states allow him to recover to the extent of consideration ***received*** by a defendant-covenantor. Other states limit recovery to the ***lesser*** of what he paid or what the defendant-covenantor received.

2. **Statutory Special Warranty Deed**
In many states, use of the word "grant" in a deed creates by implication two limited assurances against acts of the grantor (not her predecessors): (i) that the grantor has not conveyed the same estate or any interest therein to anyone other than the grantee; and (ii) that the estate is free from encumbrances made by the grantor.

3. **Quitclaim Deeds**
A quitclaim deed releases ***whatever interest*** the grantor has. No covenants of title are included or implied.

4. **Estoppel by Deed**
If the grantor purports to convey an estate in property that she does not then own, her subsequent acquisition of the estate will automatically inure to the benefit of the grantee. This doctrine applies where the conveyance was by warranty deed, or where the deed purported to convey a ***particular*** estate. It is not usually applicable to quitclaim deeds.

a. **Rights of Subsequent Purchasers**
Most courts hold that title inures to the benefit of the grantee only as against the grantor. Thus, if the grantor transfers her after-acquired title to a bona fide purchaser for value ("BFP"), the BFP will prevail over the original grantee.

b. **Remedies of**
The original g

E. RECORDING

At common law, if a grantor
prevailed. The recording acts c

1. Recording Acts—In Gener

Recording acts generally prot
provide a mechanism for "earli
utes require a grantee to record h
interest. Recording is not essentia
grantee, but can be essential to prot
constructive notice of the first conve
Any instrument creating or affecting a
acknowledged by the grantor before a n

2. Types of Recording Acts

Recording acts are in effect in every state. T ... all three,
the burden is on the subsequent taker to prove ... under the
statute.

a. Notice Statutes

Under a notice statute, a subsequent BFP (pers... who pays value and has no notice of the prior instrument) prevails over a prior grantee who failed to record. The key is that the subsequent purchaser had ***no actual or constructive notice at the time of the conveyance***.

Example: O conveys to A on January 1. A does not record. O conveys to B on January 15 for valuable consideration. B has no notice of the conveyance to A. B prevails over A. It is irrelevant whether A recorded after January 15 and before B recorded, because B had no notice ***at the time he took***. (This distinguishes notice and race-notice statutes.)

CMR **Exam Tip** Remember that under a notice statute, the subsequent BFP is protected regardless of whether she records at all.

b. Race-Notice Statutes

Under a race-notice statute, a subsequent BFP is protected only if she takes without notice ***and*** records before the prior grantee.

Example: O conveys to A on January 1. A does not record. O conveys to B on January 15 for valuable consideration. B has no notice of the conveyance to A. A records on January 18. B records on January 20. A prevails over B because B did not record first.

c. Race Statutes

Under a pure race statute, whoever records first wins. Notice is irrelevant. Very few states have such statutes.

RECORDING STATUTES		
[illegible]	Typical Language	Effect
[illegible]	"No conveyance or mortgage of an interest in land is valid against any subsequent purchaser for value without notice thereof, unless it is recorded."	Subsequent ***bona fide purchaser*** (*i.e.,* for value, without notice) prevails.
Race	"No conveyance or mortgage of an interest in land is valid against any subsequent purchaser whose conveyance is first recorded."	Grantee ***who records first*** prevails.
Race-Notice	"No conveyance or mortgage of an interest in land is valid against any subsequent purchaser for value without notice thereof whose conveyance is first recorded."	Subsequent ***bona fide purchaser*** (*i.e.,* for value, without notice) ***who records first*** prevails.

3. Who Is Protected by Recording Acts

Only BFPs are protected from the claims of a prior transferee under "notice" and "race-notice" statutes. To be a BFP, a person must be a purchaser, without notice (actual, constructive, or inquiry), and pay valuable consideration.

a. Purchasers

All statutes protect purchasers (of the fee or lesser estate). Mortgagees for value are purchasers. Donees, heirs, and devisees are ***not*** protected because they do not give value.

1) Purchaser from Donee, Heir, or Devisee

A purchaser from a donee, heir, or devisee of the record owner is protected against prior unrecorded conveyances of the record owner.

2) Judgment Creditors

Most states permit a plaintiff who obtains a money judgment to place a judgment lien on the defendant's real property by filing the judgment in the appropriate county office. The majority, however, hold that such a judgment creditor is not protected by the recording statute against a prior unrecorded conveyance by the defendant.

3) Transferees from Bona Fide Purchaser—Shelter Rule

A person who takes ***from*** a BFP will prevail against any interest the transferor-BFP would have prevailed against. This is true even if the transferee had actual notice of a prior unrecorded conveyance. This rule does not, however, help a transferee who previously held title; she cannot "ship through" a BFP to get good title.

4) **Purchaser Under Installment Land Contract**
In most states, a purchaser under an installment land contract is protected only to the extent of payment made. In a dispute with a prior claimant, the court may award the purchaser: (i) a share of the property as a tenant in common equal to the proportion of ***payments made***; (ii) a lien on the property to the extent of the ***amount paid***; or (iii) the entire property, subject to a lien on the property to the extent of the ***balance still owed***.

b. **Without Notice**
"Without notice" means that the purchaser had no actual, constructive (record), or inquiry notice of a prior conveyance at the time she paid consideration and received the interest.

CMR **Exam Tip** In determining who is a BFP for purposes of protection of the recording statutes, remember that the purchaser must be without notice ***at the time of conveyance***. It does not matter if she learns of an adverse claim after the conveyance but before recording.

1) **Actual Notice**
Actual notice includes knowledge obtained from any source (*e.g.,* newspaper, word-of-mouth).

2) **Record Notice—Chain of Title**
A subsequent purchaser is charged with notice of only those conveyances that are recorded and appear in the chain of title.

a) **"Wild Deeds"**
A "wild deed" is a recorded deed that is not connected to the chain of title. It does not impart constructive notice because a subsequent purchaser could not feasibly find it.
Example: A conveys Blackacre to B. B does not record. B conveys it to C, and C records. A conveys Blackacre to D. D does not have notice of C's claim.

b) **Deeds Recorded Late**
A deed recorded ***after*** the grantor is shown by record to have parted with title through another (subsequent) instrument is not constructive notice in most states (but is in some "race-notice" jurisdictions).
Example: A conveys to B on March 1. A conveys to C on April 1. C records on April 10. B records on April 15. C conveys to D on May 1. If D has no actual or inquiry notice of the A-B deed, he will prevail. Most states would hold that B's deed was recorded late and was not in D's chain of title.

c) **Deeds Recorded Before Grantor Obtained Title**
There is a split of authority on whether a recorded deed, received from a grantor who had no title when conveyed but who afterwards obtains title, imparts constructive notice to subsequent purchasers. Most courts say it does not, and a BFP will win on the grounds that the deed is not in his chain of

title. The minority view protects the prior grantee over the BFP on an estoppel by deed theory (*see* D.4., *supra*).

d) **Deed in Chain Referring to Instrument Outside Chain**
Reference to another instrument in a recorded document that is in the chain of title may impart constructive notice of the instrument referred to—even if it is unrecorded or not itself in the chain of title.

e) **Restrictive Covenants—Deeds from Common Grantor**
Courts are split on whether deeds to adjacent lots or lots in a subdivision, executed by the same grantor and containing restrictions and easements involving the subject lot, are within the chain of title of the subject lot. The better view is that they are not.

3) **Inquiry Notice**
Under certain circumstances, a purchaser is required to make reasonable inquiries. He is charged with knowledge of whatever the inquiry would have revealed, even if in fact he made none. References in recorded instruments to unrecorded transactions, unrecorded instruments in the chain of title (*e.g.,* grantor's title documents are not recorded), and possession unexplained by the record put a purchaser on inquiry notice. The mere fact that a quitclaim deed was used does not charge the purchaser with inquiry notice.

c. **Valuable Consideration**
To be protected by the recording statute, the subsequent grantee must prove that he is a purchaser, not a donee. The consideration need not be adequate, but it must be of some pecuniary value (*i.e.,* love and affection is not valuable consideration). Note that property received as security for an antecedent debt is insufficient.

CMR **Exam Tip** A purchaser is protected by a recording statute only from the time consideration is paid. Thus, even if the deed was delivered and recorded before the consideration was paid, a purchaser will not prevail over deeds recorded subsequently but before the consideration was paid.

4. **Title Search**
In a ***tract index*** jurisdiction, the searcher looks at the page indexed by block and/or lot describing the property and any instruments affecting it. In a ***grantor and grantee index*** jurisdiction, the searcher establishes a chain of title by searching back in time in the grantee-grantor index. From that point, he then searches forward in time in the grantor-grantee index to see if any grantor conveyed an interest to someone outside of the backward chain.

5. **Effect of Recordation**
Recordation gives prospective subsequent grantees constructive notice of the existence and content of recorded instruments. It also raises a presumption of valid delivery and authenticity. However, it does not validate an invalid deed or protect against interests arising by operation of law (*e.g.*, dower, title by adverse possession); to this extent, BFPs are still in jeopardy.

a. **Recorder's Mistakes**
An instrument is considered recorded when filed with the recorder's office, regardless

of whether it is thereafter properly indexed. A subsequent purchaser is charged with notice of a misindexed instrument, but has a cause of action against the recorder's office.

b. **Effect of Recording Unacknowledged Instrument**
Because an unacknowledged instrument is not entitled to recordation, it does ***not*** give constructive notice. A subsequent grantee must have actual notice of a deed (*e.g.,* discover it in a title search) to be bound by it. *Compare*: Where acknowledgment is ***defective*** for reasons ***not apparent on the face*** of the instrument, the better view is that it imparts constructive notice.

F. CONVEYANCE BY WILL

Another way of conveying property is by will.

1. Ademption

If property is specifically devised or bequeathed in the testator's will, but the testator no longer owns it at the time of death, the gift fails. Ademption applies only to specific bequests, which can be satisfied only by the delivery of a ***particular item***; they cannot be satisfied by money. A gift of land is always a specific devise. If the testator specifically devises property and then sells or gives away a part of that property, only that portion is adeemed; the remainder passes to the devisee.

a. **Land Under Executory Contract**
Most state statutes do not apply the ademption doctrine to the proceeds of a contract for sale of land that was executory at the time of the testator's death; *i.e.,* the devisee gets the proceeds in place of the land. These statutes take precedence over the equitable conversion doctrine. In addition, ademption does not apply when the contract is entered into by the representative of an incompetent testator.

b. **Other Proceeds Not Subject to Ademption**
When property is damaged or destroyed before the testator's death but the casualty insurance proceeds are not paid until after the testator's death, ademption does not usually apply. The beneficiary of the specific bequest takes the insurance proceeds. Similarly, ademption usually does not apply to property condemned by the government where the taking was before death but the condemnation award was paid after death.

2. Exoneration

At common law and in most states, the devisee of specific property is entitled to have the land "exonerated" by the payment of liens and mortgages from the testator's residuary estate. There is a growing trend toward abolition of the exoneration doctrine.

3. Lapse and Anti-Lapse Statutes

A lapse occurs when the beneficiary of a gift in a will ***dies before the testator***. Under the common law, if a lapse occurred, the gift was void. However, nearly all states now have statutes that prevent lapse by permitting the gift to pass to the predeceasing beneficiary's living descendants under certain circumstances. These statutes vary as to the scope of beneficiaries covered by the statute.

a. **Degree of Relationship to Testator**
Many of the anti-lapse statutes apply only when the named beneficiary is a descendant

of the testator. Others apply if the beneficiary is more remotely related, such as a descendant of the testator's grandparent. Others apply to any relative, and still others apply to any beneficiary at all.

1) Descendants Are Substitutes

The anti-lapse statute does not save the gift for the predeceasing beneficiary's estate; rather it substitutes the beneficiary's descendants for the beneficiary. Thus, property will never pass under the anti-lapse statute to a predeceasing beneficiary's spouse.

b. Inapplicable If Beneficiary Dead When Will Executed

If the beneficiary is already dead when the will is executed, the anti-lapse statute usually does not apply, and the gift will lapse and fail.

c. Application to Class Gifts

If a class member within the coverage of an anti-lapse statute predeceases the testator leaving surviving issue, the statute will apply and the issue will take the deceased class member's share of the gift.

d. Anti-Lapse Statute Does Not Apply If Contrary Will Provision

The anti-lapse statute does not apply if there is a contrary will provision; *i.e.*, the gift is contingent on the beneficiary's surviving the testator.

G. CROPS (EMBLEMENTS)

Generally, the conveyance of land includes all crops growing on it. However, exceptions exist for (i) crops that have already been harvested or severed from the land, and (ii) crops planted by a tenant during the term of the tenancy. For title to crops to remain in a tenant, the tenancy must have been of ***uncertain duration*** and have terminated ***without fault*** on the part of the tenant.

VII. SECURITY INTERESTS IN REAL ESTATE

A. TYPES OF SECURITY INTERESTS

Of the five types of security interests in real estate, the first three are the most important.

1. Mortgage

The debtor/notemaker is the mortgagor. The lender is the mortgagee. On default, the lender can realize on the mortgaged real estate only by having a judicial foreclosure sale conducted by the sheriff.

2. Deed of Trust

The debtor/notemaker is the trustor. He gives a deed of trust to a third-party trustee, who is usually closely connected to the lender (the beneficiary). On default the lender instructs the trustee to foreclose the deed of trust by sale.

3. Installment Land Contract

An installment purchaser obtains legal title only when the full contract price has been paid off. Forfeiture clauses, allowing the vendor upon default to cancel the contract, retake possession, and retain all money paid, are common.

4. Absolute Deed
An absolute deed, if given for security purposes, can be treated by the court as an "equitable" mortgage to be treated as any other mortgage (*i.e.*, creditor must foreclose by judicial action).

5. Sale-Leaseback
A landowner may sell her property for cash and then lease it back from the purchaser for a long period of time. Like an absolute deed, this may be treated as a disguised mortgage.

B. TRANSFERS BY MORTGAGEE AND MORTGAGOR

All parties to a mortgage or deed of trust may transfer their interests. The note and mortgage must pass to the ***same person*** for the transfer to be complete.

1. Transfer by Mortgagee

a. Transfer of Mortgage Without Note
Some states hold that the transfer of the mortgage automatically transfers the note as well, unless the mortgagee-transferor expressly reserves the rights to the note. In these states, the transferee of the mortgage can then file an equitable action and compel a transfer of the note as well. Other states hold that, because the note is the principal evidence of the debt, a transfer of the mortgage without the note is void.

b. Transfer of Note Without Mortgage
The ***note can be transferred without the mortgage***, but the mortgage will automatically follow the properly transferred note, unless the mortgagee-transferee expressly reserves the rights to the mortgage. No separate written assignment of the mortgage is necessary.

1) Methods of Transferring the Note
The note may be transferred either by indorsing it and delivering it to the transferee, or by a separate document of assignment. Only if the indorsement and delivery method is used can the transferee become a ***holder in due course***. To be a holder in due course of the note, the following requirements must be met:

a) The note must be ***negotiable in form*** (payable "to bearer" or "to the order of" the named payee, with a promise to pay a sum certain, and no other promises).

b) The original note must be ***indorsed*** and signed by the named payee.

c) The original note must be ***delivered*** to the transferee.

d) The transferee must take the note in ***good faith*** (no notice that it is overdue, has been dishonored, is subject to any defense by the maker) and must pay ***value*** for it.

2) Benefits of Holder in Due Course Status
A holder in due course takes the note free of any personal defenses of the maker (*e.g.*, failure of consideration, fraud in the inducement, waiver, estoppel, and payment), but is still subject to real defenses (*e.g.*, infancy, other incapacity, duress, illegality, fraud in the execution, forgery, discharge in insolvency, and any other insolvency).

CMR **Exam Tip** Remember that if possession of the note has been transferred by the original mortgagee, any payment to that mortgagee will not count. The holder of the note can still demand payment—even if the mortgagor had no notice of the transfer. For example, X borrows $10,000 from Y, giving Y a note secured by a mortgage on Farmacre. Later Y assigns the note to Z, but does not tell X. X pays the $10,000 to Y. Z may still demand payment of the $10,000, and may foreclose the mortgage on Farmacre if payment is not forthcoming. The payment to Y is no defense.

2. Transfer by Mortgagor—Grantee Takes Subject to Mortgage

A grantee of mortgaged property takes subject to the mortgage.

a. Assumption

If the grantee signs an assumption agreement, he becomes primarily liable to the lender, while the original mortgagor is secondarily liable as a surety. If no assumption agreement is signed, the grantee is not personally liable on the loan, and the original mortgagor remains primarily and personally liable. However, if the grantee does not pay, the loan may be foreclosed, wiping out the grantee's investment.

CMR **Exam Tip** Remember that once a grantee has assumed a mortgage, any modification of the obligation by the grantee and mortgagee discharges the original mortgagor of all liability.

b. Due-on-Sale Clauses

Due-on-sale clauses, which appear in most modern mortgages, allow the lender to demand full payment of the loan if the mortgagor transfers any interest in the property without the lender's consent.

C. POSSESSION BEFORE FORECLOSURE

When a mortgagor defaults on his debt, the mortgagee can foreclose on the mortgage. A mortgagee may wish to take possession of the property, or begin receiving the rents from the property, before foreclosure.

1. Theories of Title

The mortgagee may have a right to take possession before foreclosure, depending on the theory the state follows. Most states follow either the lien or the title theory.

a. The Lien Theory

According to the lien theory, the mortgagee is considered the ***holder of a security interest only*** and the mortgagor is deemed the owner of the land until foreclosure. The mortgagee may ***not*** have possession before foreclosure.

b. The Title Theory

Under the title theory, ***legal title is in the mortgagee*** until the mortgage has been satisfied or foreclosed, and the mortgagee is entitled to possession upon demand at any time.

c. The Intermediate Theory

In the few states that follow the intermediate theory, legal title is in the mortgagor until default, and upon default, ***legal title is in the mortgagee***. The mortgagee may demand possession when a default occurs. There is little practical difference between this theory and the title theory.

2. **Mortgagor Consent and Abandonment**
The mortgagee may take possession if the mortgagor gives consent to do so, or if the mortgagor abandons the property.

3. **Risks of Mortgagee in Possession**
Most mortgagees do not wish to take possession because of the risks of liability. These risks involve the duty to account for rents, the duty to manage the property in a prudent manner, and potential tort liability for those injured on the property.

4. **Receiverships**
Most mortgagees attempt to intercept the rents before foreclosure by getting a receiver appointed by the court to manage the property. Courts will generally appoint receivers for rental property upon showing that: (i) waste is occurring; (ii) the value of the property is inadequate to secure the debt; and (iii) the mortgagor is insolvent.

D. **FORECLOSURE**
Almost all states require foreclosure by sale, under which the property is sold to satisfy the debt in whole or part. While all states allow judicial sale, some states allow nonjudicial sale under a power of sale (usually with respect to deeds of trust). Foreclosure sales are usually conducted by auction, and the lender is permitted to bid at the sale.

1. **Redemption**

a. **Redemption in Equity**
At ***any time prior to the foreclosure sale***, the mortgagor may redeem the property by paying the amount due. If the note or mortgage contains an acceleration clause, the full balance of the note or mortgage must be paid to redeem. This right cannot be waived in the mortgage itself.

b. **Statutory Redemption**
About half the states allow the mortgagor to redeem the property for some fixed period (*e.g.,* six months) ***after the foreclosure sale*** has occurred.

2. **Priorities**
A mortgage's priority is usually determined by the time it was placed on the property. Foreclosure does not destroy any interests senior to the interest being foreclosed. It generally destroys all junior interests, but failure to include a junior interest holder in a foreclosure action results in preservation of that party's interest.

a. **Modification of Priority**
Although priority among mortgages is generally determined by chronology, this priority may be changed by: (i) the operation of the recording statute if a ***prior mortgagee fails to record***; (ii) a ***subordination agreement*** between a senior and junior mortgagee; (iii) a ***purchase money mortgage***; (iv) the ***modification of a senior mortgage*** (junior mortgage has priority over the modification); or (v) the ***granting of optional future advances*** by a mortgagee with notice of a junior lien (junior lien has priority over advances).

REAL ESTATE FINANCING AND FORECLOSURE

Financing

Buyer finances purchase of land using the land as collateral. Usually done by giving lender a mortgage on the property, although it could be done with deed of trust, installment land contract, absolute deed, or sale-leaseback.

↓

Default

Mortgagor-borrower defaults. Mortgagee has right to foreclose. Up until the foreclosure sale, borrower may redeem by paying off mortgage and accrued interest. (Equitable redemption)

↓

Foreclosure

Foreclosure must be by sale, usually judicial sale.

Proceeds distributed according to priorities of security interests.

↓

Post-Foreclosure

If proceeds of sale are insufficient to satisfy debt, mortgagee can bring personal action against borrower for deficiency.

About one-half of states give borrower a right to redeem for a fixed period (*e.g.*, six months) after foreclosure by paying sale price. (Statutory redemption)

b. **Purchase Money Mortgages**
A purchase money mortgage ("PMM") is a mortgage given in exchange for funds used to purchase the property. PMMs are given either to the seller as part of the purchase price or to a third-party lender. PMMs have priority over non-PMMs executed at about the same time even if the non-PMM was recorded first. As between two PMMs, a seller's mortgage has priority over a third-party's. If there are two third-party PMMs, priority is determined by chronological order. Usually two PMMs have notice of the other's existence; thus, the recording acts are of no use in determining priority.

3. **Proceeds of Sale**
Proceeds are applied first to the expenses of the sale, attorneys' fees, and court costs; then to the principal and accrued interest on the foreclosed loan; next to any other junior interests in the order of their priority; and finally to the mortgagor.

4. **Deficiency Judgments**
If the proceeds are insufficient to satisfy the mortgage debt, the mortgagee retains a personal cause of action against the mortgagor for the deficiency.

E. INSTALLMENT LAND CONTRACTS
Most installment contracts provide for forfeiture rather than foreclosure as the vendor's remedy for default, but courts use the following theories to avoid that harsh result:

1. **Equity of Redemption**
Several states give the contract purchaser a grace period to pay the accelerated full balance of the contract and keep the land after default.

2. **Restitution**
A number of decisions, while granting forfeiture, have required the vendor to refund to the purchaser any amount by which his payments exceed the vendor's damages.

3. **Treat as a Mortgage**
A few states treat installment contracts as mortgages, thus requiring a judicial foreclosure sale.

4. **Waiver**
Many cases hold that a vendor's pattern of accepting late payments constitutes a waiver of the right of strict performance. To reinstate strict performance, the vendor must send the purchaser a notice of his intention to do so and must allow a reasonable time for the purchaser to make up any late payments.

5. **Election of Remedies**
The vendor must choose only one remedy (damages or specific performance) and forgo all others.

VIII. RIGHTS INCIDENTAL TO OWNERSHIP OF LAND (NATURAL RIGHTS)

A. IN GENERAL
An owner of real property has the exclusive right to use and possess the surface, the airspace, and the soil of the property.

B. RIGHTS TO LATERAL AND SUBJACENT SUPPORT OF LAND

1. Lateral Support

Ownership of land includes the right to have the land supported in its ***natural state*** by adjoining land.

a. Support of Land in Natural State

A landowner is ***strictly liable*** if his excavation causes adjacent land to subside (*i.e.,* slip or cave-in).

b. Support of Land with Buildings

An adjacent landowner is strictly liable for damage to buildings caused by excavation only if it is shown that the land would have collapsed in its natural state. Otherwise, he is liable for such damage only if his excavation was done ***negligently***.

2. Subjacent Support

An underground occupant of land (*e.g.*, a mining company) must support the surface and buildings existing on the date the subjacent estate was created. Liability for subsequently erected buildings requires ***negligence***.

C. WATER RIGHTS

Different rules apply to watercourses, groundwater, and surface waters.

1. Watercourses (Streams, Rivers, and Lakes)

There are two major systems for determining allocation of water in watercourses: the riparian doctrine and the prior appropriation doctrine.

a. Riparian Doctrine

Under this doctrine, the water belongs to those who own the land bordering the watercourse. Riparian rights attach to all contiguous tracts held by the same owner as long as one abuts the water. Riparian owners can use water only in connection with the riparian parcel.

1) Natural Flow Theory

Under this theory, a riparian owner's use resulting in substantial or material diminution of the water's quantity, quality, or velocity is enjoinable.

2) Reasonable Use Theory

Under this theory, which is the most common, all riparians share the right of "reasonable use" of the water (*i.e.*, one owner's use is not enjoinable unless it substantially interferes with the use of other riparian owners). In determining "reasonable" use, courts balance the utility of the owner's use against the gravity of the harm. Six factors are helpful in making this determination: alteration of flow; purpose of use; pollution; extent of use; destination of water taken; and miscellaneous conduct that may give rise to litigation.

3) Natural vs. Artificial Use

Under either theory, natural uses (human uses, *e.g.,* consumption, gardening) prevail over artificial uses (*e.g.,* irrigation, manufacturing).

b. **Prior Appropriation Doctrine**
Under this doctrine, individuals acquire rights by actual use. Appropriative rights are determined by priority of beneficial use. If there is a decrease in flow, priority is accorded in terms of time of appropriation. An appropriative right can be lost by abandonment.

2. **Groundwater (Percolating Water)**
Four doctrines determine rights in diffuse underground water recovered through wells.

a. **Absolute Ownership Doctrine**
This doctrine is followed by about 12 eastern states. The owner of overlying land can take all the water she wishes, for any purpose, including export.

b. **Reasonable Use Doctrine**
About 25 states follow this doctrine. It is like absolute ownership, but exporting is allowed only if it does not harm other owners who have rights in the same aquifer.

c. **Correlative Rights Doctrine**
In California, owners of overlying land own the underground water basin as joint tenants, and each is allowed a reasonable amount for his own use.

d. **Appropriative Rights Doctrine**
This doctrine is followed in some western states. Priority of use (not ownership of overlying land) is determinative.

3. **Surface Waters**
A landowner can use surface water (*i.e.,* water without a channel that passes over land, such as rainfall, seepage, etc.) within her boundaries for any purpose she desires. Questions on surface water usually concern liability for changing natural flow by dikes, drains, etc. Liability depends on which theory the state follows:

a. **Natural Flow (Civil Law) Theory**
Under this theory, followed by half the states, owners cannot alter natural drainage patterns. This rule has been "softened" in most states to allow "reasonable changes."

b. **Common Enemy Theory**
Under this theory, followed by most of the other states, an owner can take any protective measures to get rid of the water (*e.g.,* dikes). The rule has been modified by many courts to prohibit unnecessary damage to others' lands.

c. **Reasonable Use Theory**
There is a growing trend to apply this theory, which involves balancing the utility of the use against the gravity of the harm.

CMR **Exam Tip** Remember that the above theories apply to redirecting surface water. A landowner can ***capture*** (*e.g.,* by a dam or in barrels) as much surface water as he wishes. Surface water can be diverted to any purpose on or off the land. Owners below have no cause of action unless the diversion was malicious.

D. RIGHTS IN AIRSPACE

The right to airspace above a parcel is not exclusive, but the owner is entitled to freedom from excessive noise.

E. RIGHT TO EXCLUDE—REMEDIES OF POSSESSOR

The possessor of real property has the right to exclude others. His remedies for invasions include actions for:

1. ***Trespass*** (land invaded by ***tangible*** physical object);
2. ***Private nuisance*** (land invaded by ***intangibles*** such as odors or noise);
3. ***Continuing trespass*** (land repeatedly invaded by trespasser); and
4. ***Ejectment or unlawful detainer*** to remove a trespasser or tenant. This action can be joined with a demand for money damages.

IX. COOPERATIVES, CONDOMINIUMS, AND ZONING

A. COOPERATIVES

In a cooperative, title to the land and buildings is held by a corporation that leases individual apartments to its shareholders. Because of their economic interdependence and because the individual owners are regarded as tenants, a direct restraint on the alienation of an individual interest is valid.

B. CONDOMINIUMS

In a condominium, each owner owns the interior of his individual unit plus an undivided interest in the exterior and common areas. Because condominium unit ownership is treated as fee ownership, the ordinary rules against restraints on alienation apply.

C. ZONING

The state may enact statutes to reasonably control the use of land for the protection of the ***health, safety, morals, and welfare*** of its citizens. The zoning power is based on the state's police power and is limited by the Due Process and Equal Protection Clauses of the Fourteenth Amendment, and the "no taking without just compensation" clause of the Fifth Amendment. Cities and counties can exercise zoning power only if so authorized by a state enabling act. These terms should be remembered:

1. Nonconforming Use

A use that exists at the time of passage of a zoning act that does not conform to the statute cannot be eliminated at once.

2. Special Use Permit

A special use permit is one that must be obtained even though the zoning is proper for the intended use. It is often required for hospitals, funeral homes, drive-in businesses, etc.

3. **Variance**
A variance is a departure from the literal restrictions of a zoning ordinance granted by administrative action.

CMR **Exam Tip** Zoning ordinances are generally invalid if they have no reasonable relation to public welfare, are too restrictive, are discriminatory as to a particular parcel, are beyond the grant of authority, violate due process, or are racially discriminatory.

4. **Unconstitutional Takings and Exactions**
A zoning ordinance may so reduce the value of real property that it constitutes a taking under the Fifth and Fourteenth Amendments. If the ordinance constitutes a taking, the local government must pay damages to the landowner equal to the value reduction. If the ordinance regulates activity that would be considered a nuisance under common law principles, it will not be a taking even if it leaves the land with no economic value.

a. **Denial of *All* Economic Value—Taking**
A regulation that deprives the owner of ***all*** economic use of his land constitutes a taking (unless the use was prohibited by nuisance or property law when the owner acquired the property).

b. **Denial of *Nearly All* Economic Value—Balancing Test**
If a regulation leaves property with ***very little economic value***, to determine if there was a taking the court will balance: (i) the ***social goals*** of the regulation, (ii) the ***diminution in value*** of the property, and (iii) the owner's ***reasonable expectations*** for use of the property.

c. **Unconstitutional Exactions**
Local governments often demand, in exchange for zoning approval for a new project, that the landowner give up some land for a public purpose, such as street widening. However, such demands are unconstitutional under the Fifth and Fourteenth Amendments unless the government proves: (i) the government demands are ***rationally connected*** to an additional burden the project will place on public facilities or rights (essential nexus); and (ii) the dedication is reasonably related in ***nature*** and ***extent*** to the impact of the proposed development (rough proportionality).

d. **Remedy**
If a regulation constitutes a taking, the government will be required either to compensate the owner for the property or to terminate the regulation and pay the owner damages for the temporary taking.

TORTS

TABLE OF CONTENTS

TORTS

I. INTENTIONAL TORTS

A. PRIMA FACIE CASE

To establish a prima facie case of intentional tort, plaintiff must prove:

1. Act by Defendant

The act required is a ***volitional movement by*** defendant.

2. Intent

Intent may be either (i) ***specific*** (the goal in acting is to bring about specific consequences) or (ii) ***general*** (the actor knows with "substantial certainty" that these consequences will result).

a. Transferred Intent

1) General Rule

The transferred intent doctrine applies when the defendant intends to commit a tort against one person but instead (i) commits a different tort against that person, (ii) commits the same tort as intended but against a different person, or (iii) commits a different tort against a different person. In such cases, the intent to commit a certain tort against one person is transferred to the tort actually committed or to the person actually injured for purposes of establishing a prima facie case.

2) Limitations on Use of Transferred Intent

Transferred intent may be invoked only if both the tort intended and the tort that results are one of the following:

a) Assault;

b) Battery;

c) False imprisonment;

d) Trespass to land; or

e) Trespass to chattels.

CMR **Exam Tip** Everyone is "capable" of intent. Incapacity is not a good defense. Thus, young children and persons who are mentally incompetent will be liable for their intentional torts.

3. Causation

The result must have been legally caused by defendant's act or something set in motion by him. Causation is satisfied if defendant's conduct was a ***substantial factor*** in bringing about the injury.

B. PRIMA FACIE CASE—INTENTIONAL TORTS TO THE PERSON

1. Battery
Elements of the prima facie case:

(i) ***Harmful*** or ***offensive contact***;

(ii) To plaintiff's person;

(iii) Intent; and

(iv) Causation.

a. Harmful or Offensive Contact

1) Judged by Reasonable Person Standard
Harmfulness and offensiveness are judged by a reasonable person standard.

CMR Exam Tip Contact is considered offensive only if it has not been consented to. However, consent will be ***implied*** for the ordinary contacts of everyday life (*e.g.*, minor bumping on a crowded bus).

2) Direct or Indirect Contact
Contact can be direct (*e.g.*, striking plaintiff) or indirect (*e.g.*, setting a trap for plaintiff to fall into).

b. Plaintiff's Person
Plaintiff's person includes anything connected to the plaintiff (*e.g.*, clothing or a purse).

2. Assault
Elements of the prima facie case:

(i) An act by defendant creating a ***reasonable apprehension*** in plaintiff;

(ii) Of ***immediate harmful or offensive contact*** to plaintiff's person;

(iii) Intent; and

(iv) Causation.

a. Distinguish Fear
Apprehension should not be confused with fear or intimidation (*e.g.*, a weakling can cause apprehension and thus assault a bully).

b. Apparent Ability Sufficient
If defendant has the ***apparent ability*** to commit a battery, this will be enough to cause a reasonable apprehension.

c. Effect of Words
Words alone are not sufficient. For the defendant to be liable, the words must be coupled

with conduct. However, words can ***negate*** reasonable apprehension (*e.g.*, the defendant shakes her fist but states that she is not going to strike the plaintiff).

d. Requirement of Immediacy

Plaintiff must be apprehensive that she is about to become the victim of an immediate battery.

3. False Imprisonment

Elements of the prima facie case:

(i) An act or omission on the part of defendant that ***confines or restrains*** plaintiff;

(ii) To a ***bounded area***;

(iii) Intent; and

(iv) Causation.

a. Sufficient Methods of Confinement or Restraint

Sufficient acts of restraint include: (i) physical barriers, (ii) physical force, (iii) threats of force, (iv) failure to release, and (v) invalid use of legal authority.

b. Insufficient Methods of Confinement or Restraint

Insufficient acts of restraint include: (i) moral pressure and (ii) future threats.

c. Time of Confinement

It is irrelevant how short the period of the confinement is.

d. Awareness of Confinement

Plaintiff must ***know*** of the confinement or be ***harmed*** by it.

e. What Is a Bounded Area?

For an area to be "bounded," freedom of movement must be limited in all directions. There must be no ***reasonable*** means of escape ***known*** to plaintiff.

4. Intentional Infliction of Emotional Distress

Elements of the prima facie case:

(i) An act by defendant amounting to ***extreme and outrageous conduct***;

(ii) Intent or recklessness;

(iii) Causation; and

(iv) Damages—***severe*** emotional distress.

a. Extreme and Outrageous Conduct
This is conduct that transcends all bounds of decency. Conduct that is not normally outrageous may become so if:

1) It is continuous in nature;

2) It is directed toward a certain type of plaintiff (children, elderly persons, pregnant women, supersensitive adults if the sensitivities are known to defendant); or

3) It is committed by a certain type of defendant (common carriers or innkeepers may be liable even for mere "gross insults").

b. Requisite Intent
Unlike for other intentional torts, ***recklessness*** as to the effect of defendant's conduct will satisfy the intent requirement.

c. Damages
Actual damages (severe emotional distress), not nominal damages, are required. Proof of physical injury is not required. The more outrageous the conduct, the less proof of damages is required.

CMR **Exam Tip** Intentional infliction of emotional distress is the only intentional tort to the person that requires damages.

d. Causation in Bystander Cases
When the defendant intentionally causes physical harm to a third person and the plaintiff suffers severe emotional distress because of it, the plaintiff may recover by showing ***either*** the prima facie case elements of emotional distress ***or*** that (i) she was present when the injury occurred, (ii) she is a close relative of the injured person, and (iii) the defendant knew facts (i) and (ii).

CMR **Exam Tip** Intentional infliction of emotional distress is a fallback tort position. Thus, if another alternative in your exam question is a tort that will also allow plaintiff to recover, it should be chosen over this alternative.

C. PRIMA FACIE CASE—INTENTIONAL TORTS TO PROPERTY

1. Trespass to Land
Elements of the prima facie case:

(i) ***Physical invasion*** of plaintiff's ***real property***;

(ii) Intent; and

(iii) Causation.

a. Physical Invasion
The invasion may be by a person or object (*e.g.,* throwing a baseball onto plaintiff's land is a trespass). If ***intangible matter*** (*e.g.,* vibrations or odor) enters, the plaintiff may have a case for nuisance.

b. **Real Property**
Real property includes not only the surface, but also airspace and subterranean space for a reasonable distance.

c. **Intent**
Defendant need intend only to enter on that particular piece of land (he need not know that the land belonged to another).

d. **Potential Plaintiffs**
Anyone in actual or constructive possession of the land may maintain this action.

2. **Trespass to Chattels**
Elements of the prima facie case:

(i) An act by defendant that ***interferes with plaintiff's right of possession*** in a chattel;

(ii) Intent;

(iii) Causation; and

(iv) Damages.

a. **Two Types of Interference**
The interference may either be an intermeddling (*i.e.,* directly ***damaging*** the chattel) or a dispossession (*i.e.,* depriving plaintiff of his lawful right of ***possession*** of the chattel).

b. **Damages**
Actual damages—not necessarily to the chattel, but at least to a possessory right—are required.

3. **Conversion**
Elements of the prima facie case:

(i) An act by defendant that ***interferes with plaintiff's right of possession*** in a chattel;

(ii) The interference is ***so serious*** that it warrants requiring defendant to pay the chattel's full value;

(iii) Intent; and

(iv) Causation.

a. **Acts of Conversion**
Acts of conversion include wrongful acquisition (theft), wrongful transfer, wrongful detention, and substantially changing, severely damaging, or misusing a chattel.

b. **Seriousness of Interference**
The longer the withholding period and the more extensive the use, the more likely it is to be conversion. A less serious interference is trespass to chattels.

c. **Subject Matter of Conversion**
Only tangible personal property and intangibles that have been reduced to physical form (*e.g.,* a promissory note) are subject to conversion.

d. **Potential Plaintiffs**
Anyone with possession or the immediate right to possession of the chattel may maintain an action for conversion.

e. **Remedies**
Plaintiff may recover ***damages*** (fair market value at the time of conversion) ***or possession*** (replevin).

CMR COMPARISON CHART

TRESPASS TO CHATTELS VS. CONVERSION

	Trespass to Chattels	Conversion
Act by Defendant	An interference with plaintiff's right of possession of chattel (either intermeddling or dispossession)	An interference with plaintiff's right of possession so ***serious*** as to warrant that defendant pay the chattel's full value
Intent	Intent to do the act that brings about the interference	Intent to do the act that brings about the interference
Remedy	Recovery of actual damages from harm to chattel or loss of use (if dispossession, damages based on rental value)	Damage award of fair market value of chattel at time of conversion (*i.e.,* forced sale of chattel). May instead recover chattel (replevin)

D. DEFENSES TO INTENTIONAL TORTS

1. Consent

Plaintiff's consent to defendant's conduct is a defense, but the majority view is that one ***cannot*** consent to a ***criminal act***. Any consent fact pattern raises two inquiries:

(i) Was there a valid consent (*e.g.,* no fraud)?

(ii) Did the defendant stay within the boundaries of the consent (*e.g.,* not use a gun in a boxing match)?

a. **Express (Actual) Consent**
Defendant is not liable if plaintiff expressly consents to defendant's conduct. Exceptions: (i) mistake will undo express consent ***if*** defendant knew of and took advantage of the mistake; (ii) consent induced by fraud will be invalidated if it goes to an essential matter, but not a collateral matter; and (iii) consent obtained by duress will be invalidated unless the duress is only threats of future action or future economic deprivation.

b. **Implied Consent**
Apparent consent is that which a reasonable person would infer from custom and usage or plaintiff's conduct, *e.g.,* normal contacts inherent in body-contact sports, ordinary incidental contact, etc. ***Consent implied by law*** arises when action is necessary to save a person's life or some other important interest in person or property.

c. **Capacity Required**
Individuals without capacity are deemed incapable of consent, *e.g.,* incompetents, drunken persons, and very young children.

CMR **Exam Tip** This requirement of capacity differs from the rule for the intent element of intentional torts, where incapacity is no defense; *i.e.,* everyone (even a young child) has the capacity to ***commit*** a tort, but not everyone has the capacity to ***consent*** to a tort.

d. **Exceeding Consent Given**
If defendant exceeds the scope of consent and does something substantially different, he may be liable.

2. **Self-Defense, Defense of Others, and Defense of Property**
When a question involves the defense of self, others, or property, ask the following three questions:

(i) Is the privilege available? The tort must now be or about to be committed. Already committed torts do not qualify.

(ii) Is a mistake permissible as to whether the tort being defended against (battery, trespass, etc.) is actually being committed?

(iii) Was a proper amount of force used?

CMR **Exam Tip** Keep your parties clear. In questions involving these defenses, the conduct of the defendant was prompted by the commission or apparent commission of a tort by the plaintiff. That tort is not at issue, however; the issue is whether the defendant's response itself constituted a tort against the plaintiff (usually battery, trespass to land, or trespass to chattels) or instead was privileged by one of these defenses.

a. **Self-Defense**
When a person ***reasonably believes*** that she is being or is about to be attacked, she may use such force as is reasonably necessary to protect against injury.

1) **When Is Defense Available?**

a) One need not attempt to escape, but the modern trend imposes a duty to retreat before using deadly force if this can be done safely, unless the actor is in her home.

b) Self-defense is generally not available to the initial aggressor.

c) Self-defense may extend to third-party injuries (caused while the actor was defending herself). An actor might be liable to a third person if she deliberately injured him in trying to protect herself.

2) **Is Mistake Allowed?**
A reasonable mistake as to the existence of the danger is allowed.

3) **How Much Force May Be Used?**
One may use only that force that reasonably appears to be necessary to prevent the harm (including deadly force). If more force than is reasonably necessary is used, the defense is lost.

b. Defense of Others

1) **When Is Defense Available?**
One may use force to defend another when the actor ***reasonably believes*** that the other person could have used force to defend himself.

2) **Is Mistake Allowed?**
A reasonable mistake as to whether the other person is being attacked or has a right to defend himself is permitted.

3) **How Much Force May Be Used?**
The defender may use as much force as he could have used in self-defense if the injury were threatened to him.

c. Defense of Property

1) **When Is Defense Available?**
One may use reasonable force to prevent the commission of a tort against her real or personal property. A request to desist or leave must first be made unless it clearly would be futile or dangerous. The defense does not apply once the tort has been committed; however, one may use force in ***hot pursuit*** of another who has tortiously dispossessed the owner of her chattels because the tort is viewed as still being committed.

CMR **Exam Tip** Remember that this defense is ***not available against one with a privilege***. Whenever an actor has a privilege to enter on the land of another because of necessity, recapture of chattels, etc., that privilege will ***supersede*** the privilege of the land possessor to defend her property.

2) **Is Mistake Allowed?**
A reasonable mistake is allowed as to whether an intrusion has occurred or whether a request to desist is required. A mistake is ***not*** allowed as to whether the entrant has a privilege (*e.g.,* necessity) that supersedes the defense of property right, unless the entrant conducts the entry so as to lead defendant to reasonably believe it is not privileged (such as by refusing to say what the necessity is).

3) **How Much Force May Be Used?**
Reasonable force may be used. However, one may ***not*** use force causing death or serious bodily harm unless the invasion of property also entails a serious threat of bodily harm.

CMR **Exam Tip** There is a common misperception that deadly force may be used to protect one's home. This is not strictly true. Many of the "home defense" cases are really self-defense cases. Thus, deadly force can only be used when a person, not just property, is threatened.

d. **Reentry onto Land**
At common law, one could use force to reenter land only when the other came into possession tortiously. Under modern law, there are summary procedures for recovering possession of real property. Hence, resort to self-help is no longer allowed.

e. **Recapture of Chattels**
The basic rule is the same as that for reentry of land at common law: when another's possession began lawfully (*e.g.,* a conditional sale), one may use only peaceful means to recover the chattel. Force may be used to recapture a chattel only when in hot pursuit of one who has obtained possession wrongfully, *e.g.,* by theft.

1) **When Is Defense Available?**

a) **Timely Demand Required**
A timely demand to return the chattel is first required unless clearly futile or dangerous.

b) **Recovery Only from Wrongdoer**
The recapture may be only from a tortfeasor or some third person who knows or should know that the chattels were tortiously obtained. One may not use force to recapture chattels in the hands of an innocent party.

c) **Entry on Land to Remove Chattel**

(1) **On Wrongdoer's Land**
When chattels are located on the land of the wrongdoer, the owner is privileged to enter on the land and reclaim them at a reasonable time and in a reasonable manner, after first making a demand for their return.

(2) **On Land of Innocent Party**
Similarly, when the chattels are on the land of an innocent party, the owner may enter and reclaim her chattel at a reasonable time and in a peaceful manner when the landowner has been given notice of the presence of the chattel and refuses to return it. (As noted above, the chattel owner's right of recapture supersedes the landowner's right to defend his property.) However, the chattel owner will be liable for any actual damage caused by the entry.

(3) **On Land Through Owner's Fault**
If the chattels are on the land of another through the owner's fault (*e.g.,* negligently letting cattle wander), there is no privilege to enter on the land. They may be recovered only through legal process.

2) **Is Mistake Allowed?**
Generally, no mistake regarding defendant's right to recapture the chattels or enter on the land is allowed. However, ***shopkeepers*** may have a privilege to detain for a reasonable period of time individuals whom they reasonably believe to be in possession of shoplifted goods.

3) **How Much Force May Be Used?**
Reasonable force, not including force sufficient to cause death or serious bodily harm, may be used to recapture chattels.

3. **Privilege of Arrest**
Depending on the facts, the actor may have a privilege to make an arrest of a third person.

a. **Invasion of Land**
The privilege of arrest carries with it the privilege to enter another's land for the purpose of effecting the arrest.

b. **Subsequent Misconduct**
Although the arrest itself may be privileged, the actor may still be liable for subsequent misconduct (*e.g.,* failing to bring the arrested party before a magistrate, unduly detaining the party in jail).

c. **Mistake**

1) **Misdemeanor**
If the arrest is for a misdemeanor, it is privileged only if for a breach of peace and if the action takes place in front of defendant.

2) **Felony**
For a felony arrest, a ***police officer*** may make a reasonable mistake. Citizens may make a reasonable mistake regarding the identity of the felon, but not regarding whether the felony occurred.

CMR COMPARISON CHART

ARRESTS WITHOUT A WARRANT

	Felony Arrest by Police Officer	Felony Arrest by Private Citizen	Misdemeanor Arrests
When Privileged	The officer must reasonably believe that a felony has been committed and that the person he arrests has committed it	The felony in fact must have been committed and the citizen must reasonably believe that the person he arrests has committed it	The misdemeanor must be a breach of peace and committed in the arresting party's presence
Force Allowed	That degree of force reasonably necessary to make the arrest; deadly force only when the suspect poses a threat of ***serious harm***	That degree of force reasonably necessary to make the arrest; deadly force only when the suspect poses a threat of ***serious harm***	That degree of force reasonably necessary to make the arrest, but ***never*** deadly force

4. **Necessity**
A person may interfere with the real or personal property of another when it is reasonably and apparently necessary to avoid threatened injury from a natural or other force and when the threatened injury is substantially more serious than the invasion that is undertaken to avert it. There are two types of necessity: (i) public—when the act is for the public good; and (ii) private—when the act is solely to benefit any person or any property from destruction or serious injury. Under private necessity, the actor must pay for any injury he causes.

CMR **Exam Tip** Necessity is a defense only to property torts.

5. **Discipline**
A parent or teacher may use reasonable force in disciplining children.

II. HARM TO ECONOMIC AND DIGNITARY INTERESTS

A. DEFAMATION

The law of defamation is divided into two parts: the common law elements and the constitutional requirements.

The elements of common law defamation are:

(i) ***Defamatory language***;

(ii) ***"Of or concerning"*** the plaintiff;

(iii) ***Publication*** thereof by defendant to a third person; and

(iv) Damage to plaintiff's reputation.

If the defamation involves a ***matter of public concern***, the Constitution requires the plaintiff to prove two additional elements:

(v) ***Falsity*** of the defamatory language; and

(vi) ***Fault*** on the part of defendant.

CMR Exam Tip In a common law case, plaintiff does not have to prove falsity as part of the prima facie case. Rather, defendant can offer truth of the statement as a defense.

1. Defamatory Language

Defamatory language is defined as language tending to adversely affect one's reputation. A statement of opinion is actionable only if it appears to be based on specific facts, and an express allegation of those facts would be defamatory. Name-calling is insufficient.

a. Inducement and Innuendo

If the statement is not defamatory on its face, plaintiff may plead additional facts as "inducement" to establish defamatory meaning by "innuendo."

b. Living Person Requirement

Any living person may be defamed. Defamation of a deceased person is not actionable. In a limited sense, a corporation, unincorporated association, or partnership may be defamed (*e.g.,* by remarks as to its financial condition, honesty, integrity, etc.).

2. "Of or Concerning" Plaintiff

The plaintiff must establish that a reasonable reader, listener, or viewer would understand that the defamatory statement referred to the plaintiff.

a. Colloquium

If the statement does not refer to plaintiff on its face, extrinsic evidence may be offered to establish that the statement refers to the plaintiff. This is known as pleading "colloquium."

COMMON LAW DEFAMATION

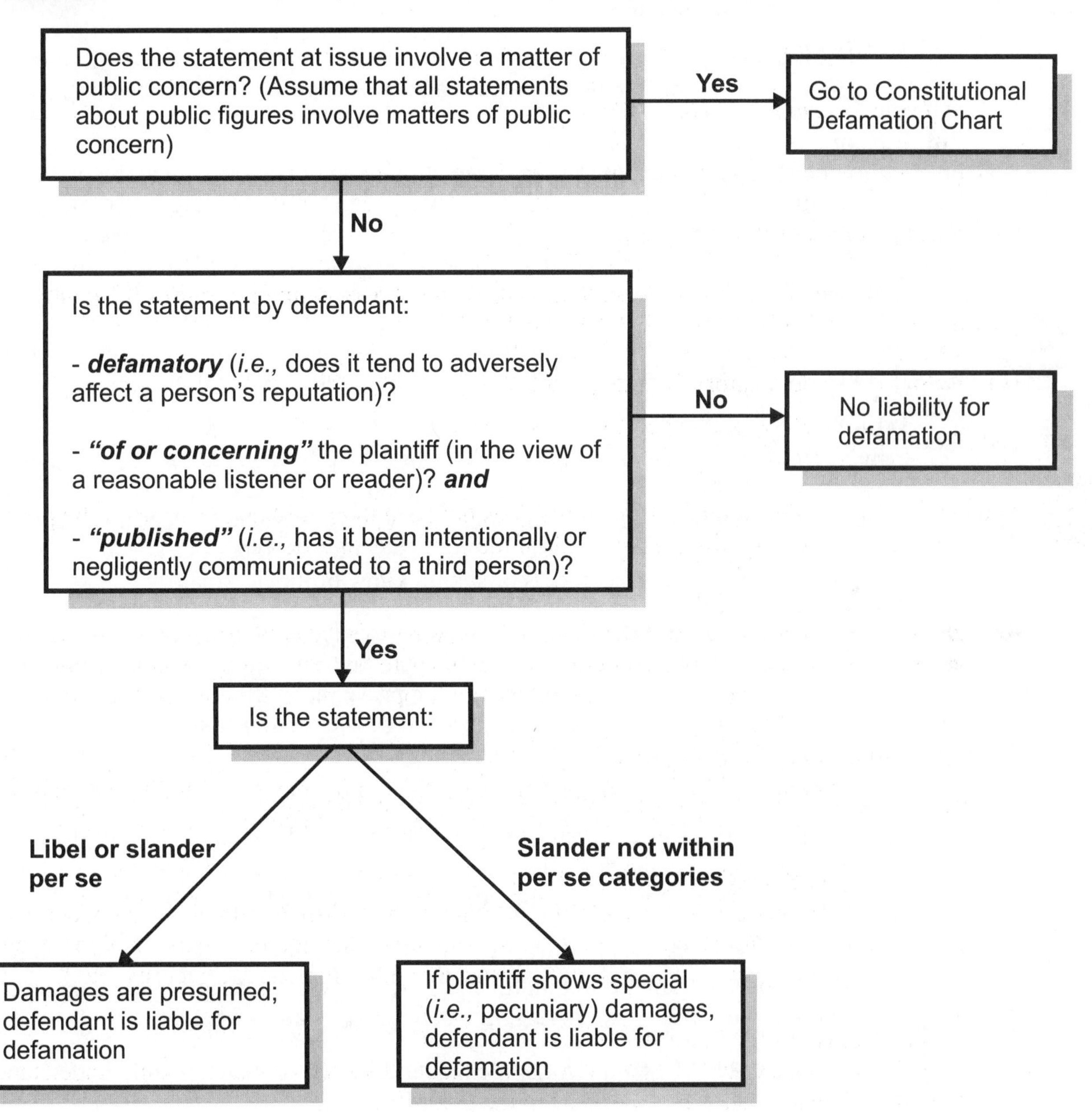

b. Group Defamation

1) If the defamatory statement refers to ***all*** members of a ***small*** group, each member may establish that the statement is "of and concerning" him by alleging that he is a group member (*i.e.,* everyone wins!).

2) If it is a ***large*** group, ***no*** member can prove that the statement is "of and concerning" him (*i.e.,* no one wins!).

3) If the statement only refers to ***some*** members of a ***small*** group, plaintiff can recover if a reasonable person would view the statement as referring to plaintiff.

3. Publication

Publication means communication of the defamation to someone other than the plaintiff. Such publication can be made either intentionally or negligently. It is the intent to publish, not the intent to defame, that is the requisite intent. Each repetition is a separate publication. However, for magazines, newspapers, etc., most states have adopted a "single publication" rule under which all copies are treated as one publication.

CMR **Exam Tip** An exam favorite is the situation where a defamatory statement about plaintiff is made only ***to plaintiff***. As a general rule, there is ***no*** publication and thus no defamation.

a. Who May Be Liable?

Primary publishers (*e.g.,* newspapers, TV stations, etc.) are liable to the same extent as the author or speaker. One who repeats a defamation is liable on the same general basis as the primary publisher (even if she states the source or makes it clear that she does not believe the defamation). One selling papers or playing tapes is a secondary publisher and is liable only if he knows or should know of the defamatory content.

4. Damage to Plaintiff's Reputation

The type of damages plaintiff must prove depends on the type of defamation (libel or slander) involved. In some slander cases, plaintiff must prove that she suffered special damages—that is, she must have suffered some pecuniary loss in order to recover anything. But once plaintiff has proved special damages, she may recover general damages as well.

a. Libel

Libel is the written or printed publication of defamatory language. Plaintiff does not need to prove special damages and general damages are presumed. The minority position distinguishes between libel per se and libel per quod (not defamatory on its face).

b. Slander

Slander is spoken defamation. Plaintiff must prove special damages, unless defamation falls within slander per se categories; *i.e.,* defamatory statements that:

1) Adversely reflect on one's conduct in a business or profession;

2) One has a loathsome disease;

3) One is or was guilty of a crime involving moral turpitude; or

4) A woman is unchaste.

c. **Slander vs. Libel**
Where it is difficult to determine whether something is slander or libel, look at the ***permanency***, the ***area of dissemination***, and the ***deliberate character*** of the publication. Where the original defamation is libel, any repetition, even if oral, is also libel. On the other hand, the written repetition of a slander will be characterized as libel. Radio and television programs are treated as libels if sufficiently permanent, premeditated, and broadly enough disseminated. The modern trend even treats "ad libbed" defamation on radio or television as libel.

5. **First Amendment Concerns**
When the defamation involves a ***matter of public concern***, plaintiff must prove, in addition to the common law elements:

(i) Falsity of the statement, and

(ii) Fault on the part of defendant.

a. **Falsity**
In cases where plaintiff is constitutionally required to prove some type of fault, plaintiff also has the burden of proving falsity.

CMR **Exam Tip** If a statement of public interest is true, plaintiff has no cause of action for defamation. However, if you see this type of statement on the exam, consider whether plaintiff may have a cause of action for intentional infliction of emotional distress or invasion of right to privacy (unless plaintiff is a public figure).

b. **Fault on Defendant's Part**
The type of fault that a plaintiff must prove depends on the plaintiff's status.

1) **Public Official or Figure Must Prove Malice**
Under the *New York Times v. Sullivan* rule, malice must be proved in defamation cases brought by public officials and public figures.

a) **What Constitutes a Public Figure?**
A person becomes a "public figure" by achieving pervasive fame or notoriety or by voluntarily assuming a central role in a particular public controversy.

b) **Definition of Malice**
Malice (as defined by *New York Times v. Sullivan*) is:

(i) ***Knowledge*** that the statement was false, or

(ii) ***Reckless disregard*** as to whether it was false.

This is a subjective test. Defendant's spite or ill will is not enough to constitute malice. Deliberately altering a quotation may constitute malice if the alteration causes a ***material change*** in the meaning conveyed by the quotation.

CONSTITUTIONAL DEFAMATION

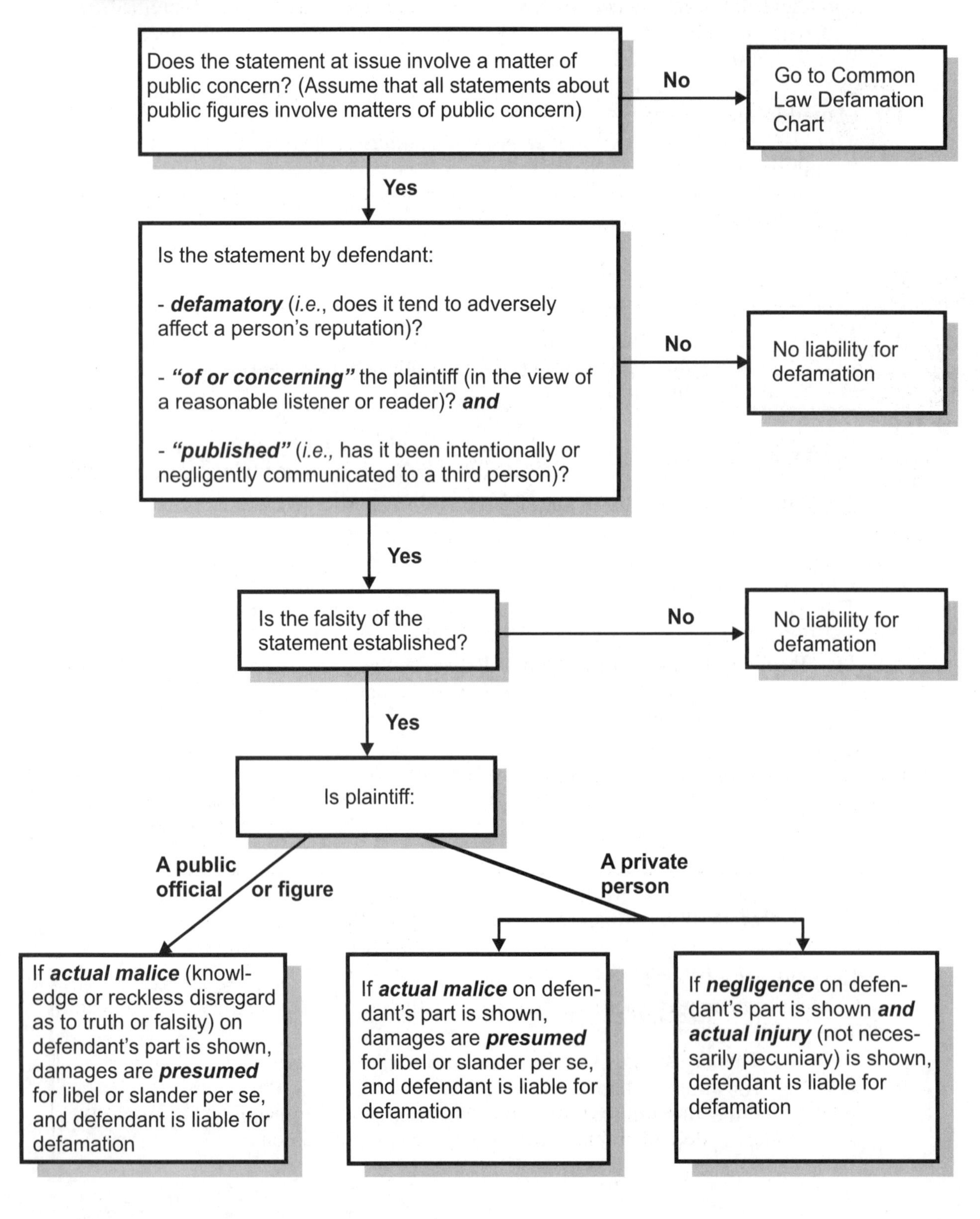

2) **Private Persons Need Not Prove Malice**
Under *Gertz v. Welch*, where a private person is the plaintiff, only ***negligence*** regarding the falsity must be proved if the statement involves a matter of "public concern." (If not a matter of public concern, constitutional restrictions do not apply.) Where the defendant is negligent, only "actual injury" damages are recoverable. However, where malice is found, damages may be presumed, and punitive damages allowed.

Exam Tip Note that the status of the plaintiff (public figure or private person) is relevant ***only*** for the degree of fault required; the element of falsity must be proved regardless of the status of the plaintiff as long as a matter of public concern is involved (and you should assume that a matter of public concern is involved whenever the plaintiff is a public figure).

CMR SUMMARY CHART

FAULT AND DAMAGES RULES IN CONSTITUTIONAL DEFAMATION ACTIONS

Type of Plaintiff/Defamation	Fault Required	Damages Recoverable
Public official or public figure	Actual malice (knowledge of falsity or reckless disregard as to truth or falsity)	Presumed damages under common law rules (and punitive damages where appropriate)
Private person/matter of public concern	At least negligence as to statement's truth or falsity	Damages only for proved "actual injury" (If plaintiff proves actual malice, presumed and punitive damages may be available)
Private person/matter of private concern	No fault as to truth or falsity need be proved	Presumed damages under common law rules (and punitive damages where appropriate)

6. **Defenses to Defamation**

a. **Consent**
Consent is a complete defense. The rules relating to consent to intentional torts apply here.

b. **Truth**
Where plaintiff does not need to prove falsity (*i.e.,* the statement is about a purely private matter), defendant may prove truth as a complete defense.

CMR **Exam Tip** Remember that falsity and fault are prima facie case elements only in a ***constitutional*** defamation case. Plaintiff does not need to prove falsity in a ***common law*** defamation case because defamatory statements are presumed to be false; defendant has the burden to prove truth as a defense.

c. **Absolute Privilege—Can Never Be Lost**
Defendant may be protected by an absolute privilege for the following: remarks made during judicial proceedings, by legislators in debate, by federal executive officials, in "compelled" broadcasts, and between spouses.

d. **Qualified Privilege—Can Be Lost Through Abuse**
Sometimes the speaker may have a qualified privilege for the following: reports of official proceedings; statements in the interest of the publisher—defense of one's actions, property, or reputation; statements in the interest of the recipient; and statements in the common interest of the publisher and recipient.

The qualified privilege may be lost if (i) the statement is not within the scope of the privilege, or (ii) it is shown that the speaker acted with malice. Defendant bears the burden of proving that a privilege exists.

7. **Mitigating Factors**
Mitigating factors (*e.g.,* no malice, retraction, anger of the speaker provoked by plaintiff) may be considered by the jury on the damages issue; they are not defenses to liability.

B. INVASION OF RIGHT TO PRIVACY

1. **Four Branches**
This tort includes four kinds of wrongs:

a. **Appropriation of Plaintiff's Picture or Name**
It is necessary to show ***unauthorized use*** of plaintiff's picture or name for defendant's ***commercial advantage***. Liability is generally limited to advertisements or promotions of products or services. Mere economic benefit to defendant (not in connection with promoting a product or service) by itself is not sufficient.

b. **Intrusion upon Plaintiff's Affairs or Seclusion**
The act of ***prying or intruding*** must be ***objectionable to a reasonable person***. Furthermore, the thing into which there is an intrusion must be "***private***." Photographs taken in public places are not actionable.

c. **Publication of Facts Placing Plaintiff in False Light**
"False light" exists where one attributes to plaintiff views he does not hold or actions he did not take. The false light must be something ***objectionable to a reasonable*** person under the circumstances. For liability to attach, there must be publicity.

1) **First Amendment Limitation**
If the matter is in the public interest, ***malice*** on the defendant's part must be proved.

d. **Public Disclosure of Private Facts About Plaintiff**
This wrong involves public disclosure of ***private information*** about plaintiff (*e.g.*, matters of public record are not sufficient). The public disclosure must be ***objectionable to a reasonable person*** of ordinary sensibilities. Liability may attach even though the actual statement is true. First Amendment limitations probably apply if the matter is of legitimate public interest.

2. **Causation**
The invasion of plaintiff's interest in privacy (under any of the four kinds) must have been proximately caused by defendant's conduct.

3. **Proof of Special Damages Unnecessary**
Plaintiff need not plead and prove special damages. Emotional distress and mental anguish are sufficient damages.

4. **Defenses**
Some defenses to the right of privacy actions are consent and the defamation privilege defenses. Truth generally is ***not*** a good defense; nor is inadvertence, good faith, or lack of malice.

5. **Right of Privacy—Miscellaneous**
The right of privacy is a ***personal right*** and does not extend to members of a family, does not survive the death of the plaintiff, and is not assignable. The right of privacy is not applicable to corporations.

C. MISREPRESENTATION

1. **Intentional Misrepresentation (Fraud, Deceit)**
Prima facie case:

(i) ***Misrepresentation*** of a material fact (no duty to disclose and opinion not actionable unless rendered by someone with superior skill in the area). Silence is generally not enough; one must make affirmative misrepresentations;

(ii) ***Scienter,*** *i.e.*, when defendant made the statement, she ***knew*** or ***believed*** it was false or that there was no basis for the statement;

(iii) ***Intent*** to induce plaintiff to act or refrain from acting ***in reliance*** upon the misrepresentation;

(iv) ***Causation*** (actual reliance);

(v) ***Justifiable reliance*** (generally, reliance is justifiable only as to a statement of fact, not opinion); and

(vi) ***Damages*** (plaintiff must suffer ***actual pecuniary loss***).

There are no defenses to intentional misrepresentation.

2. Negligent Misrepresentation
Prima facie case:

(i) ***Misrepresentation*** by defendant in a ***business or professional capacity;***

(ii) ***Breach of duty*** toward a particular plaintiff;

(iii) ***Causation;***

(iv) ***Justifiable reliance;*** and

(v) ***Damages.***

Generally, this action is confined to misrepresentations made in a ***commercial setting***, and liability will attach only if reliance by the ***particular*** plaintiff could be contemplated.

D. WRONGFUL INSTITUTION OF LEGAL PROCEEDINGS

1. Malicious Prosecution
Prima facie case: (i) ***institution of criminal proceedings*** against plaintiff; (ii) ***termination in plaintiff's favor***; (iii) ***absence of probable cause*** for prior proceedings (insufficient facts for a reasonable person to believe that plaintiff was guilty, or defendant, in fact, did not actually believe plaintiff to be guilty); (iv) ***improper purpose*** (*i.e.,* something other than bringing a person to justice); and (v) ***damages***. Prosecutors are immune from liability.

a. Wrongful Civil Proceedings
Most jurisdictions have extended the malicious prosecution action to cover civil cases.

2. Abuse of Process
Prima facie case: (i) ***wrongful use*** of process for an ulterior purpose, and (ii) definite ***act or threat*** against plaintiff in order to accomplish an ulterior purpose.

E. INTERFERENCE WITH BUSINESS RELATIONS

Prima facie case: (i) existence of a ***valid contractual relationship*** between plaintiff and a third party ***or valid business expectancy*** of plaintiff; (ii) defendant's ***knowledge of the relationship or expectancy***; (iii) ***intentional interference*** by defendant inducing a breach or termination of the relationship or expectancy; and (iv) ***damages***.

1. Privileges
Defendant's conduct may be privileged where it is a proper attempt to obtain business for itself or protect its interests, particularly if defendant is interfering only with plaintiff's prospective business rather than with existing contracts.

III. NEGLIGENCE

A. PRIMA FACIE CASE

Elements of the prima facie case:

(i) A ***duty*** on the part of defendant ***to conform to a specific standard of conduct*** for protection of plaintiff against an unreasonable risk of injury;

(ii) A ***breach*** of that duty by defendant;

(iii) The breach is the ***actual and proximate cause*** of plaintiff's injury; and

(iv) ***Damage***.

B. DUTY OF CARE

A duty of care is owed to all foreseeable plaintiffs. The extent of the duty is determined by the applicable standard of care. Therefore, when confronted with a negligence question, always ask:

(i) Was the plaintiff foreseeable?

(ii) If so, what is the applicable standard of care?

1. Foreseeable/Unforeseeable Plaintiffs

A duty of care is owed only to foreseeable plaintiffs. However, a problem arises where defendant breaches a duty to one plaintiff ("P1") and also causes injury to another (possibly unforeseeable) plaintiff ("P2"). There are two possible outcomes:

a. Cardozo View (Majority)—Foreseeable Zone of Danger

P2 can recover only if she can establish that a reasonable person would have foreseen a risk of injury to her under the circumstances; *i.e.,* she was located in the foreseeable zone of danger.

b. Andrews View (Minority)—Everyone Is Foreseeable

P2 may establish the existence of a duty extending from defendant to her by a showing that defendant has breached a duty owed to P1.

2. Specific Situations

a. Rescuers

A rescuer is a foreseeable plaintiff where defendant negligently put himself or a third person in peril (*i.e.,* danger invites rescue).

b. Prenatal Injuries

A duty of care is owed to a viable fetus. In cases of failure to diagnose a congenital defect or properly perform a contraceptive procedure, the child may not recover for "wrongful life," but the parents may recover damages in a "wrongful birth" or "wrongful pregnancy" action for any additional medical expenses and for pain and suffering from labor; ordinary child rearing expenses, however, cannot be recovered.

c. Intended Beneficiaries of Economic Transactions

A third party for whose economic benefit a legal or business transaction was made (*e.g.*, a beneficiary of a will) may be a foreseeable plaintiff.

3. Standards of Care

a. Basic Standard—The Reasonable Person

The reasonable person standard is an ***objective*** standard, *i.e.,* one's conduct measured against what the average person would do. A defendant's ***mental*** deficiencies and inexperience are not taken into account (*i.e.,* stupidity is no excuse). However, the "reasonable person" is considered to have the same ***physical*** characteristics as defendant (but remember, one is expected to know one's physical handicaps and to exercise the care of a person with such knowledge—*e.g.,* a blind person should not fly a plane).

b. Particular Standards of Conduct

1) Professionals

A professional or someone with special occupational skills is required to possess the knowledge and skill of a member of the profession or occupation in good standing in similar communities. Specialists will be held to a national standard of care.

a) Duty to Disclose Risks of Treatment

A doctor has a duty to disclose the risks of treatment to enable a patient to make an informed consent.

2) Children

Children are held to the standard of a child of ***like age***, ***education***, ***intelligence***, ***and experience***. This is a ***subjective*** test. A child under four is usually without the capacity to be negligent. Children engaged in adult activities may be required to conform to an "adult" standard of care.

3) Common Carriers and Innkeepers

Common carriers and innkeepers are held to a very high degree of care; *i.e.,* they are liable for slight negligence.

CMR Exam Tip For the higher common carrier and innkeeper standards to apply, the plaintiff ***must*** be a passenger or guest.

4) Automobile Driver to Guest

A guest in an automobile is owed a duty of ordinary care. In the few guest statute states, one is liable to nonpaying passengers only for reckless tortious conduct.

5) Bailment Duties

a) Duties Owed by Bailor

For a ***gratuitous bailment***, the bailor must inform of known, dangerous defects in the chattel. For a ***bailment for hire***, the bailor must inform of chattel defects of which he is or should be aware.

b) Duties Owed by Bailee

The bailee's standard of care depends on who benefits from the bailment: (i) for a ***sole benefit of the bailor*** bailment, there is a low standard of care;

(ii) for a ***sole benefit of the bailee*** bailment, there is a high standard of care; and (iii) for a ***mutual benefit*** bailment, there is the ordinary care standard.

6) Emergency Situations
A defendant must act as a reasonable person would under the same emergency conditions. The emergency is not to be considered, however, if it is of defendant's own making.

c. Owners and/or Occupiers of Land
The extent of the liability of owners and/or occupiers of land (and those in privity with the owner/occupier) depends on where the injury occurred and on the status of the plaintiff.

1) Duty of Possessor to Those Off Premises
There is no duty to protect one off the premises from ***natural conditions*** on the premises; however, there is a duty for unreasonably dangerous ***artificial*** conditions or structures abutting adjacent land. Also, one must carry on activities on property so as to avoid unreasonable risk of harm to others outside the property.

CMR **Exam Tip** In urban areas, the owner/occupier is liable for damage caused off the premises by trees on the premises (*e.g.,* falling branches). This has been an exam favorite in recent years.

2) Duty of Possessor to Those On Premises
In most states the duty owed a plaintiff on the premises depends on the plaintiff's status as trespasser, licensee, or invitee.

a) Trespassers
No duty is owed to an ***undiscovered*** trespasser. As to ***discovered*** or ***anticipated*** trespassers, the landowner must: (i) warn of or make safe concealed, unsafe, ***artificial conditions known to the landowner*** involving risk of ***death or serious bodily harm,*** and (ii) use reasonable care in the exercise of "active operations" on the property. (No duty is owed for natural conditions or less dangerous artificial conditions.) Easement and license holders owe a duty of reasonable care to trespassers.

b) Infant Trespassers—Attractive Nuisance Doctrine
Most courts impose on a landowner the duty to exercise ordinary care to avoid a reasonably foreseeable risk of harm to children caused by ***artificial*** conditions on his property. To establish the doctrine's applicability, plaintiff must show: (i) a dangerous condition on the land that the owner is or should be aware of, (ii) the owner knows or should know children frequent the vicinity of the condition, (iii) the condition is likely to cause injury, *i.e.,* dangerous because of child's inability to appreciate the risk, and (iv) the expense of remedying the situation is slight compared with the magnitude of the risk.

CMR **Exam Tip** For liability to attach, the four requirements above must be shown. The child ***does not*** have to be attracted onto the land by the dangerous condition, nor is the attraction alone enough for liability.

c) **Duty Owed to Licensees**
A licensee is one who enters on the land with the possessor's permission for her ***own purpose or business***, rather than for the possessor's benefit. The possessor has a duty to (i) warn of dangerous conditions (natural or artificial) known to the owner that create an unreasonable risk of harm to the licensee and that licensee is unlikely to discover, and (ii) exercise reasonable care in the conduct of "active operations" on the property. The possessor has no duty to inspect or repair. (*Remember:* Social guests are considered licensees.)

d) **Duty Owed to Invitees**
Invitees enter land in response to an invitation by the landowner (*i.e.,* they enter for a purpose connected with the business of the landowner or enter as members of the public for a purpose for which the land is ***held open to the public***). The landowner or occupier owes the same duties owed to licensees ***plus*** a duty to make ***reasonable inspections*** to discover nonobvious dangerous conditions and, thereafter, make them safe. One will lose invitee status if she exceeds the scope of the invitation.

e) **Duty Owed to Users of Recreational Land**
A landowner who permits the general public to use his land for recreational purposes without charging a fee is not liable for injuries suffered by a recreational user, unless the landowner willfully and maliciously failed to guard against or warn of a dangerous condition or activity.

f) **Modern Trend Rejects Status Rules**
A strong minority of states reject the distinction between licensees and invitees (and, in a few states, trespassers as well), and simply apply a reasonable person standard to dangerous conditions on the land.

3) **Duties of Lessor and Lessee of Realty**
The lessee has a general duty to maintain the premises. The lessor must warn of existing defects of which he is aware or has reason to know, and which he knows the lessee is not likely to discover on a reasonable inspection. If the lessor covenants to repair, he is liable for unreasonably dangerous conditions. If the lessor volunteers to repair and does so negligently, he is liable.

CMR **Exam Tip** If the guest of a tenant is injured, the landlord may be liable as lessor of the premises. But don't stop there—remember that the tenant may also be liable to the guest because of the tenant's status as the owner/occupier of the premises.

4) **Duties of Vendor of Realty**
A vendor must ***disclose*** to the vendee concealed, unreasonably dangerous conditions of which the vendor knows or has reason to know, and which he knows the vendee is not likely to discover on a reasonable inspection.

d. **Statutory Standards of Care**
A statute's specific duty may replace the more general common law duty of due care if: (i) the statute provides for a ***criminal penalty***, (ii) the statute ***clearly defines the standard*** of conduct, (iii) plaintiff is ***within the protected class***, and (iv) the statute was ***designed to prevent the type of harm suffered*** by plaintiff.

1) **Excuse for Violation**
Violation of some statutes may be excused where compliance would cause more danger than violation or where compliance would be beyond defendant's control.

2) **Effect of Violation or Compliance**
Under the majority view, an unexcused statutory violation is negligence per se; *i.e.,* it establishes the first two requirements in the prima facie case—a ***conclusive*** presumption of duty and breach of duty. In contrast, even though violation of the applicable statute may be negligence, compliance with the statute will not necessarily establish due care.

CMR SUMMARY CHART

DUTY OF POSSESSOR OF LAND TO THOSE ON THE PREMISES

Status of Entrant	Duties Owed: *Artificial Conditions*	*Natural Conditions*	*Active Operations*
Undiscovered Trespasser	No duty	No duty	No duty
Discovered or Anticipated Trespasser	Duty to warn of or make safe known conditions if non-obvious and ***highly*** dangerous	No duty	Duty of reasonable care
Infant Trespasser (if presence on land foreseeable)	Duty to warn of or make safe if foreseeable risk to child outweighs expense of eliminating danger	No duty	No duty (unless child also qualifies as discovered or anticipated trespasser)
Licensee (including social guest)	Duty to warn of or make safe known conditions if nonobvious and dangerous	Duty to warn of or make safe known conditions if nonobvious and dangerous	Duty of reasonable care
Invitee (*e.g.,* member of public, business visitor)	Duty to make reasonable inspections to discover nonobvious dangerous conditions and warn of or make them safe	Duty to make reasonable inspections to discover nonobvious dangerous conditions and warn of or make them safe	Duty of reasonable care

4. Duty Regarding Negligent Infliction of Emotional Distress

The duty to avoid causing emotional distress to another is breached when defendant creates a foreseeable risk of physical injury to plaintiff, either by (i) causing a threat of physical impact that leads to emotional distress or (ii) directly causing severe emotional distress that by itself is likely to result in physical symptoms.

a. Injury Requirement

Plaintiff can recover damages only if defendant's conduct caused some ***physical injury***. While pure emotional distress may be insufficient, a severe shock to the nervous system that causes physical symptoms is sufficient. Two cases in which a physical injury is ***not*** required, however, are: (i) an erroneous report of a relative's death, and (ii) a mishandling of a relative's corpse.

b. Zone of Danger Requirement

If plaintiff's distress is caused by threat of physical impact, most courts require that the threat be directed at plaintiff or someone in her immediate presence. A bystander outside the "zone of danger" of physical injury who sees defendant negligently injuring another cannot recover damages for her own distress. A strong modern trend allows recovery based on foreseeability factors rather than zone of danger if (i) plaintiff and the person injured by defendant are closely related, (ii) plaintiff was present at the scene, and (iii) plaintiff observed or perceived the injury.

CMR COMPARISON CHART

INFLICTION OF EMOTIONAL DISTRESS

	Intentional	Negligent
Conduct Required	Extreme and outrageous conduct by defendant	Subjecting plaintiff to threat of physical impact or severe emotional distress likely to cause physical symptoms
Fault Required	Intent to cause severe emotional distress or recklessness as to the effect of conduct	Negligence in creating risk of physical injury to plaintiff
Causation and Damages	Defendant's conduct must cause severe emotional distress	Defendant's conduct generally must cause tangible physical injury (*e.g.,* miscarriage)
Bystander Recovery When Another Is Physically Injured	Plaintiff bystander must be present when injury occurs and be a close relative of the injured person, and defendant must know these facts when he intentionally injures the other person (or defendant must have intent to cause plaintiff distress)	Plaintiff bystander must be within the "zone of danger" created by defendant's negligent conduct (*i.e.,* must be subjected to threat of impact). Modern trend allows recovery based on foreseeability factors

CMR **Exam Tip** Keep in mind that the torts for infliction of emotional distress are not the only means of recovering damages for emotional distress. If physical injury has been caused by commission of another tort, plaintiff can "tack on" damages for emotional distress as a "parasitic" element of his physical injury damages, without the need to consider the elements of the emotional distress torts.

5. **Affirmative Duties to Act**
Generally, one does not have a legal duty to act. Exceptions to this rule exist, however:

a. **Assumption of Duty by Acting**
One may assume a duty to act by acting (*e.g.,* once defendant undertakes to aid someone, he must do so with reasonable care).

Exception: Many states have enacted Good Samaritan statutes, which exempt doctors, nurses, etc., from liability for ordinary, but not gross, negligence.

b. **Peril Due to Defendant's Conduct**
One has a duty to assist someone he has negligently or innocently placed in peril.

c. **Special Relationship Between Parties**
A special relationship between the parties (*e.g.,* parent-child) may create a duty to act. Similarly, ***common carriers***, ***innkeepers***, ***shopkeepers***, and others that gather the public for profit owe duties of reasonable care to aid or assist their patrons. In addition, places of public accommodation have a duty to prevent injury to guests by third persons.

d. **Duty to Control Third Persons**
Generally, there is no duty to prevent a third person from injuring another. An affirmative duty may be imposed, however, if one has the actual ability and authority to control a person's actions, and knows or should know the person is likely to commit acts that would require exercise of this control.

C. BREACH OF DUTY

Where defendant's conduct falls short of that level required by the applicable standard of care owed to the plaintiff, she has breached her duty. Whether the duty of care is breached in an individual case is a question for the trier of fact. The main problem relates to proof of the breach. Plaintiff may use one of the following theories:

1. **Custom or Usage**
Custom or usage may be used to establish standard of care, but does not control the question of whether certain conduct amounted to negligence. For example, although certain behavior is custom in an industry, a court may find that the entire industry is acting negligently.

2. **Violation of Statute**
Existence of a duty owed to plaintiff and breach thereof may be established as a matter of law by proof that defendant violated an applicable statute ("negligence per se"). Causation and damages must still be established by plaintiff.

3. **Res Ipsa Loquitur**
In some cases, the very occurrence of an event may tend to establish a breach of duty. The

doctrine of res ipsa loquitur requires plaintiff to show that (i) the accident causing the injury is a type that would not normally occur unless someone was negligent, and (ii) the negligence is attributable to defendant (*i.e.,* this type of accident ordinarily happens because of the negligence of someone in defendant's position). This can often be shown by evidence that the instrumentality causing the injury was in the exclusive control of defendant. (Plaintiff must also establish freedom from fault on his part.)

a. **Effect of Res Ipsa Loquitur**

Where res ipsa loquitur is established, plaintiff has ***made a prima facie case*** and no directed verdict may be given for defendant. Plaintiff can still lose, however, if the inference of negligence is rejected by the trier of fact.

CMR **Exam Tip** Questions testing on res ipsa loquitur often have the defendant making a ***motion for a directed verdict***. These questions don't require you to memorize rules of civil procedure—all you need to remember is the following:

(i) ***Deny*** defendant's motion for directed verdict if plaintiff has established res ipsa loquitur or presented some other evidence of breach of duty (such as defendant's violation of a statute);

(ii) ***Grant*** defendant's motion if plaintiff has failed to establish res ipsa loquitur and failed to present some other evidence of breach of duty.

Occasionally, plaintiff may also move for a directed verdict. Plaintiff's motion should always be ***denied*** except in the rare case where plaintiff has established negligence per se through violation of an applicable statute ***and*** there are no issues of proximate cause.

D. CAUSATION

Once negligent conduct is shown (a breach of the standard of care owed a foreseeable plaintiff), plaintiff must show that the conduct was the cause of his injury. For liability to attach, plaintiff must show ***both*** actual cause and proximate cause.

1. Actual Cause (Causation in Fact)

Before defendant's conduct can be considered a proximate cause of plaintiff's injury, it must first be a cause in fact of the injury. Several tests exist:

a. **"But For" Test**

Act or omission is the cause in fact of an injury when the injury would not have occurred but for the act. This test applies where several acts (each insufficient to cause the injury alone) combine to cause the injury.

b. **Joint Causes—Substantial Factor Test**

Where several causes bring about injury, and any one alone would have been sufficient to cause the injury, defendant's conduct is the cause in fact if it was a substantial factor in causing the injury.

c. **Alternative Causes Approach**

This test applies when there are two acts, only one of which causes injury, but it is not known which one. The burden of proof shifts to defendants, and each must show that his negligence is not the actual cause. [Summers v. Tice]

CMR **Exam Tip** Distinguish these last two tests: Under the joint causes approach, both parties caused the harm. Under the alternative causes approach, although both parties acted negligently, only one caused the harm.

2. **Proximate Cause (Legal Causation)**
In addition to being a cause in fact, the defendant's conduct must also be the proximate cause of the injury. Even though the conduct actually caused plaintiff's injury, it might not be deemed to be the proximate cause. Thus, the doctrine of proximate causation is a ***limitation of liability*** and deals with liability or nonliability for unforeseeable or unusual consequences of one's acts.

a. **General Rule—Scope of Foreseeable Risk**
A defendant generally is liable for all harmful results that are the normal incidents of and within the increased risk caused by his acts. This is a ***foreseeability*** test.

CMR **Exam Tip** Questions raising proximate cause issues will not require you to make a judgment call on foreseeability in a close case. If the answer turns on the proximate cause issue, the correct choice will almost always be phrased in "if" or "unless" terms (*e.g.*, "plaintiff will prevail if it was reasonably foreseeable that . . ." or "defendant will not be liable unless he should have foreseen that . . ."). Otherwise, the facts in the question will be so clear-cut that common sense will tell you immediately whether the harm that occurred was foreseeable.

b. **Liability in Direct Cause Cases**
In a direct cause case, where there is an uninterrupted chain of events from the negligent act to plaintiff's injury, defendant is liable for all ***foreseeable harmful results***, regardless of unusual manner or timing. Defendant is not liable for ***unforeseeable harmful results*** not within the risk created by defendant's negligence. Most harmful results will be deemed foreseeable in direct cause cases.

c. **Liability in Indirect Cause Cases**
In an indirect cause case, an affirmative intervening force (*e.g.*, an act by a third person, an act of God) comes into motion after defendant's negligent act and combines with it to cause plaintiff's injury.

1) **Foreseeable Results Caused by Foreseeable Intervening Forces—Defendant Liable**
Defendant is liable where his negligence caused a foreseeable harmful response or reaction from a dependent intervening force or created a foreseeable risk that an independent intervening force would harm plaintiff.

a) **Common Dependent Intervening Forces**
The following dependent intervening forces are ***almost always foreseeable:*** (i) subsequent medical malpractice, (ii) negligence of rescuers, (iii) efforts to protect the person or property of oneself or another, (iv) injuries caused by another "reacting" to defendant's actions, (v) subsequent diseases caused by a weakened condition, and (vi) subsequent accident substantially caused by the original injury.

b) **Independent Intervening Forces**
Independent intervening forces that are not a natural response or reaction to the situation created by the defendant's conduct may be foreseeable if

defendant's negligence increased the risk of harm from these forces. Independent intervening forces include (i) negligent acts of third persons, (ii) crimes and intentional torts of third persons, and (iii) acts of God.

2) **Foreseeable Results Caused by Unforeseeable Intervening Forces—Defendant Usually Liable**
Defendant is liable where his negligence increased the risk of a foreseeable harmful result and that result is ultimately produced by an unforeseeable intervening force. This rule does not apply where the unforeseeable intervening force was a crime or intentional tort of a third person.

3) **Unforeseeable Results Caused by Foreseeable Intervening Forces—Defendant Not Liable**
In the rare case where a totally unforeseeable result was caused by a foreseeable intervening force, most courts hold defendant not liable.

4) **Unforeseeable Results Caused by Unforeseeable Intervening Forces—Defendant Not Liable**
Intervening forces that produce unforeseeable results (results not within the increased risk created by defendant's negligence) are generally deemed unforeseeable and ***superseding***. Superseding forces break the causal connection between defendant's initial negligent act and plaintiff's ultimate injury, thus relieving defendant of liability.

d. **Unforeseeable Extent or Severity of Harm—Defendant Liable**
In all cases, defendant takes his plaintiff as he finds him; *i.e.,* defendant is liable for all damages, including aggravation of an existing condition, even if the extent or severity of the damages was unforeseeable. This is also known as the "eggshell-skull plaintiff" rule.

CMR SUMMARY CHART

PROXIMATE CAUSE RULES

	Direct Cause Cases	Indirect Cause Cases: *Foreseeable Intervening Force*	Indirect Cause Cases: *Unforeseeable Intervening Force*
Foreseeable Harmful Result	Defendant liable	Defendant liable	Defendant liable unless intervening force is crime or intentional tort
Unforeseeable Harmful Result	Defendant not liable	Defendant not liable	Defendant not liable; intervening force is ***superseding***

E. DAMAGES

Damage is an essential element of negligence; thus, damage will not be presumed (and nominal damages are not available).

1. Personal Injury

Plaintiff is to be compensated for all his damages (past, present, and prospective), both special and general. Foreseeability of the extent of harm is generally irrelevant; *i.e.*, one takes one's plaintiff as one finds him.

2. Property Damage

The measure of damage is the reasonable cost of repair or, if the property is nearly destroyed, the fair market value at the time of the accident.

3. Punitive Damages

Plaintiff may recover punitive damages if defendant's conduct is "wanton and willful," reckless, or malicious.

4. Nonrecoverable Items

Nonrecoverable items include: (i) interest from the date of damage in a personal injury action, and (ii) attorneys' fees.

5. Duty to Mitigate

As in all cases, plaintiff has a duty to take reasonable steps to mitigate damages (*e.g.*, seek appropriate treatment).

6. Collateral Source Rule

Damages are not reduced just because plaintiff received benefits from other sources, *e.g.*, health insurance.

F. DEFENSES TO NEGLIGENCE

1. Contributory Negligence

Contributory negligence is negligence on the part of the plaintiff that contributes to her injuries. The standard of care for contributory negligence is the same as for ordinary negligence.

a. No Defense to Intentional Torts

Contributory negligence is not a defense to wanton and willful misconduct or intentional tortious conduct.

b. Effect of Contributory Negligence

Contributory negligence completely barred plaintiff's right to recovery at common law. Almost all jurisdictions now favor a comparative negligence system (*see infra*).

c. Last Clear Chance—An Exception to Contributory Negligence

Last clear chance permits plaintiff to recover despite her contributory negligence. Under this rule, the person with the last clear chance to avoid an accident who fails to do so is liable for negligence. (Last clear chance is essentially plaintiff's rebuttal to the defense of contributory negligence.)

1) **Helpless Peril**
In many states, where the plaintiff is in "helpless peril," defendant will be liable if he knew or should have known of plaintiff's predicament.

2) **Inattentive Peril**
In "inattentive peril" situations (*i.e.,* plaintiff could have extricated herself if attentive), defendant must actually have known of plaintiff's predicament.

3) **Prior Negligence Cases**
For the last clear chance doctrine to apply, defendant must have been able, but failed, to avoid harming plaintiff at the time of the accident. If defendant's only negligence occurred earlier, the doctrine will not apply.

d. **Imputed Contributory Negligence**
As a general rule, the contributory negligence of a third party will be imputed to a plaintiff (and bar her claim) only when the relationship between the third party and the plaintiff is such that a court could find the plaintiff vicariously liable for the third party's negligence. Negligence is imputed in master-servant, partner, and joint venturer relationships. Negligence is not imputed between husband and wife, parent and child, and automobile owner and driver.

2. **Assumption of Risk**
Plaintiff may be denied recovery if she assumed the risk of any damage caused by defendant's act. Plaintiff must have (i) known of the risk and (ii) voluntarily proceeded in the face of the risk.

a. **Implied Assumption of Risk**
Knowledge may be implied where the risk is one that an average person would clearly appreciate. Plaintiff may ***not*** be said to have assumed the risk where there is no available alternative to proceeding in the face of the risk or in situations involving fraud, force, or an emergency. Also, common carriers and public utilities may not limit their liability by disclaimer, and members of a class protected by statute will not be deemed to have assumed any risk.

b. **Express Assumption of Risk**
The risk may be assumed by an express agreement.

c. **No Defense to Intentional Torts**
Assumption of risk is not a defense to intentional torts, but it is a defense to wanton and willful misconduct.

3. **Comparative Negligence**
In comparative negligence states, plaintiff's contributory negligence is not a complete bar to recovery. Rather, the trier of fact weighs plaintiff's negligence and reduces damages accordingly (*e.g.,* if plaintiff is 10% at fault, her damages are reduced by 10%). A majority of states allow plaintiff to recover only if her negligence was less serious or no more serious than that of defendant (partial comparative negligence). "Pure" comparative negligence states, however, allow recovery no matter how great plaintiff's negligence.

Exam Tip On the MBE, you will be told to assume that pure comparative negligence applies unless the question states otherwise.

a. **Effect on Other Doctrines**
Last clear chance is not used in comparative negligence jurisdictions. Most comparative negligence jurisdictions have abolished the defense of implied assumption of risk but have retained the defense of express assumption of risk. In most states, plaintiff's negligence will be taken into account even though defendant's conduct was "wanton and willful" or "reckless," but not if it was intentional.

CMR COMPARISON CHART

NEGLIGENCE DEFENSES

	Contributory Negligence	Implied Assumption of Risk	Pure Comparative Negligence	Partial Comparative Negligence
Defined	Plaintiff's own negligence contributes to her injury	Plaintiff knew of a risk of injury and voluntarily assumed it	Plaintiff's own negligence contributes to her injury	Plaintiff's own negligence contributes to her injury
Effect	Plaintiff's claim completely barred	Plaintiff's claim completely barred	Plaintiff's damage award reduced by percentage of fault attributable to her	Plaintiff's damage award reduced if her fault is below the threshold level; otherwise, plaintiff's claim is barred
Defense Negated by Defendant's "Last Clear Chance"?	Yes	Not applicable	Not applicable	Not applicable
Defense Applies to Wanton or Reckless Tortious Conduct?	No	Yes	Yes	Yes

IV. LIABILITY WITHOUT FAULT (STRICT LIABILITY)

A. PRIMA FACIE CASE
For strict liability, the following elements must be shown: (i) existence of an ***absolute duty*** on the

part of the defendant ***to make safe;*** (ii) ***breach*** of that duty; (iii) the breach of the duty was the ***actual*** and ***proximate cause*** of the plaintiff's injury; and (iv) ***damage*** to the plaintiff's person or property.

B. LIABILITY FOR ANIMALS

1. Trespassing Animals

An owner is strictly liable for reasonably foreseeable damage done by a trespass of his animals.

2. Personal Injuries

a. Strict Liability for Wild Animals

An owner is strictly liable to licensees and invitees for injuries caused by wild animals as long as the injured person did nothing to bring about the injury.

b. No Strict Liability for Domestic Animals

An owner is not strictly liable for injuries caused by domestic animals unless he has knowledge of that particular animal's dangerous propensities that are not common to the species.

c. Strict Liability Not Available to Trespassers

Strict liability will generally not be imposed in favor of trespassers in the absence of the owner's negligence. However, a landowner may be liable on intentional tort grounds for injuries inflicted by vicious watchdogs.

C. ULTRAHAZARDOUS OR ABNORMALLY DANGEROUS ACTIVITIES

There are three requirements for the application of strict liability to ultrahazardous activities: (i) the activity must involve ***risk of serious harm*** to persons or property; (ii) the activity must be one that ***cannot be performed without risk of serious harm*** no matter how much care is taken; and (iii) the activity ***is not commonly engaged in*** in the particular community (blasting, manufacturing explosives, etc.). Some courts also consider the value of the activity and its appropriateness to the location.

Exam Tip Exam questions testing on strict liability often include a statement in the facts or in an answer choice that the defendant exercised reasonable care. Remember that no amount of due care on the part of the defendant will relieve him of liability in a strict liability situation.

D. EXTENT OF LIABILITY

1. Scope of Duty Owed

The duty owed is the absolute duty to make safe the normally dangerous characteristic of the animal or activity. It is owed to all foreseeable plaintiffs.

2. Defenses

In ***contributory negligence*** states, contributory negligence is no defense if plaintiff has failed to realize the danger or guard against it. It is a defense if plaintiff knew of the danger and his unreasonable conduct was the very cause of the ultrahazardous activity miscarrying. Assumption of the risk is a good defense to strict liability. Most ***comparative negligence*** states apply their comparative negligence rules to strict liability cases.

V. PRODUCTS LIABILITY

A. BASIC PRINCIPLES

Products liability refers to the liability of a supplier of a defective product to someone injured by the product.

1. Theories of Liability

There are five theories of liability that plaintiff may use: (i) intent, (ii) negligence, (iii) strict liability, (iv) implied warranties of merchantability and fitness for a particular purpose, and (v) representation theories (express warranty and misrepresentation).

CMR **Exam Tip** If the question does not indicate what theory of liability plaintiff is using, apply a strict liability theory because that is the easiest to prove.

2. Common Elements

To find liability under any products liability theory, plaintiff must show: (i) a ***defect***, and (ii) existence of the defect ***when the product left defendant's control***.

a. Types of Defects

1) Manufacturing Defects

If a product emerges from manufacturing different and more dangerous than the products made properly, it has a manufacturing defect.

2) Design Defects

When all products of a line are the same but have dangerous propensities, they may be found to have a design defect.

3) Inadequate Warnings

A product may be defective as a result of the manufacturer's failure to give adequate warnings as to the risks involved in using the product. For liability to attach, the danger must not be apparent to users.

b. Proving a Defect

1) Manufacturing Defects

For a manufacturing defect, defendant will be liable if plaintiff can show that the product failed to perform as safely as an ordinary consumer would expect (defendant must anticipate reasonable misuse). This test also applies to defective food products.

2) Design Defects

For a design defect, plaintiff usually must show that the defendant could have made the product safer, without serious impact on the product's price or utility.

3) Government Safety Standards

A product's ***noncompliance*** with government safety standards establishes that it is defective, while ***compliance*** with safety standards is evidence—but not conclusive—that the product is ***not*** defective.

4) **Scientifically Unknowable Risks**
Defendant will not be held liable for dangers not foreseeable at the time of marketing.

5) **Unavoidably Unsafe Products**
Manufacturers will not be held liable for some dangerous products (*e.g.,* knives) if the danger is apparent and there is no safer way to make the product.

c. **Existence of Defect When Product Left Defendant's Control**
The defect must have existed when the product left defendant's control. This will be inferred if the product moved through normal channels of distribution.

Exam Tip In virtually all products liability actions, the fact that there was no contractual ***privity*** between the plaintiff and defendant will not prevent plaintiff from recovering. Nevertheless, it is still a favorite ***wrong choice*** in products liability exam questions based on negligence or strict liability theories. Remember that any foreseeable plaintiff, including a bystander, can sue any commercial supplier in the chain of distribution regardless of the absence of a contractual relationship between them.

B. LIABILITY BASED ON INTENT

Defendant will be liable to anyone injured by an unsafe product if defendant intended the consequences or knew that they were substantially certain to occur. Products liability actions based on intent are not very common. If intent is present, the most likely tort is battery.

1. **Who Can Sue?**
Privity is not required, so any injured plaintiff can sue.

2. **Damages**
In addition to compensatory damages, punitive damages are available.

3. **Defenses**
The defenses are those available in other intentional torts cases.

C. LIABILITY BASED ON NEGLIGENCE

The prima facie case is the same as in any negligence case. Plaintiff must show (i) duty, (ii) breach, (iii) actual and proximate cause, and (iv) damages.

1. **Duty of Care**
A duty of care is owed to any foreseeable plaintiff.

a. **Who Can Sue?**
Privity with the defendant is no longer required, so any foreseeable plaintiff can sue. This includes:

1) Users;

2) Consumers; and

3) Bystanders.

b. **Who Can Be Held Liable?**
Commercial suppliers such as manufacturers, wholesalers, and retailers can be held liable.

2. **Breach of Duty**
Breach of duty is shown by (i) ***negligent conduct*** of defendant leading to (ii) the supplying of a ***defective product*** (as defined above).

a. **Proof of Negligence**
Negligence is proved the same as in a "standard" negligence case. The plaintiff may invoke res ipsa loquitur.

b. **Liability of Retailers and Wholesalers**
It is very difficult to hold retailers and wholesalers liable for negligence since they can usually satisfy their duty through a cursory inspection.

3. **Causation**
An intermediary's (*e.g.,* wholesaler's) negligent failure to discover a defect does not supersede the original manufacturer's negligence unless the intermediary's conduct exceeds ordinary foreseeable negligence.

4. **Nature of Damages Recoverable**
Physical injury or property damage must be shown. (Recovery will be denied if the sole claim is for economic loss.)

5. **Defenses**
The defenses are the same as in a general negligence action.

D. **LIABILITY BASED ON STRICT TORT LIABILITY**
The prima facie case: (i) a strict duty owed by a ***commercial supplier*** of a product; (ii) breach of that duty; (iii) actual and proximate cause; and (iv) damage.

1. **Duty**
Defendant has a duty to supply safe products.

a. **Who Can Sue?**
Privity is not required—users, consumers, and bystanders can sue.

1) **No Substantial Alteration**
For liability to attach, the product must reach plaintiff without substantial alteration.

2) **Does Not Extend to Services**
Strict products liability applies only to products. Even where a product is provided incident to a service (*e.g.,* blood during an operation), there is no strict liability. Plaintiff may, however, sue in negligence.

b. **Who Can Be Held Liable?**
Any commercial supplier can be held liable. Casual sellers will not be held strictly liable.

2. Breach of Duty

For breach of duty, plaintiff must show that the product is defective (as defined above). The defect must make the product unreasonably dangerous. Retailers may be liable even if they have no opportunity to inspect the product.

3. Causation

For actual cause, plaintiff must show that the defect existed when the product left defendant's control. Proximate cause is the same as in negligence cases.

4. Nature of Damages Recoverable

Physical injury or property damage must be shown. Recovery will be denied if the sole claim is for economic loss.

5. Defenses

In ***contributory negligence*** states, ordinary contributory negligence is no defense where plaintiff merely failed to discover the defect or guard against its existence, or where plaintiff's misuse was reasonably foreseeable. Assumption of the risk is a defense. In most ***comparative negligence*** states, courts will apply their comparative negligence rules.

6. Disclaimers Ineffective

Disclaimers are ***irrelevant*** in negligence or strict liability cases if personal injury or property damages occur.

E. IMPLIED WARRANTIES OF MERCHANTABILITY AND FITNESS

There are two warranties implied in every sale of goods that can serve as the basis for a suit by a buyer against a seller:

(i) ***Merchantability***, which refers to whether the goods are of average acceptable quality and are generally fit for the ordinary purpose for which the goods are used; and

(ii) ***Fitness for a particular purpose***, which arises when the seller knows or has reason to know the particular purpose for which the goods are required and that the buyer is relying on the seller's skill and judgment in selecting the goods.

1. Who Can Sue?

Most courts no longer require vertical privity. Most states adopted a narrow version of the horizontal privity requirement. This means the buyer, family, household, and guests can sue for personal injuries.

a. Bailee and Lessee

These warranties extend to bailments and leases as well as sales.

2. What Constitutes Breach?

If the product fails to live up to either of the above standards, the warranty is breached and the defendant will be liable.

a. Proof of Fault Unnecessary

Plaintiff does not have to prove any fault on the part of defendant.

3. **Causation**
Actual cause and proximate cause are handled as in ordinary negligence cases.

4. **Damages**
Personal injury and property damages, ***and purely economic*** loss, are recoverable.

5. **Defenses**
Defenses include assumption of risk (using a product while knowing of breach of warranty) and contributory negligence to the same extent as in strict liability cases. Failure to give notice of breach is a defense under the U.C.C. (even in personal injury cases).

6. **Effect of Disclaimers**
Disclaimers are generally rejected in personal injury cases but upheld for economic loss.

F. REPRESENTATION THEORIES

In addition to the theory of implied warranties, a defendant may be liable when a product does not live up to some affirmative representation. The two representation theories are:

1. **Express Warranty**
Any affirmation of fact or promise concerning goods that becomes part of the basis of the bargain creates an express warranty.

   a. **Who Can Sue?**
   Any consumer, user, or bystander can sue. If a buyer sues, the warranty must have been "part of the basis of the bargain." If plaintiff is not in privity (*e.g.,* bystander), she need not have relied on the representation as long as someone did.

      1) **Bailee and Lessee**
      This warranty extends to bailments and leases as well as sales.

   b. **Breach**
   Fault need not be shown to establish breach. Plaintiff need only show that the product did not live up to its warranty.

   c. **Causation, Damages, and Defenses**
   Causation, damages, and defenses are treated just as under implied warranties.

   d. **Disclaimers**
   A disclaimer will be effective only in the unlikely event that it is consistent with the warranty.

2. **Misrepresentation of Fact**
A seller will be liable for misrepresentations of facts concerning a product where:

(i) The statement was of a material fact concerning quality or uses of goods (mere puffery insufficient), and

(ii) The seller intended to induce reliance by the buyer in a particular transaction.

Liability is usually based on strict liability but may also arise for intentional or negligent misrepresentations.

PRODUCTS LIABILITY THEORIES

	Negligence	Strict Liability	Implied Warranties
Who Can Sue?	Any foreseeable plaintiff	Any foreseeable plaintiff	Purchaser and her family, household, and guests
Who Can Be Sued?	Any commercial supplier (*e.g.*, manufacturer, wholesaler, retailer)	Any commercial supplier	*Merchantability:* A merchant dealing in the kind of goods sold *Fitness for a Particular Purpose:* Any seller of the goods
What Constitutes Breach?	Negligent conduct that results in the supplying of a defective product	The supplying of a defective product	*Merchantability:* Sale of goods not generally acceptable or fit for ordinary purposes *Fitness for a Particular Purpose:* Sale of goods not fit for purpose that seller knows or has reason to know of (and knows that buyer is relying on seller's judgment)
What Damages Can Be Recovered?	Personal injury and property damage (no recovery for economic loss standing alone)	Personal injury and property damage (no recovery for economic loss standing alone)	Personal injury and property damage (recovery solely for economic loss also permitted)
What Defenses Are Available?	Assumption of the risk and any type of contributory negligence	*Contributory Negligence States:* Assumption of the risk and unreasonable misuse (failure to discover or guard against defect ***not*** a defense) *Comparative Negligence States:* Any type of fault (under state's comparative negligence rules)	*Contributory Negligence States:* Assumption of the risk, unreasonable misuse, and failure to give reasonable notice of breach *Comparative Negligence States:* Any type of fault (under state's comparative negligence rules)

a. **Justifiable Reliance**
Justifiable reliance is required (*i.e.,* the representation was a substantial factor in inducing the purchase). Reliance need not be the victim's (it may be a prior purchaser's). Privity is irrelevant.

b. **Causation and Damages**
Actual cause is shown by reliance. Proximate cause and damages are the same as for strict liability.

c. **Defenses**
Assumption of risk is not a defense if plaintiff is entitled to rely on the representation. Contributory negligence is the same as in strict liability, unless defendant committed intentional misrepresentation.

VI. NUISANCE

Nuisance is not a separate tort in itself. Rather, nuisances are a type of harm—the invasion of either private property rights or public rights by conduct that is tortious because it falls into the usual categories of tort liability (*i.e.,* intentional, negligent, strict liability). There are two types of nuisance: private and public.

A. PRIVATE NUISANCE
Private nuisance is a ***substantial, unreasonable interference*** with another private individual's ***use or enjoyment*** of property that he actually possesses or to which he has a right of immediate possession.

CMR **Exam Tip** Nuisance questions on the MBE will often flag the correct choice with a key term from the definition of nuisance—*e.g.,* defendant is liable because the activity created a "substantial" (or "unreasonable") interference with plaintiff's use of her land.

1. **Substantial Interference**
Substantial interference is interference that is offensive, inconvenient, or annoying to the average person in the community. It is not substantial if it is merely the result of plaintiff's hypersensitivity or specialized use of his own property.

2. **Unreasonable Interference**
To establish unreasonable interference, required for nuisances based on intent or negligence, the severity of the inflicted injury must outweigh the utility of defendant's conduct. In balancing these respective interests, courts take into account that every person is entitled to use his own land in a reasonable way, considering the neighborhood, land values, and existence of any alternative courses of conduct open to defendant.

3. **Trespass to Land Distinguished**
In a trespass, there is an interference with the landowner's ***exclusive possession*** by a physical invasion; in a private nuisance, there is an interference with ***use or enjoyment***.

B. PUBLIC NUISANCE
Public nuisance is an act that unreasonably interferes with the ***health, safety, or property rights of***

the community, *e.g.,* using a building for criminal activities such as prostitution. Recovery by a private party is available for a public nuisance only if the private party suffered unique damage not suffered by the public at large.

C. REMEDIES

1. Damages
Plaintiff will usually be awarded damages.

2. Injunctive Relief
If the legal remedy of damages is unavailable or inadequate (*e.g.,* the nuisance will cause irreparable injury), injunctive relief will be awarded. In this case, the court will consider the relative hardships. However, hardships will not be balanced where defendant's conduct was either willful or against an assertion of right by plaintiff.

3. Abatement by Self-Help
In the case of a private nuisance, self-help abatement is available after notice to defendant and his refusal to act. Only necessary force may be used. In public nuisance cases, only a public authority or a private party who has suffered some unique damage can seek an injunction or abatement.

D. DEFENSES

1. Legislative Authority
Legislative authority for "nuisance activity" (*e.g.,* zoning ordinance) is not an absolute defense but is persuasive.

2. Conduct of Others
No one actor is liable for all damage caused by concurrence of his acts and others.

Example: Ten steel mills are polluting a stream. Each steel mill is responsible only for the pollution it causes.

3. Contributory Negligence
Contributory negligence generally is no defense to nuisance unless plaintiff's case rests on a negligence theory.

4. Coming to the Nuisance
One may "come to a nuisance" (purchasing land next to an already existing nuisance) and, thereafter, pursue an action. It is generally not a bar to plaintiff's action unless she "came to the nuisance" for the sole purpose of bringing a harassing lawsuit.

VII. GENERAL CONSIDERATIONS FOR ALL TORT CASES

A. VICARIOUS LIABILITY
Vicarious liability is liability that is derivatively imposed. In short, this means that one person commits a tortious act against a third party and another person will be liable to the third party for this act. The basic situations that you should note for bar examination purposes are set out below.

1. **Doctrine of Respondeat Superior**
A master/employer will be vicariously liable for tortious acts committed by her servant/employee if the tortious acts occur within the ***scope of the employment*** relationship.

   a. **Frolic and Detour**
   An employee making a ***minor*** deviation from his employer's business for his own purposes is still acting within the scope of his employment. If the deviation in time or geographic area is substantial, the employer is not liable.

   b. **Intentional Torts**
   It is usually held that intentional tortious conduct by servants is not within the scope of employment. ***Exceptions:***

      1) Force is authorized in the employment, *e.g.,* bouncer.

      2) Friction is generated by employment, *e.g.,* bill collector.

      3) The employee is furthering the business of the employer, *e.g.,* removing customers from the premises because they are rowdy.

   c. **Liability for Own Negligence**
   Employers may be liable for their own negligence by negligently selecting or supervising their employees. (This is ***not*** vicarious liability.)

2. **Independent Contractor Situations**
In general, a principal will not be vicariously liable for tortious acts of her agent if the agent is an independent contractor. Two ***broad exceptions*** exist, however:

   (i) The independent contractor is engaged in inherently dangerous activities, *e.g.,* excavating next to a public sidewalk, blasting.

   (ii) The duty, because of public policy considerations, is simply nondelegable, *e.g.,* the duty to use due care in building a fence around an excavation site.

   a. **Liability for Own Negligence**
   The employer may be liable for her ***own*** negligence in selecting or supervising the independent contractor (*e.g.,* hospital liable for contracting with unqualified and incompetent physician who negligently treats hospital's patient). (This is not vicarious liability.)

3. **Partners and Joint Venturers**
Each member of a partnership or joint venture is vicariously liable for the tortious conduct of another member committed in the ***scope and course*** of the affairs of the partnership or joint venture.

4. **Automobile Owner for Driver**
The general rule is that an automobile owner is not vicariously liable for the tortious conduct of another person driving his automobile. In some jurisdictions, courts employ theories other than vicarious liability to hold an automobile driver liable.

a. **Family Car Doctrine**
In many states, the owner is liable for tortious conduct of immediate family or household members who are driving with the owner's express or implied permission.

b. **Permissive Use**
A number of states have now gone further by imposing liability on the owner for damage caused by anyone driving with the owner's consent.

c. **Negligent Entrustment**
An owner may be liable for her ***own*** negligence in entrusting the car to a driver. Some states have also imposed liability on the owner if she was present in the car at the time of the accident, on the theory that she could have prevented the negligent driving, and hence was negligent herself in not doing so. (This is not vicarious liability.)

5. **Bailor for Bailee**
Under the general rule, the bailor is not vicariously liable for the tortious conduct of his bailee.

a. **Negligent Entrustment**
As above, the bailor may be liable for her ***own*** negligence in entrusting the bailed object. (This is not vicarious liability.)

6. **Parent for Child**
A parent is not vicariously liable for the tortious conduct of the child at common law. Note, however, that most states, by statute, make parents liable for the willful and intentional torts of their minor children up to a certain dollar amount (*e.g.,* $10,000).

a. **Child Acting as Agent for Parents**
Courts may impose vicarious liability if the child committed a tort while acting as the agent for the parents.

b. **Parent Liable for Own Negligence**
The parent may be held liable for her own negligence in allowing the child to do something, *e.g.,* use a dangerous object without proper instruction. Further, if the parent is apprised of the child's conduct on past occasions showing a tendency to injure another's person or property, she may be liable for not using due care in exercising control to mitigate such conduct, *e.g.,* by allowing the child to play with other children he has a history of attacking.

7. **Tavernkeepers**

a. **Common Law**
No liability was imposed on vendors of intoxicating beverages for injuries resulting from the vendee's intoxication, whether the injuries were sustained by the vendee or by a third person as a result of the vendee's conduct.

b. **Modern Law**
Many states, in order to avoid this common law rule, have enacted Dramshop Acts. Such acts usually create a cause of action in favor of any third person injured by the intoxicated vendee. Several courts have imposed liability on tavernkeepers even in the absence of a Dramshop Act. This liability is based on ordinary negligence principles

(the foreseeable risk of serving a minor or obviously intoxicated adult) rather than vicarious liability.

Exam Tip When you see an MBE question on vicarious liability, recognizing whether the doctrine applies is only the first step in your analysis. Even where defendant is not vicariously liable, plaintiff may prevail if defendant personally was negligent in supervising the person causing the injury. Always look for this option among your answer choices.

CMR SUMMARY CHART

VICARIOUS LIABILITY

Party Committing Tortious Act	Vicarious Liability of Related Party
Employee/Servant	Employer/master vicariously liable if tortious act within scope of employment relationship
Independent Contractor	Employer of independent contractor ***not*** vicariously liable unless activity is inherently dangerous or duty is nondelegable on public policy grounds
Partner or Joint Venturer	Other partners or joint venturers vicariously liable if tortious act within scope and course of partnership or joint venture
Driver of Automobile	Owner of automobile ***not*** vicariously liable unless jurisdiction has family car doctrine or permissive use statute
Bailee of Chattel	Bailor ***not*** vicariously liable
Child	Parent ***not*** vicariously liable (except for limited statutory liability for willful and intentional torts)
Patron of Tavern	Tavernkeeper ***not*** vicariously liable in absence of Dramshop Act

Note: Even if the related party is not vicariously liable, she may be liable for her ***own negligence*** (*e.g.,* negligent selection of independent contractor, negligent entrustment of automobile, negligent supervision of child).

B. PARTIES—MULTIPLE DEFENDANT ISSUES

1. Joint and Several Liability

Where two or more negligent acts combine to proximately cause an indivisible injury, each negligent actor will be jointly and severally liable (*i.e.,* liable to plaintiff for the entire damage incurred). If the injury is divisible, each defendant is liable only for the identifiable portion.

a. **Defendants Acting in Concert**
Where two or more defendants act in concert and injure plaintiff, each is jointly and severally liable for the entire injury. This is so even if the injury is divisible.

b. **Statutory Limitations**
Many states have abolished joint liability either (i) for those defendants judged to be less at fault than plaintiff, or (ii) for all defendants regarding noneconomic damages. In these cases, liability will be proportional to defendant's fault.

2. **Satisfaction and Release**

a. **Satisfaction**
Recovery of full payment is a "satisfaction." Only one satisfaction is allowed. Until there is satisfaction, however, one may proceed against all jointly liable parties.

b. **Release**
At common law, a release of one joint tortfeasor was a release of all joint tortfeasors. A majority of states now provide that a release of one tortfeasor does not discharge other tortfeasors unless expressly provided in the release agreement.

3. **Contribution and Indemnity**
Contribution and indemnity are doctrines that determine how joint tortfeasors allocate between them the damages they must pay to a successful plaintiff.

CMR **Exam Tip** To keep these two doctrines separate in your mind, recall that generally, for ***contribution*** to apply, both defendants must have a ***measurable degree*** of culpability for the tort, but ***indemnity*** usually applies when one of the parties is ***much more responsible*** than the other. It is important to note that neither of these doctrines affects how much the ***plaintiff*** receives. Rather, they deal with how much of the total award ***each defendant*** ultimately must pay.

a. **Contribution**
The rule of contribution allows a defendant who pays more than his share of damages under joint and several liability to have a claim against other jointly liable parties for the excess; *i.e.,* it ***apportions responsibility*** among those at fault.

1) **Limitations**
The contribution defendant must be originally liable to the plaintiff. Also, contribution is not applicable to intentional torts.

2) **Methods of Apportionment**

a) **Comparative Contribution**
Most states have a comparative contribution system, whereby contribution is imposed in proportion to the ***relative fault*** of the various defendants.

b) **Equal Shares**
In a minority of states, apportionment is in ***equal shares*** regardless of degrees of fault.

b. **Indemnity**
Indemnity involves ***shifting the entire loss*** between or among tortfeasors. Indemnity is available in the following circumstances: (i) by contract, (ii) in vicarious liability situations, (iii) under strict products liability, and (iv) in some jurisdictions, where there has been an identifiable difference in degree of fault (*e.g.,* retailers who negligently rely on a product's condition may receive indemnification from the manufacturer who negligently manufactured it; one whose liability is based on a secondary duty may recover indemnification from a person who had a primary duty; one who is passively negligent may recover indemnification from a joint tortfeasor who is actively negligent).

c. **Comparative Contribution**
As noted above, most comparative negligence states have adopted a comparative contribution system where contribution is in proportion to the relative fault of the various defendants. This approach ***also*** supplants indemnification rules based on identifiable differences in degree of fault.

C. SURVIVAL AND WRONGFUL DEATH

1. **Survival of Tort Actions**
Survival acts allow one's cause of action to survive the death of one or more of the parties. The acts apply to actions involving torts to property and torts resulting in personal injury. However, torts invading intangible personal interest (*e.g.,* defamation, invasion of right of privacy, malicious prosecution) expire upon victim's death.

2. **Wrongful Death**
Wrongful death acts grant recovery for pecuniary injury resulting to the spouse and next of kin. A decedent's creditors have no claim against the amount awarded. Recovery is allowed only to the extent that the deceased could have recovered in action if he had lived (*e.g.,* deceased's contributory negligence reduces recovery in comparative negligence states).

D. TORTIOUS INTERFERENCES WITH FAMILY RELATIONSHIPS

1. **Husband-Wife**
Either spouse may bring an action for indirect interference with consortium and services caused by defendant's intentional or negligent tortious conduct against the other spouse.

2. **Parent-Child**
A parent may maintain an action for loss of a child's services as a result of defendant's tortious conduct, whether intentional or negligent. A child, however, has no action in most states against one who tortiously injures the parent.

3. **Nature of Action**
Actions for interference with family relationships are derivative. Hence, any defense that would prevent recovery by the injured family member also prevents recovery for interference with the family relationship.

E. TORT IMMUNITIES

1. **Intra-Family Tort Immunities**
Under the traditional view, one member of a family unit could not sue another in tort for personal injury. Most states have ***abolished husband-wife immunity***. A slight majority have also abolished parent-child immunity (but generally do not allow children to sue merely for negligent supervision). Those that retain it do not apply it (i) for intentional tortious conduct, and (ii) in automobile accident cases to the extent of insurance coverage.

2. **Governmental Tort Immunity**
In varying degrees, federal, state, and municipal tort immunity has been eliminated. Where it survives, immunity attaches to ***governmental***, not proprietary, functions.

   a. **Federal Government**
   Under the Federal Tort Claims Act, the United States has ***waived immunity*** for tortious acts. However, immunity will still attach for (i) assault, (ii) battery, (iii) false imprisonment, (iv) false arrest, (v) malicious prosecution, (vi) abuse of process, (vii) libel and slander, (viii) misrepresentation and deceit, and (ix) interference with contract rights. Immunity is not waived for acts that are characterized as "discretionary," as distinguished from those acts termed "ministerial."

   b. **State and Local Governments**
   Most states have substantially waived their immunity to the same extent as the federal government; about half have also abolished municipal immunity to the same extent. Where municipal immunity has been abolished, the "public duty" rule provides that a duty owed to the public at large is not owed to any particular citizen absent a special relationship between the governmental body and the citizen. Where municipal immunity still exists, contrast "governmental" functions (*i.e.,* functions that could only be performed adequately by the government) and "proprietary" functions (functions that might as well have been provided by a private corporation). Courts limit application of sovereign immunity by ***not*** granting it for proprietary functions.

   c. **Immunity of Public Officials**
   Public officials carrying out official duties are immune from tort liability for discretionary acts done without malice or improper purpose. Liability attaches, however, for ministerial acts.

3. **Charitable Immunity**
The majority of jurisdictions have eliminated charitable immunity.